The Anguish of the Jews

 A STIMULUS BOOK

Editor in Chief for
Stimulus Books
Helga Croner

Editors
Lawrence Boadt, C.S.P.
Helga Croner
Leon Klenicki
John Koenig
Kevin A. Lynch, C.S.P.

STIMULUS BOOKS are developed by Stimulus Foundation, a not-for-profit organization, and are published by Paulist Press. The Foundation wishes to further the publication of scholarly books on Jewish and Christian topics that are of importance to Judaism and Christianity.

Stimulus Foundation was established by an erstwhile refugee from Nazi Germany who intends to contribute with these publications to the improvement of communication between Jews and Christians.

Books for publication in this Series will be selected by a committee of the Foundation, and offers of manuscripts and works in progress should be addressed to:

Stimulus Foundation
785 West End Ave.
New York, N.Y. 10025

Edward H. Flannery

THE ANGUISH OF THE JEWS

Twenty-Three Centuries of Antisemitism

A STIMULUS BOOK
Paulist Press
New York/Mahwah

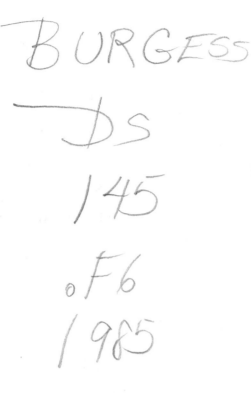

Library of Congress
Catalog Card Number: 85-60298

ISBN: 0-8091-2702-4

Published by Paulist Press
997 Macarthur Boulevard
Mahwah, N.J. 07430

Printed and bound in the United States of America

Contents

INTRODUCTION 1

1. THE ANCIENT WORLD 7

2. THE CONFLICT OF THE CHURCH AND SYNAGOGUE 28

3. A CRITICAL CENTURY 47

4. SHIFTING FORTUNES 66

5. THE VALE OF TEARS 90

6. AN OASIS AND AN ORDEAL 122

7. THE AGE OF THE GHETTO 145

8. THE STRUGGLE FOR EMANCIPATION 160

9. THE RACIAL MYTH AND ITS CONSEQUENCES 179

10. A WAR WITHIN A WAR 196

11. THE FINAL SOLUTION 205

12. RED ANTISEMITISM   230

13. POLITE ANTISEMITISM   247

14. THE LAST TWENTY-FIVE YEARS   263

15. THE ROOTS OF ANTISEMITISM   284

    NOTES   296

    INDEX   351

INTRODUCTION

The republication of this twenty year old history of antisemitism undertaken on the initiative of a Christian publishing
house is, paradoxically, a measure of both progress and failure in
Jewish-Christian understanding and dialogue of the last score of
years. A Christian publishing initiative taken on so self-incrimi-
nating a subject is obviously significant and encouraging. No less
significant but less encouraging on the other hand is the need to
republish it at all. The first objective of the original publication
of the book was to acquaint Christians generally with the immense
sufferings of Jews throughout the Christian era. The objective has
not been realized.[1] The problematic that supplied the motivation
for the first publication still obtains. The vast majority of Christians, even well educated, are all but totally ignorant of what happened to Jews in history and of the culpable involvement of the
Church. They are ignorant of this because, excepting a few recent
inclusions, the antisemitic record does not appear in Christian
history books or social studies, and because Christians are not inclined to read histories of antisemitism. Jews on the other hand
are by and large acutely aware of this page of history if for no other
reason than that it is so extensively and intimately intermingled
with the history of the Jews and Judaism. It is little exaggeration
to state that those pages of history Jews have committed to memory are the very ones that have been torn from Christian (and secular) history books. This new edition of the original volume is a

1

repeated effort to contribute toward the reinsertion of those pages.

Such a project holds more than academic interest. Indeed the fate of the fledgling Jewish-Christian dialogue is in a real sense at stake. The disparity of knowledge separating Christians and Jews in an area that touches them so closely renders authentic communication difficult. How in effect can the Jew, laden with the knowledge of his/her people's centuries-old oppression in Christendom, engage in fruitful dialogue with the Christian who is sincerely convinced that his/her partner in dialogue is simply too persecution-minded? Or, inversely, can the Christian dialogist, uninitiated to the dark pages of Jewish-Christian history, succeed any better with his Jewish partner who believes that Christians are fully familiar with these pages and yet callous concerning the persecution and suffering of his/her people? This imbalance of vital knowledge can only serve to impede, even vitiate the dialogue. The Holocaust, the Nuremberg and Eichmann trials, and many Church documents touching the problem of antisemitism have helped to increase interest in the subject of antisemitism and to rectify the imbalance, but far from adequately. The inclination to deny the reality of antisemitism and to regard the Holocaust as a latter-day aberration with little or no roots in the past or connection with the present is still widespread, and thus the problem is not faced.

This historical ignorance is pregnant with untoward consequences. It robs the Christian of grounds for motivation to take hatred of Jews as a serious social and ethical problem and to discover it in him/herself. It prevents the Christian from understanding Jews, their needs, hurts, and aspirations, many of which were shaped in the crucible of perennial oppression. Further, it blocks the way to Christian self-understanding, for antisemitism has left its mark on the Christian (and his/her Church) as much as on the Jew. It denies the Christian an opportunity to confront a capital sin of the Christian past, recapitulated in the present and in him/herself, and to undertake the *metanoia* this requires. Of grave consequence, finally, is the fact that this Christian refusal to face the antisemitic past is an important contributor to the extraordinary durability of this longest hatred of human history.

This volume then may serve as an invitation to Christian

readers to enter into the dark side of the Christian heritage, to undergo what might be called a historical psychoanalysis in the hope that by tracing out the origin and development of Jew-hatred this ageless evil will be banished from history and from the depths of the modern (and Christian) soul. For the Christian, such a venture would, in most instances, be an almost total uncovering of repressed material, a painful catharsis. Only such an exorcism of the demons of the past will permit a reassessment of the quality of our Christianity and the truth of our theology and lead to that attitude of maturity and responsibility so essential to the mutual understanding and cooperation with Jews to which the Church is committed.[2]

Basically, the present edition retains the purpose, method, and factual content of the first. It purports to present a substantially complete but succinct exposition of the data of the anti-semitic development, proceeding age by age and region by region as the course of events dictates. It is not written for the scholar but for the educated person who in his/her studies missed these important pages of history. It is the writer's hope that it will serve as an introduction to an extensive and complex subject, to an abiding interest in the struggle against antisemitism, and to the improvement of Jewish-Christian relations.

The new edition is to a certain point a revision, not of facts but of some perspectives. In a critique of the first edition in 1965 Rabbi Arthur Hertzberg wrote:

> What came through to me in Flannery's writing is his still on-going education in a very painful subject. I heard a decent man, who has been nurtured in conventional Catholic education and attitude, who was recasting these attitudes as he was confronting, for the first time, the underside of the history of the Church. This knowledge was clearly remaking him, but the process was not yet complete . . .[3]

Excluding the personal compliment, I can make Rabbi Hertzberg's words my own, but would change the "was" of his last sentence to the present tense. Rabbi Hertzberg is right. Education in the history of antisemitism is on-going, painful, and a remaking process. It is, moreover, probably never complete. The prototype and paragon of all prejudices, antisemitism is a rich source of insight into history, human nature, and into one's self. For the Christian in particular it is a valuable instrument for sounding the depths of the Christian psyche and character. The twenty years that separate this edition from the first exemplify some effects of this process. A comparative reading would show several divergences from the original. Pre-Christian antisemitism is conceded less weight in the development of antisemitism. The role of the churches is of necessity granted more. Rationalist antisemitism is also given greater importance. A tighter historical bond is found joining Christian and modern racist and Nazi antisemitism—and therefore the Holocaust—but at the same time they are sharply distinguished as opposites in their essential nature. The demonic character of antisemitism is sensed more clearly, and its spiritual and pathological depths are emphasized. Whoever will continue the journey into this cavernous hatred will find that he/she is at grips with an unfathomable evil. Those who will not do so risk remaining or becoming its prey.

The reader must be warned of the unavoidable refraction that is produced by a history of this kind that focuses relentlessly upon the negative content of the record of Jewish-Christian relations. The refraction is further magnified by the summary manner in which the seemingly endless series of negative occurrences is presented, giving off thereby an unintended suggestion that these data tell the whole story. As an antidote to this distorting effect the reading of a comprehensive history of Jews and Judaism is recommended.

Something must be said about definitions. The term "antisemitism", a misnomer, is also a problem.[4] First used in 1879 to signify racial antipathy toward Jews, it has since come to include anti-Jewish hatred of all types and of all eras. Misnomer though it is, common usage permits it to be used in the wider sense. Care however must be taken not to confuse it with anti-Jewish manifestations that are not strictly speaking antisemitic. The distinguishing mark of all antisemitism in the strict sense is hatred or contempt and a stereotyping of the Jewish people as such. In the absence of either of these qualifiers antisemitism does not exist. It should be distinguished therefore from indiscriminate hostility to which all peoples and groups have been prey; from anti-Judaism, a theological construct, with which it is often intermingled; and from anti-Jewish manifestations that may lead to—or in history have led to—antisemitism but do not possess the attributes specified above.[5] Unfortunately, even seasoned scholars have failed to respect distinctions such as these and have thus created a semantical confusion that has often rendered rational discourse on the subject well nigh impossible. In this volume we shall restrict ourselves to applications of the term in the strict sense without, for all that, discounting the fact that other manifestations, such as anti-Judaism, anti-Zionism, indifference and silence in the face of Jewish peril, etc., are usually richly laden with antisemitism or used as fronts or disguises behind which it does its damage. This strict usage, further, does not negate the fact that there are attitudes and policies which though not antisemitic in themselves are dangerous to the Jewish people and their vital interests. Some authors have effectively warned against such attitudes and policies and have entitled them the "real", the "new", and even the "ultimate" antisemitism.[6] Their emphasis on these new Jewish perils is well taken, but their use of the word antisemitism dilutes that rigor of terminology which alone will bring clarity to its meaning and dispel the present confusion. Beyond this, an overextension of the term plays into the hands of the antisemite who would divest it—and the reality it denotes—of all specific content.

It is a pleasure to express thanks to those without whose assistance or encouragement this book would have already found its last resting place on library shelves. First thanks should go to Fr. Kevin Lynch and Mr. Donald Brophy of Paulist Press for their invitation to update the book for republication. Thanks is due to Bishop Louis E. Gelineau of Providence, Rhode Island, who encouraged this effort and allowed a work schedule without which it would not have been possible; to Monsignor John M. Oesterreicher, founder of the Institute of Judaeo-Christian Studies and Distinguished Professor of Seton Hall University without whose assistance the first edition would never have been attempted; to Dr. Eugene Fisher, Executive Secretary of the Secretariat for Catholic-Jewish Relations of the National Conference of Catholic Bishops for supplying relevant materials; to Dr. Robert Michael of Southeastern Massachusetts University, the first to urge re-publication and offer help; to Donald Martin, Esq., who worked so hard and fast to acquire the author's publication rights from the former publisher; and to my secretary, Louise Pastille, who typed and retyped the manuscript repeatedly. Special thanks must be given to those thousands of Jews who in discussions following some two hundred and fifty lectures in Temples or Jewish centers, especially during the *Oneg Shabbat*,[7] gave me an insight into antisemitism and the Jewish reaction to it that could never be picked up in books and scholarly symposia.

Thanks, above all, to God, our common Father, who continues to reconcile his chosen peoples that have been so long estranged.

1
THE ANCIENT WORLD

Antisemitism is not, despite a common opinion, as old as the Jews.[1] While occupying a homeland of their own, Jews encountered the normal hostility of rival powers but nothing that could strictly be called antisemitism. This development was reserved for the Diaspora, the dispersion, and it was not until the third century B.C.E.[2] that its presence there could be clearly discerned.

Israel's Exodus from Egypt in the thirteenth pre-Christian century has been called the "first pogrom," and some historians concede it an antisemitic character.[3] And antisemitic it was if, and only if, one unduly stretches the meaning of the word. Egypt at that period had already developed a strong xenophobia, particularly with respect to the numerous Semitic tribes to the East that continued to covet her luxuriant Nile valley. The hated Hyksos had departed, leaving in their wake memories that the presence of any Semite on Egyptian soil would not fail to revive. "Look how numerous and powerful the Israelite people are growing, more so than we ourselves! Come, let us deal shrewdly with them to stop their increase; otherwise in time of war they too may join our enemies" (Exod. 1:9-10). These words of the Pharaoh actually betray a nervous national leader rather than an enemy of Jewry.

The near-millennium which extended from the Exodus to the age of Esdras and Nehemiah (fifth century B.C.E.) were years of painful spiritual and cultural formation. The people Moses led to Canaan were forged at length into a religious and social solidarity that subsequent millennia would not succeed in destroying. From the heights of Sinai, the voice of Yahweh had thundered forth the tenet of unity: "I, the Lord, am your God . . . you shall not have other gods besides me" (Exod. 20:2-3); and Israel's election was made no less plain: "I, the Lord, am sacred, I, who have set you apart from the other nations to be my own" (Lev. 20:26). From these transcending declarations a plethora of rituals, precepts, and customs were drawn that hedged Israel about and set her off as God's anointed among the nations. The Jews could have no doubt: their segregation was the will of Yahweh.

As they passed through the turbulent periods of judges, kings, and prophets, the world at large paid them little attention.[4] As late as the fifth century B.C.E., Herodotus—that meticulous observer and perambulating pioneer of history who visited many lands, including "the Palestine of Syria"—ignored the Jews in his comprehensive history of the time.[5] Obviously, their theological claims and their ethnic exclusivism neither interested nor irked the syncretic polytheists of antiquity as long as they were worked out on Palestinian soil. Nor did they attract much notice during the first years of the Diaspora. At most, these introverted communities scattered among the nations were regarded as mere curiosities. Herodotus also visited Elphantine, yet he failed to note in his *History* that the garrison there was Jewish. But the Diaspora, quietly gaining its foothold in the ancient world, was the stage being prepared for the inevitable clash between the worshippers of Yahweh and those of pagan deities.

EARLY CONTACTS

Dispersion of Jews began as early as the ninth century B.C.E., and, fed by a series of deportations and emigrations from Palestine, grew until, well before the Common era began, Babylonia, Egypt, and finally Rome became important Jewish centers. From these the Diaspora fanned out to encircle the entire Mediterranean, reaching as far as Persia, Armenia, Arabia, and Abyssinia in the East and Spain and Great Britain in the West.[6]

Though there is considerable disagreement about its size, the most reliable estimates place it at some four million persons during the first Christian century with another million in Palestine, the total comprising about one-eighth of the Roman Empire.[7]

Contrary to a widespread opinion, the Jews of the Diaspora did not occupy a special position in the economic structure of the ancient world. Their distribution among the various areas of the economy reflected fairly closely the general pattern. Coming from an agricultural nation, often as slaves and colonizers, a very large number—probably a majority—were farmers. A few, especially those who had emigrated voluntarily and had come to the cities, were engaged in commerce. They peopled all the crafts and industries of ancient times and eventually gained the monopoly of a few, for example, glasswork, weaving, and dyeing. As their separateness lessened in Hellenic-Roman times, they entered the sciences and other professions, and also had a part in public functions, particularly tax-farming and soldiery.

Early contacts of the Jews with antiquity were generally harmonious. The reluctance of many of the exiled to return to Palestine after emancipation and the ever-growing attraction Egypt and other Hellenized centers held for Palestinian Jews give adequate testimony of this. Moreover, the earliest literary references to Jews in the fourth and third centuries B.C.E., though they show no real knowledge of Judaism, were not unfavorable. Theophrastus entertained strange notions of Jewish rites and called Jews a "race of philosophers."[8] Clearchus of Soli, a disciple of Aristotle, considered them "descendants of the philosophers of India," an opinion he attributed to his teacher.[9] Megasthenus and Hermippus likewise considered them a species of foreign philosopher, the latter claiming for some of Pythagoras' tenets a Jewish origin.[10]

The razing of the Temple in the Elephantine colony (c. 410 B.C.E.) can hardly be considered an antisemitic act. Rather was it an act inspired by political motives and religious fanaticism. The Jewish garrison stationed there had been sent by Persian interests. Naturally, the Egyptian inhabitants resented Persian domination and harbored ill will for the representatives of their enemies. To make matters worse, the Jewish practice of sacrificing animals on the altars of Yahweh infuriated Egyptian priests who, as worshippers of the sacred ram, considered the Jewish rites sacrilegious.

Traditionally, the history of antisemitism is said to begin with the story of Haman, reported in the book of Esther. We are told that Haman, grand vizier of King Ahasuerus of Persia (Xerxes I, 486-465 B.C.E.) was angered by the Jew Mordecai's refusal to "bend his knee to him," and warned the king in these words: "There is a people scattered through all the provinces of thy Kingdom, and separated from one another, that use new laws and ceremonies, and moreover despise the King's ordinances" (Esther 3:8). Most exegetes, however, reject the historicity of this passage, because it reflects the Maccabean era of the second century B.C.E. rather than the Persian epoch of the fifth century. Nevertheless, the text is important since it succinctly formulates the classical reaction to the Jewish refusal to commingle and to worship national gods that was to echo throughout subsequent centuries.

THE HELLENIC WORLD

After the conquests of Alexander the Great (356-323 B.C.E.), the Jews ceased to remain unnoticed. The Macedonian conqueror, pupil of Aristotle and diligent propagator of the Grecian mode of life, left behind him a world rapidly becoming Hellenized. Against this first unification of culture, Jewish communities—now grown in size and influence—emerged in all their singularity. Unlike the rest of their Greco-Oriental and, later, Roman neighbors, Jews did not take their place as average citizens of the cities and towns. They continued to acknowledge Jerusalem as the Holy City to which they sent a *didrachma* each year as a personal tax and where stood the Temple of Yahweh, their one true God, invisible and transcendent, who refused to assume His place in the pantheons of the empire. Looking upon their host countries as profane soil and their fellow citizens as children of error and superstition, Jews grouped themselves in a quarter of their own city. The "ghetto" was a voluntary reality hundreds of years before the term was coined or legislation regarding it enacted. To the proud heirs of Pericles, Aristotle and

Homer, this aloofness was an insufferable arrogance. Convinced that all that was not Greek was barbarian, they resented rival claims to superiority or privilege on the part of a people they considered politically and culturally undistinguished. A collision between these two proud and dissimilar mentalities could only be a matter of time.

The first clear traces of a specifically anti-Jewish sentiment appeared in third century Egypt. The place is not accidental. Egypt was not only the heart of the Diaspora but the most advanced point of Hellenization outside Greece itself; Alexandria was a second Athens. Unsettled conditions in Palestine after Alexander's death brought increased deportations and immigrations of Jews to Egypt, that cradle of the Jewish nation which had never ceased to sing its siren song to Israel. The chief recipient of the inflow was Alexandria, the new "emporium of the western world" (Strabo), founded by Alexander, and fast becoming the commercial and intellectual capital of the world. Jews had been invited to populate the city by Alexander, who had given a section to them in order that they might be able to live according to their Law. By the beginning of the Common era, Jews occupied two-fifths of the city and already numbered 100,000. They were permitted a senate and ethnarch (governor) of their own, were active in commerce and possibly had a monopoly in grain and navigation of the Nile; they were conspicuous in tax-farming, and a few had grown very wealthy—an achievement that did not endear them to the envious Greeks, Syrians, and Egyptians who sought the same success. All Alexandrian Jews were not noble characters, but in this they were only typical Alexandrians, who, if we can believe Emperor Hadrian, were not of the highest caliber: "Their one God is money; Christians adore it, Jews adore it, so does everybody else."[11] The old xenophobia, moreover, was still alive, so, discontent under Greek and Roman rule, Egyptians took offense at the tolerance shown Jews. But most of all, Jewish refusal to accept common religious and social standards was resented by the strongly Hellenized population. Alexandria was manifestly predestined to become the chief center of antisemitism in the ancient world.

The first attack came from the pens of Alexandrian writers.[12] Hecataeus of Abdera, a Greek historian of the early third century

B.C.E., in an otherwise friendly but legendary account of Jewish origins and beliefs, asserted that Moses "in remembrance of the exile of his people, instituted for them a misanthropic and inhospitable way of life."[13] This theme of a humiliating origin and of misanthropy was picked up in the same century by Manetho, an Egyptian priest and historian, who embroidered it. Jews, once Egyptian lepers and diseased, Manetho wrote, were expelled by King Amenophis and led by Moses, who taught them "not to adore the gods," not to "abstain from sacred animals" and to "have nothing to do with those not of their faith."[14] It is likely that this account was current among historians of the time. Some of them must have been familiar with the biblical story of the Exodus, but since their patriotism found it unflattering they concocted their own account. Manetho's contribution was the weight he added to these tales as the official historian. From this point, the themes of leprous origins and misanthropy were rarely absent from the litanies of pagan antisemitism. They appeared in the works of Chaeremon, Lysimachus, Poseidonius, Apollonius Molon and of course in Apion and Tacitus—the two catchalls of Greek and Roman antisemitism respectively. The accusation of misanthropy was also to be used against the early Christians.

In the second century, literary antisemitism was sparse. Mnaseas of Patros holds the distinction of having originated the fable that Jews adored the golden head of an ass.[15] This charge, too, was destined for a long future and for use against the Christians. Agatharchides of Cnidus, in his *History of Asia*, noted the "ridiculous practices" of the Jews and the "absurdity of their Law," in particular, their observance of the Sabbath. Mockingly, he related how Ptolemy Lagus took Jerusalem in 320 B.C.E.: its inhabitants did not resist the invader because he attacked on the Sabbath.[16]

AT GRIPS WITH HELLENISM

During this same century, history took the lead from the men of letters and, in the growing conflict between Hellas and Judaea, Jerusalem itself became the battleground. The change from Persian to Greek domination and from the Ptolemaic to the Seleucid in Palestine exerted a corrosive influence on the strict

ethnic-religious separatism that Esdras and Nehemiah had succeeded in inculcating. Assimilationist tendencies, brought home
by Jewish emigrants, found numerous disciples in the homeland
and even expression in the sacred writings: "Let us go and make
a covenant with the heathens that are around us, for since we have
departed from them many evils have befallen us" (I Macc. 1:12).
The cause of the assimilationists was greatly aided in 198 B.C.E.
by the victory of the Seleucids, in Palestine, enthusiastic propa-
gators of the Greek way of life. Encouraged, the Hellenists in Jerusalem lost no time introducing Greek customs into the body of
Jewish practices. An extreme point was reached when the high
priest Jeshua assumed the Greek name Jason, placed Greek symbols in Jerusalem and went out to offer Temple gifts at the Greek
games near the city where naked Jewish youths disported themselves in the Grecian manner. Onto such a scene strode the Seleucid Antiochus IV Epiphanes (175-163 B.C.E.), extravagant
Hellenizer, to force a climax. Impatient with the progress of the
Hellenists in Jerusalem, he took the city. Pillaging and slaugh-
tering, he entered the Holy of Holies and dedicated the Temple
to Jupiter Olympus. The practice of the Mosaic Law was outlawed under pain of death. The reaction of almost all Jews was
violent. United behind the Maccabees, the nation rose and broke
the Seleucid yoke. For the first time since 586 B.C.E., Judaea enjoyed almost complete independence which lasted almost 75
years.

The astounding Maccabean victory fired Jewish hearts
everywhere with a new sense of independence and national pride;
it also helped to balance the unequal struggle against Hellenism.
In Palestine, the Hasmonaeans launched a war of expansion
which set boundaries for the Jewish state not reached since the
time of Solomon. The effects of the victory were hardly less palpable in the Diaspora, where the Hellenizing process was well advanced. Setting themselves against the cultural wave that
threatened to engulf them, Jewish communities launched a twofold literary counterattack. In a group of Messianic books Jewish
writers sang the glories of Israel and envisioned her ultimate
triumph over all nations under the scepter of her Messiah.[17] The
new spirit also caught up Jewish apologists, who, anxious to find
a place for Judaism in the Olympian sun, elaborated Jewish ac-

complishments with considerable bias, depicting the Hebrews as
the progenitors of all civilization and culture. Among the philosophers, Aristobulus, a Macedonian Jew, did not hesitate to declare that Pythagoras, Socrates, Plato, and Homer had derived
their ideas from an early Greek translation of the Bible. But none
of these went so far as those falsifiers who, by incorporating renowned pagan authors into their own texts, composing fictitious
quotations from them, and attributing Jewish authorship to
whole pagan works, sought to enhance the stature of Judaism.
The pseudo-Hecataeus and pseudo-Aristeas are prominent examples of this kind of propaganda.

Naturally these efforts were resented by chauvinistic intellectuals. What disturbed them even more was the success these
propagandizing efforts enjoyed. Conversions to Judaism began to
soar in this period, especially among the cultured. Many pagans
of good heart, apparently disillusioned by the spiritual poverty
and moral mediocrity of their pagan milieu, were ripe for the appeal of the pure monotheism and firm moral demands which the
Jewish propagandists espoused. And since the Jewish faith, especially in the Diaspora, had already adopted a universalist and
missionary outlook, its doors were swung wide to those who
knocked. Some entered as "true proselytes," binding themselves
to the whole Law and circumcision; but others, demi-proselytes,
called "Godfearing" or "devout," remained at the threshold, ob-
serving only the Sabbath rest and a few other Jewish customs.
The total influx must have been large, for by the first century
C.E., according to Josephus, Jewish religious observances were
practiced in every nation and city.[18] And Seneca complained bitterly that the Jews "have so prevailed that they are accepted
everywhere in the world: the conquered have given their laws to
the conquerors."[19]

The position of the Jews now little resembled what it had
been a century or more before. Then a small, clannish people,
they were now representatives of an influential and proselytizing
nation that threatened to rival the best efforts of Greek civilization
in spiritual influence and industriousness.

Hellas accepted the challenge with bad grace. In the cities
where Jews were numerous, open hostilities commenced. Josephus reports a suppression of Jews under Ptolemy Physcon in 146

B.C.E., but the account, displaying chauvinistic characteristics, is questionable. Of greater certitude is the report by Jordanes (sixth century C.E.) of the persecution in 88 B.C.E., but which Josephus places forty years earlier. Regardless of the historicity or dates of these reports, it was apparent that Jewish-Gentile tensions were now at the breaking point. The disturbances may, to a considerable degree, be attributed to reciprocal political and commercial rivalries but also to the behavior of Jews, who from the founding of Alexandria were, as Juster states, "continuously in sedition."[20] But these factors alone do not account for the point to which tensions had come. Resentment against Jewish separatism and religious claims doubtless played at least an equal part.

LITERARY ANTISEMITISM

The chief reaction again came from men of letters, who regarded themselves as the guardians of Hellenistic civilization. Foremost among them were the Stoics and Sophists, mostly Alexandrian in residence or influence. The former, fervent proselytizers themselves, were alarmed by Jewish proselytism and its success; the latter, skeptical philosophers, resented Jewish appropriation of Greek sources. Greek historians, meanwhile, continued to extol their own nation's glories at the expense of what they considered upstarts from Palestine.

Poseidonius, Stoic philosopher and historian, taking up where Hecataeus and Manethos left off, gave further circulation to the tales of Israel's expulsion from Egypt as lepers; described Jews as an "impious people, hated by the gods"; and blamed Moses for leading them into "misanthropy and perversity" and teaching them "laws contrary to humanity and justice." He related further that when Epiphanes violated the Holy of Holies he sacrificed an enormous pig on the altar and forced Jews to eat it.[21] This sardonic reference to Jewish abhorrence of pork is Poseidonius' sole original contribution to the antisemitic inventory, and one that lasted.

Apollonius Molon, a famous rhetorician of this time and teacher of Cicero and Caesar, was the first to compose an entire work against the Jews, thus launching the endless chain of literature *adversus Judaeos* that reaches down to the present day. All we possess of his work is found in a fragment of Polyhistor and a few summary references in Josephus' *Against Apion*. As do most antisemitic writers, Molon repeats almost all the charges of his predecessors: Jews are atheists, hate strangers, and hold absurd superstitions. His own contribution comprises an attack on Jewish law, which he finds "lacking in truth and justice." The rest is merely insults: Moses was a charlatan and impostor; Jews are cowardly, but also daring (Molon appears not to notice his contradiction), useless, demented, and "the most inept of all barbarians."[22]

Passing from Molon to Apion, the Mt. Everest of Greco-Oriental antisemites, we enter the Christian era, passing but a few foothills. These are Lysimachus, Chaeremon and Democritus, who merely repeated old charges. The first two merely added touches of their own to Manetho's story of the Exodus.[23] Democritus, in his *On the Jews*, repeats Mnaseas' charge that Jews adore the golden head of an ass and, according to the historian Suidas, charged that "every seven years they capture a stranger, lead him to their Temple, and immolate him by cutting his flesh into small pieces."[24] The "ritual-murder" accusation is born. To be employed against early Christians and again against Jews from the twelfth century on, it will leave a trail of blood in its wake.

Apion—naturalized Alexandrian rhetorician—takes his place in the history of antisemitism as the first of the titans. Possessed of a fierce hatred of Jews, whose influence he resented, this vain and unreliable man earned the reputation of charlatan and braggart. Pliny reports Emperor Tiberius' (14-37 C.E.) opinion of him: *cymbalum mundi* (the tom-tom of the universe).[25] Apion's attack on the Jews, found mostly in his *History of Egypt*, contained nothing that had not been said in substance before, but the wanton use he made of his material and the note of bitterness he added assured him distinction. The Exodus story is retold, but the lepers are now joined to the "blind and lame," and their number placed at 110,000. The Sabbath, he said, originated because a pelvic ailment, incurred as Jews fled Egypt, forced them to rest on the seventh day. To the usual charge of misanthropy Apion adds that Jews are held under oath "not to assist strangers, especially Greeks." He chides Jews for not adoring the gods of the city, for sedition; they are ridiculed for sacrificing animals, abstaining from pork, and practicing circumcision. Jews, he tells us, adore the golden head of an ass, as Antiochus Epiphanes discovered in the Temple.[26]

But Epiphanes discovered more. Here in full is Josephus' account of Apion's version of the terrifying tale:

> . . . Antiochus found in the temple a couch, on which a man was reclining, with a table before him laden with a banquet of fish of the sea, beasts of the earth, and birds of the air, at which the poor fellow was gazing in stupefaction. The king's entry was instantly hailed by him with adoration, as about to procure him profound relief; falling at the king's knees, he stretched out his right hand and implored him to set him free. The king reassured him and bade him tell him who he was, why he was living there, what was the meaning of his abundant fare. Thereupon, with sighs and tears, the man, in a pitiful tone, told the tale of his distress. He said that he was a Greek and that, while traveling about the province for his livelihood, he was suddenly kidnapped by men of a foreign race and conveyed to the temple; there he was shut up and seen by nobody, but was fattened on feasts of the most lavish description. At first these unlooked for attentions deceived him and caused him pleasure; suspicion followed, then consternation. Finally, on consulting the attendants who waited upon him, he heard of the unutterable law of the Jews, for the sake of which he was being fed. The practice was repeated annually at a fixed season. They would kidnap a Greek foreigner, fatten him up for a year, and then convey him to a wood, where they slew him, sacrificed his body with their customary ritual, partook of his flesh, and, while immolating the Greek, swore an oath of hostility to the Greeks. The remains of their victim were then thrown into a pit.[27]

The monstrous and deathless tale of "ritual murder" already enjoys its classical expression.

Two Jewish champions entered the lists against Apion. Flavius Josephus' work, *Against Apion*, made no attempt to conceal his contempt for Apion, calling him "a man of very bad morals and one no better in his whole life than a mountebank."[28] Philo, the great Jewish Platonist, confronted Apion in Rome in 39 C.E., where he led a delegation to plead the Jewish cause before Cali-

gula in the wake of anti-Jewish riots in Alexandria under Flaccus.
Apion, representing the antisemitic faction, had little trouble con-
vincing the half-mad emperor that the Jews' refusal to erect his
statues in their temples was sufficient provocation for the brutal
riots that had descended upon them. But here we are already in
the Roman period, another stage in the history of antisemitism.

After Apion, Greek antisemitism withered. Political and cultural hegemony had passed to Rome, and Hellenism lost much of
its proud vigor. Henceforward most Greek writers showed a new
tolerance toward the Jews, as antisemitism reverted to its original
posture: Israel was viewed as an oddity. Plutarch is charactertis-
tic. Full of misinformation about Jews, he speculated about them
with abandon.[29] Celsus, in the second century C.E., includes
Christians and Jews alike in his disdain. Even at this late date, he
could not abide that the Jews "pride themselves in possessing a
superior wisdom and disdain the company of other men."[30] Greek
antisemitism's last attack—a violent one—came in the third century from Philostratus, a Sophist, who takes us back for a moment
to Molon and Apion, but says nothing original.[31]

UNDER THE ROMAN EAGLE

Roman antisemitism, direct heir to the Greek, bore the
stamp of its predecessor. The Roman conquest failed to change
radically the cultural climate or social conditions of the Greco-
Oriental world. Greek opinion of Jews thus passed on to the Romans. Roman antisemitism, however, was more complex than
that of the Greek. The Maccabean spirit did not abate in Roman
times, and Rome knew how to discourage rebellions. Torrents of
blood were to flow from Jewish-Roman conflicts. On the other
hand, Roman policy displayed a clear philosemitic tendency.[32]
Indeed, official favor toward Jewish belief and the success of Jewish proselytism among the Romans impress the historian of the
era as much as the Judaeo-Roman wars and anti-Jewish reactions.
Only the intellectuals remained impervious to the appeal of Israel's monotheism.

The most important new element in the Roman period was
the Jewish community in Rome. A latecomer in the Diaspora, it
served as a small-scale model of all Jewry within the very shadow

of the imperial palace, thus assuming great importance as a determinant of imperial policy and popular attitudes toward Jews. Before the Christian era, the community was large and influential—second only to Alexandria. Already in 59 B.C.E., Cicero in his plea *Pro Flacco* assumed that everybody knew "how numerous they are, their clannishness, their influence in the assemblies."[33] Roman Jews enjoyed a vote in the assemblies and became something of a political power. They entered the business life of the city; they won many converts to their faith, and were endowed by the emperors with many privileges. These privileges earned the hatred of their envious neighbors; and their proselytic gains, that of the intellectuals and occasionally the government.

The principal source of tension, however, was religious. Roman religion was ritualistic and intimately woven into the daily lives of the people. Images of the gods were everywhere, and almost every act, public or private, had its supernatural accompaniment. Romans were proud of their deities and rites, which they closely associated with the glory of Rome. Generally tolerant of other religions to which they were hosts, they were uncompromising with whatever threatened to undermine their own cult.[34] They were unaccustomed, moreover, to religious competition. Most of the many foreign religionists within the boundaries of the empire were content with their freedom of worship and found little difficulty accommodating themselves to the simple requirements of inclining to Jupiter and abstaining from acts hostile to the imperial cult.

Not so the Jews. Accommodate they would in all but cult. They, too, had a religion, indeed a more demanding one than the Roman and equally entwined in their daily lives. Israel's God was a jealous God who struck no bargains. Such intransigence placed the Roman authorities in a serious dilemma: either renounce their prized principle of toleration or grant special exemptions to this stubborn minority; in Juster's phrase: "persecution or privilege."[35]

Roman realism prevailed. Jews were granted all privileges necessary for complete practice of their way of life not only in occupied Palestine but also in Rome and throughout the Diaspora. Indeed the history of Jewish-Roman relations comprises little more than the story of these privileges and the conflicts or alliances to which they gave rise.[36] Jews were accorded unique favors in order to render the practice of their monotheism possible. Exempt from many external acts of the Roman cult and released from all secular activities on the Sabbath, they were held only to prayers for the emperor. Before the Common Era began, Judaism was recognized as the only *religio licita* in the empire, save the imperial cult itself.

Reasons have been sought by historians for this exceptional status. Many factors contributed to it, but the fundamental explanation seems to be psychological. Rome and Jerusalem both admired and feared one another. Jews appear to have preferred Roman domination to any other—even that of the Herods—and more than once they sided with Rome against her enemies. But they had learned to fear Roman brutality, and the specter of 2,000 Jews crucified by Varus (139-69 C.E.) within view of Jerusalem was enough to keep the fear alive. Rome, for her part, seemed fascinated by the Jews' courageous adherence to their religion, but had similarly learned to fear their rebellions, some of which taxed its military might to the full. And yet, beyond the mutual admiration and fear, there existed little true understanding between these two radically different mentalities. Their relations were destined to be stormy.

The policies of the empire reflected the ambivalence. Some emperors were favorable to Jews, some hostile. Julius Caesar (100-44 B.C.E.), grateful for help received during the civil war, showered them with privileges. Roman Jews thus mourned Caesar bitterly at his death. His concessions, considered by historians to be the Jews' Magna Charta in antiquity, were on the whole renewed by subsequent emperors. Augustus (27 B.C.E.-C.E. 14) continued these policies and, among other things, refrained from distributing grain to Jews on the Sabbath. Tiberius (14-37 C.E.), under the influence of Sejanus, his antisemitic minister of state, deported 4,000 Jews to Sardinia because of the malfeasance of a few, but did renew their privileges after Sejanus' death. Caligula (37-41 C.E.) attempted to impose emperor worship in the synagogues, but died before his mad venture could be enforced. Claudius (41-54 C.E.) treated Jews well, though he may have expelled some because of Jewish-Christian conflicts.[37]

The savage war which brought about the destruction of Jerusalem in 70 C.E. might be expected to have destroyed Israel's official status, but it did not. The only change in this respect was the conversion of the traditional Temple tax which Jews were permitted to send to Jerusalem into a *fiscus judaicus*, a tax sent to the temple of Jupiter Capitoline in Rome. After the war the course of Judaeo-Roman relations was generally dependent upon the movements of Jewish messianism and proselytism. Still fired by visions of independence, Jews often rebelled, most seriously under Trajan in 115 C.E. and under Hadrian in 131 C.E. This last uprising brought an end to Israel as an effective political force in antiquity, although thereafter the empire still conceded to the Jewish patriarch the deference given heads of state. The final revolt under Hadrian was provoked by the emperor's interdiction of Jewish cult and the practice of circumcision and his construction of a pagan city, *Aelia Capitolina*, in Jerusalem. A zealous Hellenizer, Hadrian had become alarmed by the success of Jewish proselytizing and resolved to have done with Judaism for good.[38]

Popular antisemitism, though not the outstanding feature of the Roman period, was nevertheless rather widespread and betimes intense. Throughout the empire, the Jews' special imperial status, "alien" character, and commercial initiative earned them the envy and resentment of the non-Jewish populace. In Rome, their privileges and influence caused strong resentment, which was held in check, however, by imperial protection. In Alexandria old tensions had grown but during the first days of the empire could not risk open expression. Under the unstable Caligula, the risk lessened, and an outbreak—the first real pogrom of history in 38 C.E.—occurred in Alexandria. Unsure of the emperor's disposition, the prefect of the city abetted the mob in their riotous clamor for the erection of the imperial statue in the synagogues. In consequence, Jews were stripped of their citizenship, mocked, and finally crowded into one quarter of the city, even relegated to cemeteries and beaches. Some were tortured and murdered. It was in the wake of these proscriptions that the delegations of Philo and Apion pleaded before Caligula in Rome, to the further humiliation of the Jews.[39]

Disorders marred Jewish-Gentile relations in other cities where Jews were numerous, particularly under the reigns of Vespasian (69-79 C.E.) and Titus (78-81 C.E.). In Antioch Jewish political rights were challenged, requests were made to Rome to suppress them, and massacres of Jews took place. In Ephesus, Cyrenaica and cities in Ionia there were outbreaks inspired usually by the refusal of Jews to participate in the pagan cult. In Caesarea—founded by Herod (4 B.C.E.-40 C.E.)—disputes about political priority were rife and Jews were frequently attacked; on some occasions many were killed, especially in cities bordering on Palestine (Damascus, Tyre, Ascalon, Ptolemais, Gadara, Hippus, and Scythopolis) where Jewish religious propaganda was active.

CLASSICAL ANTISEMITISM

The true antisemites of the Roman Empire were neither the emperors nor the people, but the intelligentsia. Many of them took no notice of Israel, but among those who did Jews had few friends and many bitter enemies. A Varro might show a certain respect; a Pliny the Elder or Titus-Livy remained neutral; from the rest there was nothing but insult and contempt.[40]

This phase of our history began in 59 B.C.E. with the great voice of Cicero. The renowned orator, apt pupil of Molon, carried his Rhodesian master's prejudices back to Rome, thus supplying the thread that bound Roman antisemitism to its Greek antecedents. Occasion to display his feelings was presented in a trial for the defense of a certain prefect of Asia Minor named Flaccus who had despoiled the Jewish treasury—a defense immortalized in his *Pro Flacco*. Before the court, we recall, he whispered his fear of the number, clannishness and influence of Roman Jews,[41] and lauded Flaccus for having stood up to their "barbarous superstition."[42] "Their kind of religion and rites," he orated, "has nothing in common with the splendor of the empire, the gravity of our name, and the institutions of our ancestors; all the more now that this people has shown through arms how they feel about our rule; and conquered and enslaved, how little the immortal gods care for them."[43] The Jews, he had remarked earlier before the Senate, are "born to servitude."[44] History does not record the outcome of Flaccus' trial but does relate that Cicero was banished from Rome the following year.

During the closing years of the last pre-Christian century, literary antisemitism was scarcely kept alive by Horace's few sneers about Jewish proselytism and credulity, Tibullus' and Ovid's jibes about the Sabbath rest, and Trogus Pompey's distortions of Jewish history.[45] It is not until we reach Seneca in the following century that Cicero's pitch is again reached. This fervent Stoic and patriot railed against the prevalence of customs of that "most wicked nation," especially the practice of keeping the Sabbath. "To spend every seventh day without doing anything and thus lose one seventh part of life," Seneca averred, "is contrary to a useful life."[46] Petronius indulged in sarcasms concerning circumcision and the Jews' "reverence" for pork. Quintilian's and Martial's allusions were brief but cutting: To the first, Jews were a "pernicious nation" and their faith a "superstition"; to the latter, circumcised Jews and their Sabbath were synonymous with everything degrading. In the second century, Juvenal rued the corrupting influence of Judaizing parents on "their unfortunate offspring."[47]

The apogee of pagan antisemitism was reached in Tacitus.[48] In bitterness and breadth of attack the celebrated historian surpassed all competitors in the Greco-Roman era. No previous charge is missing from his arsenal—except that of "ritual murder," by that time in use against Christians—and each charge receives a new embellishment. Their Sabbath, he avers, commemorates the day on which they escaped and to which in their indolence they became attached. Their other institutions are "sinister, shameful, and have survived only because of their perversity." Their prosperity "stems from their obstinate solidarity, which contrasts with the implacable hatred they harbor toward the rest of men." They never eat with strangers and, though prone to debauchery, "abstain from intercourse with strange women." Among the Jews themselves, however, "nothing is illicit." Indeed, the first instruction they are given is to disdain the gods, abjure the fatherland, forget their parents, brothers, and children.

Suddenly, the tone changes, he comes close to eulogy: Jews consider it a crime to kill "a single child"; they believe in immortal life for those who die in battle, whence their disdain for death; their God is a supreme and eternal being, whence their intolerance of "any statue in the cities and especially in their temples, their adulation for kings . . . "

The lapse is momentary. What are the Jews? "Of all enslaved peoples the most contemptible . . . a loathsome people . . . at once full of superstition and hostile to all religious practice," a people whose "customs are absurd and sordid . . . " In sum: "All that we hold sacred is profane to them; all that is licit to them is impure to us."[49]

After Tacitus, Roman literary antisemitism declined. There were a few faint complaints, and then the final rattle of a pagan hatred long since in its death throes. Rutilius Namatianus, fifth-century poet, angered by a "querulous Jew" met on the road, vented his feelings in an elegy about "an unsociable animal this Jew, to whom all human nourishment is repugnant . . . " The poet concludes with an attack on the Sabbath and other Jewish rites and finally on that scourge which Judaism gave the world—Christianity.[50]

EVALUATION

Greek and Roman antisemitism resemble each other sufficiently to be considered a historical unit. The Roman phase may to a large extent be seen as Greek antisemitism continued in new political circumstances. In both phases the same basic situation obtained: a proud and conquering civilization facing a politically negligible nation, bereft—by pagan standards—of all culture and accomplishments, deeming its Torah superior to the laws and letters of the conqueror.

Despite the clash of religious views and values between the followers of Yahweh and Zeus or Jupiter, pagan antisemitism was not theological. Foreign theologies were generally tolerated, provided their adherents refrained from acts hostile to the imperial religion and gave an external nod to Jupiter. Jews were exempt from the latter requirements, and Judaism was allowed as the only *religio licita* in the Roman empire. This first antisemitism, further, was neither ethnic nor racist. Despite their haughty contempt for all the subjugated, Greece and Rome were tolerant of the motley amalgam of peoples that made up their empires. Jews, moreover, were often confused with Syrians or Orientals generally.

Nor was ancient pagan antisemitism economic, as antisemites would have it in this—and in every other—era. Economic factors were prominent in the antisemitism of Alexandria, the seaports, and the Greek cities, but they could not be considered sufficient to characterize it. Juster, who made an exhaustive study of the Greco-Roman period, found no disproportion of Jews in commerce and saw fit to conclude: "Never did a pagan author characterize Jews as merchants; never in the pagan epoch were the notions of Jew and merchant associated as if they belonged together. In this same epoch nothing indicates that they had any predilection for commerce."[51] The same may be said of Jewish wealth. Some Jews were wealthy and drew resentment, but the Jewish masses were of moderate means or poor; some of them were beggars; many began life in the Diaspora as slaves. Economic antisemitism entered history long after the pagan era came to an end.

Essentially, ancient antisemitism was cultural, taking the shape of a national xenophobia played out in political settings. It was primarily a literary phenomenon, flowing as it did, for the most part, from the pens of a proud, nativistic intelligentsia that had assumed the mantle of defenders of the imperial glory.

It is difficult, historically, to overestimate the importance of this first manifestation of the antisemitic animus, if for no other reason than that it gives the lie to the notion of an "eternal" antisemitism with its subtle suggestion that the Jew himself is always culpable of outbreaks of antisemitism. More importantly, it displays the antisemitic, we might say, in a pure culture, as yet uncontaminated by the theological or racist Judaeophobias that were to come in the Christian and modern eras. A study of this period, moreover, lends substance to the view that antisemitism rests in an important way on a positive ground: Judaism's biblical vocation to separate its faithful from the nations in witness to the one God and his Law. Jews were resented in this epoch for their separatism, their claims, and also for the higher moral and spiritual quality of their way of life. A cryptic admiration—turned into its opposite—is often discernible behind the pagan resentment. This positive ingredient at the heart of antisemitism is often overlooked by historians and analysts of the subject.[52]

The significance and import of ancient antisemitism has been acknowledged by recognized scholars in the field, notably, Theodore Reinach and Salon Baron. The first is of the view that Greco-Roman opinion of the Jews "contributed toward clarifying an entire historical development that reaches down to our own times."[53] The latter has this to say: "Almost every note in the cacophony of medieval and modern antisemitism was sounded by the chorus of ancient writers."[54] Jules Isaac warns against exaggerating the importance and influence of this early species of antisemitism, but conscientiously devotes forty percent of his work on antisemitic origins to it.[55]

Insufficient attention, however, has been accorded this first antisemitic period, even to the point of complete suppression.[56] Lovsky attributes this failure to two opposing motives. He writes:

> When the bias is Christian, the alibis of Egyptians (or Persians) are gladly featured, as if the sin of the pagan should attenuate that of the Christians; when it is anti-Christian, the protests against the existence of Egyptian antisemitism are so much the greater in order to burden the Church with an animosity that would find its inspiration to the Christian faith. Indeed because of such reservations, impartial debate seems impossible.[57]

One can indeed notice in the different accounts of this historical phase of antisemitism accounts which run from complete suppression to endowing the period as the necessary and sufficient foundation of all eventual antisemitisms. That the historian must steer clear of such apologetical or *a priori* tendencies and avoid every sort of manipulation of historical data needs no insistence.

That Greco-Roman literary antisemitism wielded an influence on modern rationalist antisemitism is evidenced by the Encylopedists' verbatim use of some of the early pagan antisemitic authors. Voltaire is one of these. Arthur Hertzberg has evinced this, and concludes:

> The notion that the new society (of the Enlightenment) was to be a reevocation of classical antiquity was the prime source of post-Christian antisemitism in the nineteenth century. The vital link, the man who skipped over the Christian centuries and provided a new, international, secular, anti-Jewish rhet-

oric in the name of European culture rather than religion was Voltaire.[58]

Samuel Ettinger has also demonstrated how early pagan antisemitic ideas and phraseology passed through the English Deists of the eighteenth century into the mainstream of the Enlightenment.[59]

How much the pagan antisemitic virus infected the Christian growth is difficult to ascertain. It appears to be minimally. It is only to be expected, however, that at least a minor infection would occur as the Church became gentilized and simultaneously de-Judaized toward the end of the first century C.E. Christian antisemitism is, as we shall see, of another kind that stood in little need of the pagan impetus to take on a life of its own that would in time develop a Judaeophobia much more virulent than that of its predecessor.

As Christianity commenced its ascendancy, pagan antisemitism was in rapid decline. The Church had come upon a new source of anti-Jewish thought and sentiment.

2
THE CONFLICT OF THE CHURCH AND SYNAGOGUE

The phenomenal rise of Christianity in the first three centuries of the Christian era paralleled a transfer of pagan animosity from Jews to Christians. At first both were indistinguishable to the contemptuous Roman eye; accordingly both enjoyed the same privileges, both suffered the same opprobrium. Once the distinction between them became clear, however, the Church fell heir to many of the charges that Jews alone had elicited in the past. It was now the Church that was a detestable superstition with absurd and extravagant rites, the new hater of mankind, the worshiper of the head of an ass, the ritual murderer, the devotee of debauchery and incest.[1] Some pagan writers, such as Celsus, Porphyry, and Dio Cassius, even found it possible to speak kindly of Jews, particularly when compared with Christians. During the bloodiest Christian persecution Emperor Diocletian explicitly exempted Jews from pagan sacrifice and connived at their illegal religious practices. It was an uneasy alliance for the servants of Yahweh who thrice daily in their prayers addressed the Almighty in the *Shemoneh Esreh*: "May the Empire of pride [Rome] be brought down without delay in our own time."

SEEDS OF SEPARATION

But before pagan antisemitism died, a new conflict was in the making. The nascent Church, having sprung from the Synagogue, proclaimed itself the fulfillment of Israel. Its Founder, of the house of David, had proclaimed that He was come "to the lost sheep of the house of Israel" (Matt. 10:6), "not . . . to destroy but to fulfill" (Matt. 5:17). But He had also announced Himself as the sole way to the Father, had asserted His priority to Abraham (see John 8:58), and had enjoined His followers to go and "make disciples of all nations" (Matt. 28:19). The new faith contained Judaic, trans-Judaic, and some anti-Judaic elements. Future developments would determine how these elements would be apportioned and the degree of anti-Judaism that would be incorporated into the teaching of the aborning Church, and finally whether this anti-Judaism would become a source of antisemitism.[2]

For the moment, while the Synagogue looked upon the new movement as just another Jewish sect and Christians still hoped that all Israel would enter the Church, there was peace. The first Christian Church, full of zeal and fervor, was a Jewish Church in the leadership, membership, and worship; and it remained within the precincts of the Synagogue. But as the universalist implications of the Gospel message (not yet fully written) made themselves felt, a series of developments gradually brought this tentative equilibrium to an end. It soon became clear that the majority of Jews would not enter the Church. This realization was disconcerting to the Christian converts, whose faith was built to a large extent on the Jewish Scriptures and the Jewish Messiah. In tones of a prophet Stephen charged the people and their leaders with infidelity to Moses as well as to the Messiah (Acts 7:2-7:53). Paul preached the inefficacy of the Law for Jew and Gentile, and in the face of Jewish opposition turned to the Gentiles (Rom 1:16, 2:10-11). Through a praeternatural communication Peter was instructed to accept the demi-proselyte Cornelius into the Church without committing him to the Law (Acts ch. 10). The council of the Apostles in Jerusalem decreed that gentile converts were not to be held to the legal observances (Gal ch. 2; Acts 15:5-11). Finally, at Antioch, Paul confronted Peter, insisting that while Jewish Christians might practice the Law, faith in Jesus Christ was necessary and sufficient for salvation (Gal. 2:11-21). This was the final disposition of the matter. Judaeo-Christianity, thus rejected, was destined to become a snare to Christian and Jew alike and a source of conflict for both Church and Synagogue.

In the mid-first century, Paul laid down the ground-plan for the Church's theology of Israel: The Law, transitory and preparatory in character, terminated in Christ. Universal salvation is found in faith in Christ, which is the fruit of grace. The burden of the Law is replaced by the hope and liberty of the Gospel (Gal. and Rom. *passim*). In his Epistle to the Romans (ch. 9-11) this doctrine was tempered: Grieving for his kinsmen—for whom he himself would be anathema—the Apostle taught that even if the Jews have failed by their unbelief, God has not cast off His people. If they have stumbled, they have not fallen. God has closed their eyes until the full number of the Gentiles enter in. In the fullness of time, they will return, and their reconciliation will be a golden age for the Church. The task of Christians is not to patronize them but to provoke them to jealousy by the holiness of their own lives. Indeed Jews "are most dear for the sake of the fathers. For the gifts and the call of God are without repentance" (Rom. 11:28-29).

This Pauline doctrine of separation and benevolence set the primary and authentic attitude of the Church toward Judaism. But, in the early years, as the Church's severance from the parent body became complete, the negative aspects stressing Judaism's replacement were greatly accentuated, and a less benevolent tradition was destined to overshadow the Pauline doctrine.

THE CONFLICT BEGINS

The Synagogue resented Christianity's claims and in the emerging conflict struck the first blow.[3] Hellenist Jewish converts to the Church were driven from Jerusalem. Stephen was killed, as were the two Jameses, James the Less by the action of the Sadducean high priest. Peter was forced out of Palestine by the persecution of Herod Agrippa I, and Paul endured flagellations, imprisonments, complaints by Jews to Roman authorities, and threats of death at Jewish hands. Barnabas' death (c. 60 C.E.) at the hands of Jews in Cyprus is unanimously reported by the early hagiographers.[4]

Nero's persecution of Christians in the mid-first century was probably instigated by Jewish delations. As yet Christians had not yet been distinguished from Jews by the empire and could not have been persecuted as a body without being pointed out. The likely informers were Poppaea, Nero's wife, a Jewish demi-proselyte, and her entourage. The motive imputed by St. Clement of Rome was "jealousy and envy."[5]

Jewish anti-Christian hostility in this era was by no means universal. Gamaliel's neutrality, reported in Acts (5:38-39), was closer to the norm: "Keep away from these men and let them alone. For if this plan or work is of men, it will be overthrown; but if it is of God, you will not be able to overthrow it. Else perhaps you may find yourselves fighting even against God." His viewpoint epitomized the usual sentiment of Pharisaism toward dissident sects. Toward the end of the first century, Rabbi Eliezer looked benignly on Christianity and voiced his conviction that there was a place for Jesus in the world to come.[6] A century later Tertullian would tell of Jews offering Christians asylum in their synagogues during persecutions. And there were cases, confirmed by archeology, where Christian martyrs were buried in Jewish cemeteries.

Jewish hostility in the early period was nevertheless strong, if sporadic. St. Justin's complaint to Rabbi Trypho a little later: "You cannot use violence against us Christians because of those in power, but as often as you could, you did . . . "[7] must be heeded but not overdrawn; early Christian historians were prone to exaggerate the scope of Jewish hatred, especially of the popular kind.

The Great War (66-70 C.E.) and the destruction of the Temple in Jerusalem proved a turning point for Judaeo-Christian relations. As the war began, Christians left Jerusalem for Pella there to remain for the duration. To Jews, this seeming disloyalty was revealing, and left no doubt in their minds that the new movement had dissociated itself not only from the practice of the Law but also from Jewish national aspirations. But the Christians saw in the destruction of the Temple the fulfillment of Christ's prophecy and a confirmation of their belief that the scepter had passed from Judaism to the Church. The new awareness on both sides served to increase tensions.

The definitive separation, for the Jews, occurred in the year

80 when the Sanhedrin at Jabne introduced a malediction in the *Shemoneh Esreh*, recited thrice daily by Jews: "May the *minim* perish in an instant; may they be effaced from the book of life and not be counted among the just." Much controversy has centered upon this malediction and in particular upon the term *minim*. All agree that the prayer was introduced in order to weed out Judaeo-Christians from synagogue services, that *minim* meant "heretics," including Jewish Christians, and that in later centuries the term came to include all Christians. But many have denied that the word included gentile Christians in the early centuries. After an investigation of pertinent talmudic texts, Marcel Simon concludes, however, that "the term applied early not only to apostate Jews, but also to Christianity of every nuance, which was considered the greatest apostasy from Judaism."[8]

At this same time, letters were sent by the Sanhedrin at Jabne to the Diaspora concerning the new malediction and the attitude to be adopted *vis à vis* Christianity.[9] Three of the Fathers—St. Justin, Eusebius, and St. Jerome—give an inkling of the content of the letters, which to some extent may be reconstructed: Jesus, a charlatan, was killed by the Jews, but his disciples stole his body and preached his Resurrection, calling him the Son of God; Jews should have no dealings with his followers. The decision at Jabne, promulgated by these letters, constituted a formal and final excommunication of Christians from the Synagogue.[10]

For Christianity the final separation was longer in coming. Paul had decided the issue doctrinally, but had allowed Jewish converts to continue practicing prescriptions of the Law, and adhered to them himself for fear of scandalizing his brethren (I Cor. 9:20). It is probable that this tolerance survived in the Church for many years after Paul's death. In the mid-second century, for example, St. Justin still exhibits leniency toward such Judaizers, though in this he is exceptional. Even after the excommunication of Jabne, apparently many Christians of Jewish parentage clung to the hope that their nation would eventually accept Jesus as its Messiah. It was not until 130 C.E., when a majority of Jews, including the influential Rabbi Akiba, hailed Bar Kokba as the Messiah that hopes were finally dashed. Even so, by 100 C.E. the Christian attitude toward Judaism had already stiffened. The hostility of the Synagogue and the refusal of the majority of Jews to enter the Church despite the apostolic preaching was regarded more and more as blindness and malice.

Historians and exegetes have noted the progressive change in tone that marked the attitude toward Jews in the New Testament as it was committed to writing during the second half of the first century, and many have sought to trace the roots of antisemitism to the sacred pages themselves. Anti-Jewish texts are singled out from many parts of the New Testament, most particularly in John's Gospel, composed toward the end of the first century, which includes numerous anti-Jewish episodes and often employs the phrase "the Jews" in a pejorative manner. John has, in consequence, been called "the father of antisemitism."

Is there antisemitism in the New Testament? The question is a complex and highly controverted one.[11] To attempt to answer it it is necessary to give strict attention to the definition of antisemitism, an attention that is often lacking, even in scholarly discussions of the issue. We shall assume in these pages that antisemitism is 1) not theological anti-Judaism, even though it may contain the latter, nor 2) negative prophetic statements delivered within a Jewish ambience, nor 3) elements that may lead—or in history have led—to antisemitism; but finally, 4) only attitudes, words, or actions that embody a hatred or contempt of the Jewish people *as such*. (The reduplicative, *as such*, is the formal and most important factor of the definition.) In light of such a definition, it is the opinion of the writer that the New Testament cannot be considered antisemitic, this despite the fact that it is replete with an anti-Judaistic theology and anti-Jewish pronouncement, prophetic in nature, that have made it a seedbed of antisemitism.

It is of importance to the historian of this period to note that the gradual composition of the New Testament during the second half of the first century C.E. was accompanied by a worsening of Jewish-Christian relations that could not but find its reflection in its books, human documents as well as divine. Paul, writing first, despite a full supply of anti-Judaistic theology, has the kindest words for Jews and Judaism. The later editors of John, writing last, are unrelenting in their anti-Judaism.[12] It is plain that the situation has changed. From Paul's to John's time, persecution of Christians increased; Christians were expelled from the Synagogue; the Temple and city of Jerusalem were destroyed (in the Christian mind seen as a sign of divine retribution). The Johannine community incorrectly interpreted its own difficult situation as merely repetition of what had happened to Jesus, the apostles, and the earlier Church. The influx into the Church of pagan converts of this time, moreoever, could only have made matters worse. It would be, historically, highly improbable that the literati among them conversant with the classical pagan antisemitic authors and the uneducated from Alexandria and the seaports where antisemitism had materialized would not import some of that animus into their new situation. Though a relatively minor contribution, it was doubtless sufficient to act as a stimulus of the existent anti-Judaism.

THE APOLOGETICAL OFFENSIVE

Of the patristic literature of the late first century, only *The Didache* and *The Letter of Barnabas* concerned themselves with Judaism, and only the latter *ex professo*.[13] The sole reference in *The Didache*, which warns Christians that they should not let their "fasts be with the hypocrites," is ambiguous.[14] The reference is probably directed against Judaizers in the Church; yet, using the New Testament designation of the scribes and pharisees (Matt. 23:13-29), it may refer to Jewish leadership or the Synagogue. Some believe that it refers to all Jews. *The Letter of Barnabas*, by resort to allegorical interpretation, attempts to show how Jews misunderstood the Old Testament, which, the writer asserts, was never intended to be observed literally, since all therein is but a prefiguring of Christ and the Church: "Do not add to your sins and say that the covenant is both theirs and ours. Yes! It is ours; but they thus lost it forever . . . "[15] With the extreme allegorism of this epistle we embark on a path from orthodoxy that will culminate in Marcion, the gnostic excommunicate of the second century, who made Yahweh into a demiurge and rejected the Old Testament entirely. The limits of orthodoxy were then clearly drawn between which the Church must tread a perilous course, between the Scylla of Marcionism and the Charybdis of Judaeo-Christianity.

As the second century opened, St. Ignatius of Antioch sent

his fervent letters to gentile communities to warn against heresy, in particular against Judaizing: There is no need of "obsolete practices" in Christian hope, for those who Judaize are like "tombstones and graves inscribed merely with the names of men."[16] "Christianity," he wrote to the Magnesians, "did not believe in Judaism, but Judaism in Christianity."[17] With this last observation and Barnabas' theory of prefiguration, a fertile theme originated: that the Church is, and always was, the true Israel.

The second century witnessed a broadening of the struggle between Church and Synagogue, as both competed for the pagan soul—the former in worsening political conditions, the latter, after Hadrian (117-38 C.E.), in generally improving ones. Christians outpaced the Jews in membership and assumed a more aggressive tone in controversy; elements of a more hostile Christian theology concerning Jewish guilt and punishment appeared. Jews, aroused by Christian claims and successes, indulged in occasional violence and slander, and participated to some extent in the imperial persecutions of Christians.

It is a difficult period for the historian. To determine the facts, especially with respect to Jewish involvement in the persecutions of Christians, is not easy. As a rule, some Jewish and non-Jewish writers have tended to exaggerate the Church's contribution to the emergent antisemitism, while many Christian scholars assume, unjustly, an unrelenting and implacable anti-Christian fury on the part of Jews in general.[18]

There is little recourse but to allow, as far as it is possible, the events to speak for themselves. For the sake of clarity we shall audit the accounts of Church and Synagogue separately.

THE CHARGE OF JEWISH HATRED

In Christian sources, the charge of Jewish hate is unrelieved. St. Justin (100-65 C.E.), in his *Dialogue with Trypho*, returns again and again to the point. On one occasion he confronts Trypho with the simple declaration, "You hate and (whenever you have the power) kill us."[19] Tertullian (c. 155-c. 222 C.E.) labels Jews "the seed-plot of all calumnies against us;"[20] and in the early fourth century, Emperor Constantine (306-37 C.E.) said, "Let us have nothing to do with the most hostile Jews."[21] Taken from many available accusations, these few samples convey the seriousness of the charge. The answer has been made that the accusers, having entertained few relations with real Jews, constructed a theological abstraction having little relation to reality. The example is given of Origen who, in the course of commenting on the words of a psalm that could be construed to require hostility of Jews toward Christians, claimed that the Jews "rage against Christians with an insatiable fury."[22] Other such cases exist among the Fathers.

There can be little doubt that in these early centuries a theological construct of the Jew was created, which by the fourth century had lost many of its human features. Even so, it would be unrealistic to attempt thus to explain away all of the Jewish hatred for Christianity. St. Justin and Origen were in close contact with living rabbis, and Constantine was not a theologian.

Sufficient incidents of Jewish violence against Christians are recorded to show that Jewish hatred was widespread and, while sporadic, often intense. In 117 C.E., under Trajan, Jews participated in the death of St. Simeon, bishop of Jerusalem. During his revolt (132-35 C.E.), Bar Kokba massacred Christians who refused to deny Christ. In 155 at Smyrna, when St. Polycarp was condemned to be burned, Jews gathered faggots for the pyre "as is usual with them."[23] In Smyrna a century later, St. Pionius, burned under Decius, addressed the Jews that derided him before his death:

> I say this to you Jews . . . that if we are enemies, we are also human beings. Have any of you been injured by us? Have we caused you to be tortured? When have we unjustly persecuted? When have we harmed in speech? When have we cruelly dragged to torture? . . . [24]

It appears from this text that the Jews were not direct participants in the martyrdom but rather its active supporters. The same may be said of the martyrdom of St. Philip of Heraclea and Hermes, the deacon, in 304. Other charges of Jewish persecution in the *Acta Sanctorum* are of too questionable historicity to be cited.

St. Justin accused the Jews of persecuting and slandering Christians on more than one occasion. He complained, for example, to Trypho: "You cast out every Christian not only from his own property but even from the whole world, for you allow no Christian to live."[25] Tertullian accused the Jews of having "attached infamy to the Name," and called the synagogues of his day "fountains of persecution."[26] Origen charged them with falsely reporting Christians guilty of cannibalistic practices and sensual orgies. And the *Letter to Diognetus* declared that Christians are "attacked by the Jews as Gentiles and are persecuted by the Greeks, yet those who hate them can give no reason for their hatred."[27]

Most offensive to Christians were Jewish insults to the person of Christ, about which St. Justin, Tertullian, Eusebius, Hippolytus, and Origen complained, and upon which Celsus, pagan anti-Christian philosopher, seized in order to cast them at Christians. Some of these insults are found in the Talmud—the Palestinian version of which was compiled during the third and fourth centuries[27]—others were of popular currency. St. Justin related that the Jews laughed at Jesus, cursed Him, and insulted Him, "as the chiefs of your synagogues instruct you to do after prayers."[28] In his *Against Celsus*, Origen provides an idea of the caliber of the insults: Jesus, illegitimate son of Panthera, a Roman legionary, was a charlatan and a magician killed by the Jews; after His death, marvels were invented by His disciples concerning Him.[29] Other tales of a still lower grade circulated, in which Jesus figured as a bandit and one possessed. At a later age, these obscenities were compiled in the infamous *Toledot Yeshu*.[30]

Rabbinical opposition in this period increased as the rapidly growing Church threatened Judaism's very existence. Before the fourth century arrived, the Church stood, according to Marcel Simon, as the "enemy *par excellence*."[31] The famous Rabbi Tarphon of Jerusalem, for example, called a curse upon himself if he did not burn Christian Scriptures regardless of the divine name therein, since Christians were worse than heathens, and Rabbi Meir termed the Gospels "a revelation of sin."[32]

Are the foregoing testimonies to be accepted as evidence of a generalized and implacable fury of Jew against Christian? Most Christian historians believe so, but Parkes believes that Jewish hatred was restrained and provoked by Christian theology. Simon concedes the reality of much of the violence, and a "high probability" of Jewish slanders; as for the Jewish persecutions of Christians, he holds that "the few sure cases of active hostility do not, it seems, go beyond the realm of individual and local actions. It cannot be a question of a general conspiracy of Judaism, nor of a determining role, but merely of actions of some Jews, who abetted or stimulated popular hatred."[33]

THE THEOLOGY OF SEPARATION

During the first three centuries, the Church's part in the struggle took the shape of a theological offensive. The refutation and debasement of Judaism progressively became integral elements of its apologetics; among its apologists, there were signs of a rising irritation, the beginnings of a certain Judaeophobia.

The challenge Judaism posed did not become fully apparent until the Synagogue regained its vitality and influence after the disasters of 70 and 135. The people the Church claimed to have supplanted continued to co-exist and, more important, laid claim to the same sources of faith, asserting its anteriority and its title to the Old Testament. To the pagan mind, always impressed by antiquity, the Synagogue's case was strong. The Church's bid for acceptance as a third way, *tertium genus*, in the empire, was not to be an easy one. Pagan writers like Theophilus of Antioch and Porphyry railed at its pretense of supplanting the older religion. Its theological task was more difficult still. In steering a course between the extremes of Judaeo-Christianity and the anti-Judaism of Marcion and the Gnostics, the Church had to prove to the Gentiles—and to the Jews—that it was the true Israel, that Judaism was a pretender that refused to abdicate a lost kingdom—and all this was from Judaic sources.[34] To aid Christian preachers and apologists in their task, *Testimonies*, or scriptural armories for refuting Judaism with Old Testament texts, were circulated.[35] Exegetical disputes inevitably arose between the apologists and the rabbinate. The latter accused the former of mutilating the text of the Septuagint (Greek version of the Old Testament), and replaced it with several new Hebrew translations. Christian polemicists countered with charges of textual suppressions by the Jews.[36]

The anti-Judaic literature was fairly uniform in content. Whether written in the form of dialogue or theological treatise, all centered on the Messiahship of Christ, the abrogation of the Law, and the vocation of the Church. Its substance may be summarized: the Church antedates the old Israel, going back to the faith of Abraham, the sacrifice of Melchizedek and even to the promise made to Adam. Thus, the Church is a Church of the Gentiles, *ecclesia ex gentibus*, at once a "new people" and "eternal Israel," whose origins coincide with that of humanity itself. The human soul is "naturally Christian"[37] and Christ is the *Logos* who "enlightens every man who comes into the world" (John 1:9). The Mosaic Law was only for the Jews, who for their unworthiness and their cult of the golden calf were given the burden of the Law. The Mosaic prescriptions hence were a yoke imposed upon the old Israel because of its sins. In short, the Church and Israel are synonymous; the Jews are an apostate nation, truant from its providential role of chosen people.

This doctrine the Jew naturally found infuriating, since it struck at the very heart of Judaism. The apologists, for their part, considering it a part of the Gospel message, were apparently unaware of the direction they were taking, away from the Pauline perspective. Less and less were Jews "most dear for the sake of their fathers."

The most important and complete Christian tract against the Jews of the second if not of all early centuries was the *Dialogue with Trypho* of St. Justin, a model of a kind of Jewish-Christian discussion that would frequently appear throughout history.[38] The Dialogue is the record of an actual discussion with a Rabbi, who some have thought, probably incorrectly, to be the well-known Rabbi Tarphon. St. Justin was apparently well acquainted with Jews and Judaism and is quite at home with his dialogist. He draws heavily on Old Testament texts and references to prove the messiahship of Christ, concedes to the Law only a preparatory role, and complains somewhat bitterly of Jewish hatred. On the whole, the tone of the *Dialogue* is irenic and maintains a "high level of courteousness and fairness."[39] The work ends as both disputants voice their friendship and promise prayers for one another.

St. Justin was the first to give voice to the ominous theme that Jewish misfortunes are the consequence of divine punishment for the death of Christ. Having referred to the exclusion of

Jews from Jerusalem, their desolated lands and burned cities, he assures his Rabbi that the "tribulations were justly imposed upon you, for you have murdered the Just One."[40] The apologist has forgotten St. Peter and St. Stephen who referred to the murder of Christ in a context of forgiveness (Acts 2:36-39, 7:60).

The *Letter to Diognetus*, of unknown authorship, applauds Jewish monotheism, but signalizes their religious practice as "hypocrisy," "a sign of folly" and "silliness."[41] *The Testament of the XII Patriarchs* speaks more kindly and hopes for the conversion of Israel. The *Clementine Recognitions* and the apocryphal *Acts of Philip* likewise show no bitterness. Not so the *Gospel of Peter*, an apocryphal work of the first half of the second century, wherein a hostile spirit prevails. *The Dialogue of Timothy and Aquila*[42] is noteworthy for its unique opinion that the book of Deuteronomy (meaning second-law), concerned with sacrifices and ceremonies of Judaism, was not inspired by God but man-made and hence never placed in the Ark of the Covenant. The unknown author discusses the death of Jesus at the hands of the Jews but has nothing to say of divine punishment.

Tertullian's *Adversus Judaeos* is the first systematic attempt to refute Judaism. Less versed in Judaism than St. Justin, but probably familiar with Justin's *Dialogue* and with one or more of the *Testimonies* in circulation, the African apologist sets out methodically to demonstrate, using Old Testament texts, the desuetude of the entire Mosaic dispensation. Writing to protect Christians and converted Jews, his anti-Judaism is purely theological and without acrimony.

Third-century anti-Judaica are dominated by St. Cyprian, St. Hippolytus, and Origen. Cyprian's contribution, *Ad Quirinum*, is no more than a compilation of Old Testament proofs for Christianity but was used as a model for later ones. Its chief interest for our purpose is that it exemplifies that in this era an exposition of the Christian faith demanded a detailed refutation of Judaism. St. Hippolytus' *Demonstratio Adversus Judaeos*, of which only a fragment survives, is important for another theme. Jews, addressed in the most brusque manner, are told that though they boast of having killed Christ they should not forget that their misfortunes were the result. From a line of Psalm 69, Hippolytus deduces that they will always be slaves. For their past sins, he says, they have found pardon, but are now to be left desolate "because they killed the Son of their Benefactor." He warns of the ills "that will befall them in the future age on account of the contumacy and audacity which they exhibited toward the Prince of Peace."[43]

Origen (c. 185-c. 254) returns the discussion to intellectual grounds. In his *Against Celsus* he wrote a critique of Judaism and a rebuttal of Celsus' *True Account* in which the pagan philosopher places in the mouth of a Jew the anti-Christian arguments current among contemporary Jewry, many of which were most disrespectful. Well versed in pagan philosophy, in the Scriptures, and in Judaism—to the extent of debate with Rabbi Simlai—Origen answers Celsus ably. In so doing, he turns his attack on Judaism, which Celsus had befriended for his own purpose. Christians, Origen argues, respect the Law more than do Jews, who interpret it in a fabulous manner, and whose practices are now trivia; their rejection of Jesus has resulted in their present calamity and exile. Moreover, he states, "we say with confidence that they will never be restored to their former condition. For they committed a crime of the most unhallowed kind, in conspiring against the Saviour of the human race . . . "[44]

Several other writings of the third century deal with Judaism only in passing. In his *Adversus Haereses*, St. Irenaeus (c. 125-202) refuted heresies of Judaic provenance. Three works, falsely attributed to St. Cyprian, are particularly interesting: an *Adversus Judaeos*, which blames the Jews for their sins and invites them to repentance; *De Montibus Sina et Sion*, a homily in which the Law is compared to the earth and the Gospel to heaven; and a letter, *Ad Vigilium*, indicting Jews but hopeful for their "return." The general attitude toward Judaism in these works is moderate; their condemnations are usually tempered with a note of sadness and hope for reunion.[45]

Perhaps the most remarkable of third-century Christian writings is the *Didascalia*, a liturgical compendium in which Jews are held responsible for the death of Christ but referred to as "our brothers," and in which Christians are instructed to fast for them during the days of the Jewish Passover: "You will fast for our brothers who have not obeyed; even when they will hate us, you are obliged to call them brothers, because it is written in Isaiah, 'Call brothers those who hate us.' "[46] The Pauline quality is unmistakable.

THE ROOTS OF THE CHURCH'S REACTION

The volume and the fervid quality of much of this literature of the third century betrays a growing concern with Judaism on the part of the Church. What lay behind it? Why, indeed, should the Church, out-pacing Judaism in membership and strength, grow also in fear and irritation toward a faltering foe? Was Judaism still a threat? Was the populace involved? Obviously, a knowledge both of popular relations of Christians and Jews and Judaism's policy toward proselytism is necessary for an evaluation of the Christian polemic.

It has been generally accepted until recently that after the catastrophes of 70 and 135, in hostile reaction to imperial curbs (the ban on Jewish proselytizing) and to the gentile world in general, Judaism forsook its universalist tendencies, and rapidly withdrew into itself to construct the world of the Talmud. Msgr. Louis Duchesne has stated the common view: "The religious life became quite closed, the era of liberal Jews, flirting with Hellenism and the government, was past and well past. No attempt is any longer made to be well thought of by other peoples or especially to recruit proselytes. This field is left open to the Nazarenes. Judaism withdraws into itself, becomes absorbed in the contemplation of the Law."[47]

In recent years, this thesis has been re-examined with particular force by Marcel Simon who has clearly demonstrated that the highly missionary and influential character of Judaism lasted well into the fifth century. The Church's debate with Judaism, in other words, was by no means purely academic, but rather the fruit of an intense and perilous rivalry.[48] Throughout the patristic era Judaism posed a threat from three directions: its appeal to the Christian masses caused strong Judaizing tendencies in the Church; its proselytizing continued unabated; Jews were associated with several of the Christian heresies. Such evidences of continuing vitality on the part of a faith the Church had considered superannuated and with which it held profound doctrinal and liturgical ties were not of a nature to engender equanimity *vis à vis* Judaism in Christian leaders.

Judaeo-Christianity, conceived as a merger of the Church and Synagogue, had been clearly renounced by the Church at the council of Jerusalem and by the Synagogue at Jabne in 80. Refusing to die, it led a complex and marginal existence within and without the confines of the Church. Condemned to an unorthodox career, it split off into many Judaeo-Christian heresies outside the Church and a variety of Judaic tendencies within. Chief among the heresies was Ebionitism, which purported to merge faith in Christ and Mosaic monotheism. Though its origin and etymology is uncertain, the term Ebionite, meaning "poor," appears to connote a doctrine of poverty.[49] St. Irenaeus used the term for the first time and outlined the heresy.[50] Not only did Ebionites adhere to the complete practice of the Law, holding that Jesus was made just by its observance, but also denied Christ's divinity and virgin birth. St. Paul was completely rejected, and a single Gospel, derived probably from Matthew's, was accepted. In time, Ebionitism veered toward Gnosticism, another heresy with Jewish associations. Other Jewish heretical groups were closely related to Ebionitism, chiefly Nazarenism. Orthodox Christians were called Nazarenes in the earliest days of Christianity, but soon the word came to signify a Judaeo-Christian sect outside the bounds of the Church. St. Irenaeus noted that they turned toward Jerusalem during prayer; St. Epiphanius, fourth century heresiologist, saw them as a milder form of Ebionite. There were also Elkasites, Symmachians, Cerenthians and other sects that partook of the general Ebionite doctrine. All were agreed on the necessity of total observance of the Law for all, but in Christology differences existed; for most of these sects, Christ was but a superior human person and Joseph was his father.

Though St. Irenaeus is wrong in labeling Simon Magus, Jewish gnostic magician, as the father of all gnostic systems, there can be no question about Jewish participation in Gnosticism in both pre-Christian and Christian times.[51] Originally a pre-Christian, Oriental product, gnosis (esoteric spiritual knowledge) became a Christian heresy when Christian concepts and doctrines were brought within its purview. The primitive Church's struggle against Gnosticism, especially of the Jewish mold, was one of its most bitter. Peter faced it in Simon Magus; Paul met it in the figure of Cerenthus; John encountered the Nicolaites (antinomian Jewish Gnostics), to whom he referred as the "Synagogue of Satan" (Rev. 2:9). In common with other forms, Jewish Gnosticism rejected faith in favor of philosophical speculation, hence repudiated the revelation of the Old Testament but did not scruple to borrow terms and concepts from it. Jewish contacts with Oriental mystery cults or Greco-Roman speculation eventually created a certain Jewish type of thaumaturge or healer who was never far removed from the practice of magic and sorcery. The consorting of Christians with these Jewish practitioners was a worry to the Church Fathers, which explains, in part, their frequent allusion to "Jewish superstition."[52,53]

A more serious worry was Judaic influence *within* the Church. It was not, of course, a question of that legacy of Judaism from which the Church built much of her doctrine, morals and liturgy, or of her early adherence to the Jewish calendar in marking her feasts, but of the tendency among the faithful to supplement their life of worship, despite prohibitions of the Church leaders, with certain practices taken bodily from Judaism. This phenomenon, known as Judaizing, is to be carefully distinguished from the Judaeo-Christianity of the pre-Pauline Church and the heretical status it subsequently took on. This was rather a Judaeo-Christianity of an attenuated sort flourishing in an otherwise orthodox setting. Some of the Fathers make this clear by their reference to *nostri Judaisantes* (our Judaizers).

Judaizing proclivities made themselves felt from the first. Paul complained to the Galatians (I:6) of those who apparently followed in his footsteps only to refute him, and in the second century many of the Fathers warned against them. St. Justin distinguished between those who imposed the Law only on themselves and those who required it for all; the second group he considered heretical. To the first he showed a leniency not found in the other Fathers. The Judaizing tendency took many shapes. Often it was no more than the superstitious use of Jewish amulets or Jewish-Christian prayer formulas believed to have miraculous virtues. More often, it was the practice of rites of the Synagogue, such as ablutions, lighting of candles, eating the paschal lamb or unleavened bread, taking Jewish oaths, asking rabbinical blessings, and frequenting synagogues. In some cases, it involved the complete observance of the Law. Judaizers fought the establishment of Sunday as the Christian day of rest as well as the dissociation of the date of Easter from that of the Jewish Passover; and after these issues were settled by the Church, many of the faithful continued for some centuries to practice the older observance. In the late fourth century, St. John Chrysostom would complain bitterly of Judaizing practices in his see at Antioch.[54]

Not all Judaizers were Jewish converts. Many gentile Christians felt the attraction of Judaism and were influenced by the Synagogue in matters of worship. Moreover, Jews and Christians commingled freely and must have felt a mutual affinity in the midst of the pagan population. The Synagogue, meanwhile, was not opposed to accepting Christians as well as pagans as demi-proselytes. The Church, sensitive to the dangers of the situation, discouraged fraternization with Jews. On another level, certainly, there was intercourse by some of the Fathers with Rabbis, whose authority in scriptural studies was highly regarded. St. Justin, St. Clement of Alexandria, Origen, Aphraates, St. Ephraim, and especially St. Jerome had recourse to them to learn Hebrew or discuss interpretations. In general, the rabbinate excelled Christian scholars in the techniques of exegesis—logically enough, since the allegorical method so popular among Christian apologists was originally Jewish.

But the "Jewish contagion" was dangerous only insofar as the doors of Judaism remained open to the gentile world—and especially to the return of Jewish converts. These doors, in effect, were open. The fall of Jerusalem, far from stifling Judaism's missionary zeal, had served only to strengthen its universalist aspirations. Hadrian's ban on circumcision had not proved effective, nor was it strictly enforced. The rabbinical attitude toward proselytes remained divided between rigorists who, distrustful of proselytes, laid down rigid conditions for acceptance, and liberals, or Hellenists, who, considering Israel's missionary role a grave obligation, relaxed these conditions. That this more lenient attitude was the dominant one—though the former was slowly gaining ascendancy—can be judged from many testimonies in Jewish, pagan, and Christian sources. It would be possible to call the Talmud, Juvenal, St. Justin, Tertullian, Origen, Chrysostom, and others as witnesses. Jewish proselytic efforts were strong late in the fourth century and, despite the losing competition with Christianity, were continued with vigor into the fifth.

It is in light of the multifaceted crosscurrents of Judaeo-Christian competition throughout the patristic era that the rising pitch of anti-Jewish writings of the first three and later centuries must be assessed. The virulence of the fourth century anti-Judaica would otherwise be incomprehensible.

CONCLUSION

Did antisemitism exist in the Church during the first three centuries? Opinions differ. It is difficult, on our part, to categorize as antisemitic: hostile Christian writings or actions effectively provoked by Jews; theological or apologetical treatises or teachings which expounded an anti-Judaism more or less integral to the dogmas of the Church; or the indignation of pastors gravely worried about the dangers Judaism posed for their often superficially Christianized congregations. While most anti-Jewish initiatives of these centuries fitted these three categories, certain excesses of another kind were also present: a stray insult in the *Didache*, Justin's *Dialogue*, and the *Epistle to Diognetus;* a generalized hostile feeling in the apocryphal *Gospel of Peter* and in St. Hippolytus. But that is about all. More ominous was the emergence of a teaching not yet fully formulated but clearly enunciated in St. Hippolytus. and Origen: that Jews are a people punished for their "deicide" who can never hope to escape their misfortunes, which are willed of God. This thesis formed the first seeds of an attitude that would dominate Christian thinking in the fourth century and greatly contribute thereafter to the course of antisemitism.

These first centuries served as a warning that theological or pastoral anti-Judaism could take either of two directions: one toward a benign, even benevolent, separation and disagreement, as exemplified in *The Testament of the XII Patriarchs* and the *Didascalia;* or wax to a level of negation and virulence that would erase that line which differentiates it from antisemitism pure and simple.

3
A CRITICAL CENTURY

No century was more fateful for Jewish-Christian relations than the fourth. The Constantinian age was at hand, and the shape that human events were to take for another thousand years was rapidly crystallizing. For the Church it was an hour of triumph. Powerful in number and influence, it was now exalted as Church of the State, a role in which it exerted a dominant influence on the political and social as well as the religious life. It was a century in ferment. The pens of Sts. Jerome, Gregory of Nyssa, John Chrysostom, Ambrose, and Augustine brought the patristic age to full flower; the Councils of Nicaea and Constantinople canonized the essentials of Catholic belief; and the empire split in two. It was also a time of peril for the Church. Christological controversies raged; paganism cast up its final defiance in Julian the Apostate; the barbarians from the North were almost at the gate. And, not least, Judaism, uncowed, challenged the very foundations of the Church and threatened to undermine it from within.

But behind the challenge Judaism had begun to agonize. Rabbinical learning had departed from Palestine and had found a new center in Babylonia; in the empire Judaism steadily lost ground in competition for the pagan soul. Under the new Christian empire, its privileges were largely withdrawn, its proselytism was outlawed, and in 425 the patriarchate[1] was abolished. The choice for Judaism was plain: either continue a losing and perilous competition or retire into the world of the Talmud. The rabbinate opted for the latter alternative, considering it the price of survival, and thus set the pattern of Jewish religious life for centuries. At how high a price only the future would tell. For Judaism, at all events, the fourth century was prelude to millennial misfortune.

The transition from the pagan to the Christian empire was swift, and its consequences for Judaism immediate. In 313 the Edict of Milan conceded toleration to all cults, including Judaism; in 323 the Church was accorded a unique position of favor and privilege; and when on his deathbed in 329 Constantine was converted to the Church, the imperial government initiated restrictive measures against Jewish privileges and proselytism. By the end of the fourth century, the Jew's civil status was precarious, and his/her image had greatly deteriorated. At the close of the previous century, he/she was no more than a special type of unbeliever; at the end of the fourth, a semi-satanic figure, cursed by God, and marked off by the State.

This rapid deterioration of the Jewish image and status can be traced to a few causes. The rising tempo of Jewish proselytism and of Judaizing in the Church was, as we have seen, one of them. The influx of the Roman middle class into the Church was another. These converts brought with them the antisemitic opinions bequeathed by classical antiquity. A third source may be seen in the rigidly verbal method of scriptural interpretation used at the time, which took every unflattering reference to Jews in the Old Testament at face value. A denigration of Jews thus assumed something of a dogmatic character.[2] A fourth and most decisive factor was the full flowering of that theology which laid Jewish miseries to divine punishment for Christ's crucifixion.

ANTI-JUDAIC APOLOGISTS

The foregoing causes reached their full efficacy through the pens and pulpits of many of the Fathers and apologists of this and the early fifth century. As paganism died and the Christian heresies waned, these defenders of the Church looked more and more upon Judaism as a threat to the faith and the final roadblock to unity. They turned upon the Synagogue with the greatest vigor.

Generally, they took up the same themes as earlier writers but felt less need than their predecessors to prove the rejection of Israel and the election of the Church which reality seemed to have confirmed. Still disturbed by Judaism's durability and the lure it held for many Christians, they set their face to the destruction of Judaic influence. They resorted to the Old Testament to demonstrate the perversity of the Jew, and drew upon passages from the prophets, psalms, and historical books which seemed to support their premise. Efforts to convince Jews of the truth of Christian doctrine gave way for the most part to consigning them the role of obdurate unbeliever doomed to bear witness to the Church from without. And in the light of the Jews' continuing dispersion and statelessness, certain New Testament texts which appeared to predict these conditions were reinterpreted to prove the inevitability of divine punishment. St. Paul's doctrine was, with rare exceptions, lost from view.

In the first half of the fourth century, Eusebius of Caesarea (d. 340) in two massive volumes[3] presented a review of Jewish history founded on the distinction between "Hebrews" and "Jews." The Hebrews were considered primitive Christians, thus the patriarchs; the Jews, a less worthy people for whom the Law of Moses was a necessity. Hilary of Poiters (d.c. 367) similarly reinterpreted Jewish history for the purpose of proving Jews a perpetually perverse people, despised by God.[4] Aphraates (d.c. 345), a Syriac apologist, wrote to warn Christians against Judaizing practices but in a mild vein, even displaying a certain Jewish influence in his own style of presentation.[5] St. Ephraim (d. 373), another Syriac, inserted contemptuous references to Judaism in his liturgical hymns calling the Synagogue, for example, a "harlot."[6] A pseudo-Ephraimic writer warned that whoever ate or mingled with the Jews became "comrades of the crucifiers."[7] St. Cyril of Jerusalem (c. 315-386), an ardent preacher, denounced the Jews from the pulpit and wrote offensively of the Jewish patriarchate, which he considered a shameful institution.[8] And St. Epiphanius (c. 310-403), one of the great early heresiologists, in his analysis of Judaeo-Christian heresies did not hide his feelings for one group, the Herodians, who are "real Jews because they are indolent and dishonest."[9]

In the second half of the century, the crescendo continued.

St. Gregory of Nyssa (c. 331-96), with wanton eloquence, describes the Jews as "slayers of the Lord, murderers of the prophets, enemies of God, haters of God, adversaries of grace, enemies of their fathers' faith, advocates of the devil, brood of vipers, slanderers, scoffers, men of darkened minds, leaven of the Pharisees, congregation of demons, sinners, wicked men, stoners, and haters of goodness."[10] St. Gregory makes it abundantly clear that this century has added a new note of contempt to the Christian image of the Jew. St. Jerome (340-420) meanwhile still exemplifies the strange ambivalence that marked Christian attitude at this time: while continuing his personal relations with rabbis and even seeking lessons in Hebrew from them, he upbraids Jews in his writings as serpents,[11] haters of all men,[12] and Judases.[13] Their psalms and prayers, he states, are the "braying of donkeys,"[14] and they curse Christians in their synogogues.[15]

CHRYSOSTOM: THE HIGH POINT

All of this is dwarfed by St. John Chrysostom (c. 344-407), who, up to his time, stands without peer or parallel in the entire literature *Adversus Judaeos*. The virulence of his attack is surprising even in an age in which rhetorical denunciation was often indulged with complete abandon. The chief venting of his ire was six sermons delivered in his see of Antioch, where Jews were numerous and influential and where, apparently, some of his flock were frequenting synagogues and Jewish homes and probably trafficking in Jewish amulets. The saint was not one to meet such a situation with equanimity. Rigid on principle, a born reformer and fiery preacher, he threw the whole of his energy and oratorical talent into castigating Judaism. How to accomplish it? There was one way: show the Jews and the Synagogue in their true colors; engender in Christians a fear and disgust of Judaism that would discourage all desire to Judaize.

Of what to accuse the Jews? "Of their rapine, their cupidity, their deception of the poor, of thieveries, and huckstering? Indeed a whole day would not suffice to tell all."[16] Chrysostom nonetheless faces up to his task. How can Christians dare "have the slightest converse" with Jews, "most miserable of all men" (*Homily* 4:1), men who are " . . . lustful, rapacious, greedy, perfidious bandits." Are they not "inveterate murderers, destroyers, men possessed by the devil" whom "debauchery and drunkenness have given them the manners of the pig and the lusty goat. They know only one thing, to satisfy their gullets, get drunk, to kill and maim one another . . . " (1:4). Indeed, "they have surpassed the ferocity of wild beasts, for they murder their offspring and immolate them to the devil" (1:6). "They are impure and impious . . . " (1:4).

The Synagogue? Not only is it a theater and a house of prostitution, but a cavern of brigands, a "repair of wild beasts" (6:5), a place of "shame and ridicule" (1:3), "the domicile of the devil, as is also the soul of the Jews" (1:4 & 6). Indeed Jews worship the devil; their rites are "criminal and impure;" their religion is "a disease" (3:1). Their synagogue, again, is "an assembly of criminals . . . a den of thieves . . . a cavern of devils, an abyss of perdition" (1:2, 6:6).

These denunciations, selected from many, convey a notion of Chrysostom's attack. Yet all is not invective. These insults interlard large segments of scriptural references and theological reasoning. Behind the invective lies a very clear theology of Judaism. It is this theology, moreover, rather than the vituperation that inflicted greatest injury on the image of the Jew.

Why are Jews degenerate? Because of their "odious assassination of Christ" (6:4). This supreme crime lies at the roots of their degradation and woes (6:1). And for this deicide, Chrysostom declares, there is "no expiation possible, no indulgence, no pardon" (6:2). Vengeance is without end. Jews, moreover, will always remain without temple or nation (6:2). The rejection and dispersion of the Jews was the work of God, not the emperors: "It was done by the wrath of God and His absolute abandon of you" (6:4). Thus will Jews live "under the yoke of servitude without end" (6:2). God hates the Jews and always hated the Jews (6:4, 1:7), and on Judgement Day He will say to Judaizers, "Depart from Me, for you have had intercourse with my murderers." It is the duty of Christians to hate the Jews: "He who can never love Christ enough will never have done fighting against those [Jews] who hate Him" (7:1). "Flee, then, their assemblies, flee their houses, and far from venerating the synagogue because of the books it contains hold it in hatred and aversion for the same reason" (1:5). Chrysostom himself gives the example: " . . . I hate the synagogue precisely because it has the law and prophets . . . " (6:6) " . . . I hate the Jews also because they outrage the law . . . " (*ibid.*).

Attempts have been made to explain Chrysostom's fury.[17] Oratorical exaggeration, genuine alarm at the extent of Judaizing among his flock, a faulty use of Old Testament metaphors and symbols, the impact of Julian the Apostate's seemingly miraculous failure to rebuild the Temple of Jerusalem (6:1), faulty applications of Old Testament denunciations of Israel, an equally faulty interpretation of many New Testament texts seemingly concerned with the destiny of the Jews—such are some of the attenuations proposed to rationalize his onslaught. They fall short of their task. Christians as well as Jews can only deplore these sermons as a grave lapse from charity and common justice. Chrysostom's historical stature as a great churchman, orator, liturgist, and saint cannot spare him a prominent niche in the pantheon of antisemitism. The effects of his preaching and his teaching of the deicide accusation wielded a baleful influence not only on the clergy and populace of his time but on those of centuries thereafter. A generalized popular hatred of the Jew was now under way; and among the literati the tone of Chrysostom's diatribes found an echo in and out of the Church for centuries.

THE THEORY OF THE WITNESS-PEOPLE

St. Augustine (354-430), a contemporary of Chrysostom, presents an ambivalence toward Judaism. Faithful to the Pauline tradition of special affection for the Jews, he is at the same time at a loss to understand their unbelief, their animosity toward Christians, and their unending misfortunes. Thus he often addresses them in severe terms. Too urbane and aware of human weakness to hate or indulge in vituperation, he gives vent to intellectual passion. A first part of his theology of Judaism is common to that of the other Fathers:[18] Judaism, since Christ, is a corruption; indeed Judas is the image of the Jewish people; their understanding of the Scriptures is carnal; they bear guilt for the death of the Saviour, for through their fathers they have killed the Christ. In one of his sermons he exclaims: "The Jews held him;

the Jews insulted him, the Jews bound him, they crowned him with thorns, dishonored him by spitting upon him, they scourged him, they heaped abuses upon him, they hung him upon a tree, they pierced him with a lance."[19] It is clear, according to Augustine, that the divine malediction they called upon themselves has been heard; they are destined to be slaves.

Augustine's original contribution resides in his theory of the Jews as a witness-people, a theological construction by which he attempts to solve the apparent dilemma of the Jews' survival as a people and their increasing misfortunes. The role of the Jews, in his opinion, is still providential; they are at once witnesses of evil and of Christian truth, *testes iniquitatis et veritatis nostrae*; they subsist "for the salvation of the nation but not for their own."[20] They witness by their Scriptures and serve as "slave-librarian" of the Church;[21] and likewise they give witness by their dispersion and their woes.[22] Like Cain, they carry a sign but are not to be killed (Gen. 4:15); as in the Scriptures, so in reality the older brother will serve the younger.[23]

And yet, Christians have a duty to love Jews and to lead them to Christ. In his *Treatise Against the Jews*, recalling Chapter XI of the Epistle to the Romans, Augustine pursues St. Paul's thought: Jesus and the Apostles were Jews; the Law of Sinai was from God; and if Israel has been replaced, Jews are still called to repentance and faith in Christ. "Thus," he concludes, "let us preach to the Jews, whenever we can, with a spirit of love . . . . It is not for us to boast over them as branches broken off . . . . We shall be able to say to them without exulting over them—though we exult in God—'Come, let us walk in the light of the Lord.' "[24]

It is a misfortune of Christian history that Augustine's admirable reassertion of Paul did not receive the same hearing as his theory of the witness-people, which was destined for theological fame and for uses never envisaged by its author. History was to produce many who took their inspiration from this theory, and felt justified in assisting the Almighty by aggravating Jewish miseries. Yet it also saved many lives.

Several minor writings of the fourth and fifth centuries are concerned with Judaism.[25] Two took the form of dialogue: the *Dialogue of Athanasius and Zaccheus*, a Greek writing, and Evagrius' *Discussion Concerning the Law Between Simon, a Jew, and*

Theophilus, a Christian, a Latin work written in the West, probably in Spain. Their tone is earnest and amicable. Evagrius' *Discussion* closes with a lengthy prayer of the newly converted Jew, the following portion of which is of special interest because of its sense of continuity between the Old and New Covenants:

> . . . Oh Lord Jesus, if I am worthy to have faith, strengthen me also for the full knowledge of Thyself. For Thou showest the way to them that wander, and callest home the lost, and raiseth the dead, and strengthenest the faithless in their faith, and to the blind Thou givest light in the eyes of their heart. Thou Thyself art the holy Tabernacle Who wast with our Fathers in the desert. Thou art the Candlestick, Thou the Golden Altar and the Shewbread, Thou the Altar and the willing Victim. . . .[26]

A text of Sulpicius Severus, a Christian historian probably writing in Aquitania at the end of the fourth century, is important as a concise formulation of the theme of the punishment of the Jews: "[Jews] are beheld scattered through the whole world, that they have been punished on no other account than for the impious hands which they laid on Christ."[27]

Christian charity was not wholly absent from the anti-Jewish literature of this highly tempered age. Even Chrysostom managed to admit that Jews possessed some moral qualities[28] and St. Augustine praised their fidelity to the Law.[29] St. Ambrose (340-97) acknowledged their chastity at a time when Jewish carnality was a stock-in-trade accusation[30] and St. Jerome saluted their generosity.[31] Prayers for the Jews in this period continued an already long tradition in the Church. Jesus, who had wept for his beloved people and uttered His "Father, forgive them"—in which Jews were certainly included—was imitated soon after by St. Stephen who died with the same prayer on his lips (Acts 7:60); by St. Paul who offered his own salvation for his kinsmen (Rom. 9:3) and by St. Justin in his *Dialogue (passim)*. The *Acts of the Martyrs* present examples of martyrs praying during their execution for their Jewish persecutors, such as Paul of Palestine;[32] the *Didascalia* prescribes the paschal fast as an intercession for the Jews.[33] In the fourth century this prayerful tradition continued. St. Jerome wrote, "the synagogues are sepulchres in the desert

. . . let us pray the Lord that these sepulchres rise;"[34] and St. Leo the Great (d. 461): " . . . he who was crucified by them, prayed for them; let us also with the blessed apostle Paul lend our prayers."[35] Juster noticed that these prayers for the Jews decreased with time.[36] The apostolate of prayer for the Jews did not die completely but diminished in periods when the Pauline tradition languished, only to enjoy resurgence in modern times.

FROM THEOLOGY TO LAW

Of more immediate import to the fate of the Jews than the opinions of the apologists and theologians of the patristic era were the legislative measures taken by both the Church and the empire. In a sense these were the translation into statutory form of what the patristic teaching seemed to call for. Some anti-Jewish legislation by the Church could be anticipated. As long as fraternizing among Christians and Jews and Judaizing among Christians were strong it is not surprising that counter-measures found their way into canons of the Church councils.

Already the council of Elvira in Spain (c. 306) forbade Jewish-Christian marriages, except in the case of conversion of the Jewish party; it banned close relations between Jewish and Christian communities; and prohibited Jewish blessings in the fields of Christians.[37] The council of Antioch (341) prohibited Christians to celebrate the Passover with the Jews,[38] an issue which the General Council of Nicaea (325) had formally decided,[39] but which would not be actually closed for many years. The council of Laodicea (434-81) grappled with the problem of Judaizing, apparently acute in the East, forbidding Christians to keep the Jewish Sabbath or to receive gifts or unleavened bread from Jewish festivals and "impieties."[40] All in all, the conciliar action of the Church appears restrained compared to the fulminations of some of the Fathers. Judaism was left severely alone except in those conditions where the faith of Christians was considered imperiled.[41]

The decline of Jewish status under the empire presents a more complex development. The imperial government was now committed to the Church and her teachings, but was also bound to the empire's historic tradition of tolerance and privilege for Judaism. This double commitment was not an easy one to fulfill.

The more difficult problem was not how to promote the interest of the Church but rather how to deal with Judaism. The task was facilitated, to some extent, by the common acknowledgment of both Church and State that Judaism possessed the right to exist and thus should enjoy a basic liberty of cult. It was aggravated, on the other hand, whenever churchmen or rulers, indifferent to legal tradition or zealous in combating the "Jewish evil,"[42] gave short shrift to equities of the traditional law. The emperors, in effect, varied greatly in their commitments, whether in promoting Christian interests or protecting Jewish rights. Constantius I (305-06), though Arian, proved more rigorous in legislating against Jews than did his predecessor, Constantine; Theodosius I acquiesced to St. Ambrose's unlawful encroachment on imperial policy; Arcadius (395-408), perhaps exasperated by Chrysostom's importunings, exiled him from his see at Antioch[43] and Julian the Apostate brutally attempted to wrest the empire from its Christian commitment altogether. But the time was not far off when ecclesiastical and imperial legislation concerning Judaism would reflect one another faithfully.

The progress of the imperial legislation may be followed in the *Codex Theodosianus*, a compilation of all laws enacted from the reign of Constantine until its eventual composition in 438.[44] Numerous statutes of this comprehensive legal corpus treat of Judaism and provide a good index of Judaic-Christian relations in this period in both the eastern and western empire. Though the statutes cannot be precisely systematized, four main categories are discernible: statutes which establish Judaism's basic rights and freedoms; those which prohibit injustices or violence against Jews or their cult; those prohibiting anti-Christian practices by Jews; and those which restrict the Jewish cult and activities. Though the last category, of more significance for our subject, comprises the larger part of the legislation, contrary to the impression given by some historians, it is not characteristic of this legislation as a whole.

That Judaism remained a *religio licita* under the Christian empire is clearly set forth in several statutes. Judaism is, we read in the Code, "not a prohibited sect" (CT 16-8-9). It enjoys, in effect, the right of excommunication for its members (CT 16-8-8); its clergy is entitled to the same privileges as the Christian clergy (CT 16-8-13); and its patriarch is to be granted his accustomed privileges (CT 16-8-15).[45] From this legal status flow certain protections: Jews who conduct themselves peacefully are not to be molested (CT 16-10-24); they are not to be disturbed on their Sabbath and feast days (CT 16-5-44); and their synagogues are not be attacked, violated, burned, or confiscated: several statutes, especially in the reign of Theodosius II in the early fifth century, reiterate this injunction (CT 7-8-2; 16-8-25 & 26; 18-8-21).

The existence of Jewish and anti-Christian hostility and violence is evinced in several statutes which forbid Jews to stone or use violence against Jewish converts to the Church (CT 16-8-5), to interfere with the sacraments (CT 16-5-44), to mock or burn the cross during the feast of Purim (CT 16-8-18), or to outrage Christianity itself (CT 16-8-1).

There can be no question that the *Codex* throws most of its weight to the service of the Church. Christian proselytism is favored by laws which ban conversions to Judaism (CT 16-8-1; 16-8-7). Converts to the Synagogue are rendered intestate (CT 16-7-3) but converted Jewish children are, conversely, not to be disinherited by their parents (CT 16-8-28). Thus was the law of Hadrian, long in desuetude, re-enacted; Jewish proselytism was again a criminal action. Outstanding is the statute which permits unwilling Jewish converts to return to their Judaism (CT 16-8-23). It was rarely to be respected by the authorities.

A series of progressively rigorous penalties proscribes the circumcision of slaves of Jewish owners. At first, slaves were forfeited; later the owner incurred the death penalty and confiscation of goods (CT chiefly, 16-9-1; 16-9-2; 16-9-4 and 5). From 384 on, a Jew was forbidden to buy a Christian slave (CT 3-1-5), a prohibition repeated in 423 (CT 16-9-5). The apparent tenacity of Jewish resistance to laws concerning slaves and the determination of the empire to enforce them point to a problem with deep social and religious roots. Jews were prominent in slave trading and also engaged in agriculture and industry, which required the use of slaves. Motivated by proselytic zeal and a wish to avoid legal impurity incurred by household contact with the uncircumcised, they were in habit of cicumcising their slaves.[46] The Church was naturally alarmed at these losses to the fold. The Empire, sharing the worry of the Church, determined to put an end to the practice.

The grave consequences for Jewry can be understood. Many were forced from agriculture and industry into smaller trades and crafts, but not without strong and prolonged resistance to the slavery statutes.

Construction and care of the synagogues were submitted to regulation.[47] In 415 Patriarch Gamaliel VI was degraded for having constructed a new synagogue without authorization, and it was destroyed. Further laws regulating the matter were enacted twice in 423, one of them forbidding beautifying or repairing the synagogue without permission (CT 16-8-27), a measure doubtless inspired by esthetic competition as well as a desire to render synagogues less attractive to would-be Judaizing Christians.

Other restrictive legislation, known as *privilegia odiosa*, curtailed the Jews' civil status. They were barred from public functions, like the army, administrative posts (CT 16-8-24), and off and on from the legal profession.[48] Marriages to Jews, seen as "shameful" and "adulterous" unions, were prohibited under the penalty of death (CT 16-8-6; 3-7-2).[49]

A law of 397 denied Jews the right of asylum granted by the Church (CT 8-45-2).[50] In the following year, Jewish tribunals, until then competent in all Jewish affairs, were invalidated with respect to all matters not purely religious (CT 2-1-10). In 425 when the patriarchate was abolished, the tax attached thereto was not abolished but simply added to the Jews' other taxes (CT 16-8-25).

The solidarity of canonical and imperial legislation is obvious. While maintaining the equities of traditional Roman law, the imperial legislation reflected the spirit and often the letter of the canons of the Church councils, and in many instances implemented them in the capacity of a "secular arm." Many offensive and denigrating references to Jews and Judaism strewn throughout the *Codex* plainly overflow the purely juridical state of mind and echo similar terminology in the canons. Judaism is referred to as a "wicked sect," a "superstition;"[51] its congregation, as a "sacrilegious assembly;" and Jews are termed "abominable."[52] Christianity is designated as the "venerable religion."[53] The ecclesiastical influence was progressive: Simon has noted in the legislation "a growing influence of the religious over the political."[54]

POPULAR OUTBREAKS

More eloquent for the historian of Judaic-Christian relations than these juridical developments were the violences perpetrated by both Christian and Jew during these years. Hostilities were brutal and frequent. Blow was met by blow in a scandalous reciprocity of provocation.

Jews were still accused of undying hatred for Christianity by many leaders and writers of the time. St. Basil complained that, together with the pagans, Jews fought Christianity.[55] St. Gregory Nazianzen accused them of an "inveterate hatred" of Christians.[56] Sozomenus, the historian, testified that Emperor Julian believed in the intractable hatred of Jews for Christians.[57] In effect, many reported happenings give substance to the accusations.

Jews lived up to their reputation for sedition and tumult.[58] At Diocaesarea in Palestine, under Constantius, they rose, massacred the Romans, and attempted to extend hostilities throughout Palestine. In the reprisal, they were themselves massacred, and Diocaesarea and other Jewish cities were destroyed. Under St. Athanasius (c. 293-373), in Alexandria, Jews joined rioting Arians against the saint, who was both a political and religious leader of the city. During Julian's short reign (361-63), Jews aided the pagan reaction against the Christian empire and were accused of burning several churches.[59] They took part in the Persian persecutions of Shapur II, in which Archbishop Simeon of Ctesiphon was killed. At Imnestar in 415, according to the historian Socrates, on occasion of a *Purim* celebration, Jews, intoxicated with wine, fastened a Christian boy to a cross and abused him until he died.[60] The report raises a question of facticity. Was it merely another ritual murder charge? Juster believes it was.[61] Or was it a real happening? Parkes sees no reasons to doubt the authenticity of the account.[62] A few years earlier (408), the *Codex* had legislated a ban against insults to the cross at *Purim* and against the allowance of the Talmud of heavy drinking on that occasion.[63] A report of drunken rioting and insults to Christ in Alexandria was also made by one chronicler.[64]

A Jewish uprising in Alexandria under the patriarchate of St. Cyril (c. 414) brought the greatest woe to the Jews.[65] Aroused against a certain Christian schoolmaster and threatened by St. Cyril, they killed many Christians. Next day Christians, encouraged by St. Cyril, attacked the synagogues and killed as many Jews as they could find. The rest fled to Alexandria, putting an end to the age-old Jewish colony.[66]

The Christian record is no more enviable than the Jewish. Parkes claims that it is worse.[67] Simon observes that pogroms in this period are no more frequent than in the pagan era.[68] With the exception of the savage murder of Hypatia, famous Jewish Neoplatonist philosopher, by fanatical Christian anchorites near Alexandria in 415, Christian anti-Jewish activities were limited to attacks on synagogues. And these were numerous. Against the attacks, the law seemed impotent; from 373 to 423, no less than six laws were enacted against such violations. Perhaps the most extraordinary and significant assault was that of Callinicus in Mesopotamia in 388, where a Christian mob, led by the Bishop, burned the synagogue. The Emperor Theodosius ordered the synagogue rebuilt by the Bishop, and the incendiarist punished. St. Ambrose intervened with a letter to the Emperor, in which he vehemently chastised the Emperor for favoring the Synagogue, a "home of unbelief, a house of impiety, a receptable of folly."[69] Laws that protect them, the letter stated, are wrong and should be annulled or disobeyed. The only reason he himself [St. Ambrose] did not burn the synagogue of Milan, he said, was because he was remiss; and he certainly would have done so if he had known he would be punished by the law of the Empire.[70] The imperial power, Ambrose asserted, must be used in the service of the faith.[71] The Emperor, threatened in the cathedral itself with refusal of the sacraments, ceded to Ambrose, annulled his order, and thus lapsed into civil illegality by accepting the latter's principle of the precedence of religious over civil law.

Attacks continued in both provinces of the Empire. In Dortona, Italy, with encouragement from the Bishop, the synagogue was destroyed and replaced by a church. In Tipasa in Africa, the synagogue was seized and turned into a church. In Rome, the synagogue was destroyed but was ordered rebuilt by Maximum—an action to which St. Ambrose accredits the Emperor's eventual downfall. At Antioch, the tomb of Maccabees with their relics was converted into a church. In Edessa, a synagogue was seized, the bishop participating. In Magona, Minorca, on the occasion of the feast of St. Stephen, a riot broke out during which the synagogue was burned. About this time, Theodosius II (408-50) ordered the restoration of a confiscated synagogue, but was strongly reprimanded by St. Simon Stylites. It was also the time that a group of monks in Palestine under Barsauma, who in his youth had been hurt by the Jews, roved through Palestine, attacking synagogues and occasionally massacring Jews.

Relations of Christians and Jews on the popular level present a confusing picture. That some degree of popular hostility toward Jews existed can be concluded from the attacks on the synagogues which could not have been instigated by mere ecclesiastical fiat without a response of anti-Jewish feeling in the populace.[72] On the other hand, it is certain that popular sympathy and respect for the Jews did exist. Judged by the persistent worry of both priests and rabbis, the social relations of both peoples must have been too close for their liking. Jews did not differ greatly from their neighbors in occupation, although it was in this period that the accusation of Jewish addiction to commerce and cupidity originated. Saints Jerome, Ambrose, Chrysostom and Cyril of Alexandria make the first accusations.[73] But it does not seem that a disproportionate number of Jews were as yet in commerce or moneylending. The patristic accusations are found in polemic writings written from an ascetic point of view.[74] Still, Jews were henceforth found in commercial enterprises in increasing proportions. The choice was only partly theirs. The slavery laws, curial charges, exclusions from functioning in government, the army, and the legal profession, as well as the incurrence of special taxes, all forced them toward commerce. Moreover, their competence in this field was greatly facilitated by their international connections in the Diaspora. Identification of Jewry with commerce and finance was, nonetheless, still several centuries off.

By the middle of the fifth century, the transformation of the Jewish status was complete. The struggle with the Church was lost, and Hellenistic trends in Judaism were defunct. The national and cultural center was now in Babylonia, and the patriarchate was gone. In the eyes of the Church, the Jew was a guilt-laden unbeliever resistant to grace and a destroyer of souls. To the Empire, he was still a citizen protected by law but now merely tolerated as a second-class citizen. Before this menacing situation, Judaism was faced with a critical alternative: further struggle with its concomitant risk of extinction or withdrawal into itself whereby its spirit could be preserved and the world outside more or less ignored. The Talmud, the Babylonian part of which was now being set in writing, became the very heart and soul of Judaism. Graetz, commenting on this period, says: "For more than a thousand years the external world, nature and mankind, powers and events, were for the Jewish nation insignificant, nonessential, a mere phantom; the only true reality was the Talmud."[75] Jewish propaganda and proselytism never fully disappeared but, circumscribed by talmudic directives, it was thereafter only half-hearted as well as unsuccessful. A new era in the history of Judaism was opening.

CHRISTIAN ANTISEMITISM

Did a Christian antisemitism exist in the patristic age? Who can deny it? There appeared in this age and thereafter an animus and violence against Jews that breaks the bounds of theological or apologetical disagreement, even of the most fervid kind, but that cannot escape the most restricted definition of antisemitism. Lovsky, a theologian of Orthodoxy who has deeply pondered Christian antisemitism, leaves no doubt:

> In a final analysis there can be no debate. There are too many signs that stake out the permanence, the importance and the gravity of Christian antisemitism: contempt, calumnies, animosity, segregation, forced baptisms, appropriation of children, unjust trials, pogroms, exiles, systematic persecutions, thefts and rapine, hatred, open or concealed, social degradation.[76]

The fourth century demonstrates convincingly that there is a certain boundary, often difficult to locate, across which Christian theological anti-Judaism is transformed into Christian antisemitism. In other words, the principal source of Christian antisemitism was the Church's theological anti-Judaism. It is apparent that there exists a certain level of theological negation or polemical intensity which, when reached, produces an effect that is no longer purely theological or polemical: ideological opposition has turned to hatred and stereotype—the life-blood of antisemitism. An example of this may be taken from the transformation of the initial polemic which held that Judaism was no longer God's vessel of salvation and, because of its infidelity, was replaced by the Church into the view that Jews, wicked and despicable, were unworthy and rejected of God from the beginning.[77] Thus were Jews not only wrong but evil. An ethnic note has been added to the original anti-Judaism.

The most ominous development in this crucial century was without question the definitive elaboration of the theme of a divine curse and punishment upon Jews for their role in the crucifixion of Christ—the deicide accusation. Broached in St. Justin's *Dialogue* in the second century and repeated in the third century, it was fully elaborated in the fourth, mainly by Chrysostom. Judaism's rapidly deteriorating socio-political situation seemed to lend weight to the opinion that Israel's rejection as the vessel of salvation entailed as punishment an endless dispersion amid punitive conditions. It was forgotten or ignored that the Jewish dispersion began many centuries before Christ and that Palestine was never completely emptied of Jews. Chrysostom, whose influence was great, made the deicidal theme central to his theology of Judaism. He was greatly impressed by Julian the Apostate's failure to rebuild the Temple in Jerusalem in 363. This event, reported by historians of the time, often in terms of miracle, he interpreted as a direct intervention of God to perpetuate Judaism's punishment and to fulfill New Testament prophecies.[78]

From this point, the theme of deicide gained wide currency and, although never accepted as a universal creedal tradition in the Church, it gained universal acceptance and lived on as a sort of socio-theological corollary of the Church's Christology. Down to the twentieth century it was to supply a pseudo-theological basis for myriad oppressions and degradations of the Jews. Multitudes of misguided Christians considered themselves called to assist the Almighty in effectuating His "curse" on Jews, free to indulge their hostilities with a divine seal of approval.

Despite its venom and its ethnic quality, Christian antisemitism retained its basically anti-Judaic, its theological character. On baptism, Jews were welcomed enthusiastically into the fold. Its fundamentally theological character—as well as that of the legislation of the time—is perhaps best shown in the relatively better position conceded to Jews in contrast to heretics. Parkes is explicit: "Certainly so far as the fourth century is concerned, it was better to be a Jew than a heretic . . . . Anti-Jewish laws were dictated as much by general conceptions as by specific hatred of the Jews, and even showed the Jew to be less hated than the heretic."[79] In truth, heretics had no protection; Jews enjoyed a measure of legal protection, and their sacred books were respected.

This preferential treatment could be partially explained as merely a derivative of Augustine's theory of the Jews as a witness-people, destined to subsist in testimony to the truth of the Church, but not adequately. This theory was fully evolved only with Augustine, a century after the legislation of the Church and the Theodosian Code had begun to protect (and curb) Jewish rights.[80] There seems no sufficient reason to doubt the motives supplied in the *Codex* for Judaism's privileges: respect for Judaism, a concession of tolerance, the antiquity of Jewish privileges.[81] The witness-people theory was a theological instrument, constructed tardily, to account for the worsening of Judaism's status that paralleled the rise of the Church in the third and fourth centuries—a theory that certain scriptural texts seemed to confirm.[82] It is more plausible to see in the preferential treatment the influence of the original Pauline tradition of Judaism's special status.

There were secondary causes of the emergence of Christian antisemitism at this time. Pagan antisemitism was one of them. Brought into the Christian community by pagan converts it helped to infect the original anti-Judaism with the antisemitic virus. Its face, however, changed as old charges appeared in new settings. Jews were what the pagan authors said they were, but for different reasons: pogroms took the form of attacks on synagogues; Jewish "impiety" or "atheism" was now their rejection of the Church; their "hatred of mankind" became hatred of Christians. Occasionally, a verbatim repetition occurs, as when Chrysostom describes Jews in terms of Claudius' letter to the Alexandrians as the "pests of the universe."[83] Pagan antisemitism was at this point in its death throes, almost completely submerged in a new and more virulent antisemitic strain.

Christian antisemitism was rooted, finally, in the survival of a vibrant and often defiant Judaism. The refusal of the Synagogue to join the Church stood forth as a serious challenge to the Christian apologia, a scandal to the Christian faithful, and a source of worry to their pastors, alarmed by the Judaizing tendencies within their flock. Antisemitism thus was not rooted only in Christian doctrine but also in a pastoral zeal which resorted to every and any means to find, in Simon's description, "a therapy for the Jewish disease."[84] Is it not possible, in fine, to assume a certain inevitability affecting this conflict which engaged these two faiths laying claim to exclusive election by the One True God and using the same source of revelation to uphold their claim? At all events, the die was cast: as the fifth century moved in, Judaism's horizons were ominously overcast. They were so to remain, for a long time—before the storm.

4
SHIFTING FORTUNES

The Middle Ages meant one thing to the Christian, another to the Jew. For the latter, they not only began earlier and ended later but assumed a direction opposite to the general current of history. The earlier period, often called the Dark Ages, was for Jews a time of shifting fortunes but, as a whole, was relatively bearable. As the medieval period reached its culmination—the golden age of the twelfth and thirteenth centuries—the dark night of Judaism began.

The Dark Ages—from the fifth to the eleventh century—witnessed a world in travail. Confusion reigned as the older Greco-Roman civilization and new barbaric elements strove to meld. A great Empire in decline, ceaseless barbarian invasions, Persian wars and Moslem encirclement—such were the elements of disarray from which the Church, sole unifying force extant, was to forge the unity that would be Christian Europe. In its civilizing efforts, it received aid from a mere handful of strong personalities, a Theodoric, a Justinian, a Gregory the Great, a Charlemagne. It was a period in which the mantle of temporal as well as spiritual governance was often thrust upon the Church, but one, conversely, in which its spiritual authority often suffered encroachment.

Judaism's situation presented a picture as chaotic as that of the times. Little can be said that applies to all Jewry or to the whole period. Hence the necessity of following the vagaries of Jewish fortunes from East to West, from Gaul to Spain, Persia to Arabia where their prosperity or degradation depended as much on the will of pope, king, bishop, council, caliph, noble, or mob as it did on law. Recalcitrant to the emerging unification, Jews received special attention almost everywhere. Jewish-Gentile altercations were the not infrequent result, but by and large, on the popular and often the ecclesiastical and political level, Jews fared well.

THE EASTERN EMPIRE

The thread of historical continuity leads, at this point (c. 450), from Rome—then in barbarian lands—to Byzantium, where the old Empire precariously subsisted under a rule of emperors of a divine-right stamp who involved themselves in spiritual affairs as much as in affairs of state. The Theodosian legislation was the juridical basis upon which Jewish affairs were regulated, but not with complete success. Jews resented and fought its restrictive measures, and Christians often ignored the statutes that protected Jewish rights. There were occasional disorders.

Many conflicts occurred at Antioch, which succeeded Alexandria as the center of Jewish-Gentile hostilities in the East. Jews suffered violence on more than one occasion at the hands of the rioting Christian factions, the "Blues" and the "Greens."[1] During the reign of Emperor Zeno (474-91), there were massacres, and the synagogue at Daphne was burned together with the bones of the dead, a deed which prompted the emperor to remark that it would have been better to burn live Jews instead. Jews, meanwhile, were not inactive. In the later fifth century, Jewish violence against an archdeacon at Laodicea and a Samaritan uprising are recorded. A few years later Severus, the Patriarch of Antioch (512-19), confessed his fear of the Jews and complained of their outrages. Jews, apparently, took advantage of the violent rivalry of the "Blues" and "Greens" to indulge their vengeance of the moment by taking sides. Under Anastatius I (c. 430-518), Jews again were massacred by the "Greens" and their synagogues burned. Attacks on synagogues continued but apparently at a slower rate. John of Ephesus (516—c. 585) boasted of converting seven of them into churches. And a monk of Amida, named Sergius, incited a mob and burned down a synagogue, in the wake of which a veritable contest of church and synagogue burning and rebuilding ensued.[2]

JUSTINIAN I (483-565 C.E.)

Of paramount import to the destiny of Judaism was the formulation of the Justinian Code in the first half of the sixth century.[3] This legislation seriously affected the situation of Jews and their cult and inspired considerable future anti-Jewish legislation. Of the fifty-odd statutes of the Theodosian Code which dealt with Judaism, Justinian retained less than half, eliminating many of those protecting Jewish rights, notably, the statute conceding Judaism legal existence. Paradoxically, many of the insulting references to the Jewish religion were omitted. In almost all areas of Jewish life the Code imposed further disabilities. The slavery laws were tightened: a Jew absolutely could not own a Christian slave (CJ 1-3-54; 1-10-2); Jewish property rights were narrowed (CJ 1-5-13; Novella 131); Jews were barred from public functions, excepting the decurionate, and also from the practice of law (CJ 1-5-12 of 527 A.D.); they were prevented from testifying against a Christian (CJ 1-5-21).

The most extraordinary innovation of this Code was the hand it laid on Jewish cult. Since he considered himself Emperor by divine right, Justinian held he could do for Judaism what he did for the Church: see that it functioned properly. For example, the Synagogue must not celebrate the Passover before the Christian Easter. (Thus ended the joint celebration of these feasts by Judaizers.) More remarkable again were the injunctions of the famous Novella 146 of 553,[4] which, in response to a suit by a Jew, the Emperor decreed: that the Bible used in synagogue services could be read in Greek, Latin or the vernacular, but not necessarily in Hebrew, as the rabbis wanted; that the Septuagint or Aquila translations be preferred; that the *Mishnah* (oral teaching) be eliminated; that those who disbelieved in the resurrection and last judgment or the existence of angels, be excommunicated and put to death. Scholars vary in their interpretations of this fantastic incursion into theology. Some view it as a new frontier of anti-Jewish persecution;[5] others, as an awkward but sincere attempt to convert the Jews. Thus Parkes, who asserts: "His law is not 'antisemitic.' It is 'grandmotherly. . . .' There is a more truly Christian spirit behind it than there is behind most of the contemporary legislation. Toleration could not, in that age, be expected to go further."[6] Be that as it may, by such legislation the Justinian Code prepared the way for encroachments on Jewish rights its Theodosian predecessor would never have countenanced. By stripping Judaism of its explicit legality, Justinian opened the door to abuses such as occurred in Borion in North Africa in 535, where Judaism was outlawed, synagogues closed, and Jews forced into baptism. Though exceptional, this action set an ominous precedent, and, under the new Code, the Jew was without legal recourse against it. The banning of the *Mishnah*, moreover, prefigured the burning of the Talmud of later times.

Justinian's excursions into theology did not bring the intended results; quite the contrary. Exasperated by the new disabilities, Jews and Samaritans (the latter were more severely treated) made common cause, massacred Christians at Caesarea in 556, and destroyed their churches, but were, in turn, cruelly punished by Justinian's legate. A half century later under Phocas (602-10), the Jews of Antioch killed many Christians, burned their bodies and dragged the Patriarch Anastatius (d. 598) through the streets before killing him. Some observers exonerate the Jews of the murder of the Patriarch, but all concede their active participation. More serious was Jewish complicity in the Persian invasions of Koshru II (590-628) in the reign of Heraclius (610-41) at the beginning of the seventh century. Smarting under the oppressions of Justinian's Code and hoping to retain control of the Holy City, Jews organized in Palestine under Benjamin of Tiberias to join the Persian invader. They helped him lay waste Christian homes and churches and assisted at the fall of Jerusalem (614). Thirty thousand Christians are said to have perished and, though it is unquestionable that the Jews aided in the slaughter, it is no doubt legendary that they purchased thirty thousand Christians from the Persians for the purpose of massacre. Following the fall of the city, Jews overran Palestine, attacking Christians and their churches. At the behest of Jewish inhabitants of

Tyre, an army of Jews laid siege to that city and destroyed many churches. The besieged Christians retaliated by beheading 100 Jews for every church destroyed.[7]

Jerusalem remained in Persian and Jewish hands for fourteen years, until Heraclius retook it in 628. Disaffected by the Persian reluctance to concede them a greater rule of the city, Jews formed an alliance with Heraclius in his campaign to regain the Holy Land from the Persians. The alliance did not prevent the Emperor—released by the Patriarch Modestus (d. 634) from his oath not to punish the Jews for their anti-Christian violence—from executing many of them and reinstating the old ban on Jews in Jerusalem. In 632, Heraclius decreed that all Jews be baptized. This astounding attempt to unify the Empire by forced conversions brought the usual reverse results: When the armies of Islam advanced on the Christian East a few years later, Jews, baptized or not, received them as welcome avengers.

COMPULSORY BAPTISM

The practice of forced baptisms opened a new and depressing chapter in the histories of Jewry and Christendom. Heraclius was not the first to try it in the East. His predecessors, Mauritius and Phocas, are accused of the practice, as are also his successors, Leo the Isaurian in the sixth century, Basil I in the ninth century, and Romanos I in the tenth; the West would supply a listing of its own. Heraclius's motivation was primarily political. So closely knit to Christianity was the socio-political order of the age that Jewish unbelief was deemed something of a crime against the State, and occasional Jewish connivance with the enemies of Orthodox Christianity—Arians, Persians, and Muslims—tended to confirm this view.

Alarmed by the threat that infidel nations posed at the Empire's borders, the Emperor proposed to impress upon the dominions a unity that persuasive measures had failed to achieve.[8] The results of his project were meager. Far from embracing Christianity, his victims fell rather into three categories: steadfast Jews willing to face death or exile rather than apostatize; tepid Jews happy to reap advantage as tepid Christians; and crypto-

Jews who, still convinced of their Judaism, simulated Christianity. In moments of imperial crisis, the last group sided with the steadfast to join the Empire's enemies, seeking relief from an observance they had never truly accepted. These early "marranos"[9] became a bane to the state, an abomination to the Church, and a sorrow to the Synagogue. The Church's opposition to forced baptisms had been made plain a generation earlier by Pope St. Gregory, who in a letter to the bishops of Arles and Marseilles, where it was reported that Jews were forced to be baptized, wrote: "When anyone is brought to the font of baptism not by the charm of preaching but by compulsion, he returns to his former superstition and dies the worse for having been born again."[10] The second general Council of Nicaea (787) later decreed that all baptized Jews who secretly observed Judaic practices be not admitted to the Church or sacraments but rather that they practice Judaism openly.[11] The Church's prohibition, reiterated many times during the next millennium, seemed powerless against the medieval urge to enforce religious and cultural unity. The history of forced conversion would be long, heartrending, and bloodstained before it reached its high point centuries later in the Spain of Ferdinand and Isabella.

From the seventh to the eleventh century, Jewish fortune in the East varied widely according to place and time. Though Judaism was no longer explicitly recognized as a *religio licita*, it remained nonetheless so in practice. The Justinian Code remained the chief basis of its rights and restraints, but further developments in the Eclogues of Leo the Isaurian tightened restrictions on public officeholding, slave trading, and proselytism. Imperial policies also varied, stretching from the benevolence of Michael II in the ninth century to the persecution of Romanos I in the tenth. The councils of the Church limited themselves to a few canonical prohibitions against Judaizing practices. Clergy and people were warned in the canons of Chalcedon (451)[12] and Trullo (691)[13] against intimacies with Jews, and the second council of Nicaea turned to the problem created by forced conversions.[14] Their canons make it evident that Jewish-Christian relations on the popular level were intimate. Judaism as a religious and social force was still active, and Judaizing was not dead.

THE WESTERN EMPIRE

Returning to the mid-fifth century in the West, we find the corpse of the Roman Empire in the hands of the invaders: Goths, Franks, Burgundians, Vandals, Lombards, and others. In general, these barbarian conquerors, minorities in their new kingdoms, accepted the provisions of the Theodosian Code as law, those pertaining to Judaism along with the rest. Jews were regarded as Roman citizens, entitled to whatever the common status provided. Such was their situation in principle, if not always in reality.

Theodoric (c. 454-562), Ostrogothic conqueror of Italy and its surrounding territory, was genuinely devoted to Roman law, which he applied with complete impartiality. None were to discover this better than the Jews. Though this Arian believer held Judaism in low esteem, he firmly adhered to a principle of toleration. On one occasion he exposed his feelings to suppliant Jews in these terms: "Why, oh Jew, do you seek for earthly peace in your petition, when you are unable to find eternal peace?"[15] Yet in a letter to the Jews of Milan he assured them: "Those who stray from the right path in matters of faith are not to be denied the benefit of justice."[16] This same letter contained his famous dictum: "We are not to coerce in matters of religion, for no one is to be held against his will to believe."[17] Opportunities to test these principles were not lacking. At Ravenna, where a synagogue was burned when Jews, probably baptized by force, were accused of casting sacred hosts into the river, Theodoric ordered the Catholic population to rebuild the synagogue and to flog the arsonists. In Rome, another synagogue was burned on an uncertain provocation. Theodoric scolded the Roman senate about the event and demanded that the guilty be punished. In reply to Milanese and Genoese Jews who sought his protection, he ruled that Christian clerics were not to interfere in Jewish rights and, inversely, that Jews were not to offend the rights of the Church. To some degree Theodoric's unusual sense of justice and rights must be credited to his well-educated secretary and adviser, Cassiodorus, whose tolerant sentiments are found in some of his writings.[18]

POPE SAINT GREGORY THE GREAT

Theodoric's kingdom collapsed at his death, and shortly after the unruly Lombards began their harassment of the shattered Empire. How the Jews fared in Lombard hands is not known. Of much greater interest and importance was the rise to the pontifical throne, at the end of the sixth century, of a man who was to leave his mark on the history of the Jews and of the West. A former Roman aristocrat and monk, Pope Gregory I, called the Great (c. 540-604), was temporal as well as spiritual ruler. The papacy had reached its greatest prestige and, moreover, there was no one on the political scene as capable of maintaining law and order in this tumultuous period. Gregory's dealing with the Jews, deducible from more than 20 of his 800 letters that survive, were a model of justice and sagacity. His cardinal principle was that the law (the Theodosian Code) should be strictly and impartially administered: To Victor, Bishop of Palermo, he wrote: "Just as Jews ought not to be allowed in their synagogues more than is decreed by law, so neither ought what the law concedes them suffer any curtailment."[19] The legal rights of the Jew, in other words, were to be respected. Gregory forbade bishops to interfere in Judaic internal affairs: To the Bishop of Napes he wrote that they were to be allowed to celebrate their feasts freely.[20] On several occasions, when synagogues were violated, the Pope intervened. To the bishops of Terracina, Palermo and Calgari letters were sent ordering that the synagogues be returned to the Jews or restored. The Bishop of Palermo was also ordered to pay for a synagogue that had already been consecrated as a church.[21] Jews, on the other hand, were not to be allowed to exceed the law. Especially in the matter of holding or trading in slaves, St. Gregory was adamant: Jewish ruses to own and traffic in Christian slaves were not to be tolerated. Here Gregory's motive was chiefly religious; he held it an insult to Christ to allow simple souls (slaves) to fall into the *superstitio judaica*, or to be "trampled on by His enemies."[22]

Gregory's devotion to law and justice in no way lessened his zeal for the conversion of Jews to Christianity. He vigorously opposed Judaizing tendencies, and exhorted his bishops to work tirelessly to win Jews to Christ, not by force or terror but by gentleness and persuasion: Baptisms or conversions were never to be forced; indeed, "those outside the Christian faith must be drawn by kindness, tenderness, admonishings and persuasion, lest those whom the charm of preaching and the fear of the future judgement may bring to believing be repelled by threats and fears."[23] The Pope did not stop short, however, of material inducements to enter the Church, such as reduction of rents and free baptismal robes, but he entertained no illusion about the quality of conversions thus obtained. He excused them on the ground that if converts, influenced in this manner, entered the Church with a "doubtful faith, their children at least are baptized with a more perfect faith."[24]

Curiously, the teaching concerning Jews that St. Gregory expounds in his homilies and scriptural commentaries little resembles that expressed in his letters. In the former, Jews hew more closely to the fourth century image of the Jew as a dark, blind, and perverse unbeliever. Apparently Gregory felt constrained to adhere to the traditional image and to the consecrated method of scriptural allegorizing in black and white extremes. The important fact is that despite this, he did not abandon the Pauline teaching of special affection for Israel or fail in practical dealing with real Jews to approach them with justice and love. No more could be expected from a Christian churchman in the sixth century.

Thanks to his immense authority, Pope Gregory's affirmation of the original Pauline tradition and the validation of the Roman Code wielded a decisive influence on Christian policy for the rest of the Middle Ages and formulated the basis of official Catholic policy toward the Jews—often heeded more in principle than practice. Jules Isaac sums it up: "Pope Gregory the Great inaugurated with respect to the Jews, a policy of humanity, equity, and relative protection, which does him honor, and will do honor to popes after him; for a tradition was thus established from which many—but not all—would have the goodness of mind and heart to find their inspiration."[25]

FIRST SPANISH ORDEAL

A highly tragic Jewish-Christian drama was played out in Visigoth Spain at this period. Jews had lived in Spain from time immemorial and had grown in number and wealth. Many of the anti-Jewish statutes of the Theodosian Code had fallen into desuetude, and others were often evaded by bribery or by the collusion of Christian authorities.[26] Apparently the council of Elvira's ban on Jewish-Christian associations had become a dead letter. The conversion of King Reccared in 587 and the new sense of national solidarity this engendered altered the state of affairs. The kingdom, the Church, and the majority of the people were now one, and a species of theocratic rule shared by Church and crown was thus founded. Against the new background, Jews stood forth in their uniqueness—chiefly religious. It was not long before anti-Jewish legislation was reinvoked.

The third council of Toledo (589) forbade Jews to own Christian slaves, marry Christian women, or hold public office.[27] Reccared, who gave his sanction to the council's canons, received a letter of praise from Pope Gregory for taking a stand against the *perfidiam Judaeorum*—the unbelief of Jews[28]—and congratulated him for refusing a large bribe to negate the legislation.[29]

Jewish woes did not really begin in Spain until the reign of King Sisebut (612-21). This monarch, struggling to free his territories from the threat of Byzantine imperialism, probably aware of Jewish "betrayals" in the East, and having attempted without success to enforce Reccared's ever-evaded anti-Jewish laws, determined to have done with the Jewish problem once and for all. Jews were given an ultimatum: baptism or exile. Thunderstruck, many fled the country, but even more were converted—one report places them at 90,000.[30]

St. Isidore of Seville (570-636), ranking Spanish prelate, strongly condemned Sisebut because "he no doubt had zeal but not knowledge, compelling by force those whom one must urge by reasons of faith;" the saint took satisfaction nonetheless that "Christ had been proclaimed."[31] Sisebut died a few years later and left the fourth council of Toledo (633) with the problem of lapsed converts, who proved a scandal to the faithful.[32] The council, presided over by St. Isidore in the presence of King Sisinand (d. 636), was as much a national assembly as a Church synod—as were almost all of the twenty Toledan councils. It ruled that force must not be used in baptism, but that those who had already received the sacrament must remain Christians and also avoid relations with unbaptized Jews; in cases where the children of unbaptized Jews had been baptized, the children were to be taken from them for Christian education.[33]

This last decision opened another sad chapter in the history of Christendom. The removal of children from their non-Christian parents occurred many times throughout Church history and found examples up to the nineteenth and twentieth centuries in the famous Mortara and Finaly cases, we shall see. Canonical justification of such actions usually referred to canon 60 of the fourth council of Toledo, which was incorporated into the corpus of canon law of Benedict XIV (1740-58). The present Code (1917) makes no reference to the matter. The medieval canonists were of the opinion that whoever did not openly manifest his opposition to baptism at the very moment of its administration was not truly forced, *vere coacti*,—even if death itself awaited such opposition— and was therefore validly baptized, incurring all the rights and duties of Christian life. Baptized children, according to the conceptions of time, were the dominion of the Church civically as well as spiritually.[34]

The canons of the council were not altogether effective, for we find Chintila in 636 banishing all but Christians from his kingdom, a decree sanctioned by the sixth council of Toledo two years later.[35] This council also imposed an oath on all future kings to enforce Chintila's edict under the threat of anathema and eternal fire,[36] and dispatched a letter to Pope Honorius (d. 638) reproaching him for allowing lapsed Jewish converts in Rome to return to Judaism.[37] Chindaswith (641-52) similarly allowed baptized Jews to lapse and unbaptized Jews to return to the country. But not so his son and successor, Recceswinth (c. 649-72), who denounced Judaism before the eighth council of Toledo (653) as "abominable and detestable" and a "pollution" of the realm and called for increased severity toward Jews.[38] Accordingly, both the crown and the council agreed that steps should be taken to rid the country of all unbelievers and blasphemers. The council passed no new legislation concerning Jews, but the king replaced the *Breviary of Alaric* with a body of laws of his own which stripped Judaism of its rights and imposed humiliating punishments like flogging and hair extraction for many misdemeanors. All Jews were forced to sign a *placitum*,[39] a lengthy oath which rendered the practice of Judaism impossible. Violators of the *placitum* were to be burned or stoned, and Christians were warned against aiding or protecting Jews. The ninth Toledan council (655) ruled that baptized Jews must spend all Jewish and Christian festivals in the presence of a bishop.[40]

The summit of oppression was reached under King Erwig (680-87), who enacted twenty-eight laws designed to make the existence of Jews and Judaizers intolerable: Jews were ordered to accept baptism; Jewish converts must obtain a permit from a priest to undertake a journey; they were forced to listen to Christian sermons and forbidden to make distinctions among meats; evasions and bribes by Jews and lax enforcement by authorities were prohibited; and, finally, blasphemies against the Christian faith were made punishable. The twelfth council of Toledo (681) confirmed these measures.[41] Toward the end of the century, with Islam menacing his kingdom from North Africa where many Jews had fled, King Egica (d. 702), after first attempting to soften their lot, decreed conjointly with the sixteenth council (693) that the Jews must abandon commerce and surrender all property acquired from Christians.[42] The seventeenth council (694), again in conjunction with the king, accused the Jews of conspiracy with their king in North Africa, reduced them to perpetual slavery, banned all Jewish rites, and ordered all Jewish children above the age of seven to be taken and reared as Christians.[43]

King Witiza (702-09) strove to alleviate the condition of the Jews and reconstruct his disintegrating realm, but too late; the hour of doom had struck. Muslim forces under Torik quickly overran Spain, and in 711 the Visigoth kingdom was destroyed. Jubilant Jews welcomed the conquerors everywhere. That they aided their advance is not certain, but neither is it improbable. There were Christian defections to the invaders too, for example, that of Oppas, Archbishop of Seville. Indeed, the frequent allusions to connivance with Jews on the part of both authorities and populace in evading the law and the apparent success of Jewish bribes indicate at best a half-hearted acceptance of the regal and conciliar anti-Jewish program. The height of non-cooperation, if not opposition, was reached under Erwig, who found it necessary to threaten priests with a fine and excommunication for laxity toward the anti-Jewish laws and to command bishop to spy upon bishop.

How explain this Visigothic persecution? It would appear that the Church, the crown, and the Jews contributed to it. The Jews were powerful and assertive enough to alarm the Church. Even the mild-tempered St. Isidore felt required to write his *Contra Judaeos* to refute them.[44] Actually it was rather to preserve than to propagate the faith that the councils and bishops legislated against Jews. And in this the State was more zealous than the Church, on many occasions taking the initiative or going beyond the action or intent of the Church. Avarice has been mentioned as a cause of this zeal, for there is no doubt that Jews were lavish in offers of bribes to their persecutors. Purely political motivation was also present. Most kings wished to unify the country, and some, usurpers, needed the good will and support of the bishops. At all events, one may conclude with Ziegler: "It is safe to say that the maltreatment of the Jews in the Visigothic kingdom was the unfortunate result of the union of Church and State."[45]

IN FRANKISH HANDS

In contrast to their Spanish coreligionists, the Jews of France lived in relative comfort. Little is known of their early days, which go back at least to the time of the Roman Republic. In the Arian period of successive barbaric kingdoms—Ostrogothic, Visigothic, Burgundian, and Frankish—the Theodosian Code founded their rights, but its restrictive measures were not pressed. Several cities, Arles, Marseilles, and Narbonne (considered a part of Spain) became important Jewish centers of trade. But as Jewish affairs were left to the councils of the Church, and the Code gradually lost ground to regional codes, Jewish activities were more closely scrutinized. The council of Vannes in 465 forbade the clergy to eat with Jews on the grounds that Jews considered the food of Christians impure and would not reciprocate the invitation, thus humiliating Christians.[46] Gondebaud the Burgundian (d. 516) banned marriages between Jews and Christians and prohibited physical attacks by Jews on Christians. The penalty for the latter was loss of a hand; if the victim was a priest, death. It is apparent from these rulings that personal relations between Christians and Jews were close, and that Jews were in no sense cowed by the Christian majority. The comment of Blumenkranz, a thorough student of this period, seems appropriate here: "Even the expulsions and other clearly characteristic violences inflicted on Jews by representatives of Christianity lose something of their horror when we discover that Jews, when conditions lent themselves, did not hesitate to have recourse to these measures themselves."[47]

After the conversion of Clovis (481-511), no immediate change took place in the Jewish situation, but the new unity of Christian faith tended as usual to single out Jews for attention.

Numerous councils during the sixth and early seventh centuries legislated on Jewish-Christian relations, the most important of which, respecting Jewish-Christian relations, were held in Orleans (five times), Epoane, Clermont, Macon, Rheims, Chalon-sur-Saône, and Paris. There was little substantially new in their canons. Most referred to Christian slaves—the perennial problem—some demanding respect for the faith of Christian slaves, others calling for their release. Mixed marriages, eating of Jews with Christians, and Judaizing were prohibited. Jews were barred from public office or from holding authority over Christians. The motivation of this last ruling was not, as is often thought, purely religious. So closely linked was the Christian faith to the political structure that a Jewish civil functionary appeared as a contradiction in terms. All in all, the canons bespeak good Christian-Jewish relations and the existence of a number of influential Jewish communities in Merovingian France.[48]

The Frankish crown was more severe than the councils. Childebert I (495-558) forbade Jews to appear in the street during Easter, or to mock Christians. This same monarch was involved in compulsory baptisms. In 558, in Uzes, St. Ferriol, Bishop of Uzes, tried to convert Jews by persuasion and used to invite them to his home, for which he was denounced and jailed for three years by Childebert. Upon return to the diocese, the bishop gave the Jews the choice of baptism or exile. In 576, in Clermont, another bishop, St. Avitus (d. 525), set about converting Jews and succeeded with only one. As this convert marched toward the font, a resentful Jew cast malodorous oil on him. A riot ensued which the bishop succeeded in quelling; but shortly after, the synagogue was destroyed. St. Avitus then offered the choice of baptism or exile to the Jews. Five hundred conversions were reported, but many Jews had fled, and many of the baptized lapsed. In 582, Chilperic II (561-84), whom Gregory of Tour calls "the Nero of France,"[49] enforced baptism, himself acting as godfather. One of his aides, Priscus, refused baptism despite inducements and imprisonment. For his obstinacy he was murdered by Phatir, a Jewish convert, but was avenged by the king and the people. Phatir was cruelly cut down as he left the church where he had taken sanctuary. In Arles and Marseilles forced conversions were prevalent later in the seventh century, for which, we have seen, Pope Gregory reproached the local bishops.

One of the most notorious examples of forced conversion was that perpetrated by King Dagobert (629-39), who summarily ordered all Jews in his kingdom to be baptized or depart. What was Dagobert's motive? Zeal for souls like that of bishop Avitus and Ferriol? Or was it part of the general seventh century wave of anti-Jewish expulsions, a Frankish model of the pattern set by Heraclius in the East and Sisebut in Spain just a few years before? A general fear of Jews as a threat from within, in the face of Persian and Arab aggression? It is impossible to know; probably it was a mixture of all these. We know, at least, that for 150 years after Dagobert's decree we hear nothing of Jews in the Frankish kingdom.

The Muslim victory in Spain in 711 brought to the Jews of that country a period of prosperity and creativity that was perhaps unequaled in the entire postbiblical history. Even outside of Spain there were unusual developments: the birth of Karaism— a scripturally inspired challenge to the Talmud—the rise of Jews to a quasi-monopoly in international commerce, and the conversion of the Khazar kingdom to Judaism, just to mention the highlights. But it was in Spain that the golden age flowered and to Spain that the spiritual hegemony of Judaism passed from the Babylonian centers. The new age reached its height in a rabbinic, literary, and philosophical revival that produced such figures as Judah Halevi in poetry, Salomon ibn Gabirol (Avincebron) in philosophy, and later the great Maimonides. Jewish-Arabic philosophical collaboration of this period constituted a foundation stone in the creation of medieval scholasticism. This meteoric surge of culture, alas, was a prelude to disaster—the zenith of a trajectory that would, by the end of the eleventh century, plunge Judaism into one of its darkest nights.

UNDER THE CRESCENT

Jews generally fared better under non-Christian than Christian governance. It was in Persian lands, after the fall of Jerusalem in 70, that Judaism first flourished in Christian times. Sura, Nahardea, and Pumbeditha became the foremost Jewish spiritual and cultural centers. Not all, of course, was peace and light. Jewish religious particularism and involvement in politics attracted some resentment and reactions. The Sassanid dynasty (226-641), under Magian influence, persecuted Jews—but Christians also. Jewish dead were exhumed, synagogues destroyed, and Jewish practices forbidden. Again in the fourth century under Shapur II, there were harassments, and in the fifth and sixth a series of persecutions occurred under Jazdegert II, Peroz, Kavadah I, and Hormizd IV. Jewish schools were closed, various vexatious laws enacted, and keeping the Sabbath was prohibited. Despite these vexations, long periods of peace and good relations obtained. Jewish subjects supported the Persian cause against the Byzantine Empire and accompanied Khosru II[50] in his campaigns. When Omar launched his attack on the Persian Empire at the beginning of the seventh century, however, Jews had recently suffered molestation under Kavadah II and, weary of harassment, joined Christians to help the Arab conqueror take the Persian throne.

Under the banner of Islam, the same oscillating fortunes awaited Jews. They had lived in Arabia since the era of the captivity and enjoyed great influence, particularly in Yemen and in Medina, the scene of future Jewish-Mohammedan struggles. They became so much a part of their surrounding culture and environment—in all but religion—that they could be taken for natives. When Mohammed founded his religion in 622, he incorporated many Jewish conceptions and practices into the new faith; when he fled to Medina, his first followers were Jews and Judaizing Arabs. The prophet held high hopes of converting all Jews and at first directed his prayers toward Jerusalem. He soon discovered how vain his hopes were. Many Jews openly derided his pretensions and misinterpretations of Judaism. Rebuffed, he became hostile, ridiculed Judaism, and headed an army against the Jews. Before his death, he sought to suppress both Judaism and Christianity completely. Omar (d. 720), Mohammed's successor, expelled all Jews and Christians from Arabia, but on extending his Empire he accepted them again. He laid down vexatious regulations which included a distinctive dress, a special tax, a prohibition against riding a horse, and others.[51] Jews were somewhat happier under the Crescent than under the Cross, but were always reminded by law and custom of the inferior status Islam conferred upon them, religiously and socially.[52]

THE CAROLINGIAN INTERLUDE

When one speaks of the golden age that Judaism achieved in the eighth and ninth centuries, the Carolingian epoch must be included. That extraordinary emergence from barbarism—an age of emancipation before its time—placed Jews for a moment on a level with Christians, indeed to a degree favored them. The restrictions of the old Code were all but forgotten, and new legislation sought merely to protect the Church from certain Jewish practices rather than to curb Judaism. Already with Pepin (714-68), an improved Jewish status was discernible, and with Charlemagne (742-814) it was unmistakable.

This great Catholic prince found no difficulty in safeguarding the interests of the Church while maintaining friendly relations with Jews. Most of his capitularies dealing with Jews were forbidden to purchase Church treasures or receive the person of a Christian as collateral in a business deal. And when he sent a delegation of three from his Empire to Harun al Rashid, Charlemagne included a Jew named Isaac. Incidentally, this man alone survived the journey, bringing back with him a gift from the eastern ruler that created a sensation in the West—an elephant. Charlemagne also had a special Judaic oath formulated for Jewish use in court.

The new toleration came to full fruition in the reign of Louis the Pious (814-40), Charlemagne's son and successor. Under this prince and his seductive wife, Judith of Bavaria—who greatly admired Judaism—Jews enjoyed a standing in society that they had not yet attained in Christendom. They held positions of trust in the State and enjoyed equal juridical rights; they were appreciated as merchants and importers of luxury products from the East and won a high reputation in medicine. Louis himself retained one as his personal physician. This last distinction Jews held at their risk, for throughout the Middle Ages their successful cures were often interpreted as sorcery, and the death of a patient, as in the case of Charles the Bald (and later of Carloman and Hugh Capet), was considered a poisoning.[53] Louis the Pious, meanwhile, granted Jews letters of protection or diplomas, one of which asserted that apostolic teaching exhorts us to "follow divine mercy and make no distinction between faithful and infidel."[54] It was during Louis's reign that the *Magister Judaeorum* (Master of the Jews) first appeared, whose function was to guarantee Jewish rights, mainly, to be free from violence, to employ Christians, to purchase slaves abroad. The murder of a Jew was penalized by the fantastic fine of ten pounds of gold. The Emperor also permitted Jews to refuse their slaves permission to be baptized when asked. Parkes is right in seeing this invasion of the missionary rights of the Church as an "insult to the Church" and a "foolish action" on the part of the Jews who abused their favored position in this way.[55] Toleration of this latitude was all but inconceivable in the ninth century and could only arouse violent reaction from men of the Church.

The reaction was not long in coming. It came first in the person of St. Agobard (779-840), Archbishop of Lyons, a city where Jews enjoyed to the full the privileges the Emperor had granted. St. Agobard, "probably the most cultured man of his time"[56] and a zealous spiritual shepherd, was profoundly disturbed by the intimate social relations of Christians and Jews in his diocese and irate over the favors the emperor had conceded Jews, particularly in the matter of slave ownership.[57] That the Archbishop's sensitivity to the dangers to the Christian faith in this situation was not unfounded is substantiated by the sensational conversion to Judaism of the deacon Bodo, the Emperor's chaplain, which took place in 839, a year before the death of both the Archbishop and the Emperor. Challenging the very concept of personal law that the Carolingian rulers had instituted, Agobard called for a reversion to the rule of the Theodosian Code.

The bitter struggle between the Emperor and the Archbishop over Jewish policy and the relative rights of Church and the Empire lasted two decades and in its course saw both deposed and reinstated. The Emperor ordered the churchman to desist from his anti-Jewish preaching, but Agobard ignored him and urged his fellow bishops to disobey the Emperor's pro-Jewish rulings. In the end, victory fell to the Emperor, but not without a protracted struggle. As it progressed, St. Agobard wrote four letters to the Emperor and a fifth to the Bishop of Narbonne—a region where Jews had lived for centuries in unusual freedom and prosperity. Two of the letters—veritable treatises—have assumed a high place in medieval *anti-Judaica*, and have received the names *On the Insolence of the Jews* and *On Jewish Superstitions*.[58] In these and his other letters, Agobard covers the entire field of anti-Judaic polemic. Scripture and canon law are invoked to prove the subordinate status of the Jews; Jews are stigmatized as devotees of superstition, blasphemy and calumny. The Archbishop was apparently familiar with certain Jewish *midrashim* of gnostic and cabalistic character and also with the *Toledot Yeshu*, passages from which he quotes.[59] Jews are accused of cursing Christ, vaunting their royal favors before Christians, effecting a change of the market day from Saturday to another day to the detriment of Christian worship,[60] building new synagogues, stealing Christian children and selling them to Arab slavers. In his final letter to the Bishop of Narbonne, Agobard launches an attack on Jews reminiscent of John Chrysostom's. Jews are charged with seducing Christian women through hatred, of being a stain on Christian society. He concludes: Jews are "cursed and covered with malediction, as by a cloak. The malediction has penetrated them as water in their entrails and oil in their bones. They are cursed in the city and cursed in the country, cursed in their coming in and their going out. Cursed is the fruits of their loins, of their lands, of their flocks; cursed their cellars, their granaries, their shops, their food, and the crumbs of their tables."[61]

Agobard has few equals in anti-Judaic literature. As in the case of Chrysostom, his antisemitic animus represents a deplorable lapse not alone from Christian charity but from basic civility as well and contributed substantially to the growth of Christian antisemitism.

In the reign of Charles the Bald, Louis's son (840-77), the struggle continued. Bishop Amulo (841-52), Agobard's successor, was now at grips with the crown. Charles appreciated the commercial benefits Jews brought to his realm even more than his Carolingian predecessors and actually imposed a slightly smaller tax on Jewish merchants than on their non-Jewish competitors. The Bishop, for his part, inherited his predecessor's animus toward Jews. Alarmed by Bodo's conversion[62] and by Jewish influence in his see, he determined to avenge Agobard's humiliation at the hands of the imperial court. He assisted at the council of Meaux (845), which reinstated many of the Theodosian restrictions only to have Charles dissolve the council.[63] It reconvened in Paris the following year but most of the anti-Jewish legislation was omitted. Smarting under the recalcitrance of the king, Bishop Amulo sent him a letter, which prolonged St. Agobard's polemic in a more detailed and formal manner. The letter, *Liber Contra Judaeos*,[64] opens with the words "Detestable is the unbelief of the Jews," and proceeds to employ the traditional testimonies from the Scriptures, councils, and Fathers to prove the fallen state of the Jews and the necessity of avoiding them. Jews are again charged with blasphemies and indignities against Christianity, and Jewish tax collectors are accused of using their powers to influence impoverished Christians to apostatize. Amulo interlards his charges with many abusive references to Judaism. His opus joins that of St. Agobard to occupy a major place in *anti-Judaica*.[65]

Though Bishop Amulo fared no better with the crown than did Agobard, from this point on Jewish fortunes showed signs of worsening. According to a letter addressed to the Emperor[66] and ascribed to Bishop Remigius, who followed Amulo in Lyons, a number of young Jews were converted to Christianity. The reason given for the conversions was that "every Sabbath the word of God is preached in the synagogues by our brothers and priests." To offset the risk of losing their children to Christianity, Jewish parents sent them to Arles. Whereupon the Bishop requested the Emperor—ostensibly more sympathetic to the efforts of the Church than his predecessors—to see to it that these children at

Arles were afforded the opportunity of baptism. The degree of force in these conversions has been questioned. There was clearly some pressure present, yet they do not appear to fit the category of forced baptisms.[67]

Charles the Bald represented the last outpost of the Carolingian age in upholding equal rights for Jews. At his death, they sank into the quicksands of feudalism, prey to every petty prince or sovereign who wished to exploit them. With the protection of the crown gone, they were more than ever strangers in society. In 897 Charles (III) the Simple (879-929)—monarch in name only—donated all the lands of the Jews to the Bishop of Narbonne. There was no recourse against the action. The Church was at this point the sole protagonist of the protections and the restrictions accorded Jews by the Roman code; so whenever a churchman joined a prince in disregarding them, the Jews' plight was precarious indeed. Charles the Simple's stripping Jews of their property was clear indication that their right to retain real property was gone. A major step had been taken toward their complete uprooting. Within a century, Jews would have to abandon agriculture, betake themselves in large numbers into the towns and, as a consequence, into commerce.[68]

The ninth century brought new forms of anti-Jewish indignities. First came a series of charges of treason. In 848 Jews were accused of betraying the town of Bordeaux to the Norman pirates, but there is little likelihood that they did. Jewish betrayals, founded on a few instances of the past, were now a full-grown myth that saw in every Jew a born Judas. The accusation that they betrayed Barcelona to the Moors is also highly improbable, since the Moors did not attack the town at this time. That they betrayed Toulouse to the Moors is out of the question: This town was never in the hands of the Moors. Nonetheless for this alleged deed, they were punished. A custom grew up in these years whereby on each Good Friday, in retribution for the crucifixion of Jesus, a Jew received a blow on his face. The custom lasted 300 years. A similar one appeared in Beziers where Jewish homes were stoned on Palm Sunday after a sermon by the bishop. In 1160 Bishop William put an end to this atrocious custom. Probably in this era also began the practice of making special mallets for a Holy Week ritual to symbolize the killing of Jews. Traces of this practice seem to have come down to the present.[69]

The omission of the genuflection during the liturgical prayer for Jews in the Good Friday services of the Roman ritual (the *Improperia*), which has drawn much comment in recent years, became almost universally accepted in the ninth century. There can be no question but that this unique omission was discriminatory and, to some measure, of antisemitic inspiration. The traditional explanation of the omission was, we know, that the gesture by which Jews mocked Jesus at his scourging should not be repeated in the service.[70] In his study of the question, Msgr. John Oesterreicher has pointed out that the reasoning behind this explanation is neither historical nor Christian, for it was the Roman soldiers who mocked Jesus—and His people—during the scourging; and, for all that, in a Christian perspective a genuflection of mockery need not preclude a genuflection of adoration.[71] At all events, the perennial issue was laid at rest by a decree of the Congregation of Rites in 1956, which restored the genuflection, thus bringing to an end a source of offense and misunderstanding to Jews. The question has been asked whether the initial suppression of the genuflection was prompted by the clergy or by the Christian congregation. An answer has been sought in a marginal note of the *Sacramentary of St. Vast* of the tenth century: *Hic nostrum nullus debet modo flectere corpus ob populi noxam ac pariter rabiem*, which has been generally translated: "Here none of us [priests] is allowed to incline his body by reason of the fault and fury of the people." On the basis of this rendering some scholars have attributed the suppression to the people's hatred of the Jews.[72] A quite different translation of the note is given by Eric Peterson, who refers the *noxam* (fault) and the *rabiem* (fury) to the *Jewish* people.[73] This interpretation of the text—which of course credits the clergy rather than the people with the suppression—is historically more satisfactory. At the time in question, the view prevailed among the clergy that the Jews raged against the Church, but relations between the Christian and Jewish people were good, especially in the Frankish empire where the suppression seems to have originated.

The tenth century records little antisemitic material. Jews

were expelled from Sens by the Archbishop. To a question put him by the Archbishop of Mayence concerning the baptism or expulsion of Jews, Pope Leo VII (d. 939) recommended that the Gospel be preached to them, but that in the case of obstinacy they be expelled.[74] With these exceptions the Jews seemed to live without a history—as if awaiting quietly the violent storm that approached.

EVALUATION

The difficulties of characterizing a period as heterogeneous as the second half-millennium are obvious. Spain and France, for example, differ as much as do East and West. And yet a *jugement d'ensemble* on the period as a whole appears possible. Observers who look for a rectilinear deterioration of Jewish-Christian relations from the first days of Christianity will be disappointed in the era. Actually, the relations of this period constitute an improvement over those of the fourth and fifth centuries. Blumenkranz's evaluation of conditions in the Occident may also be applied to those of the East: "If our period (430-1096) is not altogether a happy epoch for Jews, it is at least so in comparison with the one preceding, and more still, certainly, with the one that will follow it."[75] Hostility and violence were present, but in both East and West—save in Spain—they were temporary and topical. Popular relations were generally good; Jews were closely integrated into their societies, sharing the same language, customs, and professions. Their role in commerce in this era has been greatly exaggerated. Jews enjoyed no monopoly in trade, local or international. True, from the eighth century on, they became prominent in trading, especially international trade, but attained a monopoly only in slave trading, which they retained until slavery disappeared as an institution in the thirteenth century. There was as yet no reference to Jews as usurers.[76]

To summarize: there was in this era no popular or economic antisemitism. Yet there was a juridical or legislative anti-Judaism.[77] Jews were not opposed as persons or as a people, and indeed heretics still fared worse than they. The Church still had reason to worry about Jewish influence in social and religious life. The talmudic withdrawal of Judaism was never complete. Many

Jews, especially those who reached posts of influence in civic or economic spheres kept the doors to and from the Christian world open. The legislation of both church and state must, in effect, be seen, above all, as a defense against Jewish proselytism.[78] The perennial laws against employment of Christian slaves, holding governmental office, and Jewish-Christian intimacies were motivated by religious scruples rather than political or social considerations.[79] The policy of the Church remained substantially the one expressed in the Theodosian Code, and received its classical formulation by Pope Gregory I. A balanced policy, it was often marred by excesses of language and application inspired more by the hostile fourth century tradition than by the Pauline spirit. The dichotomy created by these two traditions was now a permanent characteristic of Christian relations with Jews. In this—as in later ages—it was necessary to distinguish a Gregory the Great from an Agobard and Amulo, a Sisebut from a Charlemagne. For all that, an imbalance of these traditions, if less noticeable in this period, is progressively in the making: the Gregorys and Charlemagnes tend to become rarities; the Chrysostoms and Agobards tend to multiply.

5
THE VALE OF TEARS[1]

During the first half of the second Christian millennium, the history of antisemitism and the history of Judaism so converged as almost to coincide. It is a scandal of Christian history that, while the Church and the Christian State were at the zenith of their power and influence, the sons of Israel reached the nadir of their unending oppression. This was the age of Innocent III and Henry II, Gregory VII and Henry VI, of the Crusades, of Aquinas and Dante, of St. Francis, of Notre Dame and Rheims Cathedrals; but it was no less the age of anti-Jewish hecatombs, expulsions, calumnious myths, *autos-da-fé*, of the badge, the ghetto, and many other hardships visited upon the Jews.

For the historian of such a period difficulties increase. Until this point, the sporadic nature of antisemitic occurrences and the relative scarcity of sources created minor problems of exposition; henceforth the profusion of events and documents necessitates a quickening pace and a greater telescoping of the facts.[2] Our limitations, too, forbid a rigid chronology, except in the case of France and Germany, where we shall follow the events in some detail. The histories of England, Spain and Italy will be treated as temporal wholes. Along with the geographical and chronological framework will run a counterpoint of themes on usury, ritual murder, demonology, the ghetto, Jewish "servitude" and more again—headings under which the greater part of the history of this period could indeed be written.

90

The year 1000 found Jews in conditions reasonably stable for the time.[3] Two centuries later they were almost pariahs; in three, they were terrorized. What occurred in this span to effect such a change? Some observers speak of the Church's "teaching of contempt" finally taking hold and suddenly seeping down to the populace.[4] True, but the matter appears more complex. The eleventh century—as a period of incubation—contained certain events that foreshadowed the future. When Hakim destroyed the Holy Sepulcher in 1009, the Jews of Orleans were accused of collusion—an improbable charge since Jews as well as Christians were persecuted by that mad caliph. Nonetheless, widespread persecution of Jews resulted. Again in 1012, when Jews were expelled from Mainz by Henry II, the expulsion was a repercussion of the earlier charge of treason, and doubtless also a reaction to the conversion to Judaism of Wecelinus, chaplain of Duke Conrad in 1006. In the "Crusade of Spain" against the Saracens in 1063, the Jews were disqualified for armed service and were attacked by the soldiers on march.[5] In short, renewed suspicions of Jewish complicity with Islam heightened the sense of the Jews' alien and infidel character, thus readying the atmosphere for the storm about to break over Judaism at the close of the eleventh century.[6]

THE INFIDELS AT HOME

To find a year more fateful in the history of Judaism than 1096 would necessitate going back a thousand years to the fall of Jerusalem or forward to the genocide of Hitler. Though often surpassed by other years in the volume of atrocities, 1096 marks the beginning of a harassment of the Jews that, in duration and intensity, was unique in Jewish history. It was the year of the First Crusade. To the Jew it was a thunderclap out of the blue. Great, ill-organized hordes of nobles, knights, monks, and peasants—"God wills it" on their lips as they set off to free the Holy Land from the Muslim infidel—suddenly turned on the Jews. There were mutterings that the Crusaders might better start their work with the "infidels at home." One chronicler, Guibert of Nogent, (1053-1124) reported the crusaders of Rouen as saying: "We desire to combat the enemies of God in the East; but we have under our eyes the Jews, a race more inimical to God than all the others. We are doing this whole thing backwards."[7] Turning this logic into action, the crusaders fell upon the Jews in Rouen and other places in Lorraine, massacring those who refused baptism.

The French Jews sent a letter of warning to their German co-religionists in the path of the oncoming crusaders, advising a day of fast; but these, confident nothing ill would happen to them, merely thanked their French brothers and offered them their prayers. They were quickly disillusioned. All along the Rhine Valley the troops, urged on by preachers like Peter the Hermit, the antisemitic Count Emicho, and others offered Jewish communities the option of baptism or death. At Speyer, thanks to the forceful action of Bishop John, only ten were killed. At Worms many Jews took refuge in the palace of Bishop Adalbert, while others remained in their homes, promised protection by their neighbors. The stronger forces of the crusaders prevailed, however, and the majority of Jews were killed.

Many Jews committed suicide rather than risk being baptized. Several hundred were massacred at Mainz,[8] as once again Jewish parents sacrificed their children and themselves to "sanctify the Name." A few, as was usual, were baptized. Cologne knew a momentary reprieve as Jews, with the aid of Archbishop Hermann, were hidden in Christian homes in seven villages of the diocese, only to be discovered later and murdered. In Ratisbon, the crusaders forced the whole Jewish community into the Danube and baptized them. Massacres occurred at Treves, Neuss, Ratisbon, in cities along the Rhine and the Danube, in Bohemia and finally in Prague where Bishop Cosmas did his best to shield the Jews. In 1099 at journey's end in Jerusalem the soldiers of Godfrey de Bouillon found the Jews assembled in a synagogue and set it ablaze.[9]

The general pattern of all massacres was the same. The perpetrators were the *pauperes*, "poor men," who had formed a sort of advance guard for the more disciplined crusaders under Godfrey. The Jews were stoutly defended by the bishops—with the exception of Archbishop Ruthard of Mainz and, to a degree, Bishop Egibert of Treves—also by town authorities, the clergy, and in many places by the people themselves. The massacres were clearly mob actions, reinforced by religious fanaticism. In most cases a few Jews were baptized voluntarily, more again were baptized by force, many were killed, and there were numerous suicides. From January to July of 1096 it is estimated that up to 10,000 died,[10] probably one fourth to one third of the Jewish population of Germany and Northern France at that time.

The massacres left a stunned Jewish population and, as the accounts of various chroniclers show, a troubled Christian conscience.[11] While Henry IV (1056-1106) returned from Italy and learned of the massacres, he punished whatever culprits he could find and permitted the forcibly baptized Jews to return to their former faith, an action which the anti-Pope Clement III (1080-1100)—considering the baptisms valid—strongly opposed. On the Jewish side, the influential "Rashi"[12] took a lenient stand toward the returned penitents in contrast with more severe rabbinical opinion. The harrowing experience left a deep scar on the Jewish psyche, especially in Germany. A spirit of depression and fear became characteristic, invariably accompanied by renewed anger against Christianity, which was deprecated in veiled terms in the liturgy but openly among Jewish writers. Christians were viewed by some as capricious assassins, ever ready to strike.[13] But out of the suffering, a new heroism was born. A cult and tradition of martyrdom was instituted whereby Jews who gave their lives "to sanctify the Name" (*kiddush ha Shem*) were greatly revered; their remembrance became a part of the synagogue service.[14] The example set by the martyrs of 1096 found thousands of imitators in later centuries. Strangely, in the wake of the massacres, popular hostility toward Jews increased and their social position suffered further deterioration. A vague assumption that the atrocities must have been deserved gradually took possession of the suggestible popular mind.

ST. BERNARD

The Second Crusade in 1146 brought the same miseries as the first, but on a smaller scale because of the more effective intervention of Emperor Conrad III (1208-61), King Louis VII (1121-80) of France, of the bishops, and especially of St. Bernard of Clairvaux (1090-1153). This time the religious motive was reinforced by an economic one. Since the First Crusade, Christians had become more active in commercial affairs and so now resented their Jewish competitors. Moreover, Jews were more deeply involved in money-lending, a practice which drew upon them the hostility of both the clergy and the people.[15] Pope Eugenius III (1145-53), who called up the new Crusade, suggested to the princes that, as an inducement to enlistment, crusaders be absolved of their debts to Jews. In France, there was no violence at the outset but merely a cancellation of debts. In Germany, a French monk Radulph, absent from his monastery without leave, went about preaching that Jews were the enemies of God and should be persecuted. Many Jews fell before the aroused mobs which rushed upon them crying, "Hep, Hep."[16] Neither Emperor Conrad nor the bishops could stop them.

Archbishop Henry of Mainz called upon St. Bernard for help. The renowned abbot, one of the chief promotors of the Crusade, insisted the Jews not be harmed, but agreed that Jews should not collect interest on crusaders' debts.[17] In a letter to the Archbishop, St. Bernard accused Radulph of "foolishness . . . unauthorized preaching, contempt for episcopal authority and incitation to murder."[18] Recalling Paul, he wrote, "Who is this man that he should make out the Prophet [St. Paul] to be a liar and render void the treasures of Christ's love and pity?"[19] In another letter to the English, he wrote, "It is an act of Christian piety both 'to vanquish the proud' and also 'to spare the subjected,' especially those for whom we have a law and a promise, and whose flesh was shared by Christ whose name be forever blessed."[20] His letter to Archbishop Henry was sent to the bishops of France and Bavaria. When these efforts failed, St. Bernard, at the risk of his life, went to confront Radulph and prevailed upon him to return to his monastery.

But the damage was done. Massacres and brutalities occurred in Cologne, Speyer, Mainz, and Wuezburg in Germany, and in Carenton, Sully, and Rameru in France. In Rameru the famous Jewish scholar Jacob Tam had five wounds inflicted upon his head in vengeance for the five wounds of Christ. Though the Second Crusade was much milder than the first, the fatalities reached many hundreds.

Of a different mind than St. Bernard was another influential abbot of the time, Venerable Peter of Cluny, who wrote Louis VII

(1120-80) an angry letter urging the king to punish the Jews because, worse than Saracens, "they defile Christ and Christianity and fleece Christians." The crusade should be financed from their money, the abbot declared. They should not be killed, but "like Cain, the fratricide, they should be made to suffer fearful torments and prepared for greater ignominy, for an existence worse than death."[21]

"SERVANTS OF THE ROYAL CHAMBER"

The era of the crusades was enmeshed in a broad socio-economic revolution which profoundly affected the lot of the Jews. Two developments, in particular, one juridic and one economic, converged to hasten their degradation: the Germanic theory of "Jewish servitude," or *Kammerknechtschaft*, and Jewish involvement in usury.

The protection Jews sought and received from emperors Henry IV and Conrad III during the first two crusades was bought at a heavy price. The crown laid claim to them as serfs of "the imperial chamber," *servi camerae*. At first, the status was conceived as a privilege and a protection against the fanaticism of the mobs and the rapacity of the barons, but before long it became a device for royal enrichment. The idea was not entirely new. Some dated it back to Titus and Vespasian, and we have seen traces of it in the letters of protection granted Jewish merchants in the Carolingian epoch.[22] Jews emerged from that era to find themselves leading a marginal existence in the feudal system, rightless "strangers," dependent on the whim of their closest overlord. Jewish rights were conceded in "charters" that were temporary and could be withdrawn at any moment.[23] The attachment to the imperial chamber reduced Jews to the status of pieces of property that could be—and were—bought, loaned, and sold as any other merchandise. Kings paid off barons and barons paid off creditors with Jews. Kings would, for a consideration, transfer to nobles or townships the right to possess "his" Jews. The theory and practice spread to other lands. In France, Jews were first the property of the barons, but finally, under Louis VIII (1187-1226), of the King. In England and Spain they were also claimed by the king. On one occasion, Emperor Albert sued the French

King Philip the Handsome for the Jews in France because according to the *Kammerknechtschaft* theory all Jews belonged to the Emperor.

Theology made a contribution to the theory which, in the course of time, more or less melded with its civil counterpart. The doctrine of Christianity's spiritual superiority over Judaism, which St. Paul exemplified by the Old Testament figures of Jacob and Esau and Sara and Agar (Rom. 9:13; Gal. 4:22-31), initiated a tradition that, over the centuries, increasingly took on temporal applications. The canons and codes forbidding Jews public office and Jewish testimony against Christians largely derived their inspiration from it. In the thirteenth century, Innocent III (1198-1216) spoke of the "perpetual servitude" of the Jews,[24] and the Third Lateran Council (1179) of the "subjection" of Jews to Christians.[25] St. Thomas Aquinas (1125-74), adhering to the feudal conceptions of his time, validated the principle of Jewish "servitude" to both Church and State, but added certain limitations. "It would be licit, according to custom," he wrote, "to hold Jews, because of their crime, in perpetual servitude, and therefore the princes may regard the possessions of Jews as belonging to the State; however, they must use them with a certain moderation and not deprive Jews of things necessary to life."[26] A little later this principle was established by law. The great English jurist Bracton wrote: "The Jew cannot have anything of his own. Whatever he acquires he acquires not for himself but for the king."[27, 28]

JEWISH INVOLVEMENT IN USURY[29]

The widespread success of the principle of Jewish servitude arose perhaps more from economic than legal or theological causes. By the end of the twelfth century many Jews were well worth owning. Not all Jews were wealthy, many still served in humble occupations;[30] but they were rapidly attaining pre-eminence in moneylending and some did possess great wealth. Everything conspired to assist their entry into usurious practice.[31] The laws governing slave-owning had gradually eliminated Jews from agriculture; the far flung Diaspora facilitated their engagement in commerce, thus preparing them for the money trade.

New economic developments in the twelfth century did the rest. After the First Crusade opened commercial routes to the Orient, money became an essential ingredient of the new economy. At first, merchants themselves handled financing and moneylending, but so great became the demand for money that full-time usurers were needed. The assumption of the role by Jews was almost inevitable.

Christians soon entered commerce in increasing numbers and began to crowd Jews out of the field. Jews were no longer considered safe on the communal trade routes. Re-employment of Jews in the usual occupations, however, was prevented by the guilds, religio-economic associations that restricted membership to Christians. Further, the Church's ban on usury to a large extent kept Christians from moneylending and acted as a spur to Jews, who were not subject to ecclesiastical ordinances, to enter the field.[32] Indeed, the Church connived in many ways at the Jews' practice of usury, even borrowing from them to build cathedrals and churches. The rabbinate also forbade usury, pointing to Old Testament and talmudic texts. But, by the beginning of the thirteenth century, the distinction was made that permitted it only if the debtor was a Christian,[33] and potential Christian debtors there were aplenty. Money was in short supply, so prince and pauper alike avidly sought Jewish moneylending services.

Perhaps the principal reason for the Jew's practice of usury was his own need for money. A prey to frequent and heavy exactions of kings and lords, who treated him as a sponge to be squeezed, refilled, and squeezed again, he was ever in need of liquid assets. At every turn, he was faced with special taxes, confiscations, cancellations of credit, expulsions, and threats of death. He had literally to buy not only his rights but his very existence.[34] Money became to him as precious as the air he breathed, the bread he ate. The high rates of interest Jews were accused of charging are explainable by the same reasoning. A frank recognition of this was given by King Vladislaw of Bohemia, who permitted Jews to collect twice the interest rates of Christian lenders.[35] On the other hand, it is undeniable that some Jewish moneylenders often plied their trade imprudently. Even Jewish chroniclers complain of their exorbitant rates, and some have deplored the stunting effects financial addictions had on the Jewish character, intellectual life, and self-respect.[36] The first sketches of the Jewish caricature made legendary at a later date by Shakespeare's Shylock were no doubt drawn in the twelfth century.

The beginnings of antisemitism among the great mass of people go back to the same century. Jewish usury was frequently practiced on the poor, who needed money in an emergency. Understandably, a resentment grew against the creditor. A usurer could be tolerated as a neighbor, but not an unbelieving, a deicidal one. It was finally his role as unbeliever that tipped the balance against him. There were Christians who were worse usurers than Jews, principally Florentines and Cahorsins, who entered commerce as early as the tenth century and finally took over moneylending from the Jew when, in the thirteenth and fourteenth centuries, his precarious situation made him unfit for that business. Many testimonies could be given of their hardness.[37] St. Bernard's was: "I will not mention those Christian moneylenders, if they can be called Christian, who, where there are no Jews, act, I grieve to say, in a manner worse than any Jew."[38] The Italian usurers, in effect, were expelled from France for their extortions in 1349.

The Jewish moneylender was caught in a vise. On one side, he was the "royal usurer" from whom kings squeezed their much needed funds. On the other, he was the local lender and pawnbroker who at large rates of interest—sometimes surpassing the amount of the capital itself—in turn collected from the peasants the money he needed to sustain his uncertain existence. It was a fatal situation. The prince protected him as long as he was useful and the anger of the mobs and creditors did not explode. When it did, the king usually abandoned "his Jews" and hypocritically joined in the clamor. By the end of the thirteenth century, Jews were expelled from France, England, and most of Germany. In almost all cases, the expulsions found their origin in the business of usury. It is unquestionable that many of the massacres which took place throughout the Middle Ages had a similarly economic motive too. Many who were killed were not only Jewish "unbelievers" but also creditors. The destruction of lists of debts either before or after a massacre are proof in point.

THE RITUAL MURDER LIBEL

The twelfth century, "as haunted by blood as by gold,"[39] brought forth the charge of ritual murder against Jews that found an echo in every century thereafter and left a stream of blood in its wake. The charge is an old acquaintance. Greek antiquity used it against Jews and Romans against early Christians.[40] Strictly defined it signifies an official murder of a Christian, preferably a child, in Holy Week for ritual purposes. A wider definition includes any murder of a Christian for religious or superstitious ends, including drawing blood for healing or magical purposes, often called the "blood accusation." Jews were first accused by Christians of ritual murder in the twelfth century.[41] In Norwich, England, in 1141, the dead body of a boy was found on the eve of Good Friday. On the testimony of a dubiously converted Jew, Theobald, that Jews plan in concert a yearly murder to deride the death of Christ, Jews were believed to be the culprit.[42] The accusation was not heeded at the time but it cropped up anew toward the end of the century in several English towns—in Gloucester, Bury St. Edmunds, Bristol, and Winchester. On this occasion Jews were not physically harmed. A cult of William, the supposed victim at Norwich, flourished for several centuries. Another similar accusation took place in Wuerzburg during the Second Crusade. At the same time there also arose the accusation of a host desecration in Belitz, Germany, when all Jews of the town were burned. This theme, also destined for a busy career, was usually embroidered with fantastic and miraculous tales concerning the desecrated species, often including the bleeding of the host and the conversion of the desecrator. A hundred instances of this accusation have been recorded, many of them prelude to massacre.[43] The accusation gives evidence of the medieval belief that Jews were actually convinced of Christian truth but stubbornly withheld their assent. It never seemed to occur to the accusers that the doctrine of the transubstantiation was a dogma completely alien to Jewish monotheism.[44]

From this point, accusations of ritual murder multiplied in England, France, and Germany. One hundred and fifty recorded cases have been counted.[45] A few stand out: In 1171 in Blois, forty

Jews were burned because the accused failed to pass the "water test."[46] In Germany the harassment of Jews became so grave on this account that both the Emperor and Pope took a hand to protect them. Frederick II (1215-50) convened a group of Jewish converts to examine the matter. They had little difficulty proving that, in complete opposition to the charge, Jewish teaching and tradition include an abhorrence of blood. In his "Golden Bull" the Emperor prohibited the accusation.[47] Pope Innocent IV also issued a bull in 1247 which exonerated Judaism of the charge, stating that "they (Jews) are falsely accused that, in the same solemnity (Passover), they receive communion with the heart of a murdered child. This, it is believed, is required by their Law, although it is clearly contrary to it. No matter where a dead body is discovered, their persecutors wickedly cast it against them."[48] Innocent IV issued three other bulls which tended to exonerate Jews of the ritual-murder charge.[49] Several popes thereafter exculpated Jews of the charge, chiefly, Gregory X in 1272, Martin V in 1422, Paul III in 1540, Nicholas V in 1447,[50] but to little avail.[51]

As late as the eighteenth century so many Jews were tried for ritual murder in Poland that Cardinal Ganganelli, the future Clement XIV (1769-74), made an exhaustive study which rejected all ritual-murder charges except two, those of Rinn and Trent,[52] and these have since been rejected by most historians. The charge left a steady trail of blood through the centuries and had a resurgence in late nineteenth century Germany, France, and Russia. Several instances of the accusation or propaganda bearing on it are on record even in the twentieth century.[53]

The course the accusation took was complicated and aggravated by popular veneration of some of its victims.[54] Six became subjects of popular devotions, including miracles and pilgrimages, which lasted in some cases for centuries.[55] Pope Benedict XIV (1740-58) issued a bull on Blessed Andrew of Rinn (*Beatus Andreas*) in 1755, but refused to commence his process of canonization or insert him in the martyrology. This document evinces his belief in murder of Christians by some Jews, inspired by a "hatred of Christ."[56]

The Church's aquiescence in these cults cannot be used to substantiate the validity of the murder accusation.[57] Essentially, what was approved was the piety of the faithful, independently of the truth or falsehood of the ritual-murder charges into which no thorough investigation was made. Modern scholarship generally repudiates the historicity of all the murders. In an intensive study of available evidence, Father Vacandard concludes: "There is not a single case of this kind that has been historically demonstrated."[58] A few students of the question concede the possible existence of cases of ritual murder in the wide sense, as might happen in cases of aberration.[59] The ritual-murder calumny stands in the judgment of history as the most monstrous instrument of anti-Jewish persecution devised in the Middle Ages. To its account must be laid many of the tortures, forced baptisms, exiles, and massacres of that and later ages. Its inception in the twelfth century, moreover, indicates the course the Jewish image was taking. Unbeliever and usurer; now ritual murderer. Gradually stripped of his human features, the Jew assumes a satanic guise.

With the First and Second Crusades over, Jews enjoyed a respite in Europe that was marred only by the Almohade persecution of Jews (and Christians) in North Africa and Spain. The first two Lateran Councils left them alone, and Louis VII of France was so kindly disposed that he was reproved by Pope Alexander III (1159-81). But it was only a brief lull during the unending storm. King Philip Augustus (1180-1223), believer in the "blood accusation," resentful of Jewish prosperity, and badly in need of money, saw in the Jew a solution to his difficulties. On a single day in 1182, he had all Jews arrested, then freed for ransom and expelled from the realm. Deprived of the advantages they offered, the king recalled "his" Jews sixteen years later and set them up as official moneylenders in the kingdom, taxing them heavily, however, and closely regulating their transactions. He found further vent for his feelings when, in retaliation for the hanging of one of his subjects who had murdered a Jew, he had a hundred Jews in Bray burned. His contribution to the Third Crusade (1189), preached at this time was a cancellation of debts owed to Jews. In Germany this Crusade left Jews relatively undisturbed, thanks to a forthright stand by the Emperor and the bishops against anti-Jewish violence. Incidents occurred later in the century, nonetheless, at Neuss, Worms, Boppard and Speyer. Par-

ticularly bitter was the action at Speyer where the synagogue was
burned.

POPE AND COUNCIL

The thirteenth century was not the "greatest of centuries"
for Jews. This high point of the medieval Christian synthesis set
them off more than ever from the commonweal. Despite the pres-
ervation of basic Jewish rights, it marked a new level of Jewish
decline.

Pope Innocent III, one of the chief architects of medieval re-
ligio-political unity and the most powerful pontiff since Gregory
I, was, respecting Jews, of a different spirit than his great predecessor.[60] If it may truthfully be said that in the Middle Ages the
popes were the Jews' best defenders, qualifications must be made
concerning Innocent III. Basically, he adhered to traditional papal policy laid down by Gregory the Great[61] and, at the beginning
of his reign, did not fail to renew the traditional *Constitutio pro
Judaeis*, adding a brief preamble of his own.[62] This papal constitution, first formulated by Nicholas II in 1061 and renewed by
numerous medieval popes,[63] provided a broad "charter of Jewish
liberties." Reiterating in its first sentence (*Sicut ergo Judeis . . .*)
Pope St. Gregory's cardinal principle that Jews should not be permitted anything not conceded by law but guaranteed all rights
and protection provided by law, the Constitution goes on to warn
Christians that they are not to kill or maim Jews, take their money
illegally, or abolish good customs enjoyed by Jews; they are not
to baptize them by force, interfere with Jewish festivals, desecrate
Jewish cemeteries, or exhume bodies for purposes of extortion.
Excluded from enjoyment of these protections are those "Jews
who plot against the Christian faith."[64] But Innocent—at grips
with the Albigensian heresy to which a Jewish tie was suspected—
was too sensitive to the dangers to the Faith not to pay special
attention to the restrictive clause of the Gregorian formula.
Throughout his writings are strewn references to Israel's rejection
and to the inferior social and political status assumed to result
from it. The cause of Jewish woe he attributed to deicide. To the
Count of Nevers, he wrote, "The Lord made Cain a wanderer and
a fugitive over the earth, but set a mark upon him, making his

head to shake, lest anyone find him should slay him. Thus the Jews, against whom the blood of Jesus Christ calls out, although they ought not be killed, . . . yet as wanderers must they remain upon the earth, until their countenance be filled with shame and they seek the name of Jesus Christ, the Lord."[65]

The Fourth Lateran Council, convoked by Innocent III in 1215, enacted the substance of the Pontiff's policy. Four canons affected Jews.[66] Their usury and high rates of interest were put under surveillance and tithes accruing from property passing into the hands of Jews were allotted to the Church; baptized Jews were forbidden to practice Jewish custom. To prevent mockery, Jews were enjoined not to appear in public at Eastertime; they were barred from public office; and a moratorium was called on crusaders' debts to Jewish creditors. Thus far, there was nothing new in these enactments, which merely extended to the universal Church what earlier centuries had applied more locally. The unique and most extraordinary measure taken by the Council was the prescription of a distinctive dress for Jews and Saracens. (At a later date, heretics, prostitutes, and lepers were included.) The enactment was new only to Christian lands. As early as the ninth century, distinguishing dress was imposed on Jews in Islamic lands, as was their restriction to a "Jewish quarter." The motivation of the prescription was given by the Council itself, namely, the prevention of concubinage and intermarriage between Christians and non-Christians. An Old Testament text was cited as a justification of the ruling.[67] It was clear from the conciliar rulings that despite tensions, relations between Christian and Jew remained intimate, that one was generally undistinguishable from the other. Judaism still represented a challenge from within Christian society.[68]

The history of the badge is a long and complicated one. That many desperate and often successful efforts were made by Jews to forestall or ignore the imposition of the "badge of shame" can be deduced from the numerous reiterations of the prescription by councils, popes, and civil rulers.[69] France was first to introduce it in the form of a yellow sphere, the *rouelle*. Spain and Southern France, where the general situation was unusually good, were the last to introduce it. Eventually it assumed many forms, such as the *Judenhut*, the Jewish hat in Germany; a pointed hat in Poland;

and emblems of different shapes and colors elsewhere. In Sicily, Jewish shops were marked by a circle—a harbinger of Hitler's Germany.[70] The effect of the badge on the Jew, naturally, was noxious. Physically marked off from his social environment, he stood out like a pariah, prey to insult in his daily life and to violence in time of crisis. (Outbreaks against Jews took place in Erfurt and Baden a few years after the introduction of the badge.) As if in keeping with the role he was forced to play, he lost his self-respect, became careless in his speech and dress, took on a timorousness and obsequiousness that characterized many Jews until their emancipation in modern times. It also nourished a resentment of his oppressors.[71]

Honorious III (1216-27), Innocent's successor, renewed the Constitution and adopted a milder policy toward Jews, lending an ear to them when they called upon him.[72] Gregory IX (1227-41) also renewed the charter, but was less friendly.[73] This Pope's reign coincided with that of King St. Louis IX (1226-70) under whom Jewish interests suffered further setbacks. The pious king disliked Jews both as enemies of the Church and as usurers—the Christian variety of the latter also shared his antipathy. He remitted interest due on debts owed them, and even expelled them temporarily from the realm.[74] Despite all this, the king respected their piety and forbade damage to their synagogues or cemeteries. Much of his zeal was spent in trying to convert them, and when he succeeded he personally attended their baptisms.[75]

THE TALMUD IS BURNED

The first great confiscation and burning of the Talmud must be credited to one of the converts of this time. Nicholas Donin, Dominican brother and former student of the Talmud, who had been excommunicated by the rabbinate, approached Gregory IX with thirty-five theses which purportedly proved that the Talmud was offensive to Christianity and the chief cause of Jewish unbelief. When the Pope ordered an investigation of Jewish books, only King St. Louis complied. A public disputation was staged in Paris in 1240 at which Donin represented the prosecution before the court and the renowned Yehiel of Paris, with three other rabbis, undertook the defense.

Donin had little difficulty exhibiting talmudic references which his Christian hearers would consider offensive. And Yehiel weakened his case at the outset by refusing to answer or, invoking tradition, to take an oath. In his defense he felt forced to distinguish between two Jesuses—the one referred to in the Talmud, and the historical Jesus; on the other hand he had little trouble exposing Donin's many misinterpretations and exaggerations. The commission ruled against the Talmud, but because of the intercession of the Archbishop of Sens the sentence was not carried out. At the sudden—and allegedly providential—death of the Archbishop, the sentence was reinvoked and twenty-four cartloads of the Talmud were burned in Paris. Later, Jews attempted to vindicate the book before Innocent IV, who showed himself to be favorable, but at the urging of the papal legate, Bishop Odo, a new tribunal under the direction of St. Albert the Great condemned it again in 1248. Many later popes renewed the condemnation.[76]

These public condemnations of the Talmud contributed to the "poisoning of all Judaeo-Christian relations in the Middle Ages,"[77] and gave birth to the theme of the "Talmud Jew," a theme erudite antisemites in later centuries exploited to the full. That exception may be taken by Christians to some passages of the Talmud can hardly be gainsaid, yet it is unfortunate that the first popular introduction to this book, so essential to Jewish religious life, was made by an excommunicated Talmudist[78] in an age when detection of heretical sources was the order of the day, an age in which Aristotle's works, translated by Jewish and Arab philosophers, were condemned several times.

The issue of the Talmud is complex. The contemptuous references in it to the *minim*[79] and *goyim*, the insulting references to Jesus as the son of Panthera, and other parts again, could only deeply injure Christian sensitivities. Even so, seen in perspective, these were products of an earlier age when Church and Synagogue were at war, and the work of individual rabbis whose opinions can be countered by opposite views. The general effect of Donin's exposé was to convey the impression that the Talmud was a book of anti-Christian hatred. The truth is that in this massive compilation of Jewish law, customs, and folklore references to Christianity are minimal. Its "conspiracy of silence" regarding

Christianity has been noted. F. Lovsky is quite right when he writes that, "On the whole, the Talmud sins much more by an evidently well guarded silence with respect to Christianity than by tendentious insults or accusations."[80] And Hans Schoeps writes concerning the offensive references: "Such material consists of a few scattered notices . . . incidental remarks, which never assumed central importance . . . . The attitude of present-day Judaism has altered decisively, and these statements possess no normative force."[81]

The Talmud reinforced traditional Jewish separatism, serving as a substitute for the lost fatherland. In the thirteenth century, this separatist spirit so prevailed that even the works of Maimonides, the great Jewish philosopher, were denounced to the Inquisition by a rabbinical group in Montpelier, which considered them imbued with the rationalist spirit of the age. Maimunists and anti-Maimunists remained at loggerheads for a long time; and in 1311 a bitter quarrel broke out when an anti-Maimunist group in Barcelona placed a ban of excommunication on the study of all human science, except medicine, undertaken before the age of 25, and consigned the works of the philosophers to the flames.[82]

The Talmud, for all this, fulfilled an indispensable role for many Jews throughout these years. It provided a *raison d'etre* and a way of life, creating a sacred sanctuary, an inner world into which a Jew could repair from the asperities and horrors of the outer one.

TWO CENTURIES OF WOE

The latter half of the thirteenth century brought no relief from pressures to the Jews of France and Germany. In 1246 the council of Bezier had invoked the common canonical restrictions, including a threat of excommunication for consulting Jewish physicians.[83] In Southern France the "Albigensian Crusade" had already brought the hitherto unmolested Jews of Provence under French domination with an understandable decline in their status. Philip III (1245-85) reintroduced the badge in Provence where it had been recently abrogated; and Philip IV (1268-1314) fleeced the Jews of the realm mercilessly. Toward the end of the century, a charge of ritual murder at Troyes and of host desecration in Paris resulted in a few casualties. Philip IV expelled from his kingdom those Jews who entered France after their expulsion from England.[84]

In Germany matters were becoming intolerable. Apparently no enormity was too great to lay at the door of the Jews. When the tale was told that Jews had recognized their own kinsmen in the invading Tartars from Mongolia and aided their brutal progress, it was readily believed. Throughout this time sundry attacks, calumnies, extortions, expulsions, and massacres variously affected almost a dozen cities across Germany. In 1267 the Council of Vienna enacted stringent rules purporting, in the main, to prevent commingling of Christians and Jews. One of them prescribed use of a horned hat (*pileum cornutum*).[85] The reign of Rudolph of Hapsburg (1273-91) witnessed further restrictions and excesses in the Rhineland and Bavaria. In desperation the Jews appealed to Pope Gregory X (1271-76), who in 1272 issued a bull which reaffirmed the Constitution and forbade forced baptisms and violences against Jews.[86] At their wit's end, many Jewish families migrated to Palestine.

Those who stayed lived to regret their decision. In Rottingen to 1298 word went about that Jews had desecrated a host. Rindfleisch, a nobleman, stirred up the mob and sent the entire Jewish community to the stake. Thence he and his *Judenschchters* (Jew-slaughterers) marched through Germany and Austria pillaging, burning, and murdering Jews as they went. Estimates place the murdered at 100,000, decimated communities at 140. The Emperor fined the cities where the atrocities occurred. The Rindfleisch massacres were, as Poliakov points out, the first attempt to hold all Jewry responsible for a crime—an aborted genocide.

But, as always, all this proved to be only a beginning. The fourteenth century had more horrors in store. In these unsettled times, tormented with political and social upheavals as well as natural catastrophes, it could hardly be expected that a people habitually blamed for every evil, great or small, would go unmolested. Before the century ended, Jewish history in France came to an end, but not before the expulsion itself became preferable to continued existence in that country. The first throes began in 1306 when, on the order of Philip IV, all Jews were quietly arrested on a single day and ordered out of the country within a month. One hundred thousand left, settling in nearby lands in the hope of recall, well aware that avarice had prompted the King's decision. But it was left for his successor, Louis X (1289-1316), to effect the recall nine years later; the "common clamor of the people" and empty royal coffers had made it necessary. Jewish moneylending, hated and proscribed though it was, had become an indispensable function of the medieval economy. New massacres followed in 1320 when a young visionary, an unfrocked Benedictine monk, led some 40,000 "shepherds" (*Pastoureaux*) in a species of crusade, which began with the Jews. Over 120 Jewish communities were wiped out, and many Jews, confronted with baptism, killed themselves and their children.

The next year, there sprang up a new legend that Jews, in league with the king of Tunis and other infidel rulers, had conspired with the lepers to exterminate Christianity by poisoning wells with a secret formula (reported to be composed of urine, herbs, human blood, and a sacred host!) revealed by the lepers under torture. The theme of a Jewish world conspiracy is born— six hundred years before the *Protocols of the Elders of Zion*. The legend took a heavy toll. In many places, arrests were made, and many Jews were tortured and killed. In Chinon, France, 160 Jews were cast in a pit and burned. Five thousand in all were reported killed. Confiscations followed most deaths, and the surviving Jews of the realm were collectively fined 150,000 livres. In 1322 Charles IV expelled them again but in 1359 they were brought back, this time with certain requested guarantees of security. Toward the end of the century, after a few prosperous years, the inevitable and final reaction set in. Both nobles and peasants, irate with Jews as their creditors, called for their expulsion; riots ensued; a Jewish convert lapsed. In September 1394, on the day of Atonement, the edict was signed: all Jews must quit the realm by November third. Thus came to an end a thousand years of Jewish life in France. The exiled went into bordering provinces, to papal Avignon, to Germany and to Italy.

The unhappy tale is taken up again in Germany. Louis the Bavarian (1314-47) attempted to protect the Jews, but rewarded himself well for his efforts by levying an additional tax on them called the "golden penny." His imperial protection proved of little worth during the cruel massacres of the *Armleder* (1336-38), followers of two noblemen called "Leatherarms" because of their custom of wearing leather bands on their arms. One of them was a visionary who believed he had received a call to avenge the death of Christ by murdering the Jews. Armed with crude weapons, some 5,000 followed these two and slaughtered Jews from Alsace through the Rhineland into Swabia. About this time in Deckendorf (today's Deggendorf) a plot to rid the community of debt to Jews and seize Jewish property was set in motion by a host desecration charge. The surprised Jews were attacked and killed, and the town council collected their assets. Emperor Albert II (1330-58) appealed to Pope Benedict XII (1334-42), who in response ruled that charges of host desecration must be duly tried in court with evidence and that false accusers would be punished. At this stage, unfortunately, the combined efforts of Church and State were impotent against the superstitious zealotry of the mobs.

THE BLACK DEATH

The Black Death (1347-50) was one of humanity's epochal scourges. For Jews it was a tragedy to which, after the fall of Jerusalem, only the horrors of 1096 and 1939 were comparable.[87] For three hellish years (1348-50) Jewish communities all over Europe were torn to pieces by a populace crazed by the plague which, before it ended, carried off one third of the population. Bewildered by the plague's ravages people looked for a cause. Before long the inevitable scapegoat was found. Who else but the archconspirator and poisoner, the Jew? This time, too, the weird formula for the well poisonings—elicited by torture—was disclosed: a concoction of lizards, spiders, frogs, human hearts, and, to be sure, sacred hosts. The story that Jews in Spain had circulated the death-dealing drug to poison the wells of all Christendom spread like wildfire. It was first believed in Southern France, where the entire Jewish population of a town was burned. From there the deathly trail led into Northern Spain, then to Switzerland, into Bavaria, up the Rhine, into eastern Germany, and to Belgium, Poland, and Austria.

The progress of the holocaust was, in a sense, systematic.

Local town councils, in communication with one another, often put their Jews on trial even in advance of the plague. The pattern was almost always the same: accusation, trial, torture, confession, and consignment to the flames. Many astounding confessions were recorded everywhere; even parents, under torture, accused their children. But there were numerous suicides and the self-oblation of whole communities. Attempts were made by authorities and members of the higher classes to defend the Jews, especially in Spain and Germany, but they were fruitless. So were those of Pope Clement VI (1342-52) who intervened twice, condemning violences against Jews, forbidding forced baptisms of Jews, and declaring them innocent of the calumnies against them since they too were victims of the plague.[88] Emperor Charles IV made efforts to protect "his" Jews, but half-heartedly. As often as he offered aid, he granted immunity to the attackers or conceded Jewish property to favorites even before a massacre took place. For example, he offered the Archbishop of Trier the goods of the Jews "who have already been killed or may still be killed"; and to a margrave the choice of Jewish houses in Nuremberg "when the next massacre takes place."[89] The Emperor was, to all practical purposes, a broker in Jewish property.

The economic motive was seldom absent in the ubiquitous trials and massacres. Confiscations of debts and property followed promptly on death in many places. One chronicler's comment is revealing: "The poison that killed the Jews was their goods."[90] In Freiburg, all Jews were burned at the stake except twelve of the richest, who were spared so that they might reveal their debtors, for all Jewish assets went to the community. In Strassburg, Jews were defended by the city council, but for its efforts the people replaced it with another which had all 2,000 Jews burned in the cemetery on the Sabbath and all records of their credits with them.

The religious motive also made its appearance. A group of "Flagellants" appeared on the scene and roamed throughout Germany and parts of France, expiating their sins by stirring up attacks on the Jews. These fanatics "ended by destroying churches, killing priests, canons, and clerics, desiring to have their goods and benefices."[91] They were condemned by the Holy See[92] and the secular rulers, but not before the damage was done.

It is impossible to determine the extent of Jewish casualties during these years. In all, over 200 Jewish communities, large and small, were destroyed. The massacres were greatest in Germany where every sizable city was affected, and perhaps least in Austria because of the wholehearted intervention of Albert II. One may imagine the scope of the tragedy by the 10,000 casualties reported in Poland, where they were comparatively light. Well over 10,000 were killed in Erfurt, Mainz, and Breslau alone.

FROM PILLAR TO POST

Not long after the massacres the Jews were missed—financially—and the survivors were invited to return to their old communities. A "Golden Bull" of the empire (1355) permitted them to be readmitted and taxed. Almost immediately, Speyer, Augsburg, and Mainz—and later almost all their old sites—brought them back with special guarantees of protection. Despite this ostensible indulgence, their condition was as pitiable as ever. Their civil status depended entirely upon the caprice of their rulers; their intellectual and spiritual life declined; their spirit was broken.[93] Money lending was still their chief occupation, but it was of a petty kind; and a new occupation was added, traffic in old clothes.

A period of comparative tranquility followed the readmission, but it was short-lived. Troubles resumed under Emperor Wenceslaus (1378-1400). Some Jews were killed in Nordlingen, Windsheim, and Weissenburg; in Nuremberg they were spared upon receipt of money.

The brunt of their troubles in this period was largely financial. Remission of debts to Jews became the order of the day. In 1385 a Swabian diet at Ulm abolished one-quarter of their credits and granted the residue to the cities, into whose jurisdiction Jews were now thrown. Five years later, Wenceslaus remitted debts to Jews; and in the Southwest a decree despoiled them of all their credits. These developments seriously affected their place in society. Their economic usefulness was greatly reduced by the impoverishment, and in consequence their vulnerability to hostile prince and populace was greatly increased. Not to be useful was a luxury Jews could ill afford in the Middle Ages.

In Strassburg the Jewish community was expelled in 1386. This was the first of a long series of expulsions in Germany that continued to the end of the fifteenth century. Their multiplicity is explained by the extreme decentralization of the empire. Since no central decree could effect a nation-wide expulsion, as in France, each region or city ejected its Jews, who often simply moved into the next province. The motivations behind the expulsions were also multiple: economic and religious considerations mutually reinforced each other. Verbally, however, religious reasons predominated in the edicts: ritual murder, Jewish thirst for Christian blood, and the honor of God were named as chief causes. In Ratisbon in the late fifteenth century, we find the Jewish community pathetically pleading against banishment on the grounds that their arrival in that city antedated the crucifixion, for which they could not be held responsible. The basic cause, however, was economic. Less needed in the medieval economy, Jews appeared more as mere competitors and owners of valuable properties than as sources of income. From the fourteenth century, the "wandering Jew," long a legend in Christian folklore, took on the substance of juridical and social reality.[94] By the end of the fifteenth century, no more than three or four German cities still harbored a Jewish population. Most of the expellees had finally left Germany for Poland and Lithuania.

Before the final expulsions occurred, however, there was still much to be suffered. In 1389 in Prague a priest carrying the sacred host was sprayed with sand by Jewish children at play. Reprisals were taken against the Jews, who in their turn retaliated. Before the affair ended, 3,000 Jews were massacred, their synagogue burned, and their Torah destroyed. Facing the choice of death or baptism, a number took their own lives. Throughout Bohemia, many Jews were imprisoned and fined by Wenceslaus, although later released. In 1389 the Jews appealed to the Pope, who condemned the action of the Christians, citing the terms of the *Constitutio*.[95] In 1400 a Jewish convert named Peter accused his former coreligionists of vilifying Christ in their *Alenu* prayer. A Talmud scholar defended the prayer, explaining that it did not refer to Jesus; nevertheless, seventy-one Jews were executed and three weeks later three were burned.[96] Another accusation of the time credited Jews with absolving themselves from all oaths on

the Day of Atonement.[97] New, humiliating punishments made
their appearance, for instance, the hanging of Jews by the feet and
imposing a special oath in court.

In the fifteenth century, traditional anti-Jewish acts continued unabated. There were arrests, pogroms, confiscations, re-
missions of debts, and expulsions. Most of these were triggered
by ritual-murder and host-desecration charges or by reactions to
Jewish usury. But this century in addition produced an antisemitism all its own, which involved the Empire and the Papacy,
the Council of Basel, the Hussite wars, and culminated in St. John
Capistrano.

Both the secular and spiritual powers vacillated in their policies toward Jews. Emperor Sigismund (1441-37) at once protected and extorted money from them, making them pay, for one
thing, his contribution to the Council of Constance (1414-18). He
was succeeded by Albert II who dealt with them severely.[98] Jews
were fortunate in the election of Martin V (1417-31) as Pope at
the Council of Constance, for this Pontiff observed the *Constitutio*
and in 1418, in answer to their plea, issued a decree which guaranteed protection of their lives, rites, privileges and festivals; forbade forced baptisms, and called upon Jews to respect
Christianity and refrain from insults.[99] His attitude is well
evinced by these words from one of his bulls:

> Since the Jews are made in the image of God, since a remnant
> of them shall be saved, since, further, they solicit our coun-
> tenance and our compassion, thus will we, in the same sense
> as Calixtus, Eugenius, Alexander, Clement, Celestine, In-
> nocent, Honorious, Gregory, Urban, Nicholas, Clement,
> and other former Popes, we command that they be not mo-
> lested in their synagogues; that their laws, rights and customs
> be not assailed; that they be not baptized by force, made to
> observe Christian festivals, or to wear new badges, and that
> they be not hindered in their business relations with Chris-
> tians.[100]

In 1422 when Jews were hard pressed by the preaching of
Dominican friars—assigned to preach against the Hussite heresy—the Pope responded with a remarkably favorable bull calling

for friendly relations between Christian and Jew and cautioning
the friars against preaching against such relations. He prohibited
compulsory attendance at sermons, and reminded Christians of
Judaism's intimate connection with Christianity.[101]

Pope Eugene IV (1431-47) did not follow in the footsteps of
his predecessor, Martin V, with regard to Jews, nor did the Council of Basel (1431-43). The new Pope was not hostile at first and
renewed the *Constitutio*.[102] But upon receiving complaints against
Jews and prompted by the Bishop of Burgos in Spain, a Jewish
convert, he annulled, in a bull of 1442, the privileges conceded
by Martin and reinvoked severely restrictive laws.[103] The General
Council of Basel revived the traditional restrictions, including the
distinctive garb, exclusion from office and forced inhabiting of a
separate quarter. To these were added prohibitions of university
degrees and compulsory attendance at Christian sermons.[104] The
ban on university degrees was original with this Council and
seems to indicate increased Jewish efforts to enter the common
intellectual life.

COMPULSORY SERMONS

Compulsory attendance at sermons was not new. Examples
of it may be found as early as the ninth century, but it was not
until the thirteenth, with the rise of the preaching orders, principally the Dominicans and Franciscans, that the practice grew.
The famous Spanish convert and Dominican preacher Pablo Cristiani strongly advocated it and procured a decree from the king
of Aragon that Jews be forced to listen to his sermons. Sts. Vincent Ferrer and Raymond of Penaforte also adopted the practice.
Support from the Church came in a bull of Nicholas III in 1278,
which laid down rules for the delivery of the sermons.[105] After the
Council of Basel, the practice spread, was taken up by the Protestant reformers, and saw service in the Church off and on until
abolished in 1848 by Pius IX. The practice gives eloquent evidence not only of the desperate desire of the Church to convert
Jews to Christianity but also of the medieval notion that the Faith
was perfectly lucid, that mere exposure to it was all that was required for conviction. One can imagine the few conversions these
enforced sermons obtained and the chagrin of the reluctant lis-

teners, who in some places had to have their ears inspected for removal of stuffed cotton placed there for obvious reasons. Others required an excitator to keep them awake throughout expositions on the truth of Christianity and the falsity of Judaism that sometimes lasted two hours.[106]

SCOURGE OF THE JEWS

Perhaps the most remarkable anti-Jewish phenomenon of the fifteenth century was the Franciscan reformer St. John Capistrano. This rigid ascetic and fiery preacher stormed about Europe inveighing against the dangers of heresy, the sensuality of his contemporaries, even clerics, and the "impiety and usury" of the Jews. So intense was his zeal that in his lifetime he received the title "scourge of the Jews" and from the Pope, the office of Inquisitor to the Jews for Germanic and Slavonic countries. His function in this office was to enforce the conciliar statutes, to which he set himself with a will. Jews were struck with terror where he went. Setting himself against the religious and political leaders as well as the crowds, he thundered against their unchristian lives and the evils of heresy; he threatened with hell-fire those who in any way consorted with Jews. His fulminations were not without effect, sometimes dramatic, as in the cases of the Dukes Louis and Albert of Bavaria and Bishop Godfrey of Wuerzburg, who after his visits showed themselves assiduous in curbing Jews, even having them banished. Only the city of Ratisbon refused to heed Capistrano's urgings against the Jews. In Breslau, where he preached, the host-desecration charge arose, and all inhabitants of the Jewish quarter—excepting some who fled—were imprisoned. A trial was set. Capistrano presided as chief inquisitor, personally supervising the torture of some of the accused from whom confessions to this and other ritual crimes were accepted. In all, forty were burned, a rabbi hanged himself, children of the deceased were taken for baptism, and the remainder were banished. From here St. John went to Poland, at the invitation of the Bishop of Cracow, so as to put an end to privileges Jews enjoyed under the reigning Casimir IV (1447-92). Even with this independent ruler Capistrano was successful; the common restrictions were put into force in this haven of Jewish exiles.

Later in the century, a regular epidemic of ritual-murder accusations rocked Jewish communities. Especially noteworthy was that of Ratisbon where a Jewish convert, Hans Vayol, accused the aged scholar Israel Bruna of the crime. The latter was jailed, but with the intervention of the Emperor and the King of Poland, Bruna was released. Vayol then confessed his calumny and was punished. One of the most famous of all such accusations occurred in Holy Week of 1473 in Trent, where St. Bernardinus of Feltre was finishing a Lenten series of sermons. The body of a three-year-old boy named Simon was found in the Adige river. An outcry immediately went up against the Jews.

St. Bernardinus' connection with the affair has been questioned. The mystically-minded Franciscan was a spiritual disciple of St. Bernardinus of Siena, a firm believer that Jews plotted the destruction of Christianity through their usuries and their physicians. Bernardinus, otherwise a mild and kindly religious, inherited the outlook of his mentor, actually describing himself as a dog "who barks for Christ" against the Jews.[107] He is recorded as having stated in his Lenten Sermons in Trent—apparently to an audience unimpressed by his warning against Jews—that "the feast of Easter will not pass before you will find something out."[108] The question has been raised whether St. Bernardinus helped instigate the murder charge or whether it was a spontaneous reaction to his preaching. Though Graetz accuses the saint with arranging the "cunning plan,"[109] it is difficult to believe this about a man who on another occasion stated: "As to the Jews, I say here what I say elsewhere: no one who has concern for his soul can injure the Jews, whether it be their persons or their faculties, or in any other way, for even to Jews, Christian piety and love must be shown since they possess a human nature."[110]

Whether the death of little Simon was a Jewish crime rather than a libel seemed to be answered by the investigation of the affair by the papal legate of the time who discouraged the cult grown about the boy's grave, which was fostered by the religious orders and clergy. For all this, at the behest of the Bishop of Trent, Jews were arrested, tried, and, under torture, confessed— all except one who persisted in retracting his confession when off the rack. At the end, all Jews of Trent were burned. Four had been baptized. A second investigation of the affair three years later exculpated the Bishop, and the Pope accepted the verdict of Jewish guilt. In 1584 the boy Simon was placed in the martyrology and three years later his cult was approved for the diocese of Trent by Sixtus V (1585-90). It was this approval by the Holy See, Father Vacandard believes, that influenced Cardinal Ganganelli in his investigation of the ritual-murder charge to accept that of Trent as justified.[111] The Trent episode imparted great impetus to the ritual-murder charges in and out of the Church throughout Europe. A memorial—complete with an artist's conception of a ritual murder—was erected at Frankfurt commemorating the martyred children. And the Bishop of Ratisbon, aroused by the Trent affair, accused Jews of having committed a ritual murder eight years previously. All were imprisoned, but after a protracted political struggle over the charge, involving the city council, the Emperor and even the Holy See, the Jews were set free, but fined.

In Passau, Bavaria, in 1478, a host-desecration charge was made on the strength of which several Jews were tried, tortured and killed; and the synagogue was replaced with a church in which the desecration was commemorated.[112]

At the close of the fifteenth century the only important Jewish communities left in Germany were those of Ratisbon, Worms, and Frankfurt. Frederick III, a weak prince, was favorable to Jews but unable to restrain the anti-Jewish antipathies of his subjects. Medieval German Jewry was moribund.

THE JEW IN ENGLAND:
A FINANCIAL PAWN

The life of the Jews in England had the briefest span in medieval Jewish history. In many ways it is the most instructive example of the instability of the position of the Jews in medieval society and of the part their economic function played in their plight. The story is predominantly one of finances. Although Jews arrived in England prior to the Conquest in small numbers, they were brought for the greater part from France by William the Conqueror (1066-87) in the late eleventh century. They rose to dizzy heights of affluence and financial power in the twelfth century, but declined rapidly and steadily in the thirteenth to encounter their first nation-wide expulsion in 1290.

The first phase of their existence in England (late eleventh and early twelfth century) was comparatively idyllic. The Conqueror's son, William Rufus, a rebel by nature, liberally indulged them, going so far as to farm out bishoprics to them. Under Henry I (1100-35) they were encouraged and became "the King's men," the chief source of sovereign income. As sole moneylenders of the kingdom, they became a middle class unto themselves and enjoyed equality and freedom at least on a par with the native Englishmen. Many of them became enormously rich and lived in palatial mansions. An idea of their wealth is gained by the 60,000 pounds they were taxed for the Third Crusade as compared with the 70,000 pounds levied on the entire Christian population. One Aaron of Lincoln built a fabulous fortune and though its coin was lost at sea, a special department of the Exchequer was still necessary for its management at his death—when it was, of course, confiscated by the crown. But their wealth was their undoing. Practically all sovereigns of the twelfth and thirteenth centuries were addicted to extorting it; the barons and the clergy—their debtors—resented their high rates of interest; the resentment of the barons was even greater because of the Jews' connections with the crown; and the populace simply envied their affluence. The tide began to turn under Stephen (1135-54). This monarch protected them during the Second Crusade, but sought in earnest to discover ways of absorbing their money, taxing them, for example, to the extent of one-fourth of their liquid assets.

The coronation of Richard I, the Lion-Hearted, in 1189, provided the critical occasion that initiated the terminal decline in their fortunes. Jewish delegations came to the coronation with handsome gifts for the king, but were refused entry by officials and pelted with stones by the mobs. Erroneously, the word spread that Richard himself wished them exterminated. Riots followed in which many Jews were killed and their stately homes burned. Richard punished the ringleaders of these disorders and ordered the Jews left alone. This fair-minded king was also appreciative of the Jews' fiscal usefulness and taxed them heavily. During his reign, a special exchequer for Jews was established.

When Richard left for France in 1190 to fight in the Third Crusade, new riots broke out and spread to most of the principal towns with Jewish communities: Lynn, Bury St. Edmunds, Lincoln, Norwich, Stamford, and York. The most tragic occurred at York.[113] There, Crusaders, before setting out to follow their King, plundered the possessions of the Jews, who fled into the royal castle where they were besieged by the warriors—many of whom were deeply in debt to their quarry. The climax was reached when a stone, thrown from the castle, killed a monk whose custom it was to celebrate Mass outside the castle every morning and urge the people to "destroy the enemies of Christ." When the Jews saw the fury of the beseigers and felt their fate to be sealed, they took their own lives, cutting one another's throats. When the mobs gained access to the tower, the few Jews left, who begged for baptism and deliverance, were slaughtered. The total casualties have been estimated variously from 500 to 1,500. From this scene of carnage, the attackers converged on the cathedral and burned all the records of financial obligations to the Jews kept in its archives. When Richard returned, he attempted to bring the guilty to book and ordered that all Jewish debts be henceforth registered in duplicate by the government.

King John (c. 1167-1216) conceded liberties and privileges to Jews but apparently only to profit from the by-products these improved conditions would bring. He imprisoned all Jews, tortured many, and in this way extorted 60,000 silver marks. One wealthy Jew of Bristol, who refused to pay his exorbitant tax, had a tooth extracted every day until he revealed his coffers. He lost seven teeth. Henry III's (1207-72) dealings with Jews is a record of pure taxation, which grew to such a point that Jews, unable to pay, sought to leave England but were refused permission. On one occasion, he mortgaged all Jews to his brother, Richard of Cornwall; on another, to the Caorsini, the Italian usurers who had become the chief competitors of the Jews in moneylending in England and abroad. By the time Edward I was crowned in 1272, Jews were impoverished enough to be dispensed with. His business now transacted with the Caorsini, Edward passed his famous *Act Concerning Jews* in 1275, which prohibited them from engaging in usury and encouraged their entry into land cultivation and the trades. Compliance with this directive was not easy, since the labor guilds would not accept Jews, and they themselves were ill prepared for the manual skills.

During the civil war of 1262, Jews were attacked in many places; in London alone 1,500 were killed. In 1279 all Jews in the city were arrested on the charge of debasing the coin of the realm. After a London trial 280 were executed.[114] New ecclesiastical curbs imposed later in the century intensified the Jews' desire to quit the country. Edward I, moreover, now saw no alternative to expulsion. Allowing them to take their movable goods, he ordered them out of the realm by All Saints Day of the year 1290. Their possessions fell to the crown. In October a month before the deadline, 16,000 left for France and Belgium, some finding death on the way, even as close as the Thames where a perverse sea captain allowed many to drown.

This sketch of English Jewry's economic oppression would be incomplete without its religious counterpart. The Jews of England had not been spared the rigors of the customary Church restrictions and popular religious fanaticism. Earlier than in other countries, the decrees of the Lateran Councils were put in force. The Council of Oxford in 1222,[115] under Archbishop Stephen Langton of Canterbury, supplemented them, enforcing the badge and forbidding commingling of Christians and Jews, even to the point of prohibiting sale of food to Jews—an ordinance countermanded by Henry III. Synagogue construction and the vocal volume of Jewish servies were regulated; blasphemies against Christianity by Jews were penalized with death.[116] In 1280 Jews were required to listen to sermons delivered by Dominicans who petitioned and received a directive from the crown that the sermons be listened to "in a diligent and friendly manner."[117] Finally, four years before the expulsion, Pope Honorious IV (1285-87) complained in a bull of remissness of the English hierarchy in combatting Jewish usuries and proselytizing.[118] Measures were promptly taken by several dioceses.

The ritual-murder accusation found fertile soil in England. It was in Norwich, we recall, that the accusation and the practice of venerating the designated victim were born. The suspicion that Jews actually crucified Christian children became deeply embedded in the popular mind. In 1255 the suspicion found another victim in Hugh of Lincoln, a Christian child of eight whose body was found in a well. A full trial was staged; ninety Jews were sent to the tower of London; eighteen were executed. An appeal by the Dominicans of Lincoln favoring the innocence of the Jews had little effect. As often happened, one of the accused Jews confessed and placed the blame on fellow Jews. Little Hugh was made the object of a cult and a pilgrimage for centuries.[119] The tale became so much a part of the nation's traditions that it found its way into Chaucer's *Prioress' Tale*, just as the "usurious" Jew of England was eventually caricatured in Shakespeare's Shylock and Dickens' Fagin.

6
AN OASIS
AND AN ORDEAL

The experiences of the Jews in Italy and Spain constitute something of a paradox. Enjoying comparable happy circumstances at first, the communities of these neighboring countries came to quite a different end. In Rome, the center of Catholic unity, Jews were never expelled and in Italy as a whole their situation was felicitous until the end of the Middle Ages, even longer. Across the Pyrenees, caught amid a desperate attempt to enforce Catholic unity, they suffered their bitterest hours and their final and most painful expulsion. To understand this paradox fully is a task as yet unfinished for historians. Pending its completion, the contrast these two histories pose both to one another and, taken together, to the rest of Europe may serve to caution against viewing the medieval scene too simply and against judging heterogeneous situations of the past in the light of doctrinaire principles of the present.

IN THE SHADOW OF ST. PETER

The case of the Roman community was particularly remarkable. Of it, Emmanuel Rodocanachi, a student of the relations of the Jews and the Holy See, writes: "Whereas everywhere else—in Spain, in France, in Germany, and even Arabia and the remotest regions—Jews were severely persecuted; in Rome, the capital of the Christian world, they were shown tolerance. This tranquility, this security of body and soul, which they enjoyed nowhere else, they found, relatively at least, in the shadow of St. Peter."[1] And Léon Poliakov says: "Rome, the only large city of Europe from which the Jews were never expelled, remained an oasis of peace for them."[2]

These opinions are borne out in reality. From an early period, Roman Jews comprised an independent organization or *schola*. And as early as the twelfth century, its representatives participated in the municipal procession on the occasion of the papal coronation, welcoming the new Pontiff and presenting him with their scroll of the Law and accepting a renewal of their rights and privileges. The custom appears to have been an old one.[3] When Benjamin of Tudela[4] visited the Roman community in the twelfth century he found it "respected and paying taxes to no one."[5] The badge did not come to Rome until late in the thirteenth century, well after it was imposed elsewhere in Europe; and then many exceptions existed. Jewish-Christian relations were intimate: Jews associated openly and intermarried with Christians and selected their occupations freely. A descendant of the Jewish convert Pedro Leonis became anti-Pope Anacletus II. These favorable Roman conditions were approximated throughout the pontifical territories, including Avignon.

That the situation of Italian Jewry in general was exceptionally good is well attested. Poliakov describes it thus: "Taken together, the Jews of Italy constitute in Europe a case apart. In the Middle Ages, their history was not a 'vale of tears'; and in modern times there was no 'Jewish problem' in Italy, but of Jews harmoniously integrated among their compatriots."[6] Scattered throughout the country but concentrated in Rome, the papal states, Lombardy, Naples, Venice, and Sicily, Jews were generally prosperous and enjoyed good relations with their neighbors. Only two popular anti-Jewish disorders are recorded, one in the eleventh century, another in the thirteenth.[7] The latter was incited by fraudulent charges against Jews, which caused Pope Alexander IV (1254-61) to side with the Jews. The storms that shook European communities during the Crusades and the Black Death left the Jews of Italy untouched. Later the peninsula became a haven for Jewish refugees from France, Germany, and Spain, so that by the early sixteenth century it "swarmed with fugitive Jews," and many *marranos* were found in the papal possessions.[8] With the advent of the Italian Renaissance, Jews participated in the cultural surge, and considerable literary converse took place between Christians and Jews, the most notable of which was that of Dante with the Jewish poet Immanuel (c. 1265-c. 1330) and that of Pico della Mirandola with Elias del Medigo (1460-97).

What lay at the roots of this exceptional state of affairs? First, there were economic causes. The feudal system, a prime cause of Jewish degradation, disappeared early in Italy, to be replaced by the free cities which more or less ignored the Jews and were, as far as their political and military exploits were concerned, ignored by them. Jews in Italy did not become singularly wealthy as in other places but were either moderately wealthy or poor. They never predominated in moneylending. Indeed, the Christian usurers of Northern Italy (chiefly, Florentines, Lombards, and Caorsini) took care that they did not. Jews found a place in the money market, however; Jewish usurers expelled from France and Germany were allowed to practice their skills. In fact, Jews were preferred, on principle, to Christian usurers who were ever at odds with the Church's directives. The Holy See actually protected Jewish lenders and gave them permission to practice, even employing them for pontifical finances, but also closely regulated their methods, their rates of interest and demands for collateral. It was not until the fourteenth century that Italian Jews devoted themselves seriously to the lending of money; and soon afterwards the Franciscans established their *montes pietatis* (mounts of piety), credit unions designed to compete with both Jewish and Christian usurers by lending without interest. In sum, the economic causes of Jewish oppression prominent in other countries—wealth and usury—did not exist in Italy to an extent sufficient to provoke the usual resentments and reactions.

Still, Italian tolerance was basically more papal than economic. We cannot agree with those historians who give it a popular derivation, attributing it to the "friendliness" or "good sense" of the Italian people, which supposedly withstood the antisemitic pressures from above [the Church].[9] The view of those historians is weakened by their willingness on other occasions to exaggerate the influence of the papacy over the people. It fails, moreover, to take into account the originality of the Italian situation, which in many ways was the reverse of the common European experience. Whatever antisemitism there was in Italy was, in reality, popular, but it was held in check by a papal policy of toleration toward Jews. Isaac Abrahams has stated the matter plainly: "Unfriendliness to Jews flowed from the higher to the lower levels. Anti-Jewish prejudice originated among the classes, not among the masses. But this statement, true of the rest of Europe, is untrue of Italy. In the latter country such anti-Jewish feeling as was prevalent in the twelfth century was a *popular* growth. But because it emanated from below, it was controllable by those in authority."[10] The practice of this toleration throughout Italy, and Italy alone, moreover, is no accident and should be explained, aside from economic factors, by "geographical proximity"[11] to Rome.

THE PRINCIPLE OF TOLERANCE

The Church's policy possessed, as already shown, a dual character, at once opposed to Jewish ascendency over, or equality with, Christians and yet protective of basic rights of Jews. This policy, though always tied to the Church's central missionary purpose, nonetheless respected temporal contingencies and thus applied its restrictive or protective clauses according to circumstances. In the Middle Ages, in face of the growing hostility of anti-Jewish mobs and rules, the protective policy predominated. This was especially true in the papal possessions where popes enjoyed a greater liberty of action than in nonpapal regimes. Papal directives concerning Jews in the latter were more severe than those issued or practiced in Rome or the papal states.[12] It is a matter of record that in their policies toward Jews popes were more lenient than local bishops and councils. Rodocanachi says: "More than once we have seen popes themselves attenuate in their own states whatever their bulls might have had that was too rigid, too ideal, or inapplicable. They amended and *interpreted* them, whereas elsewhere surprisingly, they were applied to the letter, without hesitation or, it seems, pity."[13] Many factors, social, economic, and political, might be adduced to explain the comparatively happier situation of Jews under the papacy, a few of which we have noted,[14] but finally its origin should be sought in that tradition of papal toleration which stemmed from the seventh century—from Pope Gregory the Great who set the norm of papal policy.[15] With the first issuance of the *Constitutio* by Nicholas II (1058-61), this tradition came to full consciousness and, in the main, determined papal attitudes until the middle of the fifteenth century.

If the lot of the Jews in Italy was not a martyrdom, as it so often was in other European countries, it was not, for all that, an idyll. There were vicissitudes even for the Roman community. Warnings against Jewish unbelief and usury, sometimes offensive, were scattered among the writings even of the most benevolent popes. Most of the decrees of the *Constitutio* were prefaced by strictures concerning Jewish blindness and stubbornness: "The Jews, whom Holy Church tolerates in diverse parts of the world in testimony to Jesus Christ, wish to persevere in their hardness and blindness rather than acknowledge the words of the prophets and the mysteries of the Holy Scriptures and come to the knowledge of the Christian faith and salvation; but because in their necessity they beseech our aid and favors, we do not intend to deny them of the clemency and the mercy of Christian piety . . . ."[16] There were, furthermore, popes, for example, Innocent III (1198-1216), Gregory X (1271-76) and Eugenius IV (1431-47),[17] who feared the presence of Jews in the heart of Christendom, and introduced vexatious restrictions. But even in these cases the anti-Jewish decrees were more formally than actually enforced. Cecil Roth's comment is generally true:

> Nowhere in Europe was the network of anti-Jewish regulations, elaborated by the Lateran Councils and enunciated in successive papal Bulls, less carefully studied or more systematically neglected: nowhere was the Jewish community more free in body and in mind. From Rome, the new spirit radiated throughout Italy—except the South, where foreign influences fostered a different outlook. The sun of the Renaissance was shining in its fullest splendor, and the Jews enjoyed its fecund warmth as never before.[18]

The liberal tradition was perhaps never stronger than in the late fifteenth and early sixteenth centuries when a series of popes showed Roman Jews unprecedented consideration, bringing Jewish physicians and men of culture into their immediate entourage. Sixtus IV (1474-84) sought a Latin translation of the *Kabbalah* for Christian readers.[19] Alexander VI (1498-1500) fined Roman Jews for asking him to prevent an influx of Spain's Jewish and *marrano* refugees into the city. Julius II (1503-13), Leo X (1513-21), and Paul III (1534-49) were very well disposed toward Jews, the former two employing Jewish physicians, the last extending their privileges. Clement VII (1523-34) marked the high point in favoritism. Among other things, this Pontiff suspended the Spanish Inquisition against the *marranos*, entertained close relationships with the Jewish visionaries Reubeni and Molcho, and planned a translation of the Old Testament by Jewish and Christian scholars.

With Paul IV (155-59) and the Counter-Reform, this happy chapter in Jewish annals came to a close.

GOLDEN AGE IN SPAIN

Before their fatal plunge into the abyss of the fifteenth century, the Jews in Spain promised to surpass the finest hours of their Italian brethren. Under Moslem rule, their golden age was reached in the eleventh and twelfth centuries[20] but with the ultimatum, "Islam or death," of the fanatical Almohades, those who did not remain to simulate Mohammedanism migrated to the North to join their coreligionists in the five Christian kingdoms—Castile, Aragon, Leon, Portugal, and Navarre. Most went to Toledo, the capital of Castile, the greatest of the kingdoms, where a succession of tolerant kings, beginning with Ferdinand I in the first half of the eleventh century, granted Jews equal rights with Christians and employed many of them in positions of trust in their courts. Under these excellent conditions Jews distinguished themselves in intellectual and commercial pursuits, took part freely in all occupations from land cultivation to usury, became famous as physicians, and developed a rich spiritual life. They brought to Christian Spain the spiritual and cultural hegemony of world Jewry. So enviable was their status by the end of the eleventh century that Gregory VII (1073-85) cautioned Alphonso VI (1065-1109) to cease allowing Jews to rule over Christians. They became well integrated into their communities, and under Alphonso VIII (1158-1214), who greatly indulged them, they fought shoulder to shoulder with their Christian neighbors in the defense of Toledo against the Almohades. It is true, though, that they remained a "people within a people, a state within a state,"[21] for they enjoyed considerable autonomy, retaining, for example, the right of capital punishment for their own people until they abused it in the fourteenth century. In short, Jews were very much a part of Spain and very conscious of their pre-Christian roots in Spain, yet they kept their ethnic individuality intact. In one historian's words: "They were Spain, and they were not Spain . . . . They departed from a well-Judaized Spain well Hispanicized."[22]

This early period was marred by a number of attacks by crusaders in the course of frequent campaigns to reconquer southern Spain from the Moslems, but these disorders were generally put down before they got out of hand. The crusaders' habit of attacking Jews was probably a French import, since the first attack was made by crusaders from France in 1066. On that occasion, Pope Alexander II (1061-73) urged that the Jews of Barcelona be left undisturbed, "for God is not pleased," he wrote, "by the effusion of blood, and takes no pleasure at the perdition of men, even evil men."[23]

As the *Reconquisita* continued into the thirteenth century until only Granada was left in Moslem hands, efforts were made to apply the anti-Judaic rulings of Innocent III and the Lateran Councils (in the process of application in England, France, and Germany), but with small success. The attempt to impose the badge was particularly resented. In Castile, Jews refused outright to wear it and, by gifts to the crown, had its imposition postponed. Both popes and bishops objected to these leniencies but realistically attended only to the more noticeable extravagances. The Council of Valladolid (1128) appeared satisfied that Jews should not wear the same tunic as the clergy, thus receiving undue reverence.[24] In Aragon, the prescription of the badge created less of a furor, since Jews there wore a distinctive dress of their own to which they were very much attached. Other restrictive measures were promulgated but again honored more in the breach than in practice.

Spain, in short, assimilated the general European policy slowly and Spanish Jews, unlike their European brothers, continued to grow in prosperity, prestige, and creativity. Nominally, they were considered the king's "serfs," but the status was borne lightly. Despite their great wealth, many Jews in Castile and Aragon were taxed but never used as a "sponge" for royal coffers, as in France, Germany, and England. Usury by Jews—considered a contravention of Jewish law as well as Christian—was formally forbidden but generally winked at and regulated. These well-integrated Jews shared public baths, repasts, and to a degree participated in Christian religious ceremonies and festivals.[25]

In Aragon considerable effort was made to bring them into the fold. James I envisaged the conversion by persuasion of all Jews and Arabs of his realm. He was aided by the Dominicans, appointed Inquisitors for Aragon, who taught Hebrew and Arabic in their seminaries to this purpose. The leader of this movement was St. Raymond of Penaforte, Dominican confessor to the king. One of his more famous converts was Pablo Cristiani, who became a Dominican brother and a zealous missionary to the Jews. He was authorized to preach in all Jewish synagogues. For missionary purposes, a public disputation was arranged at Barcelona in 1263 between Pablo and the learned Rabbi Nachman, who accepted the role of the representative of the Jews only on the condition that he could speak very candidly. The debate lasted four days in the presence of the king and his entourage. Nachman defended the Talmud, distinguishing its essentials from various *midrashim* which enjoyed less authority, and arguing forcefully that the Messiah could not have come, since his era would be one of peace, not of wars. Nachman was considered by some to have won the debate and actually received a prize from the king. He later suffered exile of two years for publishing an account of the disputation. At all events, Cristiani denounced the Talmud to Clement IV (1265-68) and succeeded in having all Jewish books searched for anti-Christian passages. Bodily harm did not come to the Jews of Aragon until the fourteenth century when the massacres of the Pastoreaux and of the Black Death reached their communities. Casualties were fewer here than elsewhere, however, owing to effective government intervention and to better Jewish-Christian relations.

Navarre, bordering on France, was the scene of the first defection from the general Spanish tranquility. Economic restraints were imposed in 1284 and anti-Jewish feeling spread contagiously from France and Germany. In 1328 the denunciations of a Franciscan friar, Peter Olligen, set off massacres in Estella and several other towns. Six thousand Jews died. The Pastoreaux and the Black Death took their tolls here also. Portugal, removed from the mainstream of European events, remained a refuge for Jews in this period, despite opposition from the clergy.

From Castile, the great central province, comes a story of tolerance all its own. From the eleventh to the fourteenth centuries, a remarkable succession of humanist kings, highly appreciative of the economic and creative capabilities of their Jews, showered them with honors and favors. These monarchs protected them from the envy of the nobles and the rigors of the Church, at times even holding off the hand of the papacy. No king was without his Jewish minister, councilor, or physician, and—as in Aragon—in the course of time few noble families remained without their "taint" of Jewish blood. Jewish prestige was particularly great under the reign of Alphonso X, the Wise (1252-84). This monarch surrounded himself with Jews, granted them lands and mosques for synagogues, and enlisted their aid in constructing his famous astronomical tables. And yet, in deference to the norms of his time, he incorporated among the more liberal rulings of his statutes certain disabilities such as the badge and prohibitions against employing Christian servants and holding public office.[26] During and following his rule, Jewish intellectual life flowered both in talmudic and philosophical studies. In this era of the "three religions," a degree of skepticism crept into Jewish thought that sharpened the scission—and feuds—in Judaism, opening the way simultaneously to philosophical rationalism and the mystical speculations of the *Kabbalah*.

Another height was scaled under Ferdinand IV (1295-1312) and Alphonso XI (1312-50) when Jews rose to great eminence in the court and assumed control in financial matters. Their high estate did not fail to stir up the resentment of nobles, clergy, and people. Even as they enjoyed their new golden age, signs of decline were to be seen. The Cortes (legislature) took exception to the royal beneficence, set itself against usury by Jews, and called for heavier taxation—even a cancellation of debts to Jews. Alphonso XI, making some concessions, agreed to cancel one-fourth of their credits and to forbid Jews the practice of usury. Church councils, especially that of Zamora, decreed curtailments of their freedom such as working on Sunday, circulating in Holy Week, and ignoring the badge. A famous Jewish convert of this time, Abner of Burgos, obtained a decree from the crown to have the word "Nazarene" extirpated from the *Shemoneh Esreh.*[27]

The people, meanwhile, were envious of Jewish ascendancy and placed the blame for their own poverty on the courtly Jewish financiers to whom they attributed the high cost of living, making no distinction between these wealthy and powerful Jews and the larger number of Jews as impoverished as themselves. To them, it seemed that every Jew was or would be a grandee. There was some justification for the popular reaction, for even Jewish chroniclers of these years deplored the manner in which these favored Jews lived: flaunting their silks and satins, boasting of their lineage, caring nothing for their own people, and devoting little time to their religion or to scholarly pursuits. The favored ones, inured to their fine living and oblivious to the hatred closing in upon them, rushed on toward their doom dragging their people with them.

INTO THE ABYSS

For the Jews in Spain, the last summit of glory—and precipice—was another royal favoritism. So embroiled, in fact, was the excommunicated King Pedro the Cruel (1350-69) in Jewish interests, and so loyally did Jews rally to his side in his feud with his brother Henry of Trastamara, that Pedro was dubbed the "Judaized King," and the rumor got about—contrary to fact—that he was the bastard son of a Jewess. After his death at the hands of Henry, Jews paid for their loyalty. Though the realistic new King Henry did not avenge himself too severely upon them, still allowing them to circulate in his court, their power was gone and the downward course begun. But if Henry managed to protect the

Jews from the furies that raged against them, this was only a reprieve. The Courts henceforth lost no opportunity to curb them, introducing into Spain the oppressive measures long since practiced across the Pyrenees. The badge was finally made compulsory. The nobles continued to chafe under mortgages held by Jews; the clergy, especially the Dominican friars, inveighed against their loftiness as an insult to the Church; and the people steadfastly saw the successful Jew as the source of their woes. Jewish spiritual life continued to degenerate. Cultivated Jews bore their religion lightly and many were converted to Christianity, as often as not merely to maintain their *status quo*. The stage was set for another convulsion in Jewish history which would have unique consequences.

It first appeared in the person of Ferrand Martinez, an archdeacon in Seville, who since 1378 had been waging a relentless campaign against Jewish doctrines, wealth, and activities. Some excesses occurred, and Martinez was mildly reproached by the crown but more severely by the Archbishop. Deaf to these remonstrances, he persisted in his preachings and, during a simultaneous interregnum of the crown and the archbishopric in 1391, so aroused the populace that they rushed upon the *Juderia* (Jewish quarter) and sacked it. The uprising was put down, two of the ringleaders were flogged before a rebellious crowd, and further steps were taken to maintain order, but Martinez continued to inflame the masses.

Three months later the holocaust began. With renewed fury, the mob broke into the *Juderia* of Seville and left it in ruins. Four thousand Jews were killed, but the majority including the aged Abrabanel, former minister to the king, escaped death by accepting baptism. From Seville, the carnage spread like a plague throughout all Spain, except the provinces of Granada and Portugal, engulfing some seventy Jewish communities. In some *Juderias* not a single Jew was left, and many synagogues were turned into churches. Authorities were helpless before the onslaught. To their credit, some members of the clergy and the nobility offered Jews the shelter of their homes from the impassioned mob. In three months it was over. Some 50,000 Jews were dead and several times that number baptized, including many rabbis. A few took their lives to "sanctify the Name" and a few escaped to Granada, Portugal, and North Africa. Retribution was scant. Twenty-five ringleaders were executed by John I of Aragon and Martinez was imprisoned by Henry III.

MISSIONARY EFFORTS

The most remarkable aftermath of these horrific events was the number of baptized Jews in Spain. Henceforward, the fortunes of Spanish Judaism would center almost entirely on the presence and doings of these *conversos*. A first development took the form of an intensified desire within the Church to complete the task of conversion, which the large influx into her ranks had only served to incite. The Jews remaining in Spain now appeared to the Church as a scandal and a temptation to their converted brethren, and to the state as the final obstacle to a united Christendom. Not least in the renewed missionary efforts was the contribution of Jewish converts themselves. Almost every century had its exemplar of missionary zeal among them, and fourteenth century Spain was no exception. In Paul of Santa Maria it possessed one of the most extraordinary.

Once a talented Rabbi of Burgos named Solomon Levi, this *converso* entered the Church, studied theology in Paris, specialized in scholastic philosophy, was ordained, and became Bishop of Burgos as well as keeper of the seal to the king and a regent. He labored ardently for the conversion of his people, and in both his writing and preaching his efforts to convince them of Christianity were unceasing. He was vigorously attacked by Jewish writers of the time who, suspecting his motives, saw him as a bitter enemy and laid at his door much of the anti-Jewish legislation of the day. He was greatly revered by Christians. That he maligned Jews and urged legislation against them is confirmed on the Christian side by the efforts of the Cardinal of Pampelona and other churchmen to dissuade him from his criticisms. Another brilliant convert of the time was Geronimo de Santa Fé who similarly joined in the conversionist movement.

Above these towers the figure of St. Vincent Ferrer, Dominican, miracle-worker, an excellent preacher, and totally dedicated to the conversion of the Jews. Throughout Castile and Aragon, he passed from synagogue to synagogue, the Torah in one hand, the crucifix in the other and a band of the devout at his heels. His successes were phenomenal. Some Jews were in dread of him and fled to the mountains; others followed him to the font. In one month in Toledo he made 4,000 converts. He is credited with 35,000 baptisms of Jews between 1411 and 1412. When he failed to persuade he was severe and is believed to have inspired the first compulsory Spanish ghettoes and the oppressive legislation of 1414 which narrowly circumscribed Jewish social activities. Jews considered him a scourge, but he was as much one to their enemies. He strongly condemned forced baptisms or violence to Jews, and his preaching reminded Christians of their Hebrew roots. Speaking of the contempt of the "old" Christians for the *neo-conversos*, he exclaimed:

> . . . they despise them because they were Jews. But they should not, for Jesus Christ was a Jew, and the Blessed Virgin was a Jewess before they were Christians. It is a great sin to vilify them. This circumcised God is our God, and you will be damned as will one who dies a Jew. For one must teach them the doctrine in order that they will be in the service of God . . . .[28]

Most spectacular of the conversionist projects was the disputation set up in Tortosa in 1413, certainly the most grandiose of all such debates. The Jews of Aragon and Catalonia were compelled by anti-Pope Benedict XIII to attend it. Geronimo of Santa Fé, an outstanding talmudic scholar and convert, represented the Christian cause against fourteen learned rabbis. Before Benedict and a brilliant entourage, the contest went on for a year and nine months with audiences of two thousand attending. Three thousand Jews were converted, including all but two of the rabbinic debaters, who asked for an end to the fray. At the end, Benedict prohibited the Talmud, applied further restrictions, and prescribed enforced sermons. Throughout this era, many Jews, even whole communities, joined the Church.

For the next several decades, a period of relative calm marked Jewish-Christian relations. Both ecclesiastical and civil authorities imposed severe restrictions, definitively putting Spanish Jews on a par with their brethren in the rest of Europe, but they also invoked the traditional protectionist policy which condemned forced baptisms and violence against Jews and provided guarantees for Jewish worship. The calm, however, was not complete. Occasional uprisings, massacres, and ritual-murder accusations made their appearance, but failed to dominate the situation. The attention of Christians was no longer concentrated on Jews but rather on the mass of converted Jews who had crowded into the Church in 1391 and 1411-14.

THE MARRANOS

It had become apparent that all *conversos* had not broken with their former faith. Many, adhering outwardly to Christianity, practiced Judaism in varying degrees—secretly, sometimes quite openly, even with the connivance of both ecclesiastical and civil authorities. Some, of course, were sincere, as, for example, many of St. Vincent's converts. Among the rest, two groups are distinguishable. There were those who, regretting the step they had taken, practiced their old faith clandestinely or awaited the moment when they might, in exile, re-embrace their old faith openly. Some of these even practiced rites of "de-Christianization" or "washing off" the baptism, if not other ceremonies of a less respectful kind. Others, "bad Jews before, now worse Christians,"[29] made the most of their new situation. Maintaining relations with their Jewish confreres and their customs, they threw themselves eagerly into the communal Spanish life and soon could be found in all its segments, many reaching the higher echelons of the trades and professions, of the universities, the judiciary, and even the Church. They intermarried with the Christian nobility and grew wealthy and influential.

These compromisers won the contempt of their suffering Jewish brethren, who considered them unprincipled renegades. Official Jewish policy, however, was more lenient. These *anusim* (the forced ones) were still considered Jews, and the policy of "Rashi" and Rabbi Gershom of Mainz (b. 960) of reinstating them without punishment or embarrassment was generally followed. Church policy, on the other hand, was not so simple. Baptisms, even if accepted under duress, were deemed valid and binding. For valid ministration, it was held sufficient that the recipient had not openly expressed opposition at the moment of reception of the Sacrament—even if such expression meant instant death. Such was implied in the ruling of the Toledan Councils[30] and also of Innocent III, who wrote: "Whoever is led to Christianity by violence, by fear and torture . . . receives the imprint of Christianity and can be forced to observe the Christian faith."[31]

As the fifteenth century progressed and a new generation of *Nuevos Conversos* (new converts) persisted in the duplicities of their parents, the anger of both clergy and people rose against them. The people, contemptuous of their double standard and envious of their success, hated them more than they did true Jews, and referred to them as *marranos* (swine).[32] The pulpits throughout Spain rang out against them and their defilement of the sacraments. And the Cortes in Toledo decreed that the "New Christians" could not hold civil or church posts, a decree opposed by Pope Nicholas V.

The reaction against the *marranos* broke into violence toward mid-century. In 1440 they were attacked when they attempted to collect governmental taxes—a function many of them had taken up—and though they defended themselves, several of these tax collectors were killed and many of their homes burned. In 1460 the Franciscan friar Alphonso de Spina's *Fortalitium Fidei* (Fortress of the Faith) was published, a bitter work in which he elaborated all the old libels against the Jews although he turned the brunt of his attack against the *marranos*.[33] The book strongly influenced public opinion and furthered the subtle erasure of distinction between Jew and *marrano* already taking place. Antisemitism and anti-marranism fed upon one another and the notion grew that the evil in Judaism and marranism had a common source—hereditary Jewishness, *mala sangre* (bad blood): Jews, baptized or not, were perverse and defiled. We witness here the birth of Spanish racism, which in due course grew into a veritable obsession concerning *limpieza de sangre* (purity of blood), in other words, freedom from the taint of Jewish blood transmitted by *marranos*. Even religious orders succumbed to the mania.[34] Judaism was no longer solely a theological problem but an ethnic one as well. Meanwhile attacks against the *marranos* multiplied, culminating in those of 1473-74, which may be compared to the hecatombs of 1391.

Friar de Spina was prominent among those religious who had for some time been calling for the introduction of the Inquisition into Spain to cope with the problem. This tribunal, founded in the thirteenth century by the Holy See to combat the Albigensian heresy, had already been introduced into Aragon, where it functioned at a moderate tempo. Jews were considered outside its province—except in the Maimunist feud[35]—but not so the *marranos*, who were not deemed Jews but heretical Christians. Numerous calls for the introduction of the Inquisition came from the Dominican and Franciscan orders, who had been assigned by the Holy See to supervise the orthodoxy of the Faith. Some of their members, as confessors and advisers to royalty, pressed their plea vigorously before the "secular arm." The prospect of such an introduction was opposed by the nobility and many members of the diocesan clergy, but acclaimed by the people, who, enraged by the *marranos'* ascendancy, hoped for their punishment. Why should these hypocrites, they reasoned, enjoy high station while professing Jews suffered for their faith?

In 1479, when Ferdinand and Isabella united the kingdoms of Castile and Aragon, the possibility of a unified Christian Spain became more immediate, and at this precise moment Thomas Torquemada, the Queen's Dominican confessor, importuned the sovereigns to establish the tribunal. Prominent *marranos* besought the Holy See to withhold its introduction, but succeeded in obtaining only a short delay. In 1480 after disputes about its control, permission for its introduction under secular control was granted by Sixtus IV (1471-84) with two Dominicans in charge. Wholesale arrests of *marranos* followed, and in the following year the first *auto da fé*[36] was held in which six men and women of Jewish descent were burned at the stake. It was the small beginning of a gigantic operation that would spread to all major Spanish cities, condemn thousands of *marranos* to the stake and many times more to imprisonment, public humiliation, and confiscation of property.[37]

Torquemada was appointed Inquisitor General in 1483. Under his administration the Inquisition attained an efficiency and ruthlessness that held not only *marranos* but all Spanish Jewry in a state of terror for years. Elaborate regulations were set forth for detecting Judaizers. A list of thirty-seven clues was published to help ferret them out. Failing to wear one's best clothes on Sunday or the omission of the *Gloria Patri* in prayers were typical of the detailed grounds for suspicion. The faithful were obliged, under severe penalties, to denounce suspects, and rabbis were enjoined to impose solemn excommunication on their faithful for failure to denounce. Thirty days of grace were given for self-denunciation, after which torture was employed to elicit confessions of guilt.[38] So brutal became the efficiency of the Torquemadan and later tribunals that the Holy See, which had lost all influence over them, intervened on several occasions. The first of these was the remonstrance of Sixtus IV in which he intimated that "avarice and lust for gain" motivated the operation of the tribunal more than zeal for salvation of souls."[39] Indeed, economic motive prompted so much a part of the proceedings that the skeletons of deceased suspects were exhumed for trial. In the event of condemnation, the inheritance of the deceased was confiscated, the assets accruing, as in the case of living *marranos*, to the crown.

The failure of the Inquisition to stamp out marranism quickly turned attention back to the Jews who from the start were the suspected cause of the *marranos'* obduracy. Actually the suspicion had some basis. The rigors of the dreaded tribunal, oddly, seemed to stiffen the spirit of these opportunists, whose devotion to Judaism had been as lax as was their present attachment to Catholicism, and to lead to a rapprochement between them and their former coreligionists. In the very shadow of the *Quamadero*, the place in which the *autos-da-fé* took place, they clung to as many Jewish rites and customs as they could, even circumcision of their children. One Jewish chronicler of the time told how one could ascend any tower in Spain on the Sabbath to see the many smokeless chimneys of homes of *marranos* who scrupulously observed the Jewish prohibition of lighting a fire on that day. Some of these crypto-Jews, once lukewarm in their Judaism, now greeted the flames of the stake with the *Shemá Israel* (Hear, O Israel) on their lips in a final act of faith—and defiance.

The orthodox Jews, for their part, were not unresponsive. Their original contempt for their apostatized brothers gave way, in the face of their tribulation, to a fraternal sympathy and a desire to reclaim them for the ancestral faith. The fanatical Torquemada did not fail to notice the enhanced bond between *marrano* and

Jew, and promptly sought to make the latter, hitherto immune to his jurisdiction, liable to the tribunal for encouraging Judaizing. When this attempt failed, he demanded a more radical solution— the expulsion of all Jews from the kingdom. To this end, he approached both civil and ecclesiastical authorities, but found Ferdinand and Isabella, and no less Innocent VIII, reluctant. A relentless pursuer, Torquemada was not to be put off. Two events came to his aid. In La Guardia in 1490, *marranos* were accused by another *marrano* of plotting the downfall of Christianity, of using a consecrated Host and of crucifying a boy in the process. A trial was held, the accused was burned, and a cult arose around the alleged victim, though to the present day doubt as to the boy's existence has persisted.[40] Public reaction to the case gave Torquemada the opportunity to further his plea for expulsion. And the decisive thrust to his project came the following year when Granada, the last stronghold of Moslem Spain, surrendered to Ferdinand. This completion of territorial reconquest brought with it an increased determination to unite Spain morally and religiously.

On January 2, 1492, while still in Granada, Ferdinand and Isabella issued the fatal decree. All Jews must leave the realm by July 30 under the penalty of death, since, in the words of the decree, "Jews seduce the new Christians," and expulsion is "the only efficacious means of putting an end to these evils."[41] Stunned by the edict, powerful Jews, led by Abraham Senior, chief Rabbi and tax collector, offered an enormous sum of money to the king, who was known for his avariciousness. The story is told that at the critical moment, as Ferdinand reconsidered his decision, Torquemada rushed onto the scene, holding a crucifix aloft, and cried: "Judas Iscariot sold Christ for thirty pieces of silver; will Your Highness sell him for 300,000 ducats? Here He is, take Him and sell Him"; upon which the king held fast to his decree.[42] Many, including Senior himself, were converted but the majority, brokenhearted, left within the appointed time. Jews in Spanish colonies, like Sardinia and Sicily, who had had no contact with *marranos* and were on the best of terms with their Christian neighbors, were still included in the decree despite the pleas of Christian authorities and people there.

The story of the hardships of the 300,000 refugees is told in all Jewish histories—a depressing tale of shipwreck, piracy, starvation, and enslavement. Fortunate were those who could go to Italy and Turkey—the only places they were well received. In Turkey the Sultan asked the refugees: "Do you call Ferdinand a wise king, who has impoverished his country to enrich mine?"[43] It is a question many modern Spanish economists and historians have answered in the negative.[44] Wherever these Sephardic exiles went, they carried their culture and even their language with them, evinced their cultural superiority, and assumed leadership of their communities.

Most refugees went to neighboring Portugal, hopeful of a speedy return to the land they had occupied for over 1,500 years. But theirs is another and, if possible, more painful story than the preceding. Our limitations permit only a summary. Refugees were allowed to enter Portugal for a price and for only a limited time by John II (1481-95). Many, unable to quit the country when the allotted time was over, were enslaved and deprived of their children, who were sent to St. Thomas' Island. King Emanuel, under the Spanish sovereigns' influence, after freeing the enslaved, ordered them out of the kingdom. Unwilling to forego their economic benefit, however, he determined upon the mad plan—disfavored by the clergy—to force all Jews into the Church. This was done with utter savagery. So that none might be concealed, all children were ordered baptized on one day. Whenever necessary, children were torn from their parents, baptized, and scattered throughout the land for Christian upbringing. Filled with revulsion, many Christian neighbors aided Jews to conceal their children. Adults were forced into the most deplorable living conditions as a device to compel their consent to be baptized. Some gave in, but most were dragged bodily to the baptismal font against a background of atrocities. Thus a new colony of *marranos* formed. The familiar pattern recurred: *marrano* prosperity, popular resentment, massacres[45] and introduction of the Inquisition. The Portuguese converts, even less willing Christians than the Spanish, became even more determined *marranos*. That is, perhaps, why the Portuguese Inquisition was, if possible, more brutal than its Spanish counterpart but less successful in attaining its objective. The tribunal pursued the converts until the nineteenth century, and surprisingly *marranos* were discovered in Portugal even in the twentieth.[46]

THE NATURE OF MEDIEVAL ANTISEMITISM

The link between the antisemitism of the later Middle Ages and that of earlier epochs seems clear. Most of the elements of the earlier anti-Judaism had persisted substantially unchanged. The medieval Jew was still opposed as a special kind of infidel or heretic who, at the very heart of Christendom, laid claim to religious truth and thus imperiled Christian belief and dashed hopes of a unified Christian social order. Except in the case of marranist Spain and Portugal, there was nothing ethnic or racial in this opposition. With baptism, the Jew was "forgiven" all. More than that, unlike others, upon conversion he was greeted with jubilation. Often he was accorded "baptismal splendors" in which popes and kings served as sponsors or attendants; festivals and processions marked his march to the font.[47] Conversely, the Jew retained his right to remain a Jew. Though hedged around by restrictions and disqualifications designed to remind him of his "unbelieving state," he enjoyed a unique right to worship according to his conscience. The Inquisition left him alone, except when he was charged with inducing *marranos* to return to Judaism or with matters of sorcery. This is a "tolerance of the Middle Ages"[48] often overlooked. The principle that Jews were a "witness-people" unquestionably contributed to this tolerance, but so did the Pauline principle of the Jews' special estate "because of their fathers," though perhaps to a lesser degree. The belief in the deicidal guilt of the Jews and their punishment was taken for granted. Exceptional personalities, however, especially popes, managed to transcend the general current and keep the Paulino-Gregorian tradition alive.

Medieval law maintained a *basic* justice for the Jew, and when his plight worsened this was due to other forces than the influence of the judiciary. Guido Kisch states this plainly:

> The high moral concept of law, justice and judicial office made it impossible that the rights of the Jews should be tampered with by a conscious twisting of the law . . . Thus the

treatment of the Jews in the latter half of the Middle Ages, the temporal and numerical restrictions, the designation of definite living quarters for the Jews and their exclusion from the ownership of the land, in short, their degradation to citizens of the second rank had no lawful basis but resulted from political, religious, economic and social reasons only.[49]

The most important emergence in the medieval progress of antisemitism was the Jewish role in moneylending. The question of its extent and its derivation is controverted. Parkes asks bluntly: "Was Milman's Jew a real person?"—a Jew sordidly and obsessively concentrated on the acquisition of money?[50] Sombart goes further and credits the Jews of this period with the foundations of modern capitalism.[51] Modern racists focus their attack on this period in the effort to convert the business ability of the Jews into an innate characteristic and the chief source of antisemitism. However, history indicates that a preponderance of Jews in commerce and especially in usury made a tardy appearance. Jews enjoyed a quasi-monopoly in moneylending only in the later Middle Ages and lost it soon after. Their sometimes imprudent zeal in this domain undeniably caused some of their medieval woes but, this said, the almost complete degree of involuntariness of their position must be stressed. Having first degraded them as social outcasts, medieval society then pressed upon them the role of financial "leeches" and forced them into such conditions as to render money as important to them as life itself. "Little by little," as Poliakov says, "every step and every act of daily life as a Jew were subjected to payment of a tax. He had to pay to come and go, to buy and sell, to enjoy his rights, to pray in common, to marry, to beget children, indeed for the very cadaver he carried to the cemetery."[52]

The close tie Jewish moneylending held with social and religious conditions in the Middle Ages was clearly seen in the twelfth century by Peter Abelard, in whose *Dialogue between a Philosopher, a Jew, and a Christian*, the Jew speaks these poignant words:

> To believe that the fortitude of the Jews in suffering would be unrewarded was to declare that God was cruel. No nation has ever suffered so much for God. Dispersed among all na-

tions, without king or secular ruler, the Jews are oppressed with heavy taxes as if they had to repurchase their very lives every day. To mistreat the Jews is considered a deed pleasing to God. Such imprisonment as is endured by the Jews can be conceived by the Christians only as a sign of God's utter wrath. The life of the Jews is in the hands of their worst enemies. Even in their sleep they are plagued by nightmares. Heaven is their only place of refuge. If they want to travel to the nearest town, they have to buy protection with the high sums of money from the Christian rulers who actually wish for their death so that they can confiscate their possessions. The Jews cannot own land or vineyards because there is nobody to vouch for their safekeeping. Thus, all that is left them as a means of livelihood is the business of moneylending, and this in turn brings the hatred of Christians upon them.[53]

Of grave significance was the utter deterioration of the Jewish image in the late Middle Ages. The dissociation of the imaginary from the real Jew effected earlier under theological influence was now complete. The terms "Jewish" and "diabolical" had become all but synonymous. The deliberate unbeliever and blasphemer was now also ritual murderer and poisoner of mankind, arch-conspirator, oppressor of the poor, sorcerer and magician; in short, the agent of Satan. Medieval art gave plentiful evidence of the figure: Invariably, the Jew was portrayed with horns, a tail, an evil visage; his company is that of devils, sows, scorpions, and his poses grotesque.[54] The image was further elaborated by men of letters, preachers, and apologists, and was seized upon as a motif in popular aggressions. Finally, medieval antisemitism was a mob phenomenon. Superstitious and bloodthirsty elements among the masses, suffering under the lash of socio-political and natural calamities, found in the Jew the scapegoat needed to rationalize the evils of their lot. Fresh from barbarism, much of the populace was incapable of understanding fully the nature of evil and even less capable of putting into practice the Christian ideal of universal love.

The traumatic experience of these years left its mark on the Jews; in a certain sense, a "Jewish mentality" was born.[55] To their persecutors Jews reacted with a cold fury, recoiling still further into themselves from an "adversary no longer considered human."[56] Truly malicious references to things Christian appeared in Jewish writings, and the cross became a "symbol of disaster."[57] An unbridgeable chasm between Christian and Jew was dug—a chasm the Jews as well as Christians sought to widen. To Christians, Jews, degraded, were looked upon as living proof of the malediction they were supposed to bear. Christians did not see that the despised Jew was, in large part, of Christian making. R. Travers Herford's comments are applicable to this era: "If the Jew in literary description by the Christian and in common imagination is often a cringing and despicable figure, it should be remembered how he became so, so far as he did actually become so. The traits of character are those which the Christian ancestors of the one bred in the Jewish ancestors of the other."[58]

Medieval antisemitism left its mark on both Jew and Christian that the twentieth century has not fully erased.

7
THE AGE OF THE GHETTO

The epoch-making political, cultural, and religious changes of the sixteenth to the eighteenth centuries which led Europe from the medieval into the modern world had little immediate effect on the life of the Jews. The times changed, but their situation did not. The great forces of the Renaissance, the Reformation, the geographical and cultural discoveries, which swept feudalism away, shook the Church, and opened new intellectual paths, seemed to bypass the sons and daughters of the Synagogue, hermetically sealed off from their hostile environment. For the Gentile, the Middle Ages were ended; for the Jew, fixed in the historical process, the old instabilities and vexations endured to the very threshhold of the nineteenth century. A period of prodigious developments for one was for the other a time of wandering, stagnation, and isolation. For Jews, in short, it was the age of the ghetto.

LIFE IN THE GHETTO

The ghetto[1] of course was not entirely new. Jewish quarters had existed in ancient times as creations of Jewish separatism; and even segregation of a legal kind could be found as early as the eleventh century. The latter was imposed—and accepted—as a protection rather than an incarceration. It was sometimes looked on as a privilege, as in the case of the one conceded by Bishop Rudiger of Speyer in 1804.[2] Some Italian Jewish communities actually celebrated the establishment of their ghetto by an annual festival, and in the eighteenth and nineteenth centuries, as the ghetto died, many rabbis, especially in the East, rued its disappearance for understandable reasons. The Church, for her part, had, almost from the outset, encouraged voluntary separation of Christians and Jews and also favored a forced segregation of Jews and Muslims from Christians. The Council of Basel prescribed that Jews live apart from Christians, so as to "avoid excessive converse."[3] But it was not until the sixteenth century that the old "Jewish quarter" was made into a ghetto under lock and key. At this point in history, as has been suggested, it may have served as a compromise between expulsion and free concourse, the Jew being at once both wanted and unwanted.[4]

Patterns varied, but usually the ghetto was located in a poorer region of the city and enclosed by high walls, its gates guarded by Christian gatekeepers, paid by the confined. Some of the most famous ghettos were those in Prague, Venice, Frankfurt-on-Main, and Rome. Most were unbelievably overcrowded, often comprising a single street of abnormally tall houses, crammed with people who lived ever in dread of plagues and fires that frequently struck. The ghetto of Rome, for example, held as many as 10,000 inhabitants within less than a square kilometer and that of Frankfurt, 4,000 in 190 houses on one street. The Roman ghetto was on the banks of the Tiber, which overflowed annually; it was occupied at the price of a yearly permission.

The effects of ghetto living on the Jew were not all unfortunate. In its earlier and, what has been called, formative period, it fostered among Jews an ethnic solidarity, an attachment to the Synagogue, and a devotion to study—by no means new to the Jew—which in time became the very basis for survival. But, by and large, the effects of the ghetto were deleterious. Within its narrow confines, Jewish introversion reached a high point. Cut off from participating in the larger world about, life was concentrated on the past. A ghettoized mentality was the inevitable result. Most inmates looked upon gentile outsiders with suspicion and hatred; a few, with envy. Even physical injuries were suffered. Perhaps no one has described some of the evil results better than Cecil Roth:

> The results were what might have been imagined. The circle of human interests was intolerably confined. Life became indescribably petty. There was a superlative degree of inbreeding, both physical, social, and intellectual . . . By the time that the ghetto had been in existence for a couple of centuries, it was possible to see the result. Physically, the type of Jew had degenerated. He had lost inches off his stature; he had acquired a perpetual stoop; he had become timorous and in many cases neurotic. Degrading occupations, originally imposed by law—such as moneylending and dealing in old clothes—became a second nature, hard to throw off. His sense of solidarity with his fellow-Jews had become fantastically exaggerated, and was accompanied in most cases by a perpetual sense of grievance against the gentile who was responsible for his lot.[5]

THE MARGINAL EXISTENCE

The Jewish role in the economy of this age was considerably altered. A new capitalism had come into being which further dispensed with the earlier dependence on Jewish moneylending and trade. More than ever Jewish merchants and financiers were resented as competitors rather than monopolists. Most trades and professions remained closed to them, which resulted in their monopolizing such occupations as pawn-brokerage, the second-hand clothing trade, and peddling, which were accessible. A fortunate few managed to escape the common lot; some Jewish physicians, court advisers, and men of wealth could yet be found. But the majority were poor and unable to pay the heavy communal taxes imposed on the Jewish community without the aid of their more privileged brethren. The old scoldings against Jewish usury—now of a petty sort—were still heard, while new charges of sharp practices, price cutting, and traffic in stolen goods were added.

The insecure conditions growing out of enforced segregation were not without influence on Jewish intellectual and spiritual life. The ghettoes, for one thing, became centers of talmudic and midrashic study, which served as a spiritual haven from the rigors of an unkind environment.[6] Abraham Heschel does not hesitate to call these years the "golden period of Jewish history, in the history of the Jewish soul"[7]; yet he does not fail to point out the "one-sidedness of learning, neglect of manners, provincialism," which affected eastern Jews.[8] Other scholars, Jacob Katz for one, have noted the baleful effects of the ghetto on Jewish intellectual life. Speaking of the sixteenth century, he writes: "Judaism now became more and more a closed system of thought. As is well known, Ashkenazi Jewry produced at this time no comprehensive thinker with the sole exception of Rabbi Judah Loeb (Maharal). Instead the period was prolific with preachers who moralized and admonished."[9] As secular learning was generally eschewed, Jewish scholarship lost contact with the great currents of learning outside the ghetto. There were exceptions to the rule, of course, like Spinoza and Moses Mendelssohn, but these men did not sit well with most Jewish communities; in fact, the former was formally excommunicated. While the ghetto intensified traditional studies and deepened Jewish spiritual life, this self-imposed intellectual segregation caused Jewish scholarship to lose much of its breadth. In Roth's words:

> Keen intelligences were wasted by dealing with trivial themes. That which was meant for mankind was confined to a simple bleak street. The intellectual fecundity which can result only from the constant fertilization and cross-fertilization of human intercourse became impossible.[10]

In this age a certain softening of the lot of the Jews was, despite all, under way. Massacres were now comparatively rare and, moreover, Jews suffered in common with other social classes. The new humanism abroad increased the spirit of tolerance—and of skepticism—which favored their tranquility. On the other hand, Jews were more submissive. The image of the Jew continued to deteriorate and take on new attributes. The Jew as a treacherous skinflint, an avaricious Judas, became an archetype that needed little root in reality for its sustenance. This was the era of the Shylock figure who demands his "pound of flesh" nearest the heart of the Christian debtor—a figure taken by the Bard and other writers from an older Italian tale in which the cruel creditor was a Christian.[11]

To sum up: The status of the Jews in this era was greatly reduced. No longer hated and feared as a grave peril to Christian society, they were made into objects of aversion and derision. This age which stripped them of all self-respect was, Levinger believes, the "lowest point of their long and tragic history."[12]

AGE OF WANDERING

The expulsions from Spain and Portugal had initiated a period of wandering for the Jewish people that vastly changed the face of the dispersion. There was a general shift to the East, toward the Balkans, Poland, Turkey, and Palestine where the main thread of their history continued. Antisemitism did not follow them there, however. In Palestine and Turkey they lived happily, indulging liberally in mystical and messianic enterprises. Poland became a blessed refuge.

Oddly, it was in France and England, where one might assume that the virus had departed with the expelled, that antisemitism seemed to flourish. In these Jewless lands Poliakov finds antisemitism in its "pure state": Where the Jew did not exist, he was invented. In a fine analysis of the situation in France[13] this historian finds a plethora of anti-Jewish material in catechisms, dictionaries, sermons, writings. There were even instances of popular agitation in which, for example, second-hand clothing dealers, falsely suspected of being Jews, were harassed and insulted. Contemporary literature, too, was rich and eloquent in *anti-Judaica*. The great Pascal (1623-62) saw the misery of the "carnal" Jews as proof of Christianity.[14] So did the foremost preachers of the time. The voice of Bossuet (1627-1704) could be heard above the rest. In his sermons and his influential *Discours sur l'Histoire Universelle*, Jews are presented as an accursed and hardened race, hated of God, and in misery for their deicide. "Monstrous people," he cried from the pulpit, "that has neither hearth nor home, without country, and scattered in all countries; once the happiest of the world, now the butt of every fancy, the object of hatred of the whole world . . . . In their misery wrought by divine malediction, they are the laughing stock of all sensible people."[15]

By the end of the Middle Ages, antisemitism was endemic in France.

England presented a similar development. When Manasseh ben Israel came from the *marrano* settlement in Amsterdam in 1655 to negotiate with Cromwell for the readmission of Jews to England—whence they had been absent since 1290—his project encountered stiff opposition. Jews held a certain affinity with English Puritans who laid a heavy accent on the Old Testament in their worship; so in his appeal to Cromwell, Manasseh stressed millennial considerations, pleading that if the final ingathering was to occur, the Jewish dispersion must be complete and should include England. Cromwell, with an eye to the benefits Jews might afford the economy of the country, presented a proposal of re-entry to the Parliament. It was hotly debated and aroused great public stir. Stories went about that Jews were buying up cathedrals—that St. Paul's was to be sold for 800,000 pounds—and inevitably the traditional accusations were revived. Pamphleteers went into action, arousing the populace, on one occasion almost to the point of violence. Cromwell saw the futility of his project and dropped it. Instead he allowed the *marrano* group to remain in London, establish a synagogue, and increase. Thus was laid the foundation of the future English Jewish community. The Jews were readmitted to England, it has been said, by the back door.

THE CULTURAL AND RELIGIOUS REVOLUTIONS

The chronicles of the Jews in Germany at this time have more to do with the great religious and cultural movements than with flesh and blood dealings between Christians and Jews, which though less violent, were not different in kind from those of previous years. The center of the stage was shared by the humanist and the Protestant revolutions.

The new humanist learning, which first blossomed in Italy, turned attention to Hebrew as a language and literature, and witnessed the appearance of several Christian Hebraists. The invention of the printing press added impetus to this development:

Jewish printing houses circulated the Hebrew Bible, the Talmud, a variety of Hebrew studies, and Jewish and Christian scholars met on the academic level. Germany was not immune to the new spirit but did not take to it enthusiastically. A Jewish convert, Joseph Pfefferkorn,[16] alarmed by the circulation given the Talmud—to which he attributed the stubborn Jewish refusal to accept the Church—obtained a mandate in 1509 from Emperor Maximilian I to seize the work. He was backed by the Dominicans of Cologne, but encountered opposition from the Archbishop of Mainz in whose diocese he had initiated operations. The Archbishop demanded of Maximilian that the Hebrew books be examined by a board of experts rather than by Pfefferkorn.

A board was formed and on it sat Johann Reuchlin, one of the most highly regarded humanists of the day. This man had studied Hebrew under Jewish scholars and gained a great love and appreciation for Hebrew literature. Oddly, like other humanists of his day, he was not free of the traditional prejudices; he considered Jews barbaric and blasphemous. Another notable example of humanist prejudice is that of Erasmus of Rotterdam, who candidly asserted: "If it is Christian to hate Jews, then we are all good Christians."[17]

However Reuchlin undertook a vigorous defense of the Talmud against Pfefferkorn and his supporters, and became embroiled in a fierce controversy that lasted several years. Before it was over, the Talmud became the center of a fray that included a war of treatises between Reuchlinists and anti-Reuchlinists and a contest that was brought time and time again before the court of the vacillating Emperor and the throne of the Pope himself. Reuchlin was accused of Judaizing, of receiving money from Jews, and was cited before the Inquisition—actions he bitterly resented. In one of his tracts, "Augenspiegel" (Spectacles) he defended himself in these words: "The baptized Jew writes that Divine Law forbids our holding communion with Jews; this is not true. Every Christian must go to law with them, buy from them . . . . It is allowed to converse with and learn from them, as St. Jerome and Nicholas de Lyra did. And lastly, a Christian should love a Jew as his neighbor; all this is founded on the law."[18] When things began to go badly for him, Reuchlin appealed to Pope Leo X and was acquitted.[19] But the controversy raged on, as humanist

and "obscurantist"[20]—the Jews and the Talmud now forgotten—
fought each other as traitors to Christianity. At the end, Reuchlin
was vindicated and the Talmud was spared, Pope Leo actually
encouraging its printing. This by no means ended the feud, but
soon after a new voice was heard in the defense of the Jews which
swept the affair aside. It called for nothing less than the abolition
of Catholicism.

The voice was that of Martin Luther (1483-1546). Like Mohammed, he too courted the Jews as he founded his new faith,
confident that with Christianity stripped of "popery and mon-
kery" they would be won to the Gospel in its pure and primitive
form. In a pamphlet of 1523, entitled "Jesus Christ Was Born a
Jew," he defended Jews and urged humaneness toward them,
writing,

> They (the papists) have dealt with the Jews, as if they were
> dogs rather than human beings . . . If the Apostles, who were
> also Jews, had dealt with us gentiles as we gentiles deal with
> the Jews there would never have been a Christian among the
> gentiles . . . we in our turn ought to treat the Jews in a broth-
> erly manner in order that we might convert some of them . . .
> we are but gentiles, while the Jews are of the lineage of Christ.
> We are aliens and in-laws; they are blood relatives, cousins
> and brothers of our Lord.[21]

When Jews did not meet his expectations—or worse, when
some of his followers showed tendencies to Judaize—Luther's attitude toward Jews took a dark turn. In 1542 he published a tract
"Concerning the Jews and Their Lies"[22] and shortly thereafter
another entitled "Schem Hamphoras,"[23] in which he raged at
them in a language that at least equalled in violence anything uttered against them before or after. With biting sarcasm and occasional scatological insult, he renewed all the old charges of the
past: Jews are poisoners, ritual murderers, usurers; they are parasites on Christian society; they are worse than devils; it is harder
to convert them than Satan himself; they are doomed to hell.
They are, in truth, the anti-Christ. Their synagogues should be
destroyed and their books seized; they should be forced to work
with their hands; better still they should be expelled by the
princes from their territories. Such were his outpourings, though

in fairness, it must be noted that his diatribes were interspersed with a random prayer and a merciful word for Jews. During his last years Luther made repeated efforts to have the German princes oppress or expel Jews. In his last sermon, delivered a few days before his death, he called urgently for their expulsion from all Germany.[24] The devil the reformer would have exorcised from the Church seemed to have taken full possession of him.

Though Luther's emphasis on the Old Testament and his principle of private interpretation tended eventually to alleviate the lot of the Jews, his immediate impact on the Jewish community in Germany and its surrounding territories was small and negative. Protestant Germany, listening rather to his denunciations, maintained the vexations of the past. Sanguinary violences were fewer, but not totally absent, as the savage attack in 1614 by Vincent Fettmilch and his cohorts on the ghetto of Frankfurt-on-Main clearly shows. This pastry cook turned reformer, at odds with Lutheran officials, vented his animosity on the Jews. A similar attack was made by this gang on the Worms ghetto shortly after, but this time Fettmilch and his leaders were punished, and the Jews were returned to both ghettoes. There were further expulsions. In 1670 Jews were ordered to quit Vienna, and many made their way to the new settlement of Berlin. The last expulsion was from Bohemia in 1747, when Maria Theresa ordered them out. Her order was not carried out, however, thanks chiefly to the intercession of *Hofjuden* (court Jews) before several European sovereigns, who interceded with Maria Theresa.

These court Jews were financiers who administered the economic affairs of the court. They appeared after the Thirty Years War when numerous petty princes sought fiscal aid as they competed for power and wealth. Every prince had his court Jew, as did even many cardinals and bishops. These Jews acquired great prestige and wealth, and some became quite famous, such as Wolf Wertheimer, a Munich banker, who organized the petition to Maria Theresa. But these were the exceptions. The rank and file languished in the ghetto where lives were rigidly regulated. To the traditional restrictions were added new civil vexations of a most picayune nature: Jews could not walk in twos, appear in public when a prince was in town, buy ahead of a Christian at the market, or frequent certain streets. To travel, they had to have a safe-conduct pass and had to pay a body tax in transit. Some of their clothing was prescribed and the number of guests at their weddings were limited.

More drastic was the regulation of their marriage designed to prevent a too rapid multiplication of Jews. In some cases Jewish marriages were limited to the number of deaths; in others, only the eldest son was allowed to marry; or again only one or two sons were allowed to inherit. Socially, things went from bad to worse: Jews were often made the butt of coarse jokes, and on any street the most educated Jew could be accosted with a "Jew, where are your manners!" and made to doff his hat in deference to his challenger.

Anti-Jewish literature received new life from Luther's attacks. A flow of pamphlets and books took up the cudgels anew, refurbishing old charges and adding new ones: Jews consume Christian blood to be rid of their bad odor; they indulge in secret crimes and vices of a sexual nature. A new direction can be sensed here. From the more mythological and moralistic antisemitism of medieval writers, a step has been taken toward the ethnic and racial: Jews are not only bad actors but constitutionally bad.

The Talmud, without fail, attracted attention. Assiduous efforts were made to turn up blasphemies and evidence of ritual murder or systematic poisoning. The greatest of the sleuths was Johann Eisenmenger (d. 1704), a first-rate Hebraist and Orientalist, who, filled with anti-Jewish prejudice, accepted all the older slanders against the Jews and combed through the Talmud for further suspicious references. In 1700 his book *Entdecktes Judentum* (Judaism Unmasked),[25] a veritable, antisemitic encyclopedia, was published in Frankfurt-on-Main, but through the good offices and munificence of the court Jew Samuel Oppenheimer it was suppressed. At Eisenmenger's death, permission for publication was given by Emperor Frederick of Prussia and the work was issued in Knigsberg in 1711. It has served as a treasure trove for antisemites ever since.

TWILIGHT IN ROME

The Counter-Reformation in the Church was of no help to the Jews. Jewish influence as well as pagan elements in the humanist movement were blamed for the defection of the Reformers. Had not Luther supported Reuchlin in his defense of the Talmud? The liberal policies of the Renaissance popes were abruptly terminated by Pope Paul IV (1555-59), who set himself the task of closing ranks in the Church.[26] There are few popes who compare with him for severity toward the Jews. As Cardinal Caraffa, he had already manifested his zeal in combatting the Talmud and the influence of the *marranos*.[27] As Pope, he reversed the indulgent policies of his predecessors Clement VIII and Paul III toward the converted Jews and allowed sixty of them to be burned by the Inquisition. Many draconian measures were introduced during his pontificate. The Roman ghetto was established; a yellow badge was imposed; Jews were not permitted to own land, practice usury, or enter any trades or professions except the most menial; one synagogue was allowed, all others were destroyed; converse with Christians was banned; conversionist sermons were ordered; and the campaign against the Talmud was sustained. Jews, lastly, were forbidden to enter Christian religious orders, into which some *marranos* had apparently betaken themselves.[28]

After Paul IV, papal policy varied according to the temperament of the popes, existing conditions, and activities of the Jews. Pius IV (1559-65) relaxed Paul's severities, enlarged the ghetto and removed most restrictions. Pius V (1565-72) expelled all Jews from papal territories except Rome and Ancona. Sixtus V (1585-90) annulled almost all of Paul's policies and granted Jews a status of tolerance, conceded them many privileges, and taxed them equally with Christians. From this time, the conditions of Italian Jews improved slightly, but no longer could be distinguished from the depressing state of Jewry in other European countries.[29]

RISE AND FALL IN POLAND

The sole ray of light in this age of wandering and forced enclosure came from Poland, where Polish Jews enjoyed a new golden age and earned for themselves the spiritual hegemony of all Judaism. But it was a ray quickly and brutally to be extinguished.

From the beginning of the Middle Ages, Poland (and Lithuania) had been a happy haven for the steady flow of German refugees from the Crusades, the Black Death, the Rindfleisch massacres, and other calamities. The refugees were well received and allowed to constitute, by themselves, a middle class of traders and financiers between the nobles and peasants. Considered a boon to the economic progress of the country, they were granted access to all occupations and were even appointed official agents and tax collectors of the crown. In 1264 King Boleslav V gave the refugees a charter of rights, which was renewed in the following century by Casimir the Great (1333-1370), who allowed them considerable self-government. Before long, they were accepted as an integral part of Poland by kings and nobles but not by the clergy or the people.

The Church was alarmed by the ascendancy of the Jews and the preferential treatment they received from the crown, and worked to impose the canonical restrictions. In 1267 the Council of Breslau published a canon that expressed the fear of Jewish influence on the recently converted Christians of the country.[30] The fourteenth century was marked by a hostile attitude from the crown and the appearance of numerous host-desecration and ritual-murder charges, which took their usual toll. In the reign of the lenient Casimir IV in the fifteenth century, Capistrano, we saw, came to the aid of the Archbishop of Cracow to remedy the situation.[31] At the end of the century, the ghetto was introduced into the capital by Jan Albrecht. Persecutions also commenced in Lithuania about this time.

From this point, the story does not follow the usual pattern. In lieu of the customary further decline and expulsion, we find Polish Jews in the sixteenth century rising to rare heights. Apparently they were too well integrated into the socio-economic complex of the nation to be dispensed with. They grew in number at a rapid rate—indeed during the period 1500 to 1648 from 15,000 to 50,000. King Sigismund II (1548-1572) and his successors granted them almost complete autonomy. A "Council of the Four Lands," a species of Jewish parliament, was formed to represent all *Kahals* (communities) and to legislate for them according to Jewish Law. Responsible only to the king, this Council provided a measure of self-government, unparalleled since the Sanhedrin of ancient times. Meanwhile, Jewish education and talmudic studies attained so high a degree of excellence and univer-

sality as to influence profoundly the quality of European Judaism
for many years. Yet all was not enviable. Charges of ritual murder
and host desecration continued in this land where they seemed to
have found a natural habitat, and some popular uprisings resulted. The Jewish image was further tarnished by suspicions of
Jewish complicity with Turkey and with certain Protestant heretical sects that had taken refuge in Poland, such as the Unitarians and Socinians, who were dubbed "half-Jews." Judaizing
tendencies in some areas and a few conversions to Judaism increased the concern of the Church.

It was not from within Poland, however, that finally came
the "deluge" that submerged Polish Jewry and introduced into
Jewish history perhaps its bloodiest decade (1648-58) since Biblical times. Again the Jews were caught in a crossfire. In the
Ukraine the Eastern Orthodox Cossacks hated not only the Polish
Catholics who oppressed them but also their middlemen of alien
faith, the Jews. In April 1648, under Bogdan Chmielnicki, their
hetman, they allied themselves with the Tartars and the Zaporozhti and ravaged Poland in a most barbarous fashion, reserving
their worst cruelties for the Jews. Margolis and Marx describe the
happenings:

> Estates were devastated, manor-houses reduced to ashes, and
> human beings barbarously done to death. The victims were
> flayed and burned alive, mutilated and left to the agony of a
> lingering death. Infants were slit like fish or slaughtered at the
> breasts of their mothers or cast alive into wells. Women were
> ripped open and then sewed up again with live cats thrust into
> their bowels; many, married or unmarried, were violated be-
> fore the eyes of their menfolk, and those that were comely
> were carried away. Thousands of Jews perished in the towns
> east of the Dnieper.[32]

The atrocities in Poland continued for more than a year. On some
occasions, Jews were given the option of baptism, but when King
Jan Casimir (1648-1669) was crowned he permitted the baptized
to return to their faith. Fresh massacres and expulsions took place
during the Swedish invasion of 1655-58. During that invasion,
Polish Jews were attacked in turn by Russians, Cossacks, and

Swedes and, when these departed, by the Poles, on the ground that they had aided the invaders.

The toll of the decade was staggering. Estimates of Jewish deaths range from 100,000 to 500,000;[33] and 700 Jewish communities were destroyed. Refugees, starved and impoverished, swarmed over Europe as the dispersion turned again toward the West. European Jewry rose to the occasion. Some communities took in the refugees; others offered prayers and raised money to aid them and to ransom those sold as slaves in Constantinople, suspending for this purpose the annual tax sent to Jerusalem. In return, the refugees "polonized" European Jewry by assuming spiritual leadership of many of the host communities.

The Jewish community in Poland never recovered from the blow it had received. For the decimated remnant things got steadily worse. Though the crown was again favorable, the Diet was hostile, and autonomy of the "Council of Four Lands" was abolished. Jews were heavily taxed and their *Kahals* were chronically in debt. Riots, manned by students from Jesuit schools, plagued the *Kahals* and became so prevalent that the Jews instituted a custom of paying an annual sum to the headmasters to suppress the "schoolboy raids." In this period a new surge of messianism took hold as Sabbatians and Frankists stirred vain hopes in a miserable populace; and Hasidic piety emerged as if in answer to the need for immediate spiritual succor.[34] The Hasidic movement created in Judaism the greatest crisis since the Karaite schism in the eighth century.

Ritual-murder and host-desecration charges increased alarmingly in the eighteenth century to become almost an annual affair, with the usual executions in their wake. So grave was this situation that Jews appealed to Benedict XIV in 1758, who, we have noted, assigned Cardinal Ganganelli (the future Clement XIV) to study the charges.[35] In his report the cardinal called for protection of Polish Jews. The papal nuncio of Warsaw conveyed his directive to the Church in Poland.

SEEDS OF HOPE AND DESTRUCTION

With the exception of the Nazi period in XXth century Germany, the sixteenth to the eighteenth centuries constituted the nadir of post-biblical Jewish history. Christian antisemitism had come to full fruition, and its bitter fruits wrought devastating effects on Jewish life and personality. New factors could be discerned through the devastation. A new humanism was germinating that portended an alleviation of Jewish woes and possible liberation from oppression. A less discernible, and ominous, emergence took the shape of insinuations of bodily and mental inferiorities in the Jew that assumed a place in the ever-waxing antisemitic stereotype. Christian theological antisemitism was no longer alone in the enterprise of shaping Jewish destiny.

8

THE STRUGGLE
FOR EMANCIPATION

In the closing years of the eighteenth century, Jews enjoyed economically and socially improved conditions in most countries. The capitalist revolution, then in the course of development, had swept aside the static structures of the feudal economy with its guilds, its ban on usury, and its doctrine of an unalterable *just price*. These changes placed the role which many Jews played in the economic life in a better light. Their involvement in money-lending, international commercial connections, and willingness to speculate were now better appreciated, at least by those states-men who were anxious to improve the economies of their countries and by the new large-scale capitalists less sensitive to ethnic or traditional considerations in economic matters. Moreover, many Jews had left both peddling and usury to become shopkeepers and craftsmen. The general economic conditions were also improved, so that Jewish wealth, wherever it existed, no longer stood out amid the higher and more common prosperity. These developments could only lead to a lessening of the prevalent restrictions on Jewish trading and travel. Thus the ghetto walls, so carefully designed to cut off the Jew from all Christian contact, began to crumble well before the political edicts of the late eighteenth and nineteenth centuries abolished them altogether. The old complaint that Jews constitute a "state within a state" also lost force in an age when the concept of a unified "Christian state," where only Christians could enjoy full citizenship, was under sharp attack. The idea of citizenship as a title acquired by all inhabitants of a certain territory regardless of class or religion was swiftly gaining momentum.

There were, of course, other less palpable causes for the change in climate. The Christian conscience, so long dormant, was becoming—ever so slowly—aware of the contradiction separating its attitudes toward Jews and Judaism and the mandate of universal love of the Gospel. But the spirit of skepticism engendered by the Enlightenment, which encourages indifference to religious beliefs, was also coloring the atmosphere. From all these factors in ferment Judaism profited—but not without a prolonged struggle with its own soul as well as with the world outside. Mutual hatred between Christian and Jew, still strong, rendered the entrance of Jews into Christian society doubly difficult.

THE INNER CONFLICT

It is customary to speak of this stage in Jewish history as the age of emancipation and to credit the emancipating to the great revolutions in America, France, and elsewhere. And yet it is possible, from another perspective, to see it as the age of assimilation, the fruit of a profound cultural and religious revolution within the confines of Jewry itself. Even before the political emancipation, a moral emancipation was under way in the heart of Judaism; before the door of gentile society was opened to the Jew, he stood before it and knocked. Cracks in the wall of Jewish separatism were evident long before the eighteenth century, but it was not until that century that the decisive breach was made.

The vanguard of the assimilationist movement was in Berlin, the Prussian capital, where a number of cultured and "protected" Jews longed to emerge from the ghetto, walk erect as political and cultural equals among their Christian neighbors, and participate in the Germanic-Christian culture about them. These revolutionaries fought against the grip in which the rabbinate held Jewish intellectual life by its all but exclusive concentration on talmudic studies. They were, accordingly, bitterly opposed by the traditionalists who looked upon mingling with the outside world as a peril to faith, and upon participation in Christian civilization as an infidelity. Their fears were not groundless. During the French terror, some Jews joined the revolutionaries and abjured all faith except that in reason, and some others in the Berlin salons entered the Church a few years later when becoming a Christian was the fashion. "During the first eighteen years of the nineteenth century," writes Valentin, with some exaggeration, "more German Jews were baptized than in the previous eighteen hundred years put together."[1]

No one better symbolized the effort to work out a compromise between fidelity to the Mosaic faith and loyalty to the common culture than the brilliant Jewish thinker and man of letters Moses Mendelssohn (1728-86). This amazing man was a revolution all by himself. Emerging from the poverty of the Dessau ghetto he rose by sheer talent to the heights of German cultural life. His literary intimacy with Gotthold Lessing (1729-81)—who modeled his play *Nathan the Wise* upon Mendelssohn—his besting of Immanuel Kant in a philosophical competition, and the adulation he received from the fastidious Berlin society were enough to force both German Christians and Jews to review their attitudes toward one another. Mendelssohn's translation of the Pentateuch and the Psalms into a fine German prose was an event of importance; it built a bridge between the Hebrew and German cultures. It was not only the first forceful challenge to an incubated and Yiddish-speaking Jewry to enter the world of German literature but also an invitation to the German literati to recognize the Bible as literature as well as a source of faith. The translation caused general consternation among the Orthodox and was banned. A group of young Jews welcomed the innovations heartily, however, and formed a society devoted to promoting the nexus between the two cultures through a promotion of Hebrew literature and a reformation of Jewish education. It was Mendelssohn, moreover, who prevailed upon the Christian Wilhelm Dohm, counselor of state, to plead for Jewish emancipation. This Dohm did in his *Concerning the Civic Amelioration of the Jews* (1781), wherein he indicted the Christian world for the degradation and social stagnation of the Jews.[2]

POLITICAL EMANCIPATION

A year later came Austria's Emperor Joseph II's Patent of Tolerance abolishing the Jewish badge, the body tax, and other disabilities; granting Jews access to schools and universities; and ruling that Hebrew schools include the German language and liberal subjects. Jewish Orthodoxy fought the educational provisions fiercely while the Mendelssohnians enthusiastically urged their acceptance. Other efforts were made at this time to further Jewish emancipation in Alsace, Tuscany, and England, where, in 1734, a proposal of emancipation had been killed by the very clamor it created.

Juridically speaking, emancipation first came to the Jews in the American colonies. Religious freedom was postulated by Roger Williams at the founding of Rhode Island in 1688, and in 1789 universal religious and civil freedom was guaranteed in the federal Constitution and its Bill of Rights. But these enactments were not immediately or effectively applied in all the colonies. They had to be won gradually, and were not fully established in all states until after the mid-nineteenth century.

The most dramatic and self-conscious emancipation project—and the first in Europe—was that of the French revolutionaries.[3] The resounding proclamation of religious freedom of the Declaration of the Rights of Man in 1789 did not exclude the Jews, but it did not include them specifically either. Jews, wary of pious generalities about liberty, did not leave the matter there. For two years they had worked toward the legal removal of disabilities and for the concession of equal civic rights, and did not stop until fully rewarded in 1791. They pleaded before Louis XVI's royal commission, presided over by Malesherbes, and importuned the assemblies of the Revolution on several occasions. They had a number of gentile supporters, notably, Mirabeau, Abbé Gregoire, Pastor Rabaud, St. Étienne, Robespierre, and Abbé Mulot, president of the assembly of 1791; but they were opposed by the legation from Alsace and Lorraine—where anti-Jewish disorders still occurred—and by Abbé Maury and the Bishop of Nancy.[4] The Jewish cause was not aided by the divisions between the Sephardim and Ashkenazim or the separate, sporadic, and sometimes contradictory efforts of the legations from Alsace, Bordeaux, and Paris. Still, after long delays, in September 1791, just before the close of the Assembly, jubilant Jews were granted complete civic freedoms in all of France. Subsequently, many Jews worked assiduously for the Revolution, while others suffered in the indiscriminate blood-letting of the Terror. When the new Republic took an imperialist turn, Jewish emancipation followed the path of French armies into Holland, Belgium and Italy. In Italy the gates of the ghetto of Venice were burned, and in Rome where Jews had been particularly unhappy since 1775, the gates were destroyed amid jubilation, as Pius VI was taken a prisoner of war.

Napoleon Bonaparte meddled mischievously in Jewish affairs, yet his conquests gave the cause of emancipation its greatest advance. He had but one interest in the Jews: to make them into Frenchmen. Complaints had come to him, mostly from Alsace, about their practice of usury and avoidance of conscription. Incensed, he suspended all debts to Jews in the eastern provinces for a year. But then, in typical Napoleonic style, he determined to settle the Jewish problem once and for all and called an Assembly of Jewish Notables, which was followed by a convocation of the Sanhedrin, the first one in more than 1,500 years. Napoleon's objective was "to revive the civic morality of the Jews lost during the long centuries of degrading existence."

To the Assembly of Notables gathered at Paris in 1806 twelve questions were put concerning Jewish patriotism, marriage practices, occupations and tolerance of other faiths. The notables answered with enthusiasm in the manner desired by the Emperor, assuring him that they would defend France even unto death. They closed their sessions with a vote of thanks to the Holy See for its protection of Jews over the centuries. In the following year, the Sanhedrin confirmed these assurances, and a year later Napoleon, acting on his findings, issued his "infamous decrees," which rigidly regulated Jewish economic life and conscription into the army. The regulations remained on the books for ten years, and were enforced by Jewish consistories formed to supervise Judaism throughout French territories. Many Jews were ruined by the decrees, and all were deeply offended.

If the Jews of France now looked upon Napoleon as an enemy, those in Germany and Prussia hailed him as a liberator. Wherever French domination and influence went in these countries, Jewish emancipation followed—to the newly formed Westphalia, Frankfurt, Baden, and Hanseatic cities. In Prussia, progress toward emancipation was slower; begun after the Revolution, it was not complete until 1812. Prussia formed the battleground for the ideological struggle between the Jewish assimilationists of the Mendelssohnian stamp and a phalanx of philosophic and literary antisemites of whom Friedrich Schleiermacher (1768-1834), Johann Fichte (1762-1814), and, a little later, Goethe (1749-1832) were chief luminaries.

Fichte, in effect, is considered by many as the originator of the racist antisemitism that was later to engulf Germany. From this point Germany became the undisputed cultural center of antisemitism and the source of an endless stream of antisemitic books and pamphlets. In 1819 one pamphleteer went so far as to propose massacres, castrations, and consignment of Jewesses to prostitution. These extravagances moved Graetz—no friend of Catholicism—to state: "Protestant theology and German philosophy proposed regulations against Jews unrivaled by the canonical restrictions of Innocent III and Paul IV."[5]

In this same period Catholic traditionalists in France, represented by Chateaubriand and de Bonald, were fighting emancipation in a more sophisticated manner.

Emancipation did not reach Austria—which had completely forgotten Joseph II's reforms—or other eastern European countries.

The downfall of Napoleon brought antisemitic reaction in its wake and undid whatever emancipation had achieved in Germany, Prussia, and the Papal States. Jews learned to their sorrow that their liberation was not achieved by mere governmental fiat or by theories of enlightenment. In 1815 at the Congress of Vienna, dedicated to re-establishing the old order, Jews pleaded their cause once again. The congress adopted a resolution favoring Jewish civil rights granted "by" the various states, but their enemies cleverly had the term "by" changed to "in," in this way opening the door to new restrictions. It was clear that a new anti-Napoleonic nationalism was in the wind that would sweep away Jewish gains as well as all vestiges of liberal reform. Agitation against Jews rose and in 1819 reached a point of violence in many German cities. Again excesses occurred accompanied by an old cry: "Hep, hep, death to the Jews!"[6] The masses, too, had obviously resented the new fellow-citizens. In Prussia the old restrictive conditions returned, and in Italy under Pius VII the ghetto was reestablished. Despite all, the regression did not leave the Jews as badly off as they were before the French Revolution. Though disappointed, they now stood more erect, and there was consolation in suffering harassment in common with other liberal groups.

The next half century or so recorded a tortuous struggle between the friends of the old order and the apostles of liberal constitutionalism. The fate of emancipation was intimately tied up with that of the latter. In France Jews lost least ground. The revolution of July, 1830, brought state support to Judaism, and from this point Jews were found in all phases of French national life.

Oddly, England—where Jews had fared best, and perhaps because of this very fact—was most reluctant to grant equality. Time and again a proposal to naturalize Jews (called "The Jew Bill") was made in Parliament but without enactment. Full emancipation in England did not arrive until 1858 when Baron Lionel de Rothschild was seated in Parliament by a special oath formulated for the occasion. Thus did the law catch up with the realities. Jews had long been prominent and powerful in English life, and the anachronism of their continuing disabilities had earned the scorn of some of the foremost writers, including Macaulay.

In Germany progress was slow despite the herculean efforts of the brilliant Jewish orator and diplomatist Gabriel Riesser. Thoroughly Germanized and as equally convinced as Napoleon's Sanhedrin that Judaism was a religion not a nation, Riesser worked tirelessly to align German culture and Jewish faith and to obtain civil emancipation for Jews. Full emancipation finally came in 1848 when, under the impetus of the French revolution of that year, uprisings spread throughout Germany and Hungary and advanced the cause of constitutionalism. Thereafter Jews were admitted to the legislative assemblies. The reaction that followed had no serious adverse results for Jews.

The emancipation struggle followed somewhat similar lines in Austria and Hungary. The Hungarian government, obviously grateful for the aid given General Kossuth by a Jewish regiment, made concessions.

Italy gave in piecemeal to the emancipation movement. Sardinia, first to grant equality in 1848, was followed by the northern provinces, then Sicily, Naples, and Venice. Emancipation came last to Rome where Pius IX, at first of liberal leanings, clung tenaciously to the old order, maintaining the ghetto and compulsory sermons until the Papal States were seized in 1870.

THE ECONOMIC REVOLUTION

Political developments were not the sole factors in the achievement of emancipation. Their importance was rivaled by developments in economics. Abram Sachar does not hesitate to state: "Economic changes were more crucial in winning political equality for Jews than all the glittering generality about the rights of man and the sanctity of the human personality."[7] Jews emerged from the ghettoes into a world in the midst of an industrial revolution that opened unimagined vistas of social and material progress. Well equipped by their past struggles for the rugged competition the situation provided, many Jews entered commercial and financial enterprises and distinguished themselves. A few rose to the top of the financial world. Most countries had a powerful Jewish financier, and the house of Rothschild spread its operations throughout Europe. The influence these captains of finance exerted on the expanding economy reflected benignly upon the cause of Jewish liberation. It also prepared the ground for the charge of a world-wide Jewish financial conspiracy. According to the charge, Jews had seized control of the international traffic in gold in order to wield power over Christians. The suspicion remained long after the power of the Rothschilds dwindled.

Actually, nineteenth-century Jews did not enjoy the monopoly in the money trade they had had for a while in the Middle Ages. Though they were again over-represented in the field, there was no question of international conspiracy or control.[8] More Jews were occupied in international trade than in finance. As city dwellers and traders Jews could only be expected to take advantage of the opportunities that the industrial revolution presented.

At first their talents were appreciated by the Christian capitalists. But here again their proficiency cut in two directions. Appreciation soon turned to resentment. To their competitors, the newcomers seemed, in Bernard Lazare's words, to enter society "as conquerors."[9] It was in those days that the complaint arose that Jews were "unproductive middle men," "economic parasites." It was shaped for the most part by socialist writers and became a favorite theme with later racist antisemites of a socialist stripe.

In reality the majority of Jewish *emancipés* were members of the proletarian class. Many had organized and joined guilds and unions, taking an active interest in the labor movement and the socialist cause, some even abandoning Judaism to do so. Thus when Karl Marx gave Socialism a new radical framework, antisemites were well prepared to label his movement "Jewish Marxism" or "Jewish radicalism" despite the fact that Marx's inspirers and followers were all gentiles. Marx himself, of Jewish parentage but baptized as an infant, was a particularly caustic antisemite who considered Jews worshippers of mammon, the very soul of the corrupt capitalism he fought. The following passage is typical:

> What is the object of the Jew's worship in this world? Usury. What is his worldly God? Money. Very well then; emancipation from usury and money, that is, from practical, real Judaism, would constitute the emancipation of our time . . . . The social emancipation of Jewry is the emancipation of society from Jewry.[10]

Other Jewish architects of Socialism, Ferdinand Lassalle (1825-64) and Bruno Bauer (1809-82), for example, held little or no ties with Judaism throughout their lifetime.[11] Upon emancipation, in short, many Jews left their ghettos to join the ranks of both capital and labor, but in no sense could they be considered originators or controllers of either.[12] Their effective participation in both movements undoubtedly quickened the process of their emancipation, but at the same time forged new ammunition for the economic and nationalist types of antisemites about to emerge.

TWO UNFORTUNATE AFFAIRS

Toward mid-nineteenth century two events occurred which profoundly disturbed Jewish-Gentile relations throughout the world. Among other results, they gave rise to a protectionist and eleemosynary era in Jewish history during which many notable Jewish personalities and organizations devoted themselves to the defense of Jewish interests.

The first occurred in Damascus in 1840 when Father Thomas, superior of a Franciscan monastery, disappeared without a trace. A Turk was said to have threatened to kill him some time before, but the priest was seen in the Jewish quarter the day before he vanished. This one fact was enough to instigate the charge that he was murdered by Jews for their Passover rites— still several weeks away. Arrests were made, and under torture a Jewish barber blamed six wealthy Jewish families, who were also tortured. One of the accused died under torture, another was converted to Islam, and the rest accused themselves. Sixty Jewish children were confined without food by the authorities in hope of influencing their parents to confess.

The matter rapidly turned into a full-blown international scandal, variously involving Louis Philippe, the British House of Commons, Metternich, and the Pasha of Egypt. World opinion was aroused, and a Jewish deputation comprised of Sir Moses Montefiore, Adolphe Crémieux, famed lawyer, and Solomon Munk, noted Orientalist, left London, with British encouragement, for the Near East and sought a reopening of the case, but were opposed by the French consul of Syria. Protest meetings were held in New York, Philadelphia, and London. The Jewish delegation obtained from the Pasha of Egypt the release of the nine prisoners who survived; and a little later, when Syria passed into Turkish hands, a firman was issued by the Sultan declaring the ritual-murder charge a libel and guaranteeing Jewish rights throughout the empire. The spectacular success of the delegation and the wide support it received from Jews everywhere inspired all Jewry, demonstrating as it did the deep solidarity that existed among dispersed Jewish communities.

The second event, the Mortara affair, occurred in Bologna in 1858. It began when Edgardo Mortara, a Jewish boy of seven who had been surreptitiously baptized by a nurse, was removed from the custody of his parents by papal gendarmes. The boy was taken to Rome and made a ward of Pius IX, who manifested a tender solicitude toward him. Edgardo's parents made several unsuccessful attempts to regain their child, even as late as 1870 when they appealed to King Victor Emmanuel II. But at this point Edgardo was steadfast in his Catholic faith. He had entered the novitiate of Canons Regular of the Lateran, taking Pius as his name in religion. He was ordained three years later, and throughout his priestly life displayed a fervent zeal for the conversion of his family and people. From the outset, the case stirred impassioned international comment which reached as far as Russia and the United States.[13] Jewish and Protestant opinion was indignant, while Catholics generally, but not all, strove to defend the removal.[14] Protests to the Vatican came from Cavour in Sardinia, Napoleon III in France, and Franz Joseph in Austria. Montefiore went to see the Pope, whose answer was always the same: *Non possumus* (We can do nothing.), meaning that he was bound by doctrinal considerations.[15] The Mortara case was the chief factor contributing to the formation of the *Alliance Israelite Universelle* (1860), for many years the foremost international Jewish organization devoted to the "defense of Jewish rights wheresoever attacked." Some historians see it, further, as contributing to the downfall of the Papal States.

CZARIST ANTISEMITISM

Russia, where at least half of world Jewry now lived, remained altogether refractory to the movement of emancipation. From almost the beginning of her history, a tradition of autocracy, Pan-Slavism, and devotion to Eastern Orthodoxy shaped a policy of distrust toward European influence and especially toward Judaism. Jews were forbidden under penalty of the law to enter Central—Muscovite—Russia. Their chances of entry were not improved when, in the fifteenth century, under Ivan III, some Jews who had managed to gain access to Novgorod and Moscow set about converting the people to Judaism. A Judaizing sect resulted which counted among its adherents members of the clergy, the nobility and even Zossima, metropolitan of Moscow.

When the Judaizers were discovered, a Church council was invoked and several were burned, others imprisoned. The experience served to redouble Russian fears of Jewish influence and to tighten the official exclusionist policy. This policy continued from ruler to ruler, with the exception of Peter the Great, who allowed Jews to be admitted to the provinces. The empresses who followed him were particularly fanatical in their anti-Jewish fervor. Their common sentiment was voiced by the Empress Elizabeth who, when asked to admit Jews for commercial purposes, replied, "From the enemies of Christ I accept no profit."

By a curious turn of destiny, with the partition of Poland in the late eighteenth century, Russia became governor of the largest body of Jews in the world. Far from terminating her policy of ostracism this unanticipated development gave rise to another policy which restricted Jews to the newly won provinces, now called the "Pale of Settlement." The order for confinement took place under Catherine II, who at the same moment extended an invitation to foreigners to enter Central Russia, an invitation to all "except the Jews." The phrase was to appear often in future legislation. Even within the Pale itself, Jews suffered restrictions, extra taxes, and other hardships. Many of them first lived as innkeepers and liquor dealers in the countryside but were forced back into the cities whence the Poles had chased them earlier.

For the next hundred years, Czardom wrestled with its newly acquired "Jewish problem." It was, admittedly, a formidable one. Russian reactionary Pan-Slavism faced a Judaism just as reactionary and exclusivist. By European Jewish standards these eastern Jews were considered unenlightened, impervious to the winds of change whether in the world about them or in Judaism itself. The Russian solution to the problem was simple: Russification of the Jews. To this end, a series of "investigations" of their situation was started. G. R. Derzhavin set the tone of these investigations when, in 1800, he pointed to Jewish "economic parasitism"—many Jews were middlemen—and talmudism as the chief cause of the problem and proposed that it be removed by imposition of economic and educational reforms.

The reign of the liberal-minded Alexander I (1801-25) witnessed relatively benign efforts to wean Jews from their occupation as middlemen to agriculture and the handcrafts and to break the hold of the rabbinate by educational reforms and governmental control of the *Kahals*. The Emperor envisioned eventual emancipation by assimilation. He listened to his minister Speranski, a rare Russian friend of the Jews, who advocated allowing them to improve themselves by reducing their disabilities. But after Napoleon's defeat Alexander changed, and drove the Jews further into the Pale.

With his successor Nicholas I (1825-55) Jewish history under the czars reached its nadir. This tyrannical xenophobe introduced hundreds of disabling laws to curb Jewish activities and in a ukase of 1827 established the infamous military conscription of Jewish youths at the age of twelve, extending their service to as long as eighteen years. These youngsters, called "cantonists," were transported to the farthest outposts of the empire, tortured, and traduced in an effort to have them abandon their faith. Many apostatized but most held out heroically. Quotas were put on each *Kahal* for its "cantonists," with the result that Jewish "catchers" went about abducting young Jews without passports in order to fill the quota.

When his economic and social reforms failed to break Jewish separatism, Nicholas turned his attention to Jewish education, which his minister Count Uvarov considered the chief root of "the Jewish problem." Schools in which Russian and secular subjects were taught were established in the hope that Jewish children might be enticed to forsake rabbinic traditions. This "enlightenment from above" attracted the interest of many liberal Jews, both in and outside of Russia, who deplored the quality as well as the plight of eastern Jewry. Some, such as Max Lilienthal, arrived to aid Uvarov in his plans, but departed once they detected the conversionist intent of the government. The educational project failed because it lacked the cooperation of the majority of Jews, steeped in the older traditions. Repressive measures followed, and so pitiable became their plight that considerable sympathy was stirred abroad. Montefiore came to Russia from London and was allowed to visit the Czar and also the *Kahals*, but with no practical results.

The advent of Alexander II to the throne in 1855 "ushered in one of the most hopeful and promising periods in Russian history"[16] and accordingly aroused Jewish expectations. A liberal reformer and freer of the serfs, the new monarch relaxed Nicholas' draconian measures, repealed the juvenile conscription laws, and opened Russian schools to certain classes of Jews. Alexander hoped to reverse tradition and westernize Russia; he included Jews in the plan. Having abandoned hope of converting them, he directed his efforts to their Russification, both social and cultural. Interestingly, under this benevolent paternalism Jewish Russification progressed of its own accord. Jewish intellectual and literary life thrived somewhat as in the Mendelssohnian era in Germany. But, as in that country, the prospects of enlightenment created even more severe tensions between the traditionalists and the progressives, between the young and the old. Finally, the assets derived from Alexander's reforms proved meager enough: the masses of Jews in the Pale remained untouched. As years went on, Alexander grew disillusioned with the progress of his Jewish policies and resentful of Jewish involvement in liberal movements, which he feared. Investigations began anew; a few Jewish schools were closed and restrictions were reinvoked, including a ban on Jewish advancement in the military and in local government.

In 1867, in a series of articles, a Jewish convert named Jacob Brafman made the charge that Jews were linked in a world conspiracy aimed at the exploitation of the gentile world.[17] The charge helped to bring new government efforts to destroy Jewish communal solidarity, and before long it had become a staple of antisemitic propaganda, serving later as the basis for the notorious *Protocols of the Elders of Zion* (1919). Ritual-murder trials were held at Saratov in 1857 and Kutais in 1878.

Russia's only rival in oppressing Jews was Romania, where some 200,000 Jews lived in conditions reminiscent of the worst days of the Middle Ages. As soon as the country won its freedom from Turkey in the early nineteenth century, anti-Jewish restrictions went into force. Most applied to occupations and residence. Forming a goodly proportion of the commercial middle class in a society more than 90 per cent peasant, Jews were eyed jealously by the peasants and resented as competitors by the bourgeoisie. These economic motives were fanned by the winds of a fierce nationalism conceived in the Russian style. Anti-Jewish pressures reached a climax in the expulsions and numerous blood libels of

1867 and after. Protests were heard in France and Great Britain; U.S. President Ulysses S. Grant appointed a legate to plead the Jewish cause in Romania, but to no avail. Following the Turkish-Russian war, the Berlin Treaty embodied a provision—against Russian opposition—for religious freedom for minorities in the countries of the signatories, including Romania. But Romania found a loophole in the provision and persisted in denying citizenship to Jews, and imposed restrictions on them well into the twentieth century.

THE BALANCE SHEET

Political emancipation proved a mixed blessing to the Jews of Europe. While unquestionably one of the greatest advances and acquisitions of their history, it was nonetheless a disappointment. The Jews of traditionalist persuasion who stepped cautiously, even fearfully, from their ghettoes to assume full citizenship in their respective countries were perhaps wiser than others who, believing that the Gordian knot of antisemitism had been cut, rushed headlong into the main current of European economic and cultural life, confident that the idealism of the emancipators was at one with historical reality. They soon found the rugged elements of traditional antisemitism had not withered away before the legislative enactments. Instead of disappearing, antisemitism merely changed its guise. An old form was on the wane, another in the making. The theological bias was fainter but the national, economic, and ethnic resentments were stronger. Less hated as a "deicide people," Jews became abhorred as supposedly unassimilable economic parasites. Clearly, their emancipation had a proviso attached: that they dissolve in the gentile melting pot. So when, against the rising tide of nationalism, they held on to their religious and cultural identity and, worse, proved formidable competitors in the industrial and financial revolutions—as many did—all the old animosities remained.

If these animosities were to survive, however, a new frame had to be found for them. As religious faith declined, so did the inclination to attribute Jewish "perversity" to unbelief or deicidal guilt. As the spirit of rationalism and skepticism rose, the need to justify the discrimination in purely secular terms grew. To the secularized antisemite it was simple logic that if the plight of the Jews did not stem from the crucifixion, it came from themselves, their ethnic makeup; Jews, in a word, were innately perverse. Thus there emerged a new brand of antisemitism, rationalistic and ethnical in character.

RATIONALIST ANTISEMITISM[18]

Rationalist antisemitism was not wholly new. There were traces in previous epochs on occasions when Jews were deemed inherently hateful, but they were relatively rare and never became a dominant influence. Celsus, second century pagan apologist, who at first favored the Jews and fought Christianity but turned against both later, thus became the prototype of the nineteenth rationalist hater of Jews. It was not until the rise of rationalist thought in the seventeenth century, however, that non-religious antisemitism emerged in force. At its beginning, rationalism, rejecting revealed religion and impugning the Christian *Weltanschauung*, appeared as an ally of the Jews, oppressed as they were for reasons of creed or considerations of a unified Christian state. Much of the support Mendelssohn received was, in this sense, of rationalist inspiration. But such an alliance was not destined to endure. Sooner or later, rationalist thinking had to follow its basic presuppositions to their logical conclusion and repudiate Judaism as well as Christianity. For if priests are imposters, so are rabbis; if the New Testament is an illusion, so is the Old; if organized Christian religion is a lie, so is the Synagogue. The rationalist skeptic, ultimately, could argue in no other way.

The first of the great modern anti-Judaists of the rationalist school was himself a Jew, Baruch Spinoza. This seventeenth century metaphysical giant, working on purely rational premises, discarded traditional Judaism as a gross superstition and believing Jews as worshipers of a God of hate. In his "Theological-Political Treatise," he describes Jewish patriotism in these terms: "The love of the Hebrew for their country was not only patriotism, but also piety, and was cherished and nurtured by daily rites till, like the hatred of other nations, it must have passed into their nature. Their daily worship was not only different from that of other nations (as it might well be, considering that they were a peculiar people and entirely apart from the rest), it was absolutely contrary. Such daily reprobation naturally gave rise to a lasting hatred deeply implanted in the heart: for of all hatreds none is more deep and tenacious than that which springs from extreme devoutness or piety, and is itself cherished as pious."[19]

Rationalist antisemitism found another champion in the French philosopher of the Enlightenment, Voltaire. This prince of skeptics, sworn enemy of the Church, held Jews and Judaism in utter contempt. It is possible his views were influenced by unhappy business dealings with Jews; nonetheless, his angry assaults on the Old Testament, which he considered full of error, cannibalism, and folly, stress the rationalist grounds of his hatred.[20] His antisemitism, as we have seen, also found its inspiration in classical pagan antisemitism.[21] The great liberator from superstition actually approved the endless persecutions and massacres of the Jews[22] and gave credence to the blood accusation.[23] No insult to Jews was too gross: Jews are, Voltaire ranted, "the most imbecile people on the face of the earth," "enemies of mankind," a people "most obtuse, cruel, and absurd," whose history is "disgusting and abominable."[24] "In short, we find in them only an ignorant and barbarous people, who have long united the most sordid avarice with the most detestable superstition and the most invincible hatred for every people by whom they are tolerated and enriched."[25] We are not far from his *Écrasez l'infâme* here.[26]

Emperor Frederick II, freethinking ruler of Prussia and friend of Voltaire, was as poorly disposed to Jews as his fellow-skeptic and shackled them with restrictions throughout his reign (1740-86). It is noteworthy that Hitler familiarized himself with the Frederick-Voltairean discourses as he formulated his theories.[27]

Voltaire's type of antisemitism was not rare during the Age of Enlightenment or after. To Diderot, Jews were capable of any villainy; to D'Holbach, they were the vilest people on earth; to Rousseau, furious fanatics.[28] During the French Revolution one of the most stubborn opponents of Jewish emancipation was Rewbell, an anti-clerical representative from Alsace. More important than these and more decisive for the future was the antisemitism of the German philosophers and biblical critics: Fichte, Hegel,

Herder, Schleiermacher, and Harnack, illustrious names in the school of German rationalism, as well as contemnors of Jews and their interests.[29] The great influence they exerted had a serious bearing on the course of antisemitism in Germany.

Another important offshoot of rationalist philosophy, economic in orientation, was Alphonse Toussenel's elaborate attack, contained in *The Jews, Kings of the Epoch* (1840).[30] In this highly influential and original work, the author took up Voltaire's attack on the Old Testament and, describing Jews as the "people of Hell,"[31] elaborated the complaint against "Jewish capitalism" and proposed economic penalties against Jews. Toussenel ranks high among the high priests of socialist antisemitism, which enlisted in varying degrees such names as Pierre Proudhon, Karl Marx, Bruno Bauer, and lesser lights, all of whom trained their guns on Jewish "unproductiveness," "parasitism," and the like. The association of Socialism with antisemitism came to an end officially with the condemnation of the antisemitic movement at the Internationalist Socialist Congress of 1891, but this did not spell its end in socialist reality. On the other hand, increasingly and more consistently antisemitism became an attribute of conservatism and the anti-democratic Right.[32]

As the last quarter of the nineteenth century approached, Jews stood on the threshhold of another major phase of antisemitic history, that of racist antisemitism. In Christian times antisemitism had passed through a long theological phase during which Jews were harassed because of their "unbelief," and which extended from the mid-patristic era to the end of the Middle Ages. As modern times approached and religious unity dwindled, Jews were hated more as an ethnic or cultural group. This ethnological phase received strong support from the growth of nationalism in the nineteenth century and from rationalist philosophy as these further cut away the religious underpinnings of the older antisemitism, thus permitting a heavy accent on ethnological factors. It reached its culmination in the negative reaction to Jewish emancipation in the first half of the nineteenth century. By the 1850s the troubles ahead were predictable. A spirit of "scientism" was regnant and the pseudo-science of racial differences had already been launched. It was too much to expect antisemites to surmount the temptation of endowing their racist designs with the authority of scientific theory. To this transformation of antisemitic theory, many were to lend a hand in the years ahead.[33]

9
THE RACIAL MYTH
AND ITS CONSEQUENCES

Racial antisemitism broke out in Germany in the 1870s, spread to Austria-Hungary and France, reverberated in Russia, then subsided before its bloody climax in Nazi Germany. Germany gave the world the term "antisemitism," which first appeared in 1879 in Wilhelm Marr's *The Victory of Judaism Over Germanism*,[1] a German racist's somber warning of Jewish domination of German life. The theory of racial inferiority can be traced to Hegel's apotheosis of the German state and spirit[2] and to Christian Lassen's (1800-76) extension of the linguistic distinction between Aryan and Semitic to racial characteristics. In France, Ernest Renan, biblical critic and devotee of science, (1823-92) followed Lassen in his relegation of the Jews to an inferior racial status.[3] Arthur de Gobineau in his *Essay on the Inequality of Human Races*[4] warned against crossbreeding the races. In the racist purview, the Semitic race was deemed physically, morally, and culturally inferior to the Aryan. Jews in particular were signalized as incomparably inferior to Germanic Aryans, and unassimilable and corruptive as well. In the closing years of the century, a host of philosophers, pseudo-scientists, demagogues, and pamphleteers richly varied and orchestrated this theme.[5]

There were, further, socio-economic causes that gave teeth to the racial theories. The Hegelian school had engendered a

fierce German nationalism that fought Jewish assimilation—
which had been going on apace—and yet resented Jewish separatism. The specialization of Jews in finance—fostered by the
government—set a number of Jews apart as a banking clique,
much as in the case of the court Jews in past centuries. But it was
this very specialization which drew the resentment of the populace, the bourgeoisie, and the socialist theorists. In addition, the
prominence of a few Jews in liberal and even revolutionary circles
earned the label of radicals and revolutionaries for Jews as a
whole. Clerics, both Catholic and Protestant, still looked upon
Jews as aliens and catalogued them with the secularist and anti-
clerical enemies of the Christian order. All these causes—pseudo-
scientific, social, economic, and religious—set the Jew apart as
the whipping-boy for the troubles that Germany, and later Austria-Hungary and France, were about to face.

RACISM ENTERS POLITICS

In was not surprising that Marr's treatise received an enthusiastic hearing in 1879. The ground would not have been so fertile
for his notions a few years earlier, but in the wake of the German
victory over France it was quickly made so by postwar developments. The Kulturkampf was started and already in 1871 the antisemitic Father August Rohling had published his scathing
assault on Judaism in *The Talmud Jew*[6]—little more than a re-
casting of Eisenmenger's view—which went into edition after edition even after its thoroughgoing refutation by competent
scholars. In 1873 at the time of the financial crash—in which some
Jews were involved—the acceptance of Marr's views was assured.[7] From this point, a veritable literary war raged as antisemitic and prosemitic pamphlets flew. The furor might have spent
itself had not Bismarck—having made peace with the Church and
turned against the National Liberal Party—given the nod to the
antisemites to strike at the Jews as a means of rallying the disparate political factions against the liberal, democratic cause.[8]
The antisemitic movement was off to a fast start.

Jews were put upon from all sides as a wave of physical as
well as verbal violence swept the country. There were many denunciations in the Reichstag. The government's chief whip was

the Protestant court chaplain, Stoecker, who founded the anti-semitic Christian Social Worker's Union to fight "Jewish Socialism" and "domination of German life" by Jews. In 1881 a petition with 300,000 signatures called for renewed restrictions against the Jews, but this was countered by another befriending them, with twenty-six of the most respected names in Germany as signatories. The renowned historian, Treitschke,[9] fanned the flame by his oft-quoted remark: "The Jews are our misfortune." Meanwhile, Jews were insulted on the streets, disorders multiplied, anti-Jewish boycotts were organized, antisemitic congresses held, and university restrictions imposed. A synagogue was burned and two ritual-murder trials were held.

The furor was as fierce on the intellectual front, where antisemitic ideologies proliferated. Lazare was able to distinguish five such ideologies: Christian-social, economic, ethnological and national, metaphysical, and anti-Christian. The Christian-social type flourished principally in France; its foremost products in Germany were Rohling's anti-talmudism and Stoecker's "Christian Socialism." Economic antisemitism, of long ancestry, received new analysis and impetus from Otto Glagau's attack on Jewish bankers and brokers. Ethnological and nationalist antisemitism, never entirely absent from any antisemitic writings of this period, formed the chief basis of Marr's and Treitschke's contributions. In this category Theodor Fritsch's vicious *Anti-Semitic Catechism*,[10] which had many editions, must be placed. But by far the most formidable effort in this direction was Houston Stewart Chamberlain's *Foundations of the Nineteenth Century*.[11] This naturalized German of English descent pushed the highly inventive pseudo-science of Teutonic racial superiority and its correlate, Jewish baseness, to their limits. His massive volume became the accepted textbook for all future antisemitic academicians. Philosophical antisemitism, continuing in the Hegelian tradition, was prominently represented by Max Stirner who held that Jews never surpassed the "Negro stage" of human evolution (by which he meant the most primitive).[12]

Perhaps the most significant of all these was anti-Christian antisemitism, that final fruit of rationalist antisemitism and in many ways forerunner of Nazi antisemitism. Only adepts of this brand of Jew-hatred could frankly face the embarrassing fact that

Christianity had Hebrew roots, that Jesus and his apostles were Jews, that the Old Testament was a Christian as well as a Jewish book; only they followed their antisemitism to its logical conclusion and rejected Christianity together with Judaism. Some Christian antisemites, contrariwise, were forced into most awkward positions in order to skirt the problem: proposing that Jesus was of no human race at all, or that Jesus and the disciples were Nordic. Atheist Eugen Duehring, more consistent, attacked Christianity as the final expression of the Semitic spirit and inimical to the Nordic spirit. Nietzsche opposed both Judaism and Christianity as purveyors of the "slave morality" and foreign to the "master morality" of Romans and Teutons.[13] And in France, Tridon and Regnard expounded an atheistic and anti-Christian antisemitism which, as did all ideologies of this type, made common cause with that of the racists.[14]

These divisions at the heart of the new antisemitism, joining Christian with anti-Christian, were among the main causes of its decline. After a final paroxysm in the early 1890s, which witnessed a ritual-murder trial at Xantes, the fanatic ravings of an Ahlwardt and boycotts against Jews in Galicia, the movement lost ground rapidly. Other events contributed to the decline. Antisemites were found involved in the very type of scandals and swindles that they had broadcast as the handiwork of the Jews. In 1890 a defensive society against antisemitism was formed and in 1893 Jews organized to combat anti-Jewish libels. In 1894 the Catholic organ *Germania* disavowed the antisemitic movement.

German antisemitism spread to Austria-Hungary at the end of the 1870s, where it followed a course akin to that taken in Germany. In the Hungarian half of this confederation, Jews were caught in a conflict between liberal and conservative parties and were made the butt of an attack on the liberal and progressive movement. They were also caught up in the many national rivalries that plagued this fragile federation of Czechs, Slovaks, Poles, Hungarians, and Germans. Considered a tool of the Hapsburg rulers, the Jews were the target of the anti-monarchial reactions of the national groups. When the *Union Génerale*, an international "Christian" banking organization, failed in 1882, Jews were blamed and revenge was sought against them. Part of the revenge were the teachings of the notorious Father Rohling, who was given a professorship at the University of Prague. This priest waged a stern battle against the "Talmud Jew" and did his utmost to spread the ritual-murder accusation before he was finally discredited by the talmudic authority Rabbi S. Bloch and by others. But not before his efforts bore fruit. In 1882 in Tisza Eszlar a sensational ritual-murder trial was held. Before its end a year later, as it gradually became plain that it was a methodical attempt to discredit all Jewry, the trial collapsed. The fiasco dealt a fatal wound to the antisemitic cause in the Hungary of this era.

In Austria the movement proved a hardier plant. Antisemitic parties, socialist in outlook and under the leadership of Georg Schoenerer, one of Hitler's mentors, were formed around 1880. Restrictions against Jews in commerce and universities were invoked, causing student riots in the latter. Rohling's influence was felt here, too, and several ritual-murder charges were made throughout this period, such as the trial staged in Polna in 1899. In the 1890s the antisemites were joined by the clerical parties under the guidance of Karl Lueger of the Christian Social party, who was elected burgomaster of Vienna despite the opposition of the Archbishop and the Emperor. Lueger held office until his death in 1910, and at one point received a visit from the young Adolf Hitler, an admirer who came to Vienna to study the "Jewish problem." Christian organizations to defend the Jews appeared in Austria, as in Germany, but were ineffective. Minor disorders were frequent and a serious riot took place in Prague in 1897. With Lueger's death in 1910 the movement died.

THE FRENCH DEVELOPMENT

France, birthplace of Jewish emancipation in Europe, succumbed to the antisemitic epidemic a trifle more slowly than did Germany and Austria-Hungary, but was perhaps the most profoundly affected. There were few Jews in France, and these were patriotic and, for the most part, poor. For a while it seemed the storm to the East would pass them by. Hostile socialist writers—among whom the French were well represented by Proudhon, Toussenel, and Fourier—had not enjoyed extensive influence, nor had the conservative Gobineau and Gougenot de Mousseaux.[15] There were hostile rumblings in the 1870s when Boutoux founded the *Union Génerale* to counter Jewish financial interests and more unrest when it failed in 1882. Though the failure stemmed from over-speculation by its members, the Jews and the Republic were blamed.

But if little overt antisemitism appeared before the mid-1880s, the lines of battle, between which the Jews would eventually be caught, were being drawn. On one side stood the Third Republic, third generation offspring of the great Revolution of 1789 which, though more conservative than its grandparent, was strongly anti-clerical and, in the minds of the traditionalists, too alien and radical. It held the favor of most Jews, obviously grateful for their emancipation by the First Republic. Opposing these were the anti-Republicans: royalists looking nostalgically toward the past and the re-establishment of the monarchy; most Catholics, who resented the anti-clericalism of the Third Republic and its "infamous laws" (to which they attributed the Church's loss of influence); finally, the army, with a reactionary caste-system of its own. These three forces were one in their conservatism, their anti-Republicanism and, in varying degrees, their antisemitism. All frowned upon Jews as a power in France bent upon dominating French life and subverting French traditions; they considered the Third Republic a "Jew Republic." Thus stretched the lines of conflict in 1885, as if awaiting the sudden and strident tocsin sounded by the evil genius of French antisemitism, Edouard Drumont.

This man's *La France Juive*,[16] which appeared in 1886, acted as the detonator of long-suppressed energies. Written with a felicitous style in two bulky volumes, it heaped charge upon charge on the Jews and led to one conclusion: since medieval times the Jews had been responsible for the woes of France. Drumont's inspiration was frankly racist but supposedly "Christian," for much of his attack was against anti-clericalism. The book won an enormous public. It was plain that Drumont had touched a vital spot and had forced the cleavage between *les deux Frances* fully into the open. He wrote several anti-Jewish pamphlets, founded an antisemitic League in 1889, and finally edited the daily *La Libre Parole* in 1892, all devoted to his original goal of focusing censure on the Jews and their supposed ally, the Republic. His cause was conveniently helped by the Panama Canal scandal in which hundreds of thousands were ruined financially and which involved some Jews in briberies. It was just the proof Drumont needed to substantiate his "myth of Jewish power." In 1893 the Catholic scholar Anatole Leroy-Beaulieu presented a strong case against Drumont in his *Les Juifs et l'antisémitisme*, proving the laicizing or secularization of the Jews was the result not the cause of the "de-Christianization" of society.[17]

L'AFFAIRE DREYFUS

But all this was yet prelude. It was as if a play had been written, a director chosen, the stage set, and the cast rehearsed. The only missing part was the leading man. Whether this man was systematically picked for the role, as Hannah Arendt tends to believe,[18] or was one who merely fell afoul of a roguish circumstance and thus became the victim of a judicial error that assumed vast political proportions, is not certain. At any rate for twelve long years France was the scene of a melodrama that revolved around Alfred Dreyfus and had the world for its audience. The Dreyfus affair has been seen as a dress-rehearsal for Hitlerism. Certainly it was the most extraordinary exhibit of modern antisemitism outside Germany. Briefly, the facts are as follows.

Late in 1894 Captain Alfred Dreyfus, sole Jewish member of the French general staff, was accused of spying for the Germans; he was tried behind closed doors and, by unanimous verdict, convicted and sentenced to life imprisonment on Devil's Island. Dreyfus vehemently protested his innocence. The principal evidence against him, and the only piece published, was the famous *bordereau* (unsigned letter), allegedly in his handwriting. In mid-1895, Colonel Picquart, new head of the counterespionage section, reported to the chief of staff that he had reason to believe that Major Esterhazy, a dissolute adventurer, not Dreyfus, was guilty of the espionage and the forgery. Picquart was warned to keep silent and assigned to a perilous post in Tunisia. At this time, Bernard Lazare wrote the first pamphlet attacking the Dreyfus trial. In June 1897 Picquart had the vice president of the senate advised of his suspicions. At this point, Clemenceau took up the fight for a reopening of the case and shortly after Emile

Zola wrote his famous *J'Accuse* in Clemenceau's journal. Zola was tried for libel and convicted but fled to England. Picquart also was arrested. Esterhazy, meanwhile, with further evidence of espionage against him, was tried and acquitted. But in 1898, he was dishonorably discharged for swindling, whereupon he confessed to an English reporter that he had forged the *bordereau*.

To bolster the army's case, a certain Colonel Henry forged new documents that incriminated Dreyfus and, following exposure, Henry committed suicide. Forthwith the court of appeals ordered the Dreyfus case reopened. In June 1899 at Rennes the original sentence was annulled, but, incredibly, a new sentence of ten years imprisonment was imposed by reason of "extenuating circumstances." Within a week, the president of the Republic pardoned Dreyfus. In the following year, the Chamber of Deputies, by a large majority, voted against further consideration of the case. In 1903 however, Dreyfus asked for a revision to clear his name. It was not until July 1906 that the court of appeals set aside the Rennes sentence and acquitted Dreyfus of all charges.

Although the Dreyfus case ended justly and dealt a death blow to all hopes for an organized, official French antisemitism—Drumont had been elected to the Chamber of Deputies in 1898 to join nineteen antisemites there—it was nonetheless responsible for the growth of antisemitism in France. Hatred of Jews was transferred, one might say, from the professional level to the streets.

As the trial began, antisemitism was mostly an affair of polemicists and a smattering of special groups, but as it progressed and passed into the pages of *La Libre Parole* the general public was drawn in. At first everyone believed in Dreyfus' guilt but, as evidence mounted courageous individuals of both the political and intellectual community joined Picquart, Clemenceau, and Zola in their campaign for a revision of the verdict. Their efforts, however, only aroused opposition. Each gain by the Dreyfusards was greeted by agitation of anti-Dreyfusards, and for a while no Dreyfusard was safe in all France. The affair left deep wounds and an enduring bitterness in France, of which hate for Jews was no small part. The Vichy regime of the forties was one of its legatees.

And yet anti-Dreyfusard antisemitism was not a pure strain,

mixed as it was by nationalist, clericalist, and militarist passions. The antisemitic aspect does not rest on the fact that Dreyfus' enemies acquiesced to a terrible miscarriage of justice in order to protect the respective object of their allegiance—army, nation, church—but on the hard truth that their fanatic defense of all these was determined to a large extent by the fact that the victim was a Jew. To the partisans, Dreyfus the Jew represented all the liberal, alien, and de-Christianizing pressures on the traditional Christian order of France. The case was not only a fine example of the scapegoat theory but still more of the projective or symbolic nature of antisemitism and its paranoid character. The Jew here is no longer a human being—an Alfred Dreyfus—but an archetype. The determination of the anti-Dreyfusards to sacrifice an individual for the nation, combined with their over-valuation of Jewish influence, provided a foreglimpse of Hitler's National Socialism. But it was an abortive Nazism. To the glory of France the individual Jew was at last exonerated even at the risk of injury to what was considered by most the welfare of France's most hallowed institutions.

The affair exerted fateful effects on world Jewry as well as Jews in France. It was, in a sense, the first birth-pang of that extraordinary movement called Zionism, which within a half century would realize the wild dream of a Jewish homeland in Palestine. One of the news correspondents at the trial of Dreyfus was a half-assimilated Jew named Theodor Herzl. The ordeal of the Jewish captain convinced Herzl that emancipation was not the answer to the problem of antisemitism, and that the ultimate solution was political and national: The Jews must have a state of their own. He left the trial transformed and before he died in 1904 Zionism was well on its way.

No institution was injured more gravely by the Dreyfus case than the Church, compromised as it was by zealous but misguided defenders. On the heels of the affair, the Church was disestablished. Its influence on public life permanently declined; and anti-clericalism became an integral part of the government. The main cause of the decline was undoubtedly the almost fanatic support given the army against Dreyfus by the large majority of Catholic opinion, particularly the Catholic press. Because of this unfortunate commitment, the Church became more than ever identified with reaction and anti-Republicanism. It was quickly forgotten that during the affair the hierarchy had maintained silence; that Picquart and Leroy-Beaulieu were practicing Catholics; that the Catholic—and antisemitic—minister of war, Cassignac, was an early revisionist; that one of the two who voted for Dreyfus at Rennes was a devout Catholic; that the *Cahiers de la Quinzaine*, largely Catholic in inspiration, had vigorously supported Dreyfus; and that a considerable number of Catholic writers were also in his camp.[19] There was no evidence of a "clerical plot" against Dreyfus and the Republic, as charged by some. Catholic opposition was entirely spontaneous and explainable on historical and socio-political grounds.

Nor is there sufficient evidence to attribute, with Hannah Arendt, a preponderant role to the Jesuits—scapegoats of the anti-clericals.[20] The Society of Jesus had earned a reputation for antisemitism by its activities in Poland in the seventeenth century[21] and also by excluding candidates of Jewish blood from their Society, a policy later rescinded. But their antisemitism was actually but an aspect of their stout post-Reformation defense of the Faith against every and any agency they considered a peril. Miss Arendt is correct in her observation that among the staunchest anti-Dreyfusards in the affair there were certain "cerebral" Catholics, "Catholics without faith," whose loyalty to the Church comprised little more than an attachment to a traditional political and social order which they thought expressed the best spirit of the nation. Drumont fitted this category.

The existence of this species of Catholicism is an important key to the Catholic commitment to the anti-Dreyfusard cause. It stemmed from an already long tradition, which might be traced to theological beginnings in medieval French anti-talmudism. Advanced by Bossuet and his seventeenth-century emulators, whose great influence helped to make anti-Judaism something of a national tradition, it took a more ethnological and political turn with Bonald's traditionalism. Its first major modern prophet was Gougenot de Mousseaux, who elaborated the theme of "de-Christianization" of society by "talmudic" Judaism.[22] After Gougenot, clerical writers took up and varied his theme with special emphasis on the notion of a world-wide conspiracy on the part of Freemasons and Jews, both singly and combined, to de-Christianize the world. Much notice was given the fact that Jewish emancipation and the laicization of society ran apace, and thus the suspicion grew that republican and non-conservative movements were of Judaeo-Masonic derivation.

Drumont, needless to say, was the high priest of this tradition and gave "cerebral" Christianity, or the antisemitism of *ressentiment*,[23] its ultimate expression. It was from him, not from the Church—Leo XIII (1878-1903) had worked in vain for a *rapprochement* with the Republic—that the Catholic anti-Dreyfusards derived their unity and inspiration. The misfortune was the dearth of Catholic voices in France at the time to expose the flaws of the "Catholic position"; to point out *inter alia* the secularized character of "cerebral" Christianity, the unChristian character of *ressentiment,* the highly nationalistic and essentially political stamp of the devotion to the Christian order, and the invidious nature of the fear of Jewish economic power. Too few were on hand who understood that the laicization of the temporal order was the work of Gentiles and that Christians were secularized first, then Jews. In Lovsky's words, there were "indications of a Jewish apostasy which paralleled the Christian apostasy—the first being only the fruit of the second."[24] Undeniably, Jews were commonly found in the anti-clerical, anti-Christian, and revolutionary camps. Yet it is myopic for Christians to wonder at this. Secularist liberals had shown themselves the Jews' emancipators and friends, while conservative Christian parties remained closed to them. The emancipated Jew was left little choice.

THE XENOPHOBIC ART

By 1881 the epidemic reached Russia where Jews, despite some reforms, still lived in depressed conditions, and where the slightest spark was enough to rekindle the old Judaeophobia. The age of pogroms[25] was at hand. Alexander III, under the influence of Pobedonostsev, his antisemitic chief advisor, turned Russia back to the depths of absolutism and reaction. There were enough Jews associated with liberal or radical movements for the government to make all Jewry the chief target of its anti-revolutionary program. Pobedonostsev made no secret of his formula for solving the Jewish problem: one-third was to emigrate, one-third was to die, and one-third to disappear (that is, be converted). The first great pogrom commenced on Easter of 1881 and spread rapidly through southern Russia. A hundred Jewish communities were struck; masses of Jews were maimed, murdered, and impoverished as the police stood idly by. The attacks occurred almost simultaneously and followed the same general pattern everywhere.

Though it cannot be said for sure that the government deliberately instigated the pogroms, it is certain that they were perpetrated with its connivance. The peasants made no secret of the fact that they believed they were doing the will of the Czar. The government placed the blame for the pogroms on Jewish "exploitation" of the peasants—a charge that, whatever its foundation, was vastly exaggerated and incommensurate with the brutal remedy. Ignatiev, the minister of state, set up investigations, not of the pogroms but of the "exploitation." World reaction was one of great shock: protest meetings were held in London, and the United States government complained to the Czar. Many more pogroms took place before the end of the year. The most savage was held under Russian direction in Warsaw where condemnations were voiced by Polish civic and religious leaders.

Russian Jews, in a state of panic, initiated at this period the vast emigration that was to become the greatest exodus in Jewish history.[26] During Alexander III's thirteen-year reign, about 100,000 Jews departed each year, and later the numbers increased, most emigrants going to the United States. By 1900 a million Jews had left Russia, Romania and Galicia, and not long after that the egress almost doubled. Spain, interestingly, extended an invitation of entry to the refugees, doubtless from a long-festering remorse. At first the Russian government opposed the emigrations but later encouraged them. Pogroms continued in 1882 until finally the government was forced to intervene and stop them. It had now become plain that Czardom had discovered a new tool for dealing more or less vicariously with the "Jewish problem"—the pogrom. Ignatiev promulgated his "Temporary Laws" in May, which narrowed the area of the Pale, forbade leases and mortgages to Jews, banned residence in villages, set up a *numerus clausus* (educational quota) for Jews, and reduced professional opportunities for them. These supposedly "Temporary Laws" remained in force until 1914. Until the end of the century, sporadic pogroms continued, and further oppressions and expulsions were recorded.[27] Though there were some 650 exceptional laws concerning Jews on the books, Viacheslav Von Plehve, minister of the interior, prepared further enactments. Again protests came from England and the United States.

Under Nicholas II (1894-1917), absolutist and fervent antisemite who looked upon Jews as Christ-killers, Jewish conditions grew, if possible, worse. Our limitations permit only a summary of this litany of oppression. Pogroms and forced emigrations continued. At the turn of the century, as the revolutionary movement gathered momentum, anti-Jewish efforts were intensified. Von Plehve openly declared that he would drown the revolutionary movement in Jewish blood. In 1903 it was clear that he was not joking. The great pogrom at Kishinev, well prepared and organized, was staged as a clear warning to all dissenters. It surpassed all previous attacks in barbarity and endured for three days until finally word came from St. Petersburg to end it. Protests were heard in most civilized countries, and even in Russia prominent figures, such as Tolstoy, upbraided the government.

Toward the close of 1904 the "League of the Russian People," known as the "Black Hundreds," was organized to combat constitutionalism—and the Jews. Though this group undisguisedly perpetrated assassinations and pogroms, Nicholas II gave it his blessing. In 1905 a series of the cruelest pogroms of Russian history was launched, in preparation for which antisemitic pamphlets were printed in government printing offices. In one week during October, 670 pogroms counted hundreds of Jews killed, thousands wounded, and tens of thousands homeless. The Duma condemned the pogrom of 1906, but it was a futile gesture: the Duma was dissolved, pogroms continued, and anti-Jewish restrictions were tightened. Russian antisemitism had so attracted world attention at this point that the United States cancelled a trade pact of some seventy years' duration, and the British statesman Sir Herbert Samuel cancelled a trip to Russia.

In 1911 at Kiev, one of the most notorious of ritual-murder trials shocked world opinion when a common laborer, Mendel Beilis, was accused and prosecuted by the ministry of justice. Indignant protests poured in from religious and civil bodies of many countries, and Russia's foremost writers spoke out. The trial lasted two years and brought antisemitic agitation to its peak. Despite falsified evidence and a clearly packed jury, Beilis was finally acquitted. Russia stood wholly discredited before world opinion.

THE HOAX OF THE CENTURY

The *Protocols of the Learned Elders of Zion,* the "greatest forgery of the century," were the handiwork of Russian antisemites of this period. They are important as one of the chief source books for twentieth century antisemitism, and because of the insight they furnish into its nature. The *Protocols* first appeared in 1905—printed by the government press—as part of a book by a Russian mystic, Sergei Nilus. Nilus claimed that he received them in 1901 from an acquaintance and presented them as extracts of the 1897 World Zionist Congress in Basel which allegedly dealt with plans for world conquest that date from Solomon in 929 B.C.E. In substance the *Protocols* contain a series of twenty-four lectures by the so-called "Elders" on plans and techniques for subjugating the world and establishing a Jewish world state. They comprise a motley array of supposed examples of secret Jewish domination in history and plans for the future, including methods of stupefying Gentiles, controlling the press, finance, and government. Realistic details related to Jewish activities on the contemporary scene are added to impart an aura of plausibility. Actually, the lectures abound with contradictions and absurdities from beginning to end. In no sense whatever could they be entertained as a possible program for world domination.

Even so, they enjoyed a phenomenal influence both before and after their exposure as a crude forgery. Despite several re-editions of the original, they obtained no real notoriety until 1919 when they received excited attention in Germany and England. It is strange that the *Protocols,* which failed in their original purpose of influencing the Czar against the growing and allegedly "Jewish-Masonic" constitutional movement at the turn of the century, attained singular success after the war in many countries where Jews achieved a certain prominence in public life. With the German translation in 1919, the *Protocols* spread throughout the Western world. Translations were made into French, English, Polish, Scandinavian, Italian, Japanese, and Arabic. Three editions appeared in America where, thanks to the efforts of Henry Ford and his *The Dearborn Independent,* they were given the widest circulation.[28] After the exposure, antisemites went to desperate lengths to prove the authenticity of the *Protocols,* and continued to use them into the thirties. Their peak of influence was reached in Nazi Germany.

Exposure came in 1921 when a London *Times* correspondent noticed the close parallel between the *Protocols* and a satire on Napoleon III by a French lawyer named Maurice Joly. Almost fifty per cent of the *Protocols,* in effect, was a direct plagiarism of Joly's work. The idea of the secret meeting of "Learned Elders" was borrowed from an adventure story by Hermann Goedsche, the plot of which was laid in a Prague cemetery where the princes of the twelve tribes of Israel, no less, met to discuss plans of world conquest. And there were other sources. It is now all but certain that the compiling of the *Protocols* was done by an unknown antisemite of the Parisian office of the Russian *Ochrana* (secret police) near the turn of the century, whence they came into Nilus' hands.

The triumphant course of this "silly humbug which millions of readers have taken to be a system frighteningly wise and around which there has been raised the cry of world peril"[29] renders a valuable insight into the profoundly irrational nature of modern antisemitism. When otherwise brilliant minds are so deceived and when some, even after irrefragable disproof, persist in believing, we are at grips with a collective psychosis, with a will to hate and destroy well beyond the pale of human rationality. We have in the *Protocols,* in Valentin's words, a "sort of diabolism in a new form, a secularized diabolism."[30]

REVERBERATIONS

In Romania where a strong pan-Romanianism and an economic protectionism obtained toward the close of the century, Jews suffered conditions similar to those in Russia. An antisemitic league was formed in 1895 and, shortly after, boycotts were instigated against Jews. Many Romanian Jews emigrated, but most lived on in misery, many of them joining liberal parties, seeking betterment. There was little relief until after World War I.

In Russian Poland throughout the nineteenth century mutual religious fanaticism of Christian and Jew conspired with a Christian resentment of Jewish prominence in economic life to depress the condition of the Jews. Organized antisemitism broke out with the formation of the National Democratic Party at the end of the century. From 1905 to 1912 anti-Jewish agitation followed the general pattern of that of Central Europe, but also included an economic boycott in 1909 which ruined many Jews. When Jews helped to elect a socialist candidate to the Duma in 1912, anti-Jewish agitation was particularly intense and the boycott rigidly applied.

The antisemitic wave failed to reach Italy or other countries where Jews were few. Though England received many Jewish refugees—thus tripling the Jewish population there—no antisemitism resulted, a fact that may be attributed to the prestige of the Earl of Beaconsfield, Benjamin Disraeli, a baptized Jew who brought much glory to England.

The generalization that Jews were happier under the Crescent than under the Cross breaks down in the modern era. Even after the sixteenth century, examples of anti-Jewish measures and violence in the Near East could be multiplied, but despite all Jewish life there was fairly tolerable.[31] This was particularly true of Turkey, where religious liberty was granted in 1839. It was not true of Persia, where for centuries Jews had been hard pressed by forced conversions, violences, and restrictions. Pogroms were recorded in 1831, 1834, and 1891, and a special Jewish headgear was required as late as 1905. Morocco witnessed a pogrom in 1912. And in Yemen conditions worsened with time so that, with the advent of the Israeli state in 1948, the Yemenite Jews were happy to repatriate. The Zionist movement meanwhile gave rise to a "Semitic antisemitism" on the part of Arab states which finally made war on Israel. This Arab anti-Zionism, at first merely political and chauvinist, was in time to take on attributes of antisemitism, *tout court.*[32]

When the antisemitic wave had spent itself—in all countries save Russia and Romania—Jews were a thoroughly chastened people. A minority still believed that "the Jewish problem" was on the verge of solution along the lines of political enlightenment and assimilation. Others, despairing of this, turned to Zionism. As could be expected, the support of Zionism on the part of Jews who were to remain in their native or adopted countries stirred up anew the old charge of Jewish double loyalty, even disloyalty. The double-standard at the root of this charge was apparently lost on those who levelled it.

When oppression began in the 1870s, a new spirit affected Jewry everywhere. A number of new protective, philanthropic, and colonizing societies, modelled on the pioneering *Alliance Israelite Universelle*, were formed: the Anglo-Jewish Association in England, the *Israelitische Allianz* in Austria, the Jewish Colonization Society in London, and eventually the American Jewish Committee (1906), all of which dedicated themselves in various ways to succor oppressed coreligionists wherever they existed. They rendered yeoman service, but their early members scarcely realized what fragile stopgaps their organizations would prove to be before the demonic forces that the twentieth century was to unleash on Jews.

10
A WAR
WITHIN A WAR

It is no exaggeration to say that World War I and its aftermath comprised a period of savagery and misery that has had few equals in Jewish history. The universal disaster of 1914 dealt with the Jews more harshly than with any other group or nationality. Over and above the common hardships suffered by all soldiers and civilians, Jewish civilians suffered a war within a war on both sides of the fighting lines, especially in the eastern zone where the battle lines swept back and forth over an area in which most of world Jewry lived. At the beginning of the conflict, there was temporarily—and expediently—a truce in the unrelenting course of antisemitic activity. But when reverses developed on either side, the "eternal scapegoat" was made to account.[1] Moreover, the armistice and the peace, despite guarantees of "minority rights" and pledges that Palestine could become a national home for Jews, brought little respite; rather, these developments created conditions that spawned a fresh current of antisemitism, which, in turn, contained seeds of still greater catastrophes.

THE WAR

The greatest oppression, not surprisingly, came from the hands of the Russians. When the war was declared the "Temporary Laws" were abolished in Russia and Jews enlisted in the defense of their unkind Fatherland. But with little thanks. Almost at once they were suspected of being pro-German, of engaging in espionage and treachery, and, in consequence, were ruthlessly deported—often in boxcars—to the East and Siberia. Many Jews fled before the Russian advances but received a poor welcome wherever they went. When the demoralized Russian forces finally retreated they vented their humiliations upon the remaining Jews with pogroms, shootings, and looting.

In Germany the Kaiser launched the war with an appeal to all groups to defend the country, and Jews responded loyally. Of the 600,000 Jews in Germany, 100,000 had served the colors before the end of the war, eighty per cent of them at the front. And yet, again as reverses developed, antisemites circulated the charge that the Jews were shirkers. In consequence, the ministry of war instituted a census of Jews in 1916 which was followed by a wave of antisemitic feeling. The charge obviously offended Jews and occasioned counter-surveys by them to prove the adequacy of Jewish war participation in Germany and other warring countries. Jewish statisticians doted on showing the disproportionately high number of Jews not only among the soldiery and casualties but, in some countries, among those who earned military advancements—this despite antisemitic discrimination in the military.

Though native Jews were not unduly disturbed in western countries their immigrant brethren from the East were discriminated against as aliens. Belgium and Turkey expelled such aliens while England finally gave them the option of expulsion or enlistment in the armed services. Many Jewish relief and welfare agencies sprang up at the time to cope with the refugee problem, both in combatant and neutral countries, but their efforts were overshadowed by the unstinting services of relief agencies in America, which were in a better position to help. Most remarkable was the work of the American Joint Distribution Committee, often called "The Joint," organized in 1914.

THE AFTERMATH

The cessation of hostilities, following the usual pattern, only exacerbated the Jews' troubles. They were accused by some of starting the war, by others of losing it. And as postwar nationalist tempers rose, Jews were ostracized from the common life. Again the first backlash came from Russia. The Revolution of 1917, which granted Jews civil equality, was heralded with premature joy. The overthrow of Kerensky's moderate regime by the Bolsheviks in the following year was destined to bring trouble to Jews everywhere. The prominence of several Jews like Trotsky, Kamenev, Radek, and Zinoviev in the Bolshevik revolution was immediately seized upon as proof that Bolshevism was Jewish in origin and nature. After that, there was hardly a country where antisemites did not use this charge to the full, adding details from local situations.[2] The fact that Jewish leaders in the revolution were alienated Jews, that they were later liquidated, that the vast majority of Jews in Russia and elsewhere were either Social-Democrats or non-Communist had little influence on the course of the charge.

In the civil war between the White and Red Armies (1918-20), Jews were caught between the hammer and the anvil: Each side attacked them as enemies of its particular revolution, but they suffered more from the White forces, who fought Jews as strenuously as they did the Reds. Lenin, recognizing antisemitism as a device of reaction, outlawed pogroms, but the Red armies could not so easily overcome their instinctive and traditional anti-Jewish feelings or their estimate of Jews as bourgeois oppressors. Lenin's policy merely added to the Red stigma attached to Jews by antisemites and further embittered the White revolutionaries. The worst excesses occurred in the Ukraine under Hetman Petlyura and General Denikin where "the Orthodox Jewish masses to which Bolshevism was a godless abomination were put to the sword as—Bolsheviks."[3] Valentin gives this description of the horrors:

> To save ammunition soldiers often used only cold steel. Thus the Jews were literally butchered by the thousands. The troops went systematically to work, street by street, and the butchers, or ravishers as the case might be, distinguished themselves by a bestiality scarcely ever surpassed. It was considered a mercy to be killed outright instead of being gradu-

ally tortured to death. A father gave all he possessed that his son might "only" be shot. Parents were forced to witness the torturing of their children, children that of parents. One's pen refuses to record the atrocities committed upon women . . . .[4]

No less than 60,000 Jews were killed, and many more wounded.

THE PEACE

The peace conference at Versailles in 1919 was anxiously awaited by Jews in all countries; and their delegates combined their efforts to beseech the peacemakers to procure or protect Jewish rights in the various treaties. That the efforts of delegations coming from so many different places and conditions were rent by conflicts is not surprising. In general, eastern Jews insisted on "minority rights" permitting them to preserve their religious and ethnic traditions intact, while Jews of the western countries were satisfied to seek equal citizenship. Almost all pressed for incorporation of the Balfour Declaration (1917), a British statement that enunciated the principle of a "national Jewish home" in Palestine. In the end the various peace treaties guaranteed both equal civil rights and "minority rights" but deferred the Zionist question. This question was not settled until, in 1920, the San Remo Conference granted the British a mandate over Palestine on the basis of the Balfour principle. At this point, Arab rioting in Jerusalem had already begun, and it soon became apparent that the Zionist experiment had a rocky road to travel.

If the peace treaties brought little more than a truce to the world, they brought even less to the Jews. It was not from Versailles but the Ukraine that the cue was taken for the interwar era, and the guarantees of minority and equal rights were hastily sabotaged. A general recrudescence of antisemitism took place in almost all countries with Jewish communities. Many facts conspired to produce that unrest and insecurity which invariably proves fertile soil for the antisemitic seed; unstable new states, inflation, immigration barriers, and the growth of Communist and Nazi propaganda. To these may be added the prominence

Jews had attained both in nationalist and Communist politics. The very presence of Jews at or near the helm of the new governments, especially the Communist ones, paved the way for the heyday the *Protocols of the Elders of Zion* enjoyed during these years. Reciprocally, the *Protocols* riveted the attention of antisemites on the rise of these few Jewish leaders.

In newly-formed Poland, where some 3,500,000 Jews still lived, Jews soon learned that they had merely passed from one kind of oppression to another. In their revived nationalist fervor, the Poles looked on unassimilated Jews as strangers and proceeded to squeeze them out of the national economy. In the Galician part of the country several pogroms erupted and during the war with Russia in 1919, as the conviction spread that godless Bolshevism was a Jewish movement, there were more. Only the concern of President Wilson and some of the Allied governments brought the onslaught to a halt. Still, for years after, sporadic assaults continued. In the universities a system of *numerus clausus* was practiced whereby registrations were restricted and special seats assigned. It is true that here, as in Germany, Jews—anxious to become Europeanized and conditioned by a religious tradition devoted to creating "an aristocracy of learning"—applied to higher institutions of learning in excess of their ratio to the population.[5] This development aroused nationalist suspicions and resentments; and it tended to foster the charge of Jewish domination of professional life, a charge that Nazi Germany was to spotlight later. When General Pilsudski assumed power in 1926, antisemitic violence ended but the policy of impoverishment—called the "cold pogrom"—continued to the point of destitution for tens of thousands of Polish Jews. When the depression of 1929 struck, one million Jews were unemployed.

Romania's endemic Judaeophobia was little affected by the provisions of the minority treaty. Its ink was hardly dry when, despite protests from the Allied governments, 200,000 Jews—former immigrants—were denationalized. Jewish educational and welfare activities were disallowed, and in the university the *numerus clausus* was applied. Nativist groups attacked Jews everywhere with the complicity of the police. After a brief respite under the Maniu government (1928-30) a new antisemitic campaign in the thirties served to distract attention from the country's unsettled and uneven economic conditions.

Postwar developments in Hungary were fateful for Jews of all provinces. This battered country fell into the clutches of a Red dictatorship in 1918 under Bela Kuhn, a Jewish parvenu, who brought other Jews into his cabinet but struck down so-called capitalist Jews in his purges at the same time. When his regime fell in 1919 a white terror under Admiral Horthy replaced it and Jews suffered grievously. They were not allowed to forget that Kuhn was a Jew by birth, and antisemites missed no opportunity to din into the ear of the populace that Bolshevism was a Jewish invention. No attention was paid to the fact that Jews had been well integrated into the Hungarian national life for many generations, and that Jews as well as Gentiles suffered in Kuhn's purges. In 1919 some 5,000 Jews were slain in riots and massacres and many more injured while thousands were variously humiliated and ostracized. When this terror ceased the usual chauvinistic measures continued to dog Jewish life in commerce and education; riots and harassments sprang up sporadically. In 1925 antisemitism was condemned by the government, and Jews enjoyed a brief relief. But when the depression came and Nazism took root, a new wave of antisemitic agitation propelled Hungary toward the Hitlerian camp.

In Austria anti-Jewish violence occurred immediately after the war, and with the victory of the Christian Socialist Party the government included many antisemites. Jews were excluded from the government; strong antisemitic pressures were applied in the universities. Even the socialist Viennese government, with Jewish leaders like Viktor Adler and Otto Bauer, brought no lessening of Jewish troubles. In other countries, with the exception of Germany,[6] antisemitism was less general and severe. Czechoslovakia, after some difficulties during the formation of the new state, quit Jew-baiting, thanks to Thomas Masaryk's leadership, and saw its steady decline until Hitler's coup.

Quite opposite was the case of Salonika, a Greek possession since 1912. This age-old city, more than sixty per cent Jewish, was systematically de-Judaized. Having economic difficulties of their own, the Greeks purported to make it a "Greek" city at the expense of the Jews. In Bavaria, Jews were smeared with a Red brush in the wake of the socialist uprising in which Kurt Eisner, a Communist Jew, served as Prime Minister for a few months until his assassination. A pacifist, Eisner blamed Germany for the war and thus earned another accusation of "disloyalty" for his people. Turkey, smarting under defeat in the war and spurred to a new nationalist spirit by Mustafa Kemal Pasha, set out to Ottomanize its territory and in so doing showed little regard for the Jews, who had been woven into the fabric of the country for centuries. Restrictions, pressures, and even riots forced a majority of the Jews out of the country and made life miserable for those who remained. In Muslim lands generally, anti-Zionism fanned out from Palestine once the Jewish state became a possibility. There were restrictions and pogroms in the Moroccos, Algiers, Tunis, and Tripoli as the Hitlerian era approached. Anti-Zionism and Fascism combined to make the Near East a cauldron of anti-Jewish feeling that would survive even the Nazis. In Italy there was practically no antisemitism. In his early years, Mussolini termed antisemitism a "product of barbarism," but in 1937 the dictator did an about-face when he turned Italy into a Nazi minion. In France where Jews were an intimate part of the nation, there was little antisemitism. The literary Jew-baiting of Léon Daudet and Maurice Barrès was more than offset by the nation-wide adulation of the philosopher, Henri Bergson, the choice of Léon Blum as premier in 1936, and by the 1926 acquittal (after thirty minutes' deliberation) of a Parisian Jew who had assassinated Petlyura, the scourge of Jews in the Ukraine. Belgium saw anti-Jewish commotions in 1931 and the formation of a Nazi party by Léon DeGrelle in 1936. England, which had been a refuge for Jews from the East and an outspoken contemnor of antisemitic tyranny in Europe, remained faithful to democratic ideals with minor exceptions. There was a flurry about the *Protocols* in the twenties and then the thin, detached sort of antisemitism of G. K. Chesterton and Hilaire Belloc. The most serious breach came in 1932 when Sir Oswald Mosley organized his Fascist brigade on the Nazi model. It agitated and postured until 1936, when a bill was passed prohibiting uniformed organizations that simulated police powers.

ANOTHER PRELUDE TO DISASTER

Antisemitism in the interwar period manifested most of the traditional characteristics. The religious motive was weak, except in Poland and Hungary, where it took the form of reaction to "godless Bolshevism." Economic antisemitism, which was strong, stemmed from prevailing conditions. The war and its resultant upheavals left all countries in a desperate struggle for solvency; competition from a supposedly alien and active minority like the Jews was sure to be resented. This resentment was aggravated by the nationalist surge during and after the war which took exception to all elements that seemed to offend against national solidarity. For the moment, save in Germany, the racial obsession diminished only to be replaced by an academic antisemitism which reigned in the universities. There, chauvinist and conservative intellectuals, much as in Greco-Roman days, set themselves up as defenders of the spirit and traditions of the nation against inroads of change. The most significant antisemitic growth was political. Demagogues and assorted patriots, seeking extraneous causes for the frustrations and failures of these terrible times, pounced upon the ready-made scapegoat, the Jews. Incriminating them was greatly facilitated by the spectacular ties of a number of Jews with the Communist International and by the vogue enjoyed by the conspiracy theory popularized by the propagandists of the *Protocols*. In default of an effective program of reconstruction, what simpler expedient for ignoring myriad economic and political problems than dispossessing or neutralizing the Jews?

Though more than one government succumbed to this facile ruse, they were unable to stop the progress of Jewry. Despite all harassments Jews not only survived but advanced the cause of their complete emancipation and Europeanization. Before Hitler struck, they had entered into the mainstream of the cultural, economic, and political life of nations to a degree that is astonishing in light of the attendant conditions. Suffice it to point out that of the thirty-eight Nobel Prize winners before Hitler, eleven were Jews, or refer to the level of influence of an Einstein, a Freud, and a Bergson. Salo Baron does not hesitate to write: "On balance, future historians are likely to call the first third of the twentieth century the golden age of Ashkenazi Jewry in Europe, just as they will see in it the beginning of the modern Sephardi renaissance."[7] And, in truth, in the early thirties, the prognosis of Jewish recovery was, despite ominous developments in Germany and Russia, excellent. But the powers of destruction were already in motion, and who at that point could foresee the madness that would seize the world and destroy almost one third of all Jews?

11
THE FINAL SOLUTION

The chronicler of antisemitism is beset at every turn with the problem of superlatives. Long before reaching the contemporary scene, he has exhausted his supply and has been forced to re-enlist many for double duty, certainly at the risk of straining the reliance of his reader. The problem is not only verbal but real. From the first literary strictures against Judaism in ancient and early Christian times to almost any major manifestation of anti-Jewish animus in a later epoch, a crescendo in violence has unfolded. The progression from early riots to the Crusades, to the Black Death, to Chmielnicki, to Czarist pogroms, to World War I has comprised an ascent in horrors, each grade of which promised to be the upper limit but which unfailingly paled before what followed.

With the coming of Hitler the problem is infinitely aggravated, for suddenly events no longer resemble those of the past and the usual comparisons no longer convey the new realities. To say, for an example, that Hitler's persecution of the Jews is unparalleled in Jewish history is a trite understatement when we consider that it may very well be "unprecedented in history" altogether.[1]

Some writers circumvent the difficulty by simply calling the period "The Catastrophe" or "The Holocaust," signifying that for Jews the Nazi persecution was the ultimate in disasters. Less close to the horrendous happenings—and thus more easily taken in by the banality of words describing the events—the non-Jew may fail to comprehend the gigantic and the grotesque character of a persecution that became an inverted religion, the chief catalyst in the building of a fearsome totalitarian regime, a dominant of international politics, and the first experiment in total genocide. Thus in approaching Hitlerian antisemitism a shift of focus is necessary for the reader, while for the historian there is a problem of communicating and evaluating in a new dimension. A historian may ask, moreover, whether the fact that the postwar world has not grasped the magnitude of Nazi antisemitism—as the quibbling over the Eichmann trial has amply shown[2]—may not in itself point to an unrecognized antisemitism.

THE ROOTS OF GENOCIDE

The extreme unrest in interwar Germany could hardly be expected not to revive antisemitism in this favored spawning ground of anti-Jewish activity. Humiliated by the loss of the war and crushed by reparations imposed by the Versailles Treaty, the nation was plagued by an economic depression that led to the disastrous inflation of 1923. The middle class was ruined and unemployment widespread and chronic. The instrument created to cope with this deeply troubled period was the Weimar Republic. Though a sturdy democratic structure on paper, this ill-starred government, born in humiliation and confusion, failed to rally support from large segments of German society and lacked the necessary forcefulness in dealing with both its enemies and its problems. The *Junkers,* the military, the industrialists, and the laboring class—each pursuing its own particular interests— tended to look upon the new government as anti-nationalist and too attentive to Allied powers. In growing despair many looked about for some face-saving explanation for German misfortune and a new promise of national salvation. Neither was hard to find. A revival of antisemitism provided the first: the Jews; and the rise of a fierce nationalism produced the second: National Socialism and Adolf Hitler.

Jews were blamed for every ill: the loss of the war, the *Diktat* of Versailles, and the inflation, from which Jews were said to have profiteered.[3] In short, they were accused of the "stab in the back" from which Germany lay prostrate. Another cause for the rise of antisemitism was an influx of eastern Jews at this time, who were looked on as aliens and suspected of swindling. Later studies showed that the influx had been fantastically exaggerated in the anti-Jewish propaganda and few if any of them were implicated in financial manipulations. On the other hand, in this age of the *Protocols* all Jews, though the large majority espoused middle-class values, were suspected of ties with Communism, which was commonly referred to as "Jewish Bolshevism."

This many-sided rise of anti-Jewish feeling merged with the general antipathy to the liberal Weimar Republic, which came to be known as the "Jew Republic." Hugo Preuss, a Jew, had drawn up its constitution in which the old imperial ban on Jews in public office was abolished; its first efficient and devoted foreign minister, Walther Rathenau, was also Jewish. These were reasons enough for the antisemites to impugn the government as a tool of a Jewish conspiracy against Germany. The prominence that a highly integrated German Jewry had attained in many spheres of German life added fuel to the fire. Their prominence was easily translated into "domination." True, Jews—for historical reasons—were overrepresented in commerce and in some areas of the nation's professional life, but there was no justification for the outlandish exaggerations of antisemitic propaganda which "proved" statistically that Jews "dominated" commerce, medicine, law, the press, and the theater.[4]

Emerging from the seething ferment were a number of extremist and semimilitary organizations, nationalist and anti-republican in character, which recruited their numbers chiefly from among the young and the unemployed. One of these, the National Socialist German Workers' Party (Nazi), was destined to change the face of the earth before two decades had passed. Formed in 1919, this small group, whose seventh member was Adolf Hitler, dedicated itself to the rebirth of the German nation along totalitarian and racial lines.

From the start, the Nazi party pursued a strong antisemitic policy and in 1920 incorporated seven planks in its platform which, in sum, called for denial of citizenship and public office to Jews, expulsion of Jews who had immigrated since 1914 (an exception later repealed), exclusion of Jews from the press, and categorizing all German Jews as "foreigners" and "guests" of the nation. The emblem chosen for the party was the swastika, erroneously thought to be an Aryan symbol.

The growth of the Party was extraordinary. By 1923 it had 20,000 members, and in 1930 captured 107 seats in the Reichstag election, polling nearly 2,500,000 votes. Its adherents were the young, the unemployed, and the disaffected. These last are divisible into two main groups: the anti-Weimarist malcontents and the pan-Germanists. The latter comprised a conglomeration of racists and militarists who were infected with the old Teutomania and drew their sustenance variously from the superman philosophy of Nietzsche, the Aryanism of Chamberlain *et al.*, the neopaganism of the Wagnerian group at Bayreuth, the anti-democratism of Spengler, and the Prussian militarism—all of which anticipated a triumphant destiny for the German *Volk*. The Nazis apparently had discovered the secret of the radical and romantic temper of these bedeviled times.

Throughout the twenties the rise of the Party paralleled a tragic decline of Jewish status. Nazi ruffians roamed the streets agitating against Jews, singing antisemitic songs, and daubing Jewish property with obscenities, and antisemitic pamphlets proliferated. Rathenau was murdered in 1923 by two zealots who fancied that he was one of the "Elders of Zion." Between 1923 and 1932 one hundred and twenty-eight Jewish cemeteries and fifty synagogues were desecrated. Meanwhile, Jews were gradually elbowed out of economic and social life, while a species of "re-ghettoizing" was effected. On another level there was the cultural attack. Jewish artists and writers were openly derided; and a movement was launched to establish a Teutonic neo-paganism in the place of Christianity as well as of Judaism.

THE ARCHITECT AND HIS PLAN

Nazism's victorious advance was due, more than to any other factor, to its evil genius, Adolf Hitler. This Austrian firebrand, well endowed with organizing skill and demagogic gifts, took control of the Party almost from the outset, organizing an armed guard and exhibiting a recklessness of speech and purpose that overwhelmed his associates. He added little that was original to the Party's ideology[5] but reinforced its antisemitism with a fanaticism he had nurtured in Vienna under the influence of Karl Lueger and Georg von Shoenerer.[6] In 1923 he led an abortive *putsch* against the Bavarian government in Munich and landed in jail. There he wrote the Nazi bible, *Mein Kampf*. This book, an autobiography and a program, expostulates in a turgid and repetitious style, well embroidered with vulgarities, the blueprint of the Nazi plan for propagandizing the masses against the menaces of Marxism, Socialism, democracy and, above all, world Jewry.[7] On release from prison, Hitler, now something of a hero, took charge of the Nazi drive for power. He harangued the masses and shortly became the foremost issue in Germany. The depression of 1928 assured his ultimate victory. Hundreds of thousands flocked to his banner until in 1933 President von Hindenburg was constrained to offer him the chancellorship. He accepted and, calling an election against a background of terrorist tactics and a planned Reichstag fire, he succeeded in winning fifty-two per cent of the vote. With this victory he demanded and received full dictatorial power as *Fuehrer* of the German nation. The fate of European Jewry was sealed—as was that of the world.

The rapidity of Hitler's rise to power has raised the question of his appeal. How did this man, mediocre in so many ways, so quickly attract to his standard such disparate elements as laborers and industrialists, *Junkers* and intellectuals, socialists and capitalists, radicals and conservatives, young and old, even religious leaders, particularly in a nation where many other competing groups preached substantially the same radicalism and nationalist romanticism as he?[8] Political intrigue, of which there was plenty, cannot explain it adequately. There can be no doubt that his hypnotic influence over the masses was an important factor. His mastery of crowd psychology is clearly seen in *Mein Kampf*,[9] but more effectively still in his obvious ability to turn huge throngs into roaring submission. Nor is there any doubt that Hitler told his hearers much of what they wanted to hear. But, all things considered, the one catalyst that above all else enabled him to reconcile oppositions and finally transform Germany from a liberal republic into a totalitarian state in a single decade was his antisemitism.[10]

Though it had many precursors in the nineteenth century,

Hitlerian or Nazi antisemitism was something beyond the older kind, which for the most part constituted little more than a reaction against liberalism or an expression of nationalist or racial aspirations. This radical and nihilistic Jew-hatred preached with a boundless fury and coarseness was new.[11] No longer was the Jew a mere scapegoat or member of an inferior race, but the cause of every problem, the destroyer, the poisoner of Aryan blood, the epitome of evil. And he was all this inherently and uneradicably; neither baptism nor renunciation of Judaism could redeem him. The solution to the Jewish problem was also new and simple, and concisely summarized in the Nazi slogan, *Juda Verrecke!* (Jewry perish!).

Here at last was a transcendental antisemitism that lent itself to every purpose, that appealed to all sections of German society. The Jew, identified with both a "parasitic capitalism" and a menacing Marxism, was at the root of debilitating liberalism, the hated Weimar Republic, the Versailles Treaty, not to mention immorality, inflation, racial corruption, and irreligion. Cleanse the country of Jews and there would be jobs for the unemployed, outlets for professional talent, a new world for youth; industrialists would be more secure in their profits, German maidens would be safe, German nationalism would thrive, and Aryan blood would remain uncontaminated. Indeed the Almighty Himself would be pleased: Hitler did not fail to woo the Christians and assure them in *Mein Kampf:* "I believe that I am today acting in accordance with the will of the Almighty Creator: by defending myself against the Jew I am fighting for the work of the Lord."[12]

The days of the Almighty in the Nazi pantheon were numbered, however, since Christianity as well as Judaism stood in the way of Hitler's designs on the human mind and spirit. More and more, the *Fuehrer* and his theoreticians veered toward a pantheistic apotheosis of race; more and more, Nazism took on the features of a religion, subsuming a cryptic theology and way of salvation that left no room for true religious spirit or practice. Pure Aryan blood was the new God and the German *Volk* his incarnation. The new devil was the Jew, incarnation of the anti-race, the ultimate embodiment of evil. Salvation rested in the avoidance of racial impurity and total submission to the *Fuehrer,* the Savior, for whom life itself must be sacrificed on demand. The ultimate limit of antisemitism—as an *ersatz* religion—was reached.[13]

Did Hitler believe in these extravagant implications of his propaganda and program? It is certain that he was aware of the pragmatic value of his antisemitic policies as a political unifying force,[14] but it is equally certain that of all his convictions his antisemitism was the most durable, as can be readily seen in his writings, wherein his excoriations of Jewry are unrelieved. It may be seen in the fact, apparent further on, that he actually allowed his supreme war effort to suffer from his pursuance of the "final solution of the Jewish problem." But no conceivably better proof is there than the incredible restatements of policy in his last will and testament written in 1945 in the Berlin bunker that would on the morrow be his grave. In the first section entitled "Political Testament," he attacks "international Jewry" time and time again, and in the second concludes:

> Above all I enjoin the government and the people to uphold
> the racial laws to the limit and to resist mercilessly the poi-
> soner of all nations, international Jewry.[15]

Never had such a monomania so engrossed a man in whose hands the power to destroy was so great.

What is true of Hitler's obsessive antisemitism to a considerable extent was true of most of his closest associates of the Nazi regime, with the possible exception of Hermann Goering, a clever careerist who, playing his Nazism like a game of cards, was antisemitic according to policy. Joseph Goebbels, propagandist to the masses; Alfred Rosenberg, in charge of the intellectual brainwashing; Julius Streicher, pornographic editor of the newspaper *Der Sturmer;* R. Walter Darre, minister of agriculture; and Heinrich Himmler, commander of the police—to a man these were ferocious antisemites in need of little coaxing from Hitler to abuse Jewry each according to his role and talent.

THE DIALETICS OF GENOCIDE

With Hitler's assumption of total power in March 1933, the Jewish agony began, taking the form of a progressive terror which stretched over twelve years. At the beginning, there was a pretense of legality, an affectation of national self-defense, a simulation of popular spontaneity in the measures taken. A few weeks after the assumption of power, the program accelerated and progressed, in general, from ostracism to impoverishment, impoverishment to expulsion and finally from expulsion to extermination. There were several reasons for the gradual approach. A too hasty attack on Jews would have offended German public opinion and invited international reactions, eventualities the new regime wished as yet to avoid. There were also dangers of inflicting economic hardships on Germans by precipitate action. And, of course, there was need of keeping the Jew present as a scapegoat. As these reasons played themselves out, the death-knell of Jewry sounded.

But even the year 1933 was a dreadful one for German Jews. Before the government acted, Nazi storm troops, police, and Party members took things into their own hands. Outrages against Jews, including beatings and killings, became regular occurrences. In preparation for the government's first large-scale move, the propaganda mills ground out a barrage of complaints and threats concerning the Jews' role in the economic life of the nation. Then on April 1st a general boycott, organized and enforced by Party troops, was staged. The government pointed to it as a spontaneous popular demonstration against "Jewish domination." The boycott, which lasted only a day, was actually a dress-rehearsal for a permanent "quiet" boycott aimed at the complete ruin of Jews. Protests were heard from several countries.

A few days later, the progressive elimination of "non-Aryans" from public life commenced. The process began with civil service posts. Commenting on the action Hitler asserted that the Jews held a majority of civil service positions—a fair sample of the big lie. Next, the "non-Aryan" test was applied to the hospitals, the courts, the government, education, the cultural life, and even sports. Jewish lawyers, doctors, scholars, and artists were ostracized; universities were allotted a quota for Jews (1 1/2%), and the press was "de-Judaized." Jewish teachers were dismissed; Jewish children were taunted in class by pupils and teachers and often returned home pale and shaken. "Non-Aryan" was defined legally as a person with one Jewish grandparent in order to affect many more than the full-blooded Jews in Germany.[16] Thousands of thoroughly integrated Jews—some of them Christians—who had no contact with Judaism found themselves cut adrift. Jewish books were collected by Storm troops and burned in a public spectacle at which Goebbels addressed the crowd. A yellow badge was imposed, and Jewish shops and offices were marked with a "J" or "*Jude.*" Before 1933 was over German Jews were a community of "despairing men, weeping women and terror-stricken children."[17] Suicides—not allowed to be publicized—were frequent, and emigrations began, reaching some 50,000 by the fall of 1933. Emigrants included Albert Einstein, whose life had been threatened, and several Nobel prize winners.

In September 1935 the Nuremberg Laws, announced at a Nazi rally, cancelled the citizenship of all Jews, forbade marriage or sexual intercourse between Jews and Aryans as well as the employment by Jews of Aryan women under forty. Nazi propaganda duly accused Jews of sexual designs on German women. Nazi fanatics added contributions of their own by forming Aryan associations which denounced and reviled Jews everywhere.

Extraordinary efforts were made by the propaganda ministry to mask these brutalities or to give them an allure of rationality. In addition to Goebbels' outpourings to the German masses—through the press, pamphlets, schools, and speakers' platforms—propaganda on a "scientific" level was organized under Rosenberg. He set out to win the intellectuals, indoctrinate the oncoming generation, and prepare Nazi antisemitism for export. Professors were appointed in the universities to lecture on the "science of race" and the supposed superiority of the Aryan to the Jewish race, spirit, and scholarship. A number of research projects on Judaism and Jewry were established, and an Institute of Research on Judaism featured a library of 350,000 volumes on Judaism amassed for documenting antisemitic measures and laws. Even Streicher employed a staff of experts on Judaism for culling materials for his scurrilous attacks. In the wake of Nazi military advances chairs on Judaism and race were established in universities of Paris, Cracow, Lodz, and finally Italy. Meanwhile, contacts with Nazi groups in many countries of Europe, Arab territories, and America were diligently used to implant the antisemitic virus abroad. The little difficulty the Nazis had in founding their "science of race" among so many German intellectuals and scientists forms a melancholy chapter in the history of this macabre period. The cowardice of the intellectual community accounts to a considerable extent for the acquiescence of the German people to Nazi standards and to the postwar recrudescence of antisemitism.

Only a swiftly moving summary of the anti-Jewish events of the last half of this decade is possible here. Racial antisemitism, intimately woven into German life at that juncture, had a wild growth. Established social and economic ostracisms and brutalities continued. Anti-Jewish riots, often ensuing from a Nazi speech or rally, were frequent, and Jews were humiliated at every turn. New measures were taken. Jews were forbidden to play the music of Bach, Beethoven, Mozart, and other German composers. They were required to add the names "Israel" and "Sarah" to their names on all records. A rewriting of history was undertaken by a "race bureau," which tied all the would-be misfortunes of history to the Jews. An antisemitic handbook was distributed to teachers. And so it went.

One can imagine the mentality of the Jews living under this terror. Many feared to appear on the street by day and, so frequent were the arrests, many, unable to sleep, walked the streets at night or sought shelter with friends or relatives. At one point the suicide rate rose to twenty per day. Few were those who still believed that "the storm would pass." After the enactment of the Nuremberg Laws, the number of emigrations continued to rise, reaching a total of 215,000 persons by 1939. But even departure from the country was beset with obstacles. Not content with the expulsion of its Jews, the government sought to profit by it, taxing emigrants twenty-five per cent of their income and in 1938 prohibiting them from taking a mark out of the country—a measure inspired as much by the wish to make them unwelcome elsewhere as to profit by their departure.

The year 1938 marks the high point of the Jewish ordeal prior to the extermination program. Over 300,000 Jews were still in the country, some still eking out a living. These more fortunate ones irked the Nazi overlords, who contemplated the total destitution of German Jewry. In April it was decreed that all Jewish assets in excess of 5,000 marks should be registered, an obvious preliminary to future appropriations. All that was needed now was an occasion to strike, and this was not long in coming. Hitler's dramatic and successful bullying of England and France at Munich in September put an end to whatever scruples he still had concerning international reaction to his antisemitic program. In response to an ultimatum of Poland to her subjects abroad that they obtain special visas immediately—obviously in order to exile most of them—the Nazi government rounded up all Polish Jews in its confines in a single raid and literally dumped 12,000 of them on the Polish border. Five thousand of these, having failed to find aid from philanthropic organizations, remained in a pitiably exposed condition for weeks while negotiations on their fate went on.

One family thus treated had a seventeen-year-old son in Paris, Herschel Grynspan. Distraught by his family's plight, Grynspan took revenge on the Nazis by shooting Ernst vom Rath, a minor Nazi official in the Paris embassy, who died on November 9, two days later. This was the awaited occasion, the perfect pretext for stepping up the antisemitic timetable, the first two stages of which—impoverishment and expulsion—had not yet been completed. In a rage Goebbels decried Vom Rath's death as a defiant counter-attack by the international Jewish conspiracy—an interpretation that the extensive grilling of Grynspan by the Parisian police in no way substantiated. The Jews awaited the Nazi vengeance in trepidation. At 1:20 A.M., November 10th, it came. Simultaneously all over Germany the *Krystallnacht*, the night of horror, which the Nazis described as "popular demonstrations," began. The following excerpt provides a glimpse of what happened:

> . . . A nun in one of the hospitals which were soon filled with the maimed and the wounded declared that she had never dreamed that men could do such things; she felt as though she were in a slaughterhouse. The attacks on Jewish business establishments went on all through the night, the troopers wearing gloves as protection against flying glass. Goods and furnishings were thrown out into the street. By dawn the crowds that followed the wrecking crews had become so great that the police began to divert traffic. There was much looting

> . . . . At noon the streets where the main Jewish business was
> centered in Berlin looked as if there had been an aerial bom-
> bardment. All through the long day the man-hunt continued.
> Every little while the Jew was seen running, panic-stricken,
> with a Nazi pack in pursuit . . . .[18]

The spirit of the "Isaac affair," as the Nazis designated the pogrom, is caught in one of the announcements given over a loud-
speaker at its height: "Any Jew who intends to hang himself is
requested to have the kindness to place a paper with his name
thereon in his mouth so that we know who he is."[19] The pogrom
lasted until evening, when it stopped as suddenly as it began. The
toll: over 100 dead, 35,000 arrested (many of whom were sent to
concentration camps), 7,500 shops looted, 600 synagogues
burned.[20] Many Germans expressed their horror at what had happened but were reproved in the Nazi press.

The aftermath of the pogrom was used for further impov-
erishing of the Jews. Goering imposed on them the cost of repairs
for the huge property damage, appropriated the indemnity pay-
ments of their insurance policies, and placed a collective fine on
the whole Jewish community of a billion marks. But even this was
not enough. Hitler clearly intended to use the Vom Rath affair to
the full. Jews were forbidden access to certain streets, parks, mu-
seums, and other public places. On January 1, 1939, all Jewish
businesses were liquidated. Thus pauperized, Jews were then
made "hostages" to tap money abroad—money much needed for
rearmament on the eve of World War II. Dr. Hjalmar Schacht
went to London to notify the government there and the League
of Nations of a Nazi proposal to exchange 150,000 Jews over a
period of three years for 1,500,000 marks. Negotiations began but
were never concluded. Hitler moved into Czechoslovakia, then
Poland. The war was on and the Jews were forgotten by the Allied
powers.

The *Krystallnacht* marked a new phase in Nazi antisemitism—and a point of no return. It was a phase characterized by
reckless abandon and an internationalist turn.[21] When the civilized world voiced its shock at the pogrom, Hitler brushed this
off as the machinations of the world Jewry conspiracy. From this
point, he paid no attention to criticism of his antisemitic program.

On the contrary, as in his 1930 attempt to rally all factions in Germany to his standard by an antisemitic appeal, so now he wooed world opinion on similar grounds. He presented himself as a world leader fighting for a new order against the forces of international Jewry which, in league with the Red menace, sought to dominate the world. His conflict was no longer merely between German and Jew, but a cosmic struggle between a Jewish-Bolshevik conspiracy and the civilized world, represented by himself. Every political means was judged in the light of this struggle. Opposition to his efforts Hitler saw as the work either of "Jewish pacifism" or of "Jewish warmongering." Antisemitism thus became a full-blown instrument of international politics. Even enemy or neutral nations were expected to acquiesce, if not cooperate, with his antisemitic campaign. And wherever his armies went the conquered nation was constrained to institute an antisemitic program modeled on that of Germany. In Austria, where 200,000 Jews still lived after the *Anschluss* of 1938, the terror, manned mostly by Austrians, surpassed, if possible, that of Germany. In Czechoslovakia, with over 300,000 Jews, the Nazi program was implemented in a matter of weeks following the take-over of March 1939. After the outbreak of World War II the Nuremberg Laws, ghettoization, the badge of shame, and other antisemitic paraphernalia of oppression employed by the Third Reich were installed on the heels of the *Wehrmacht*. Even before the extermination program formally began, thousands of Jews in Europe thus died of starvation, disease, overwork, and varied abuses.

But Hitler's propaganda was not wholly successful. More than once his anti-Jewish barbarities led to international complications. There were two protests made to the League of Nations, the first contributing toward Germany's withdrawal from the League, the second occasioning the formation of a commission on refugees from Germany under an American high commissioner. On the occasion of the 1938 pogrom Chamberlain expressed his dismay in the House of Commons and President Roosevelt recalled the U.S. Ambassador. Nazi propaganda countered the latter action by claiming that Roosevelt was Jewish. There were anti-German boycotts by labor and liberal groups in Britain and the United States. But Nazi propagandizing had not been without effect. Fascist groups and quislings cropped up in every country, and the antisemitic program enjoyed the complicity of local governments in almost all occupied countries. Indeed it is hardly possible not to discern some degree of antisemitism in the widespread appeasement of Hitler before World War II.

THE SCIENCE AND PRACTICE OF GENOCIDE

Even before the Nazi occupation of the greater part of Europe was accomplished, preparations were under way to render Europe completely free of Jews (*Judenrein*). The expression, "the final solution of the Jewish problem" (*Endlösung*), was in use among Party chieftains from 1938, but at that stage it signified no more than total expulsion. Toward this objective a small bureau was set up in Berlin in January 1939, which at the outbreak of the war in September was incorporated as a sub-division of the Gestapo section of the Reich Main Security Office. It was known as the Bureau IV b, RSHA. The chief of the RSHA was Reinhardt Heydrich, a cold-blooded antisemitic sadist, who was subject to Heinrich Himmler, chief of the political police (SS), directly responsible to Hitler. Section IV b was under the direction of a colorless SS Major named Adolf Eichmann. This unpretentious Berlin office was the heartbeat of the first experiment in total genocide in history.

The operations of the bureau broke into two main stages. The first envisioned the total emigration of European Jewry, which at the outbreak of the war comprised approximately 10,000,000 people, practically half of whom were under Axis domination (some 4,500,000 were still under Russian control). Deportations began at the start of the war. Jews in the main centers were rounded up and transported to a "reservation" at Lublin near the Polish-Russian frontier; those in rural areas were herded into ghettos in large cities, principally Warsaw, Lodz, Cracow, and Kovno. After the conquest of France, the "Madagascar Plan" for the total emigration of Jews to the large African island was worked out with the cooperation of the Vichy regime. These projects, never brought to completion, imperceptibly merged with the second stage of the Final Solution—total extermination.[22] At what moment the genocidal decision was made is not certain, but the end of 1940 or the beginning of 1941 are the most probable dates. The task was handed over to Heydrich, to whom all sections of the government were ordered to give their fullest cooperation. There was little question about the priority enjoyed by Bureau IV b. The greatest secrecy marked the inception and pursuance of the project; at first, even high officials knew little of it. Then vague pronouncements were made.

It is certain that the decision was made by Hitler himself or by him in conjunction with his chief aides—probably Goering, Goebbels, Himmler, and Heydrich. These men were fully cognizant of the extreme gravity of the decision and, reversing the more recent bravado concerning antisemitic policies, they sought in every way to conceal their intent from the German people, from international opinion, and from the Jews themselves. Though oblique hints had been given, it was not until the *Grosse Wannsee* conference in January, 1942, that Heydrich told a few of the Party members of the extermination project. He stated bluntly that Jews who survived the sundry murderous measures planned for them "must be dealt with accordingly," since they must not be allowed to go free. A year later Himmler addressed a small group on the Final Solution and said: "We have written a page of glory in our history, but it must never be put on paper."[23] Not until the Nuremberg trials did some of the details of the decision and the magnitude of its prosecution come to light.

Though conceived in Berlin the extermination program began in Russia and progressed westward. When he planned the Russian offensive, Hitler himself gave the order that all Communist officials and all Jews were to be killed. For the latter assignment a special contingent in the SS, the *Einsatzgruppen*, was organized. These exterminators followed the lightning advance of the *Wehrmacht*, which entrapped 1,500,000 Jews in Nazi toils; another 2,000,000 escaped to the East. The *Einsatzgruppen* acquitted themselves of their task with dispatch, using non-Germans, even Jews, for rounding up and disposing of their quarry. Their methods were simple—machine-gunning and mass burial.

One of the documents discovered at the close of the war over the name of a certain Hermann Graebe gives a description of a scene of October 5, 1942:

. . . We went directly to the trenches without trouble. As we approached the embankment, I heard a rapid succession of machine gun fire. The people, who had left the trucks—men, women, and children—were forced to undress under the surveillance of an SS soldier, whip in hand. They were obliged to deposit their effects in certain places: shoes, clothing and linens separately. I saw a heap of shoes, about 800 to 1,000 pairs and a large pile of underwear and clothing. Without weeping or murmuring, these people undressed and stood about in family groups, embracing one another and making the last farewells while waiting for the signal from the SS soldier who stood at the edge of the trench, whip still in hand. For the quarter of an hour that I stayed there I did not hear a single complaint or plea for mercy. I watched a family of about eight members, a man and wife of about 50 years of age, encircled by their children of about one, eight and ten years, and two older daughters of about twenty and twenty-four. An old white-haired lady held the baby in her arms, rocking it and singing it a song. The parents watched the group with tears in their eyes. The father held the ten-year-old boy by the hand and spoke to him softly. The little fellow struggled against his tears. Then the father lifted his finger toward the sky, caressed the boy's head and seemed to explain something to him. At this moment the SS man who stood near the ditch called out several words to his comrade. The latter counted off a score of persons and ordered them to go behind the embankment. The family of which I have been speaking was among the group. I still remember the young daughter, a slim brunette, who as she passed very close to me identified herself with her finger and said, "Twenty-three." I went around the embankment and found myself in front of a horrendous common grave. Tightly packed bodies were piled one upon the other in such a way that only the heads were visible. Almost all had a head wound with blood flowing onto their shoulders. A few still were moving. Others lifted their hands and turned their heads to show that they were still alive. The trench was about two-thirds filled. I put the number of bodies at about a thousand. I looked for the man who had performed the execution. He was an SS soldier. He sat, legs dangling, on the narrow edge of the trench. A machine gun was placed on his knees and he was smoking a cigarette. The people, completely naked, descended a few steps dug in the clay wall of the trench and took the place indicated by the SS man. Lined up in front of the dead and wounded, they spoke to them quietly. Then I heard a series of shots . . . . On the way back, as I circled the embankment I saw a new truck filled with people that had just arrived . . . . This time it contained only sick and invalids. Some women, already naked, were in the process of undressing an old woman, whose body was fleshless and whose legs were of a frightful thinness. She seemed to be paralyzed and was held by two persons. The naked ones led her toward the embankment . . . .[24]

The scene was multiplied month after month. Then in 1942 "gas trucks" arrived from Germany. Asphyxiation—Hitler's suggestion—was more efficient and less bloody. By 1943 the task was fairly complete, and the RSHA turned to the problem of destroying the traces of their accomplishments by fire and dynamite. Eichmann placed the number of dead in the Soviet Union at 2,000,000, but more reliable statisticians place it at 1,500,000 or less.

How did the *Wehrmacht* react to the atrocities? Their orders were not to interfere with the work of the *Einsatzgruppen*. Most generals, it seems, maintained a passive attitude, but some cooperated actively. Only a few showed disapproval. Von Rundstedt, for one, forbade his soldiers to take part in it or to photograph the hecatombs, doubtless in order to maintain the secrecy of the operation. The military, too, had learned their lessons well about the "race of monkeys" in human form.

The liquidation of Polish Jews comprised act two of the hideous drama. They had been crowded into the large city ghettoes— 500,000 into the Warsaw ghetto, which ordinarily held 145,000. The first extermination efforts were informal. Jews were given 800 calories a day and trading was forbidden, so that before long as many as thirty per cent of the ghetto populations died of starvation or disease. But this death rate was not fast enough for the Nazi schedule. Death camps were organized, principally at Chelmo, Maidanek, Treblinka, Belzec, Sobibor, and the transfer from the ghettoes to the camps began at a rate of as many as 10,000 a day. Only top military priorities were allowed to interfere with this cargo.

The first operations were of the most brutal kind. The following account of an evacuation of Zamosc is an illustration:

> . . . The brutes on horseback in particular created panic.
> They raced through the streets hurling insults, lashing left
> and right with their whips . . . In the twinkling of an eye,
> before they could realize what was happening, a crowd of
> 3,000 people, men, women, and children, caught by surprise
> in the street, were chased toward the railroad station and de-
> ported to an unknown destination . . . The sight the ghetto
> presented after the assault drove the survivors almost mad
> with horror. The killed were everywhere, in the streets, the
> courtyards, and inside the house. Babies thrown from the sec-
> ond and third floor lay crushed on the pavement. The Jews
> themselves had to gather up and bury the dead.[25]

As time went on these savage round-ups gave way to ruses designed to induce compliance in the victims, such as falsifying pictures and forging postcards from "resettled" relatives. Thus were the victims persuaded that they were being transported to other places with improved working and living conditions; in other words, "resettled."

Despite these exertions, by mid-1942 there were still 2,000,000 Polish Jews alive; whereupon the program was given the benefits of German science. Experts came from Germany to improve on the "gas trucks," now worn out and obsolete. A refined production was finally devised by the scientists and the engineers of the *Wehrmacht*—a bunker equipped with "shower rooms" for asphyxiation and a second level for cremation. When Jews arrived at the camps, they were stripped and divided into two groups. Those with sufficient vitality left were ranged in a queue reserved for those destined to slave labor for a few months preceding their extermination. The weaker ones were asked to deposit their eyeglasses, false teeth, watches, and other valuables for "safe-keeping"—the doomed were expected to pay for their extermination. Many of them entered the "shower rooms" still unsuspecting of their fate. The frightful scenes within the chambers have been described and can scarcely be imagined. In 1943, as the military situation worsened in Russia, the operation was speeded up and in the following year the few remaining Jews were sent to

Auschwitz for gassing. No Jews were to fall into Russian or Allied hands.

Adolf Eichmann took personal charge of the extermination program in Europe west of Poland, possibly because he considered the task there more delicate than that in the East. This man had been appointed by Heydrich—now assassinated—to take general direction of the IV b program, but he had left its execution in the East to others. Since the chances that the extermination program might be discovered were greater in the West, increased caution was necessary. Native German Jews were sent to the camp at Theresienstadt for slave labor where conditions were a trifle more humane than elsewhere, but at the end they were not spared. The rest, for the greater part, were transported to Maidanek, Belzec, and Treblinka, camps considered a safe distance from German eyes. By the end of 1942 the Greater Reich was "cleansed of Jews." Those of the occupied countries were usually sent to Auschwitz, an enormous and well-disguised camp in southern Poland in Rudolph Hoess' charge where it was possible to cremate 10,000 corpses a day. The torture and inhuman conditions in this infamous place were such that a majority of the more than 2,000,000 Jews who died there did so before they ever got to the gas chambers. Another million or more non-Jews also died at Auschwitz.

NO GREATER LOVE

In the occupied countries of *Festung Europa*, Eichmann was less squeamish and evacuated their Jewish populations with dispatch. But in countries with puppet governments, the Final Solution ran into its only serious difficulties, which took the form of an unwillingness to hand over the Jews. Some governments cooperated to the full, like Romania, which at first actually anticipated Hitler's wishes but later rejected the program. Others, like Bulgaria, refused to surrender a single Jew. Popular resistance in France, in both occupied and unoccupied sectors, was strong, with the result that only twenty-five to thirty per cent of the French Jews met death. This country became notorious for hiding Jews, especially children. In a few cases the children were baptized against the will of the parents or relatives—or simply without their consent—which sometimes led to painful postwar complications, as in the famous Finaly case of 1951.[26] Contrariwise, there were priests who instructed children in Judaism and even, like Father Joseph André of Namur, conducted *seders* to their great peril. In Hungary a struggle against the deportation program was carried on by the Horthy regime until it was replaced. This explains why the Nazi program was not completed there until 1944. Finland rebuffed Himmler to his face and refused to surrender a Jew. Denmark would have nothing to do with the entire antisemitic program, and King Christian himself threatened to wear the badge of shame if it were imposed. All Danish Jews were smuggled to Sweden. In Holland a general strike was staged to halt deportation, and hiding Jews became a matter of patriotism, just as it did in France and Belgium. The famed Anne Frank diary tells part of this story. Even Fascist Italy became a haven of refuge for Jews as its imported antisemitism met with widespread popular opposition with which the government connived. But in Italy, as in other countries subsequently occupied by the Nazis, these successes were only a reprieve.

The hundreds of thousands of Jews that escaped the doom decreed for them owed their survival more to the rescue activities of individuals and private groups, than to resistance by governments or churches. Indeed, the story of these heroic efforts is the only believable page in the black book of the Hitlerian era. It is a story yet to be fully told.[27] Many courageous individuals, inspired by humanitarian as well as religious motives, risked and often lost their lives in daring attempts to rescue Jews or hamper the progress of the genocidal juggernaut. These heroes were found in every country and came from every area of life: there were teachers, doctors, lawyers, clerics, laborers, housewives, politicians, even soldiers who hid, fed, smuggled Jews, or merely manifested their sympathy by small kindnesses. Many organized underground systems, even factories, to provide counterfeit visas, identity cards, and ration books. This heartening story is a study in human ingenuity; no ruse was left untried to outwit the wily Nazi hunters.

The record of the churches is one marked with ambivalence.[28] Given the loftiness of their declared purpose and the primacy of their central mandate of universal selfless love, by any standard of expectation they failed in face of the Nazi onslaught, especially during the Holocaust. Yet some distinctions are necessary. The failure rested for the greatest part on the side of the official, the institutional churches, and even here it was not complete. Some Catholic bishops did not participate in the silence or collaboration of many of their peers: a Saliege and Gerlier in France; a Roncalli in Turkey; to an extent, a Faulhaber and von Galen in Germany; and others again. The Catholic Church, equipped with an expert diplomatic corps and an international network of chanceries, was best equipped to help, but was also burdened with an intense anti-Communist fervor, a Concordat with Germany, and a tradition of patriotic obedience to civil authority, all of which grieviously hampered it in meeting a situation that cried out for a heroic prophetic initiative. For all this, Poliakov, an attentive student of the efforts of the Church, reminds us: "The Church's tireless humanitarian efforts in the face of the Hitler terror, with the approval or under the stimulus of the Vatican, can never be forgotten;" and his is perhaps the ultimate encomium: "The Churches were the only moral authority whose power grew rather than diminished amid the turmoil of Nazism . . . ."[29]

Much has been made of the "silence of Pius XII" during the Holocaust, and understandably.[30] But perhaps not enough has been made of the concentration on *his* silence to the exclusion of that of so many others who remained as speechless yet did much less than he: German churches, the Allied governments, and other religious leaders again.[31] The excessive singling out of the Pope partakes to some degree in scapegoating, in a diversion of attention away from the all but universal silence, complicity, and inaction of others. The Pope's silence is better seen as the apex of a triangle that rested on the much wider acquiescence of the German episcopacy, his most immediate "constituents," which, in turn, rested on the still wider apathy or collusion with Nazism of German Catholics—or Christians—themselves so ill prepared for any better response by accustomed antisemitic attitudes so often aided and abetted in the past by the churches themselves.[32] The triangle continues to widen as we include a Europe and a Western world, impregnated with an indifference, if not, an antipathy to Jews. There is hardly a country or government in the Western world against which a case cannot be made in this respect.[33] The base of the triangle is reached when we consider the centuries-old Judaeophobia that conditioned the growth of the Western civilization itself almost from its beginnings. For all his moral authority and papal prestige, Pius XII must have been aware that he could count on no firm constituency in Catholic—or Christian—Germany in the eventuality of a strong and specific denunciation of Hitler and Nazism or of those who supported and collaborated with him. The Pope's "subjects" in Germany were little prepared to heed any such denunciation or prohibitions. Perennial Christian antisemitism, now intertwined with a vicious racist Judaeophobia, had already taken its toll. We have in this dark symbiosis the deepest root of the "silence of Pius XII."

Professor Yosef Yerushalmi sees in Pius' silence a break with the medieval papal tradition of protecting Jews, and therefore a modern phenomenon.[34] Meanwhile Professor Pinchas Lapide has accumulated a vast volume of evidence to defend Pius' caution and accredits his quiet working behind the scenes with saving from 700,000 to 860,000 Jews. He goes on to say, "These figures . . . exceed by far those saved by all other churches, religious institutions or all other organizations combined."[35] And yet Fr. John Morley concludes his archival study of the question with this verdict:

> It must be concluded that Vatican diplomacy failed the Jews during the Holocaust by not doing all that it was possible for it to do on their behalf. It also failed itself because in neglecting the needs of the Jews, and pursuing a goal of reserve rather than humanitarian concern, it betrayed the ideals that it had set for itself. The nuncios, the secretary of state, and, most of all, the Pope share the responsibility for this dual failure.[36]

Poliakov, though regretting that the Pope maintained his silence, comes to a more nuanced conclusion:

> One must recognize that experience has shown on the local level that public protestations could be immediately followed by merciless sanctions . . . . What would have been the effect of a solemn condemnation pronounced by the supreme authority of Catholicism? On the level of principle the import

of an intransigent attitude would have been immense. As to the practical immediate and precise consequences, whether for the work and institutions of the church or for the Jews themselves, is a question on which it is more hazardous to form an opinion.[37]

RESISTANCE AND DESPAIR

Throughout the Holocaust, Jewish resistance was scant but heroic. That of the Warsaw ghetto reached epic proportions. Toward the close of 1942 the population of that ghetto had been reduced to 40,000 and, despite all Nazi deceits, the true meaning of the deportations had at last become clear. A resistance organization was formed and trained; bunkers were built; and a few arms were smuggled into the ghetto. When General Stroop arrived with his men at the ghetto on April 19, 1943, he was repulsed, and thus began a thirty-three day battle between tanks, flamethrowers, a block-to-block obliteration on the one side and a pathetic sniping warfare on the other. Even Goebbels expressed astonishment at the resistance. Many of the rebels—women as well as men—who survived to the end of the action took their own lives. Nazi reports put German fatalities at fourteen, but Jewish estimates put them in the hundreds. Between 100 and 150 is a probable figure. Some 7,000 Jews in all were shot, and 20,000 sent to Treblinka. Many died in the debris; a few escaped to fight as partisans. Similar revolts occurred on a smaller scale in the ghettos in Vilna, Cracow and Bialystok.

More effective, if less dramatic, were the operations of the Jewish partisans who managed to evade or escape from the camps. Unfortunately, their efforts were greatly hampered by the hostility and betrayals of native partisans and populations, particularly in Poland. They were more effective in the West, especially in France, where they comprised between fifteen and thirty per cent of the resistance on all levels. The most extraordinary Jewish resistance of all was that of the Palestinian paratroopers, a group of Zionist Jews who, in 1943, when they had become fully aware of the extermination program, parachuted into the Balkan countries for rescue and intelligence operations. Some of their feats have become legendary. Finally, there were the brave gestures of those

Jews in various camps, especially Treblinka, who met instant death by falling upon their guards or sabotaging the chambers.

These genuine heroisms have not, however, concealed the general passivity of the Jews in their collective agony, and much ink has flowed especially from Jewish pens to condone, condemn or seek explanations for it. Poliakov has probed deeply their "dying in silence,"[38] and Hannah Arendt has trained her guns on Jewish participation in the extermination.[39] Apparently many have wondered at the spectacle of millions of Jews going meekly to their deaths. How explain it? There seems to be little need of defending Jewish courage. It is easily vindicated if one turns to those pages of Jewish history that recount the Great War of A.D. 66-70 or relate the incredible repulse of five Arab armies by the infant Israeli state in 1950. The causes of Jewish passivity lay rather in the peculiar situation of the Jews both in the past and under the Nazis. Their situation in the past, which Poliakov has compared to a species of concentration-camps system, was a poor preparation for revolt against the Nazi war machine which swept over whole countries in a matter of days.

Through the centuries Jews were kept defenseless and scattered, so that their only expressions of courage remained in heroic self-immolation in face of dilemmas of conscience. A certain Jewish pacifism of necessity grew from these trying circumstances. Under the Nazis, Jews were more defenseless than ever; the futility of revolt was absolute. Besides, there is no question but that most Jews were deceived or at least in grave doubt about the Nazi pretenses at "resettlement," often to the last moment. In their eyes, the option was not between death by revolt and death in the gas chambers but rather between death by revolt and a possibly improved situation under the Nazis. Usually as soon as the reality of the extermination plan became clear, Jewish resistance took shape. Moreover, every consideration of revolt had to take into account collective reprisals. No Jew could forget the Vom Rath affair in which the death of one minor Nazi official instigated a nation-wide pogrom.

For the greater part, Miss Arendt's indictment of Jewish collaboration fails for most of the above reasons. The Jewish Councils (*Judenräte*) and other functionaries that cooperated with the Nazis did so because they were compelled or because they hoped to save not only themselves but their people. It is undeniable that in some cases the motive of self-salvation and self-aggrandizement predominated, as in the case of Chaim Rumkowski, president of the Lodz *Judenrat*, who was permitted to reign as a monarch in the ghetto, but who was packed off in the final evacuation like everyone else. Some of the lesser Jewish collaborators were doubtless the dregs of the Jewish community. But most were sincerely inspired and simply suffered from the common illusions. There were heads of the *Judenräte* who, once they discovered the net into which they had been drawn, committed suicide.

It was not until the war ended and the Nuremberg trials started that a stunned world began to realize the magnitude of the horror of what had happened to the Jews. For the first time racial antisemitism was fully seen for what it is: an attack not alone on Jews but on the human personality as such. To the greatest antisemite of history, Adolf Hitler, falls the credit of having stripped antisemitism of all its disguises and shown it in its quintessence. For this lesson by the "master," the price of 6,000,000 Jewish lives were paid.[40]

It was a lesson poorly learned. Antisemitism survived the war in Germany and throughout the world. In Germany, antisemitism subsided as the country wrestled with its guilt, yet a residual, underground Nazism continued to surface from time to time. In Soviet Russia and its satellites, it not only survived but took on new life in ways which, though less sanguinary than under Hitler, were nonetheless ruinous of Jewish life.

12
RED ANTISEMITISM

Within five years of Hitler's death in 1945 Soviet antisemitism was at its peak. As Communists throughout the world continued to pipe the tune that "there is no antisemitism in the Soviet Union," reports of purges and deportations of "cosmopolitans," "bourgeois nationalists," "homeless wanderers," and the like—all synonyms for Jews—seeped through the Iron Curtain. These reports came as a surprise to many, even to anti-Communists, who, appreciative of the Soviet legal ban on antisemitism, had believed that the "Soviets put an end to antisemitism." Others were incredulous. Doubts and incredulity were dispelled in 1951, in any case, by the Slansky trial in Prague, an antisemitic showcase in the course of which every device was used to vilify Jews as a group, and again in 1953 by the famous "Doctors' Plot" in Moscow during which the anti-Jewish charges greatly resembled those of the *Protocols*. There could remain no reasonable doubt but that Jews in the Soviet empire were being oppressed, deported, and executed, above all else because they were Jews. At last Stalin had openly shown his hand and, following in Hitler's footsteps, started down the road to genocide. Only the death of the "Terrible One"—as Jews had come to describe Stalin—called a halt, at least temporarily, to this march.

Since then the Soviet government has reverted to its original plan of liquidating the Jew's soul instead of his body in order to swell the ranks of its classless and faceless society. Despite Khrushchev's protestations to the contrary, Jews continue to suffer unique discriminations against their person and their religion. Today only two groups deny that there is antisemitism in Russia: extreme rightist antisemites who still believe that Bolshevism is a Jewish conspiracy that cannot possibly be persecuting itself[1] and hard-core Communists who insist on ignoring the facts and take the assurances of Soviet law and Communist leaders at their face value.[2]

PREHISTORY

To the careful observer of Soviet affairs the "new Red antisemitism" came as no surprise. Rather it was seen as a further and intensified step in a development that had never been fully absent from the Communist world. The cleavage between the Jewish policies of the Romanov and Communist tyrannies was, in reality, by no means as absolute as some historians would have it. The cleavage is absolute only on paper; in historical fact, similarities between the two regimes are considerable. Nor are we, in this context, merely confusing a self-acknowledged and official Soviet anti-Judaism or anti-Zionism with antisemitism, properly speaking. Here more than ever caution must be exerted to restrict our definition of antisemitism to especially discriminatory treatment of Jews or of their religion. In the Soviet empire every non-Communist group suffers oppression of one kind or another.

To trace Soviet antisemitism to its beginnings it would be necessary to go back to the czarist policies of the nineteenth and earlier centuries when Jews were subject to alternating attempts to Russify them by force and xenophobic measures to segregate them. One might also go back to Karl Marx whose deep distrust of the Jew's role in society we have noted,[3] and to the nineteenth century socialist complaint about Jewish "unproductiveness."[4] Poorly disguised, these elements—distrust, Russification, xenophobia, economic complaints—all turn up again at one stage or another of the evolution of the Soviet regime.

More specifically and concretely, germinal Communist-Jewish tensions occurred in the first decade of the twentieth century during the struggle between the Jewish Bundists and other revolutionaries of the Social Democratic Party, especially the Bolsheviks. The withdrawal of the Bundists from the party was caused mainly by Bolshevik opposition to the Bund's espousal of the concept of ethnic or national self-determination for all peoples in the empire, a concept strongly repudiated by the Bolsheviks in favor of that of centralization. Their leader Nicolai Lenin did not conceal his contempt for the Bundists' views—or, for that matter, for those of the Zionists. To him, Jews, lacking a territory, were not a nation but a caste; Jewish nationalist aspirations were a "clerical or bourgeois fraud." On one occasion he stated that "the idea of a separate Jewish people, which is utterly untenable scientifically, is reactionary in its political implications"; and on another, that "Jewish national culture is the slogan of rabbis and bourgeois, the slogan of our enemies."[5] Lenin's view, despite much future oscillation on the part of the government in this regard, remained the chief guideline of Soviet Jewish policy. Although lip-service continued to be paid to the concept of national self-determination and although its equivalent was incorporated into the constitution and public law of the U.S.S.R. when the latter came to power, in practice the concept was narrowed down almost to the vanishing point, especially with regard to the Jewish minority.

When the revolutions of 1917 came, it was clear where Jewish sympathies lay. The vast majority favored the Mensheviks, the liberal-socialist opponents of the Bolsheviks. So true was this that Josef Stalin once told of a Bolshevik of the early days who supposedly in jest stated that "Mensheviks were a Jewish faction while the Bolsheviks were a truly Russian one, and it might be a good idea for us Bolsheviks to start a pogrom in the Party."[6] The common belief that Bolshevik leadership was predominantly Jewish is mythical. True, there were an unusually large number of Jews on the highest rung of the Soviet government, namely, Trotsky, Radek, Zinoviev, Kamenev, Kaganovitch, and others. This is explainable by the large number of Jewish intellectuals who were forced by czarist anti-Jewish educational policies to study abroad, where they were imbued with Marx's thought. These leaders, moreover, though estranged from every part of Jewish life, were undoubtedly also influenced by the traditional Jewish messianic hope of secular redemption, as well as by Jewish dedication to the "aristocracy of learning." All these factors propelled them toward positions of leadership in the Revolution. At no time, however, did the Red regime enjoy support of the Jewish masses. Some Jews, understandably, were won to the Red cause by the anti-Jewish cruelties of the White Terror, as were more again because of Lenin's public opposition to antisemitism. The Bolshevik leader condemned antisemitism as counter-revolutionary, and in 1921 it was made a criminal offense with severe penalties.[7] Eventually antisemitism was condemned in general terms in the Soviet constitution.[8] This stand was no doubt dictated to some degree by principle. The principle involved was the illusory conviction that if antisemitism would die out both Jew and anti-Jew would unite in the common supranational solidarity of the classless society. But expediency undoubtedly played an important role in Lenin's policy: in the years of civil war and reconstruction, gaining the co-operation of the minorities was imperative.[9]

THEORY VERSUS PRACTICE

On the morrow of the Revolution, the Soviets had a difficult if not contradictory task ahead of them, which may explain the vacillations of their policy toward the Jews. The Jews had to be won to Communism but, at the same time, they had to be de-Judaized so as to enable them to take their place in the classless society. The second of these goals, of course, was primary but the Soviets soon learned that converting Jews to Communism would have to be given a practical priority. So a Jewish Commissariat was established under Stalin to administer Jewish affairs. This act in itself was a relaxation of principle, since Jews, as a "caste without a territory," should not have enjoyed a special administration. In any case, later this Commissariat was reduced in importance and finally abolished. Another concession to Jewish sensibilities, as well as to the realities of the situation, was the acknowledgement of Yiddish as a national language permissible in government administrations and schools as the official language wherever Jews were numerous. The concession was tempered, however, by the standard that whatever was rendered in a national language had to be "socialist in content." For all practical purposes, Jews were later recognized as a nationality, acquiring separate listing among other Soviet nationalities and having "Jewish" stamped on their passports.

In its plans to de-Judaize the Jewish minority, the Soviet government was more assiduous. Jewish sections manned by young militant Jewish Communists were formed to make the "dictatorship of the proletariat" prevail "in the Yiddish street."[10] These aggressive bodies (*Yevsektsiya*) did their utmost to shake Jews from their traditional national, cultural, and religious loyalties. The government meanwhile suppressed the synagogues (and also the churches), and though groups of fifty or more citizens could seek permits for religious devotions, those who attended church or synagogue were stigmatized. Religious instruction of the young was made legally punishable and Hebrew was outlawed as a language. Jewish children were forced to attend the state schools, some of which used Yiddish but otherwise completely ignored the fact of Jewish existence. They were open, for example, on the Sabbath and carefully avoided references to the Jewish religion or history. The Yiddish press which had thrived under the Czar dwindled sharply until in 1935 a mere four or five newspapers remained. Courts in which Yiddish was permitted also gradually disappeared. The Jewish theater, considered more or less free of "Jewish clericalism" and an effective purveyor of Soviet ideas, fared better and did not decline until the mid-thirties.

By 1930 the job was largely completed. Jewish religious congregations had shrunk greatly, and most of what was left of Orthodox religious life was underground. It is possible to conclude, with Schwartz, that, "no political, administrative, or cultural organization representing the Jewish minority as a distinct national or ethnic group has existed in the Soviet Union since the dissolution of the Jewish Sections [in 1930]."[11]

Most of what happened to the Jewish community, to be sure, was suffered also by other minorities and religions, but with respect to no other group was the Soviet government so efficient in the enforcement of its anti-religious and anti-national program. In all these efforts there was as yet no question of overt, official antisemitism.

The first signs of overt antisemitism appeared in the mid-twenties and were popular in character. Soviet opinion attributed the outcropping of a return to pre-Soviet Jew-hatred but, in reality, it was something quite different from older forms. Czarist antisemitism was more official than popular; this newest growth was popular and, at least on higher governmental levels, unofficial. Its cause ought to be sought in the "trauma of collectivization"[12] which marked this era and from which Jews suffered most of all. At the end of the Revolution, when Communization of the economy began, the 2,500,000 Jews in Russia, most of them middlemen, were entirely dislocated. Some 400,000 found a place in the vast Soviet bureaucracy and another 750,000 entered the factories. The rest, comprising nearly a million, were, economically speaking, suspended in mid-air and suffered great hardship. The government turned to the problem of their resettlement, first by an agricultural program whereby Jews were given land grants in the Ukraine and the Crimea; later in 1926 steps were taken to create a Jewish autonomous province in far-off Birobidzhan on the Manchurian border—another retreat from original Soviet principle.[13] The latter project failed, for the resettled never became more than a minor fraction of the indigenous population of that inhospitable land. The entire administration of the autonomous province was liquidated in the purges of 1937, and after 1948 Birobidzhan was shrouded in secrecy, probably becoming a concentration camp for Jews.

The New Economic Policy (NEP)—the great retreat from Communism—begun in 1923, absorbed many Jews into semi-private enterprise. In the competition that ensued, Jews were branded as "intruders" or "NEP profiteers" and became the butt of popular antipathies, particularly on the part of the dispossessed urban middle class. They were accused of invading the cities, occupying "soft jobs," land grabbing, taking over the Crimea—the Russia Riviera—infiltrating the government, and shirking work. Statistical evidence has shown these charges to be unfounded.[14] Nonetheless, the charges were powerful enough to incite much violence and bring indignities upon Jews, especially in the factories. The animus spread to the universities and became prevalent among the Communist youth; it even worked on government officials. Slogans such as "Kill the kikes and save Russia" gained wide currency. One Party member even spread the story that

Jews use Christian blood to make matzoth. In the allotment of housing and the imposition of taxes, there were many instances of discrimination against Jews. The government was slow to enforce its laws against antisemitic abuses but was finally forced to take a strong hand, especially after it was known that local officials and government agencies were involved. Educational and penal measures were taken but on the whole they were halfhearted. *Pravda* also took the matter up—for the first and last time—and called for a halt to the disturbances.

The epidemic declined in the early thirties but did not entirely disappear. A low-toned resentment persisted and there were sporadic episodes. The decline was not so much caused by the government's intervention as by the replacement of the NEP by the Five Year Plans, which created millions of jobs and thus relieved the pressure on the so-called intruders. The *Stakhanovist* speed-up of production and the emergence of the "great-power chauvinism" of this period drained off the energies that normally fed the antisemitic impulse. Throughout the first half of the decade, the government, faced with a furtive persistence of the problem, kept a strict silence concerning it on the home front while widely publicizing condemnation of it abroad. Many liberals were deceived.

Soviet antisemitism reached its lowest point during the midthirties—as could be expected in this era of the Popular Front when the Kremlin set out to attract Western and, in particular, liberal opinion. Semblances of democracy were feigned; a more liberal constitution was written; and pronouncements against antisemitism by the ruling clique increased. Molotov called it "bestiality."

DE-JUDAIZING, SOVIET STYLE

It was a last philosemitic gasp. By the summer of 1936, the short-lived flirtation with democracy was over and the reign of terror nigh. Apparently Stalin had finally opted for a total dictatorship and for the ruthless eradication of the old guard of the Revolution. In the great purges that followed many Jews of such stature as Trotsky, Zinoviev, Radek, Kamenev, were denounced as traitors and killed. The impression was thus conveyed that the great Russian fatherland was being strangled by "Jewish internationalism." Besides the great ones a large number of the lesser Jewish leaders who managed Jewish affairs were liquidated. The purges "virtually terminated the organized life of the Jewish group as a recognized cultural and ethnic minority."[15] Concomitant with the bloody purges of Jewish leaders ran another current of antisemitism which manifested itself in the elimination of Jews from influential posts and in a general social ostracism. Unobtrusively, the Jews were being squeezed out of Russian life. In the post-purge period, antisemitic incidents again went unpunished and unpublicized.

The Soviet-Nazi pact, understandably, did not help Russian Jews. While it lasted, the existence of antisemitism, whether in Russia or Nazi Germany, was totally ignored, both in official Soviet pronouncements and in the press; and attacks on Nazism were strongly disapproved. Molotov now said that "to wage war for the 'annihilation of Hitlerism' is not only senseless but criminal."[16] Because of this policy of silence, Jews remained tragically unaware of what was in store for them when the Nazis occupied western Russia. The lack of warning often led to their entrapment. During the occupation, Nazi propaganda found a willing ear among the masses; frequently Russians were employed to start pogroms in advance of extermination. It was no less successful in unoccupied sectors where it was beamed by radio. Jews fleeing the German advance were resented and often molested; and there was evidence of renewed anti-Jewish feeling in the Russian army and government circles.

After the war, Soviet propaganda, chiefly through its well-Sovietized Jewish mouthpiece Ilya Ehrenburg, recounted tales of Russian rescues of Jews as demonstrations of Soviet solidarity. In actuality, the proportion of rescues was well below that of other occupied countries. This fact is partly explained by the supine attitude the Russian people were conditioned to adopt in the face of violence; it is also attributable to an underlying antisemitism among them. The ill-treatment of Jewish partisans and Jews in family camps in the Russian forests during the war appears to have prevailed over the rescues. Indeed, the existence of pervasive antisemitic conditions was further confirmed by the alacrity with which almost all Jewish refugees quit Soviet territory for Poland after the war.

In the postwar years, neither government spokesmen nor the press acknowledged the scope of Jewish casualties at the hands of the Nazis. In all accounts, Jews were listed indiscriminately among other nationalities that so suffered; and in the records of some regions where massive Jewish massacres had occurred, Jews were not mentioned at all. As late as 1961 a non-Jewish Communist poet, Yevtushenko, complained in his poem *Babi Yar* that the mass grave at Babi Yar near Kiev, containing the remains of 100,000 Jews slaughtered in 1941, was still unmarked by a monument. The poem created a sensation, and Yevtushenko was denounced by the official guild of Soviet writers.

THE BLACK YEARS

The last five years of the Stalin era (1948-53) made up the "Black Years" of Soviet Jewry. By 1947, it was evident that Soviet antisemitism was on the threshold of a new stage. The legal ban remained and there was less of the earlier popular Jew-baiting, but now anti-Jewish discrimination took on an official stamp that plainly emanated from the highest levels of government. All communications media and finally Stalin himself indulged openly in eulogies of the Russian people to the unmistakable denigration of minority nationalities. Again Jews, receiving the brunt of the new spirit, were further relegated to the hinterlands of Soviet life. Curiously, the very nationalism that Soviet theory had once condemned as "great-power chauvinism" now held full sway. In 1948 the anti-Zionist campaign was launched in *Pravda* with an article by Ehrenburg, who denounced the new Israeli state, Zionism, and all Jewish ties with the outside world. To those conversant with totalitarian methodology, it was an ominous development: The ideological attack had begun, the liquidations would follow. It did not take long to see that anti-Zionism meant little more than antisemitism; that Jews of every hue and strain, even anti-Zionists, were the targets. As Peter Meyer puts it: "Moscow said 'Zionist' but hit Jews."[17]

The new chauvinism next emerged as a campaign against

"cosmopolitanism"—against "cosmopolitans without ancestry" according to one variant. Another favorite bugaboo of the campaign was "bourgeois nationalists." It was not hard to surmise who was meant. Had not Ehrenburg called Israel a "bourgeois state"? The inevitable purges followed upon the denunciations. The first victims were writers and artists; and though a minority of this group were Jewish, nonetheless the large majority of the purged were Jewish. Every effort was made to emphasize this fact. Such expressions in official statements and the press as "men without a country" and "alien elements" helped to point the finger at Jews as a whole. Much was made of the fact that many of the accused Jews had adopted a Russian alias—just as had Lenin and Stalin and a multitude of other Soviet citizens. Thereafter their original Jewish names were affixed to their Russian names to signalize their Jewish origin. The last Yiddish—and loyally Communist—newspaper was suppressed at this time; and until 1959 no books were published in Yiddish. Jews disappeared from the foreign service and foreign trade; they were almost completely eliminated from the Supreme Soviets. Here, as in other spheres, an odd Jew was retained for propaganda purposes. Reports circulated of mass deportations of Jews to the East, possibly Birobidzhan, but these were neither admitted nor denied by the government.

In the satellite countries of Central Europe—mainly Czechoslovakia, Romania, Hungary, and Poland—the pattern of events in the U.S.S.R. was faithfully reflected. The same charges were hurled; Jews were arrested as embezzlers and saboteurs; first, the Jews in high echelons of government were eliminated, then the lesser lights. Mass deportations with a disproportionately high number of Jews were openly carried out. Communist antisemitism was less subtle in the satellites than in Russia.[18]

In the international sphere, tensions increased steadily between the U.S.S.R. and Israel until the death of Stalin in 1953. Oddly, thirty years after the Revolution which promised that antisemitism and Judaism would disappear, the Soviet government developed what Fejto has called a veritable "Israel complex"[19]— not totally dissimilar to the Nazis' obsession with "international Jewry."

The Slansky trial of 1952 in Prague provided the best exhibit of Soviet antisemitism in its true colors, and gave the *coup de grâce* to Soviet dissembling about racial discrimination in Communist lands. It was, moreover, the point at which Stalinian and Hitlerian antisemitism might have intersected. The Communization of Czechoslovakia had run into trouble toward the turn of the century and its economic condition was not healthy. Scapegoats were needed. Purges had been in progress for some time and already in 1951 the finger of Kopecky, the antisemitic Minister of Information, had pointed at the Jews and some were jailed. Finally in November 1952 Rudolph Slansky, former Secretary General "of Jewish origin," was brought to trial with thirteen other defendants, ten of whom were Jews.

The trial was certainly the most astounding anti-Jewish concoction since the ritual-murder trial of Michael Beilis in Czarist Russia forty years before. In short, the prosecution set out to prove that Slansky and the others were tools of a world-wide Jewish plot aimed at the destruction of the Czechoslovak Communist state and economy. Named in this far-flung network of international intrigue were "American imperialists," French, British, Israeli diplomats, and a multitude of Zionist spies, of whom Truman, Acheson, Morgenthau and Baruch formed the American contingent. Slansky, the Jew, his Jewish codefendants and the three non-Jews who "surrounded themselves with Jews," were charged with such crimes as betraying state secrets, promoting sabotage, undermining the economy and currency, exporting food so as to starve the workers, and so on. In true Communist style, the crimes were "confessed" by these unfortunate defendants whose only crime had been to serve as loyal and anti-Zionist Communists for years. Eleven were hanged and three received life imprisonment. If any possible doubt remained concerning the antisemitic character of the trial it was quickly dispelled by the subsequent purges of Jews in the government, in the Party, and in industry, and perhaps more effectively still by the wave of Jewish suicides that swept through most satellite countries.

The crescendo of antisemitic mania contorting the Stalin regime next led to Moscow, its fountainhead. There in the following year, the ultimate in phantasmagoria was reached in the so-called "Doctors' Plot." An Orwellian model, it was first reported in

Pravda in January of 1953. The charge was broadcast that nine doctors, six of them Jews, had taken the lives of two members of the Politburo: Alexander Schervakov, who had died in 1945 and Andrei Zhandov, who had died in 1948. They were further accused of "shortening the lives" of several other Soviet officials. The case of Zhandov casts the necessary light on the whole affair. Before his death he had been considered heir apparent to Stalin's post and was, moreover, more popular than his chief—a perilous position in the land of the Kremlin. Zhandov's death was reported in *Pravda* as from natural causes and the death certificate was signed by five doctors, none Jewish. Three of these doctors were named in the "Doctors' Plot," and for some inexplicable reason six new Jewish doctors were added. The official rationale of the trial was that the "murderer-doctors" were in the service of Zionist espionage. The ghost of the medieval Jew-poisoner was back to haunt the "workers' paradise."

The public trial of the doctors, set for March 1953, was undoubtedly meant to serve as a justification for the massive deportations of Jews that were still under way. But the trial was never held. Stalin died that same month in what was described by one commentator as an "antisemitic madness," thus bringing the Soviet genocide to at least a temporary halt. The "terrorist doctors" were released.

SINCE STALIN

After Stalin's death, a general *détente* in the persecution of Jews was evident. Many victims of the antisemitic campaign were released from custody and others rehabilitated. U.S.S.R.-Israeli relations improved. There was a general return to legality. But these improvements were deceptive. The basic policy of the government toward Jews and their religion had not changed; only the terror was gone. On their side, Jews, especially the young, had lost confidence in Soviet emancipation and the legal guarantees of equality. The official ban on antisemitism still remained on the books and assurances of cultural freedom continued to be made, even, for example, at the Twenty-Second Party Congress of 1961: "The Communist Party guarantees the complete freedom of each citizen of the U.S.S.R. to speak and to rear and educate his chil-

dren in any language—ruling out all privileges, restrictions or
compulsion in the use of this or that language."[20] Nonetheless, all
but total dissolution of Jewish cultural life that had thus far been
effected was not undone. The Yiddish theater remained practically defunct; Yiddish schools stayed closed; many Jewish poets
were never rehabilitated; no Yiddish newspapers were reinstated.
The new "liberalism" of the Khrushchev era extended little of its
benefits to Jews. Indeed, it was significant that in 1956, when
Khrushchev exposed the crimes of the Stalin era, he made no reference whatever to those committed against Jews or their culture—something that even *The Daily Worker* of New York
complained about.[21] Khrushchev's attitude toward Jews has been
considered enigmatic, but there is little enigma in the remarks he
reportedly made in Warsaw in 1956: "Even a second-rate Ko-
walski is more useful than a first-rate Rosenblum," and "You
have too many Abrahamoviches here."[22] It appears that the Red
leader, true to his Ukrainian background, entertained little love
for Jews.

The important fact of this postwar era was not the hardships
Jews shared with other minorities and religions but rather the denial of rights granted other legally co-equal groups. In the cultural
area, discrimination was very clear. Every effort was made to cut
Jews off from their history and culture and also to isolate them
from Jewish institutions outside the U.S.S.R. From 1948 to 1959,
a total of six books was published in Yiddish and most of these
were for export. It was not until 1961, apparently in deference to
world opinion, which had begun to notice the Jews' plight, that
a Yiddish literary journal, *Sovietish Heimland*, was published. It
was a small concession. From its first issue, the new organ hewed
strictly to the official Party viewpoint. Moshe Decter has compared the Jewish situation with that of two other minority groups:

> The Maris and Yakuts are two tiny primitive Asian groups
> which number 504,000 and 236,000 respectively. In 1961
> alone, Soviet printing presses produced 62 books for the
> Maris and 144 for the Yakuts, in their own languages . . . .
> This state of affairs is again to be contrasted with the press
> available to the Maris and Yakuts. The former has 17 news-
> papers, the latter 28.[23]

The official explanation for this state of affairs was that Jews, now fully assimilated, had no desire for a culture of their own. Ehrenburg, for one, has parroted this line. Yet all evidence points in the opposite direction. Numerous visitors to the U.S.S.R. have testified to the vitality of Soviet Jewish aspirations and to the solidarity of spirit uniting the scattered communities. According to Fejto, it is actually the "existence among many Jews in the U.S.S.R. of a nostalgia, a hope, a quasi-mystical 'national' passion that converges on Israel" that is at the root of the Soviet government's anti-Israeli and pro-Arab policy.[24] Khrushchev's further contention that Jews have no cultural institutions because they are so widely dispersed is refuted by examples of other tiny minorities which, though possessing no territory of their own, have newspapers and schools in their own languages.[25]

In religious affairs, where all faiths suffer extreme hardships in the Soviet Union, the Synagogue is singled out for special discrimination. Other religious groups, for example, are permitted a central organization, but not so the Jews. Other faiths, again, may employ their particular liturgical language for service, but Hebrew, the liturgical tongue, has been under ban from the beginning. No Hebrew Bible has been published since 1917, whereas the Orthodox and the Baptists have been permitted to publish their own. In the matter of seminaries and houses of worship the same discrimination exists. The Orthodox have five seminaries and two academies; the Muslims have two *"Madrasehs"*; but until 1957 the Jews had no houses for the training of rabbis. In that year a *yeshiva* was permitted as an adjunct to the great synagogue in Moscow. Its maximum number of students has been fourteen; and in 1962 the number dropped to four, owing to denials of residence permits to students from Georgia and Dagestan. The campaign against houses of worship bore down heavily on synagogues. Of the few that remained, several have been closed and others are in danger of closing on legal pretexts. It is little wonder then that the ratio of Jewish faithful to licensed rabbis, 15,000 to 1, compares poorly with that of other faiths. Even the practice of gathering for private prayer in Jewish homes has drawn the fire of the government and participants are harassed openly. Religious articles necessary for divine service, such as prayer shawls and phylacteries, have not been allowed, while

other religious groups have been permitted their candles, cruci-
fixes, ikons, and the like. In 1962 and 1963 this type of discrimination went so far as to ban the sale of matzoth, required for
celebration of Passover. It is the same story in the case of prayer-
books. A mere 3,000 copies of the Sabbath prayerbook were finally permitted in 1958, but Christian churches have enjoyed a
relatively wide selection of pious publications. Most disturbing of
all have been offenses against the person, which in the early sixties
involved the deposition of synagogue presidents and imprisonment of communal leaders for alleged conspiracy with visitors
from abroad.

Discrimination in employment and the professions tells a
similar tale. There are no Jews in the diplomatic service and practically none in the armed services. Quotas are set in the universities which peg Jews downward. And in political leadership they
continue to dwindle in ratio, comprising less than one half of 1%
in 1962 as against their composition of 1.09% of the total population. All of this has been unabashedly rationalized in Khrushchev's statement of 1956: "In the beginning, Jewish intellectuals
occupied important posts in the administration of the Soviet
Union, whereas Russian intellectuals were scarce. But today this
default has been remedied so that we can dispense with Jewish
functionaries"[26]—a transparent justification of previous purges
and discriminations and a tacit inference that Jews constitute an
alien body in Russian life.

More insidious still has been the treatment of Jews in the
campaign against "economic crimes" begun in 1961. Apparently
in the Soviet's scarce economy, considerable purloining of state
property, bribery, and currency speculation goes on. To discourage these practices, the guilty have been made liable to capital
punishment or long jail sentences. The campaign as such has
nothing to do with antisemitism, but certainly the trend it has
taken has. Jews have been singled out in many ways. They are
punished more severely than others, sixty per cent of those executed thus far were Jews. In some trials, all Jews are condemned
to death, whereas others—even though in more responsible positions—are given light terms. The International Commission of
Jurists has discerned "racial overtones" in the situation. During

the trials, the Jewish aspect, so to speak, is well featured both in the court and the press. Jews are usually presented as cunning manipulators who prey upon the innocent Soviet workers in order to fleece them. Whenever possible, links between the accused and the Synagogue are dragged in, as is also any possible relationship with Israel or the United States.

The bias of the trials is a fair reflection of the vicious anti-semitic campaign conducted in the Soviet press for some years, particularly in the provinces and large cities where Jews are numerous. In frequent articles, the Jew has been tarred anew with an old brush. Most of the ancient stereotypes reappear: Jews are money worshippers, cheats, immoral, unpatriotic, and generally disagreeable; their rites are absurd and their synagogues centers of ribaldry, dishonesty, and subversion. "Judaism kills love for the Soviet motherland," asserted one journal, echoing a favorite theme.[27] It is again to be noted that it is only the Synagogue that is suspected or accused of unpatriotism and subversion. There can be no question but that the press campaign as well as the trend of the "economic" trials receive their inspiration from the highest authorities.

In present-day Russia, Jews are a thoroughly chastened sect. Far from fulfilling its claim to have solved the age-old Russian antisemitic problem, Communism has aggravated it. Decter has summed up the matter well:

> Soviet policy places the Jews in an inextricable vise. They are allowed neither to assimilate, nor live a full Jewish life, nor to emigrate (as many would wish) to Israel or any other place where they might live freely as Jews. The policy stems, in turn, from doctrinal contradictions abetted by traditional anti-Jewish sentiments. On the one hand, the authorities want the Jews to assimilate; on the other hand, they irrationally fear the full penetration of Soviet life which assimilation implies. So the Jews are formally recognized as a nationality, as a religious group, and of full equality as individuals.
>
> Soviet policy as a whole, then, amounts to spiritual strangulation—the deprivation of Soviet Jewry's natural right to know the Jewish past and to participate in the Jewish present.

And without a past and a present, the future is precarious indeed.[28]

Decter's words were prophetic. Five years were not to pass
before Soviet antisemitism was to take on a new guise and vitality
and capture first place on the contemporary roster of history's
most durable hatred.[29]

13
POLITE ANTISEMITISM

Antisemitism as we have seen it in Germany, Russia, and elsewhere in Europe never managed to root itself in the United States, though more than one attempt to implant it here met with spectacular temporary success. If the old rabid hatred of the Jews found the American climate less hospitable, a certain species of social discrimination against Jews, or "polite" antisemitism, became identifiable as a typically American outgrowth. Interestingly, the same conditions that tended to stave off the first kind engendered the latter. A land of immense natural resources and dynamic economic growth had less need for scapegoats upon which to heap failures—if only because failures were fewer. But these favorable conditions produced a species of status-seeking and social snobbery from which the immigrant Jew was bound to suffer more persistently than his fellow immigrants. On the other hand, the American experience did not fully contradict the European. In the period following World War I, when all the prerequisites of antisemitism appeared, one violent campaign against the Jews followed upon another until the affluent postwar period of World War II brought back the deceptive calm of restrictive covenants and "gentlemen's agreements."

This dual character of America antisemitism helps to explain the split among researchers of the problem. One group views anti-Jewish discrimination as a conservative phenomenon stemming mainly from economic causes and traces its history more deeply into the American past.[1] While it is a view that risks overemphasizing the antisemitic data, it has, on the other hand, the merit of completeness; there are few instances of anti-Jewish activity that do not have a strain of the pure antisemitic culture. A second, and minimalist, approach, making light of mere social discrimination, finds little antisemitism in America before the latter half of the nineteenth century or even later. Some historians would, for example, begin this chapter with the post-World War I era. Thus Lee Levinger in speaking of antisemitism in late nineteenth and early twentieth century Europe, concludes: "But all this time there was no anti-Semitism, as a literary, political or economic movement in the United States. That was a product of the period after the World War [I] . . . . It seemed as though antisemitism was a movement foreign to American life and institutions."[2] This viewpoint, looking rather to ideological causes (myths and stereotypes) than to economic factors, attributes American antisemitism largely to European influence and, restricting its scope, tends to idealize the Jewish experience in America.[3] It is an overly optimistic outlook which employs too coarse a net to catch, let us say, the antisemitic minnows that, despite their size, merit a place in the great sea of antisemitic aggression. A balance of both approaches does least violence to the originality and heterogeneous nature of American antisemitism.

A note of caution. If it is true that a history of antisemitism is necessarily a distortion of an integral Jewish history, this is especially true of the chapter that deals with the United States. Despite the persistence of anti-Jewish social discrimination and the extent reached by some antisemitic campaigns, antisemitism remains a minor chapter in American Jewish history. An adequate account of Jewish life in America—its contributions to the commonweal, its successes, its harmonious relations with non-Jews, and the like—greatly surpasses the dimensions of the antisemitic story. To these more heartening aspects our limitations will unfortunately permit only random hints.

COMPARATIVE IDYLL

The words that grace the base of the Statue of Liberty are those of a Jewish poet:

> Give me your tired, your poor,
> Your huddled masses yearning to be free,
> The wretched refuse of your teeming shore.
> Send them, the homeless, tempest torn, to me.
> I lift my lamp beside the golden door.[4]

It was to Jews fleeing troubles and persecution in Europe that such words held most solace. But, curiously, it was not from Europe that the Jewish fugitives who first settled on the North American shore came; nor was the reception given them in accord with the promise the "mighty woman with a torch"[5] would one day hold forth. The first fugitives, twenty-three Sephardic Jews, impelled by a dread of the Inquisition, fled from Brazil in 1654 aboard the SS. *Caterina* and sought asylum in New Amsterdam. Peter Stuyvesant, the governor, did all in his power to prevent this "deceitful race," these "hateful enemies and blasphemers," from "infecting" his colony.[6] Only a decree by the colony's directors in Amsterdam finally permitted their entry. It was not until 1727 that a Jew could be naturalized in the colony, and later still before he could vote. When the first Jews arrived in North America, alas, their old-world image was there to greet them.

The few Jews who scattered themselves through several of the colonies received a better reception than their kinsmen in New Amsterdam. Wherever they went they enjoyed, as a rule, freedom of worship and economic opportunities, although not full political rights. In some colonies, they fared as well or better than other minorities, particularly Catholics, Lutherans, and Quakers. Reacting enthusiastically to the unforeseen tolerance, they quickly became part of the community. Several made a name for themselves in social and economic leadership. Yet there were colonies in which Jews were outlawed, in some cases exclusively, in others together with other dissenters. Civic disabilities of one kind or another existed almost everywhere; in many instances the right to vote or hold office was not conceded until the nineteenth century.

But the realities of the American experiment—chiefly the need for unity amid ethnic diversity—kept ahead of the law. The guarantees of equality granted by the Constitution in 1787 only put a seal of approval on what had long been evolving in fact. Church establishment was dying, and more and more Jews were recognized as just another religious sect entitled in principle to full citizenship. Thus trades, professions, universities, voting booths and the assemblies gradually opened up to them. In the first years of the nineteenth century, the Americanization, so to speak, of the earliest Jewish immigrants was complete.

Paradoxically, the ones to disturb this Jewish idyll, however innocently, were Jews. The age of immigration was at hand and what started as a trickle took on the proportions of a flood. First, about 1820, came the German and Austrian immigrants. Thousands of them fleeing "hep hep" riots, marital restrictions, impoverishments, and a growing European population came to join their brothers and sisters who had written so glowingly of the New World. This influx reached a peak after the revolution of 1848, and when it subsided around the 1870s a quarter million or more of the expatriates made up the majorities of Jewish communities on the eastern seaboard and established new communities inland. Like their predecessors, the newcomers adapted themselves easily. Some grew prosperous, but many never went beyond peddling. In either case, for the first time in America Jews as a group drew attention, and it was not always favorable. The Jewish image slowly underwent a change. To the accepted concept of Jews as the people of the Law and as industrious workers was added that of the Jew dispersed by God, the cunning Shylock, the vagrant peddler. In the ante-bellum era, these caricatures did not predominate or cause serious discrimination, yet they pointed to a nativist feeling (at the time preoccupied with Catholics) that foreshadowed things to come. Several allusions to ritual murder were made. On the other hand, a storm of protest greeted news of the Damascus libel in 1850.[7] During the Civil War, Jews served faithfully on both sides of the conflict according to their location, but again the antisemitic demon made its presence felt in frequent charges of disloyalty.

THE PURSUIT OF STATUS

In the 1870s the stereotype of the Jewish parvenu appeared, and with it the practice of social discrimination against Jews was born, never fully to depart again. Many factors contributed to the new image. The great spurt of industrial progress in the postwar years generated a spirit of economic and social rivalry, or status-seeking, that was not discernible before the war. Meanwhile, a few of the German-Jewish immigrants had skyrocketed to riches and social prominence. Their prominence was magnified—both Jews of the time as well as critics admitted[8]—by a certain ostentatiousness and social initiative that they had brought from central Europe and to which the non-Jewish social-climbers did not take. The native middle class, having grown rich—and ostentatious—at a slower pace, resented the rapid rise of the immigrants. And what better object on which to project its own aggressiveness and ostentation than the Jew, already tacitly burdened with the Shylock image and a note of foreignness? Thus was the Jew marked for ostracism. Some historians date the beginnings of American antisemitism from the rude refusal of the management of the Grand Union Hotel in Saratoga to accommodate the New York banker Joseph Seligman and his family in 1877. But it is possible to point to other episodes or attempts at exclusion during the 1860s and early 1870s in the armed services, the government, and hotels.[9] Among these, General Ulysses Grant's quarantining of Jews from his military lines during the Civil War made history. The Saratoga incident brought into the open and supplied a precedent for what had been practiced clandestinely and sporadically for some time but which the American tradition of tolerance and individualism had held in check—and in silence. From Saratoga the restrictive policy spread rapidly to other resorts, then to clubs, and private schools. A veritable battle of hotel and club exclusivism ensued as excluded Jews proceeded to establish their own facilities, often on the very doorsteps of the excluders.

The situation was further complicated and worsened by the new immigration of eastern European Jews, principally from Russia, who from 1881 fled Czarist brutality, first by the thousands, then by the millions, literally inundating the relatively small communities of Sephardic and Germanic Jews.[10] The new-comers brought with them their unfamiliar customs and dress, which upset many of their own kinsmen as much as others of the American middle class. A cleavage was thus created in the Jewish community itself, which was not to heal for decades. Yet this did not deter Jewish philanthropy from lending a helping hand to the new arrivals until they were on their feet. The non-Jewish community at first ignored them or viewed them with petty annoyance or pity.

It was not until near the turn of the century, when a number of the new Jewish population began to compete for clerical jobs, seek entrance to college, and in some cases reach higher financial brackets, that reaction set in. Existing social discrimination was reinforced and extended so that in the first years of the new century Jews found access to fashionable resorts, clubs, schools or fraternities almost impossible. In urban areas, where the limits of the "ghetto" pressed outward, restrictive covenants in housing were initiated and beatings of Jews by hooligans were frequent in such places as New York, Brooklyn, and Boston.

New notes were added to the Jewish stereotypes. The Jew was now seen primarily as an alien, a mysterious stranger out of tune with "American" standards and inferior to the native stock, including the Jewish. As a palliative, the distinction was drawn between "good" (among whom some of one's "best friends" might be selected) and "undesirable" Jews. The notion of Jewish conspiracy rose about that time. The remarkable advances of the benighted immigrants excited the imaginations of the gentile nativists, who probed for explanation in the realm of "invisible money powers." The more candid spoke openly of Jewish international control of gold. In 1891 Ignatius Donnelly, in his utopian fantasy *Caesar's Columns*, wrote of domination by a Jewish oligarchy under which Christians would pay dearly for their persecution of Jews in the past.[11]

Those years formed a critical juncture in American life. During their course, the deep-seated and half-recognized split in American ideals came fully to light.[12] As always, the original ideals of freedom and equality for all were officially and publicly paeaned, but now intolerance toward minority groups, hitherto practiced more or less furtively except by extremist organizations such as the Know-Nothings and the American Protective Association (A.P.A.), was so openly discussed as apparently to enjoy the dignity of a counter-tradition. This tradition took on a racist tone and pointed more directly at the Jew. More than merely socially unacceptable, he was now viewed, though vaguely, as inferior to and corruptive of the "original American stock." The movement calling for a cessation of the influx from Europe originated in this atmosphere. This movement was not without influence on government policy, for at this time a series of restrictive measures were initiated that included higher head-taxes and more stringent requirements on health and literacy, and finally culminated in the drastic shut-down by the immigration law of 1924.

These developments, however, should not be overdrawn; they were, as yet, relatively superficial manifestations. As the century closed, Jews on the whole enjoyed amicable relations with their neighbors and were highly appreciated by many. And the government, despite signs of relaxing its standards of equality with respect to immigration, continued, as in the past, to condemn injustice against any minority and in particular against the Jews. In 1903 for example, in a note to Romania the government spelled out American rejection of any distinction between Jew and non-Jew in unmistakable terms.

The first decade of the twentieth century witnessed no radically new developments on the antisemitic front, but rather, as the flow of eastern immigrants continued unabated, a stealthy widening of existing discriminations both in scope and geography. The next marked aggravation took place in 1910 and was characterized by several new developments. As the nativist animus shifted its focus from the Irish, Slav, and Latin minorities, the Jew caught up with the Negro, so to speak, as a prime target of concern. In 1916 an antisemitic writer was able to report: "The antipathy for the Jew is only surpassed by the general recognition that the Negro should be kept in a state of perpetual inferiority."[13] Other developments conspired to bring about this state of affairs. For the first time discrimination took an economic turn, at least on a sizable scale. Ads specifying "Gentiles only" and "Christians only" began to appear, starting with clerical jobs, then spreading to other areas of employment. A less advertised discrimination barred Jews from scholastic, military, and political employment. In 1913 the Anti-Defamation League of B'nai B'rith was formed to combat these developments.

AMERICAN RACISM IS BORN

Meanwhile, the literati supplied an ideological padding for the practices. First, sociologists of note and in considerable number produced findings whose only possible interpretation categorized Jews as pathological and inferior. Eugenicists followed this lead and, undoubtedly under the influence of European racist writings, set themselves to providing a racist ideology for the American frame of reference. Of these attempts the most noted was that of Madison Grant, whose *The Passing of the Great Race*[14] became the American counterpart of H.S. Chamberlain's *Foundations*. Grant's book, which uninhibitedly expatiated on the inferiority of peoples and the democracy that tolerates them, wielded great influence and ran through four editions. Its chief successors were Dr. Lothrop Stoddard's *Revolt Against Civilization*[15] and Burton V. Hendrick's *The Jews in America*.[16] Despite minimizing tendencies, Oscar Handlin concedes that "by 1920 a full-fledged racial ideology colored the thinking of many Americans."[17]

Anyone who still believed the American brand of racial antisemitism to be a benign growth was painfully disillusioned in 1915 when a young Jew, Leo Frank, on the flimsiest evidence, was convicted of the murder of a 14-year-old girl in Atlanta, Georgia, and was lynched. The antisemitic quality of the incident is best evinced by the fact that the principal testimony against the accused was the word of a Black who himself was the only other suspect—an incredible inversion of order in the South. Shocked protests in the American press greeted Frank's conviction, and his lynching sent a shudder through the nation.

One of the most strident voices clamoring for Frank's death was that of Tom Watson, a man whose past was distinguished by failure in politics and anti-Catholic vitriol. In 1913 he suddenly turned his attacks on the Jews. In his publication, *Watson's Magazine*, he laid down a barrage of violent charges and invective, drawing special attention to supposed Jewish physical filthiness and practice of extortion and fraud. In 1915 when students of law and the press protested against the conviction of Frank as a travesty, Watson jumped into the fray, charged Jewish influence, and excoriated Frank as a typical example of Jewish lust. "Every student of sociology knows," he ranted, "that the black man's lust after the white woman is not much fiercer than the lust of the licentious Jew for the gentile."[18] Watson was able to call upon one of the sociologists of the time for corroboration of this statement. After Frank's death, though all unbiased observers exonerated him, Watson continued his attack against the deceased, again including all Jewry. Ritual murder, he insisted, was a Jewish custom, and Mendel Beilis, the "Russian ritual murderer,"[19] was acquitted only by Jewish "pressures" such as had been exerted to free Captain Dreyfus. Later Watson turned his guns on Jewish wealth and domination and at one point accused Jews of being in league with Rome. That this demagogue's phrenetic antisemitism struck a responsive chord in others besides lynchers may be deduced from his election to the U.S. Senate in 1920 and from the extravagant eulogies by some of his fellow-senators at his death.

THE SUPERPATRIOTIC AGE

The end of the war fought to end all wars and establish democracy everywhere brought disillusionment to the world and a strong case of xenophobic isolationism to the United States. The League of Nations and the World Court were rejected, tariffs went up, and a wave of fear of foreigners and subversion swept across the country. This was the heyday of "100% Americanism"—a bad day for minorities, especially Jews. Were not the Jews disqualified from seeking title to the august classification, indeed the very danger against which "100% Americanism" must defend itself? Thus thought the Ku Klux Klan, most spectacular of the nativist organizations of the period. This ghoulish order, founded in the 1860s to terrorize Blacks in the Reconstruction era, and reformed in 1915 to keep the country free of Black, Catholic and Jewish influence, came into prominence again in 1920. Until its decline in 1925, this lawless organization, among its other aims, incited hatred against Jews wherever it could, especially in New York City, emphasizing their would-be dominance, alien character, and unassimilability.

Foremost hero of the "super-patriots" was the famous industrialist, Henry Ford, whose weekly, *The Dearborn Independent,* took up a campaign of defamation of Jews which lasted seven
years. The campaign, launched in 1920, concentrated its attacks
on alleged financial, commercial, and political Jewish monopo-
lies, which, according to this paper, reached also into the communications and cultural media. Well before Hitler, the
"international Jew" was born, a Jew who is the "conscious enemy
of all that Anglo-Saxons mean by civilization."[20] The *Independent's* chief source of inspiration was the *Protocols,* which Ford was
persuaded to publicize by a member of an antisemitic group of
Russian *émigrés* in Washington. Even after they were exposed as
a forgery, Ford's publication continued to use them. The damage
done by the *Independent,* with a circulation of 700,000, was com-
pounded by a re-issue of all its antisemitic materials in four volumes totaling 746 pages. Numberless copies of an excerpt of
these, entitled *The International Jew,*[21] circulated in the United
States and throughout the world. Ford finally recanted in 1927
when brought to account by a law suit by Aaron Shapiro. In a
statement to Louis Marshall, well known Jewish spokesman, he
confessed his mortification at having allowed the *Protocols* to be
employed in his publication and for having given injury to Jews.
He expressed his wish to make amends and forbade further circulation of the booklet under his name, but to little avail: It continued to circulate in Hitler's Germany and elsewhere, and again
as late as 1963 in an antisemitic hate-sheet in the United States.[22]
Carey McWilliams could say: "In one sense, Hitler began where
Ford left off."[23]

Although *The Dearborn Independent* overshadowed the rest,
it was but one of a large number of books and periodicals that
berated the Jews in the postwar years. The *Searchlight* in Atlanta,
the *Fellowship Forum* in Washington, and *The American Standard*
in New York were the more conspicuous among them.

This widespread popularization of racist and anti-Jewish literature contributed to a rich harvest on the active level. Ethnic
discrimination was advanced on all fronts, this time with Congress taking an initiative. Dozens of bills to restrict immigration—still at a high level—inundated Congress. In 1921 under the
newly elected Warren Harding, a temporary measure was passed

that effected a curtailment of the influx from southern and eastern Europe. In 1924 came the Johnson Bill which "slammed the door" by limiting immigration to two per cent of the quota base of 1890. Little effort was made to hide the fact that the main target was the Jewish influx. From 1924 to 1929, the Jewish annual immigration rate was cut from over 100,000 to 49,000, and finally to 11,000. By contrast, many of the immigrants from northern and western Europe could not even fill their quotas. The paradox was complete: The nation of immigrants had moved to preserve its "native stock." The Madison Grants had won the day.

Educational institutions were not to be outdone. In 1922 when President Lowell of Harvard suggested some kind of quota system for admittance he was merely verbalizing what had already been practiced in many schools by various sifting devices. And although his proposal was defeated by the overseers he succeeded in giving the *numerus clausus* an air of respectability in America. Before long many universities and colleges set limits on Jewish enrollment. Most professions and employment agencies did the same. Restrictive covenants among real estate owners and agencies closed off large areas in cities and suburbs to persons of "Hebrew descent."

Thanks to the postwar boom, this antisemitic outcropping did not reach the populace and though it declined somewhat toward the end of the twenties many disturbing incidents were still reported across the country. The most extraordinary was the ritual-murder charge in 1928 in Massena, New York; the most puerile, perhaps, the dragging of three Jewish interns from their beds to douse them with ice water in Kings County, New York, the previous year.

The depression ushered in a new wave of antisemitism which, before it subsided, reached the high mark of its American course. Voices were heard blaming the economic collapse on Jewish machinations, and Roosevelt's New Deal was whispered as the "Jew Deal." The nativist spirit, which had slackened in the late twenties, rose to a high pitch. Its new focus was for the most part anti-Communist, but also anti-democratic and antisemitic. The Jew on this occasion was portrayed by the superpatriots as the disseminator of international Communism and radicalism, and democracy was seen as his tool. Scores of Nazi organizations sprang up and the KKK was revived.

The most notorious of these groups was William Pelley's Silver Shirt Legion, which sported all the trappings of Hitler's storm troopers. Through books and periodicals, Pelley aped his Nazi counterparts and emitted a stream of savage scoldings about Jewish intrigue, radicalism, megalomania, insolence, and the like. He ran for the presidency as the candidate of the Christian Party in 1936 and proclaimed: "We Americans now have a political party openly and fiercely anti-Jewish. The newly organized Christian Party gives us our opportunity to register effective protest to the way in which Jews are taking over our industries, property and our money."[24] Pelley was investigated by the government, charged as a racketeer, and sentenced to jail for 15 years.

There were many other similar organizations, notably George Deatherage's Knights of the White Camellia, dedicated to struggle against both Jewish Communism and "Jewocracy" (democracy), the Order of Seventy-Six, The American Vigilante Intelligence, the Green Mountain Boys, and the Khaki Shirts. A historian of the time counted 121 organizations peddling antisemitic propaganda between the years 1933 and 1939. Particularly obstreperous among the antisemites of these years was the Rev. Gerald B. Winrod, a delver into the occult, who imbibed of the *Protocols*, and, among other activities, ranted against the Jews as "Christ killers," eulogized the Nazis, and charged that "Jesuits and Jews controlled most of the Administration."[25] He ran for the Senate in Kansas and lost, but received a sizable vote.

As the depression settled in, the assault took a political turn. Roosevelt was denounced as a descendant of Dutch Jews named Rosenfeld and Bernard Baruch was decried as the boss of the country. For the first time in American history, naked antisemitism reached the floor of the U.S. Congress when Republican Representative Louis V. McFadden of Pennsylvania inveighed against international Jewish money powers. Defeated for re-election after 20 years' service in the House, he ran for the presidency in 1936 on a platform one of whose planks was "Christianity instead of Judaism." In this same campaign Alfred M. Landon of Kansas was forced on several occasions to discountenance antisemitic support. And it was in these same years that the spurious letter of Benjamin Franklin urging the exclusion of Jews from the country first saw the light of day. It appeared in *Liberation*, the official organ of Pelley's Silver Shirt Legion.

NAZI INTERLUDE

The most important contribution to antisemitism in the thirties came from Nazi Germany. The Nazis' rise to power not only gave encouragement to the home-grown nativist organizations but gave direct aid to set up Nazi groups in the United States. The German government itself established a division of foreign propaganda, and Hitler approved of a Nazi unit for German-Americans. Another organization called the Friends of the New Germany—later to become the *Bund*—was organized as a federation of all pro-Nazi societies. This organization received funds and propaganda materials from headquarters abroad and was under the direction of Heinz Spanknoebel, a Nazi agent, who finally fled the country to avoid possible imprisonment. When the Friends of the New Germany were reorganized as the German-American *Bund*, Fritz Kuhn became its *Fuehrer*. This organization was fully equipped with a uniformed guard which drilled, held regular meetings, and distributed Nazi propaganda on a wide scale. Needless to say, antisemitism was one of the most prominent features of the *Bund* campaign.

These crude operations, both Nazi and nativist, were not destined to survive. They earned the contempt of the American people and were found by government investigation to have all the earmarks of fraud. Hitler's excesses caused a further revulsion of American opinion. Ultimately Nazism itself struck the lethal blow to organized racist antisemitism in the United States.

BACK TO POLITICS

Father Charles E. Coughlin, famed radio priest of the thirties, succumbed to the antisemitic virus. From 1926 he had won himself an audience of some 3,500,000 listeners, mostly Catholic, and wielded considerable influence. As time went on his interests became more and more political and partisan; and, finally, upon the defeat of his third party and the election of Roosevelt in 1936, his talks took on an antisemitic coloring. In 1936 he founded a weekly paper, named *Social Justice*, in which he called for the formation of a Christian Front organization aimed, among other things, "to curb the Molochs of international finance." In 1938 in *Social Justice* he spoke of a: "Christian Front which will not fear being called anti-Semitic because it knows the term 'anti-Semitic' is only another pet phrase of castigation in Communism's glossary of attacks."[26] The radio priest then took up the cause of the *Protocols* on the plea that their authenticity was unimportant since "we can't ignore the news value of their strikingly prophetic nature . . ."[27] He singled out Jews as leagued with Communism, and yet suspected them of controlling international finance. On one occasion he asserted that "because Jews reject Christ, it is impossible for them to accept His doctrine of spiritual brotherhood in the light in which Christians accept it."[28] Toward the end of the thirties he attracted sharp opposition from many quarters, not least of all from his own coreligionists. He left the air in 1940, but his work was carried on by *Social Justice* and its organizational adjuncts, the Christian Front and the Christian Mobilizers. In several instances the activities of these groups led to provocative and antisemitic incidents. In 1942 in the wake of the fracas, the American Catholic bishops declared in their annual statement: "We feel a deep sense of revulsion against the cruel indignities heaped upon the Jews in conquered countries and upon defenseless peoples not of our faith."[29]

In 1941 political antisemitism was renewed by a flurry of charges that Jews were forcing the country into war. Senator Burton K. Wheeler of Montana and Congressman John Rankin of Mississippi openly voiced this opinion. But the most influential voice on the scene was that of Charles A. Lindbergh, who had earned his place in history by his solo flight across the Atlantic in 1927. An isolationist and one of the chief figures of the America First Committee, Lindbergh showed no antisemitic leanings at first, but showed some tolerance for the Nazi regime when he accepted an Order of Merit award from Field Marshall Goering in Berlin in 1938. In a speech in September 1941, however, he charged Jews, together with the Roosevelt administration and the British, with seeking to force America into war. He warned that "their [Jews'] greatest danger to this country lies in their large ownership and influence in our motion pictures, our press, our radio and our government."[30] Severely criticized on many sides, he retired into silence.

During World War II, organized and political antisemitism declined, not to be revived. Actually, it had not substantially affected the status of American Jews but nonetheless had caused them grave anxieties and, further, gave to all Americans a warning that, under sufficiently adverse conditions, the rabid anti-Jewish agitation which marked so much of European history was possible in America. The more lasting and serious result of the depression period was the further increase of economic disabilities for Jews. As early as 1930 one observer was able to conclude that "the normal absorption of Jews within the American economic structure is now practically impossible."[31] From that point until the declaration of World War II, things went from bad to worse. In the competition for jobs, the Jew became more and more a marginal worker—the last hired and the first laid off. These years helped to crystallize a pattern of employment that allotted a low ratio of Jews in certain professions, such as teaching and engineering, and crowded them into others like law, medicine, and dentistry, access to which was not determined by social status. Discrimination in the academic field continued.

This socio-economic discrimination, while diminishing, survived the war and has remained the hallmark of American antisemitism. In the fifties, it reached its lowest point in decades, yet in 1962 a study of anti-Jewish discrimination found that a quiet but effective exclusion of Jews in housing, social facilities, schools, and employment persists despite many legal measures taken against them.[32] Overt or radical antisemitism meanwhile is far from defunct. In the early sixties the United States joined many other nations in a "swastika epidemic," in which some 600 incidents of synagogue desecrations in this country alone were reported. Nor were antisemitic organizations lacking. There was a revival of the KKK, the National States Rights Party, and the Defensive League of Registered Americans, to mention only the more notorious. Anti-Jewish hate literature became plentiful. Particularly vicious were *The Thunderbolt,* published by the National States Rights Party, Conde McGinley's *Common Sense,* Gerald K. Smith's *Cross and Flag,* and the *Rockwell Report.* Chief among the agitators was George Lincoln Rockwell, chief of the American Nazi Party, who tramped noisily about this country and abroad threatening to finish what Hitler began. He was emulated by many imitators.[33]

EVALUATION

This rabid antisemitism has failed, actually, to catch on in America. Even in the fertile soil of the thirties it did not take root, and at present it is the exclusive property of the lunatic fringe. To what are we to attribute this partial American immunity to an almost universal cancer? Superior enlightenment or ethics? Certainly American political ideals of freedom and equality, lucidly enunciated from the first days of the Republic, were not without influence on the course of American prejudice. But probably more decisive has been the opulence of resources and opportunities that Americans have enjoyed. Prolonged and gruelling poverty—breeder *par excellence* of the antisemitic growth—has never found a hospitable home in most parts of America. It is a sobering fact, however, that the relatively short-lived economic depression of the thirties was productive of a brand of antisemitism that in many ways resembled the European kind at its worst. Another distinguishing mark of American antisemitism has been the absence of religious motivation. Some degree of prejudice based on theological considerations has colored the antisemitism of several of the rabble-rousers; but even in their case it was not the mainspring of motivation. When the antisemitic animus reached its peak in the thirties it was to Nazi Germany, not to the medieval world, that the Jew-haters turned.

But the fortunate economic conditions that have impeded the growth of rabid antisemitism have, may we say, taken their revenge by producing a social hostility that is uniquely American. In an atmosphere of social snobbery and economic class-consciousness, the Jew is destined to suffer more discrimination than others, not so much because of his "difference," but by reason of his achievements. It is an observable fact that discrimination grows in virulence as the group discriminated against enters more vigorously into competition with the discriminators.

14
THE LAST TWENTY-FIVE YEARS

Twenty-five years ago there were glimmers of hope that the ageless phenomenon of antisemitism was, after all, a terminable disease and might at last be on the road to extinction. Three events in the 1960s gave promise that this might be so.

The Eichmann trial in 1961 exacerbated anti-Jewish feeling in antisemitic circles, particularly in Argentina, and sounded a mild, latent antisemitism in otherwise unbiased quarters.[1] But for many the trial held seeds of promise. It effected what could be called the "return of the repressed," bringing many for the first time to a full consciousness of the diabolism of the Holocaust and of the complicity in it of so much of the civilized world. Where the Nuremberg trial failed, it appeared that the Eichmann trial might succeed.[2]

A second seminal event was the issuance of the statement on the Jewish people (*Nostra Aetate*, 4) of the Second Vatican Council in 1965. Though the final statement was weaker than a preliminary draft presented to the Council Fathers, taken by itself, it can only be gauged as an epochal move forward on the part of the Church on the road toward Jewish-Christian understanding and reconciliation. The document stressed the common patrimony binding the Church and Israel, deplored hatred and persecution of the Jews, and forbade representing the Jewish people of old or of today as guilty of the death of Christ, and called for fraternal

263

dialogue and biblical studies between Christians and Jews. Such a statement on the highest level of the Church could, if heeded and implemented, deal a lethal blow to Christian antisemitism. Since the issuance of *Nostra Aetate* three further documents have been issued by the Vatican elaborating the principles and aims of that document, and some national Catholic hierarchies have issued documents of their own, as have also many of the mainline Protestant churches, especially in the United States.[3]

A third event, the Six-Day War of 1967, generated a surge of empathy and admiration in many countries for the plucky fledgling state of Israel that managed to repulse so promptly the onslaught of Soviet-equipped and trained Arab armies. In the minds of many the image of Israel as David confronting Goliath was conjured up again—a simile that for most people reflected positively on the image of the Jews everywhere.

It is necessary today in the mid-1980s to acknowledge that the promise of those hopeful events has not been realized. The antisemitic devil still roams the world. There is hardly a country where a Jewish population of any size exists that does not exhibit some form of antisemitism. Some of the older forms, true, have declined, others have not; and new forms continue to emerge.

Two score years after the Holocaust, despite the Nuremberg and Eichmann trials, a strong reluctance to confront the subject of the Holocaust pervades much of non-Jewish thinking. Worse, as the Jewish community and a few more sensitive non-Jews struggle with this unique manifestation of human evil, most non-Jews attempt to deflate it as merely another statistic on the indiscriminate listing of man's inhumanity to man. Today everyone, it would seem, has his/her favorite "genocide," but little to no interest in the Holocaust. Some resent Jewish attention to it, others even strive to deny its historicity.[4] In 1978, the four-part, nine and a half hour drama "Holocaust" reached 120 million people on the television screen, one of the largest audiences in television history. For a while the showing aroused a serious interest in the subject and occasioned some educational projects in schools and elsewhere. But as the memory of the series receded, the common indifference returned. For the historian of antisemitism it is difficult not to discern in this recurring insensitivity an element of latent antisemitism.

CHRISTIAN ANTISEMITISM

The hopes laid upon *Nostra Aetate, 4* and other churchly documents on Jewish-Christian relations also failed to bring about expected results. That they initiated a new era in Jewish-Christian understanding and a productive dialogue is beyond question, as is also the fact that there has been a general decline in Christian antisemitism. Official church antisemitism is a thing of the past, and if we regard certain idiosyncratic "Identity Churches" that preach racial superiority and antisemitism as pseudo-churches and pseudo-Christianity, one can affirm that no organized antisemitism exists in Christianity today.[5]

On the popular plane, however, antisemitism is still observable. Much of the traditional anti-Judaic theology and teaching is gone, and yet a correlation between certain conservative Christian beliefs and antisemitic myths and stereotypes of a secular character has been demonstrable.[6] That this conservative-theological link with antisemitism, on the other hand, is not a necessary one is evident in the friendship for Jews and Israel that has developed of late in the Evangelical Churches, all of which remain conservative in theology and scriptural exegesis.[7] On this new bond Rabbi Mark Tannenbaum, director of Interreligious Affairs of the American Jewish Committee, has commented that the "evangelical community is the largest and fastest growing block of pro-Israeli, pro-Jewish sentiment in the country."[8] Conservative or "orthodox" theology and antisemitism are obviously dissociable. Indirect support for this opinion *per contra* may be deduced from the increasing disfavor with which liberal or leftist Christians greet Israel and Jewish attachment to that state. Liberation theologies and others again of a Third World stamp have also often taken on something of an anti-Judaic coloring.[9]

The emergence of a revisionist Christian theology of Judaism in recent years promises to become a potent factor in the decline and disappearance of Christian antisemitism. Though begun in pioneering efforts of a mere handful of scholars in the 30s and 40s,[10] its present impetus has derived in the main from the growth of the ecumenical spirit in the 50s and 60s, the establishment and survival of the State of Israel, and from a postwar realization of the horrors and implications of the Holocaust. These crucial events brought some Christian theologians and scholars to the recognition that the anti-Judaism of Christian teaching and scriptures played a crucial role in the origin and growth of antisemitism throughout the Christian centuries and, if to a lesser degree, contributes to its course still. It became evident that a revised Christian theology of Judaism was imperative, not for the defeat of antisemitism alone but for the integrity of the Christian message as well.

Though still in its infancy, this new theology has increasingly attracted a broad and reputable band of theologians,[11] and more recently has enlisted the attention of some first-rank theologians of international reputation.[12] The objective these theologians have set for themselves is the correction and emendation of Christian theology of a kind to excise as far as possible the anti-Judaic elements of traditional teachings and to accord Judaism its proper theological validity and importance from a Christian perspective. Thus far the beginnings of a consensus have materialized. Virtually all agree that any Christian theological consideration of Judaism must include a full appreciation of the Jewish heritage of Christianity, the Jewishness of Jesus and the primitive Church; the rejection of offensive teachings, such as the deicide accusation and the divine repudiation and replacement of Judaism; invidious comparisons of Christianity with Judaism; and repudiation of antisemitism as sinful and unchristian. Beyond this, consensus tends to disappear. Opinions diverge in two directions. The larger number of theologians who work in this area of research generally take a liberal or progressive turn and call for a reconsideration of traditional Christology as central to the anti-Judaic problem. The problem they confront is that of reconciling the uniqueness (not superiority) of Christianity while "making room" for Judaism's ongoing role (its uniqueness) in the divine plan. Dr. Rosemary Ruether in particular has had the merit of pressing the theological dialogue vigorously in this direction[13] and has catalyzed a rich outgrowth of creative theologizing on the relationship of Judaism to Christianity—often in reactive opposition to her views. Most respondents have found her analyses too radical and unnecessary and sought more moderate positions that do not cut so closely to the heart of traditional Christology.[14] On another side of the present theological effort stand more conservative theologians and thinkers who eschew all alterations of Christology and limit their revisions to the contents of the aforementioned consensus. Basic to their thinking is the assurance that antisemitism is not inherent to Christianity or Christology and that the consolidation of Jewish-Christian friendship and understanding can be achieved on a personal and social level. They consider Christological revision an accommodation that no dialogue can require.[15]

The net worth of this theological enterprise as a whole will ultimately depend, it would seem, on its ability to create a wider consensus that will recommend itself to the theological community at large and finally on the ability of the theological community to persuade church leadership to introduce the results of its research into the pulpits and classrooms of the churches.

The blueprint for the extinction of Christian antisemitism is, ostensibly, already on paper. It is to be found in the statements and guidelines of the churches and in the work of the revisionist theologians. When this corpus will have been sufficiently disseminated and implemented on all ecclesial levels, Christian antisemitism will for all practical purposes have come to naught, or become wholly absorbed in its disowned offspring—secular antisemitism. Regrettably, the present pace of its dissemination and implementation is slow. Most of the Christian populace has not been reached.

ANTI-ZIONISM

The Six-Day war was critical for Israel's survival and a watershed in the course of contemporary antisemitism. The admiration that Israel's brilliant military success elicited in all but Arab and Soviet countries was short-lived. In short order, a fickle reversal of perspective turned Israel into a Goliath in confrontation with the pan-Arab world cast in the role of David. Anti-Zionism's hour had come. Hitherto a sporadic and anemic movement outside of Arab countries, it now took on a fresh, sustained vigor. According to one observer, anti-Zionism has become the third wave of antisemitism in this century, the first of which took the shape of pogroms in Russia and the Dreyfus Affair in France at the turn of the century, the second, Nazism.[16]

After the Holocaust, openly professed antisemitism lost whatever "respectability" it had mustered in the public forum and had thenceforth to look for "respectable" disguises behind which to find expression. Anti-Zionism was the perfect answer. High-minded citizens, politicians, intellectuals, clergymen, could now vent their hatred or distaste for Jews under the cover of sympathy for Arab refugees, Arab national aspirations, Third World ideologies, and other laudable causes again. And all could proclaim they were not antisemitic, but merely anti-Zionist.[17] Thus does antisemitism seem to disappear, as anti-Zionism thrives. In the mid-1980s, anti-Zionism stands out as the foremost front upon which the antisemitic attack is pressed—with surprising success. It has proved, moreover, to be an incredible unifier, often bringing Arabs, Communists, Protestants and Catholics, Leftists and Rightists, Blacks and Whites under the same banner, thus demonstrating the same virtuosity that the age-old antisemitism it disclaims enjoyed.

At the core of the anti-Zionist rationale is a fallacy and a refusal. The fallacy consists in defining Jewishness as *only* a religion, not a peoplehood or a nation, whereas it is essentially all of these; the refusal, in not allowing Jews to define themselves. Throughout their long history Jews have identified themselves as a people wedded to a Law, a homeland (Israel), and a nationhood. Zionism originated in the Torah, Judaism's most sacred book, not, as some think, in the political movement launched by Theodore Herzl and his collaborators in the twentieth century. For the committed Jew, an attack on Zionism, on Israel, is an attack on his Jewishness and his Judaism.[18]

There are, of course, degrees of anti-Zionism. One cannot place in the same category the genocidal intent to destroy Israel found among some Arabs, Soviets, and extremists and that undefinable tendency to disfavor Israel that is so widespread. Yet in a wide sense both are expressions of anti-Zionism, and both are almost always to some degree antisemitically motivated; in the first case consciously, in the second, unconsciously. Can we compare, for example, the sentiments of a Yakov Malik, Soviet ambassador to the United Nations, who declared, "The Zionists have come forward with the theory of the Chosen People, an absurd ideology," thus exposing the antisemitism of his anti-Zionism—can we compare this with what has been called "another silence" of the churches in the face of the danger to Israel's survival during the Six-Day war?[19] Hardly. The difference is great, but it is still one of degree. It was ethically possible to be anti-Zionist before the State of Israel became a reality, and it is possible to be so today in the sense of criticizing Israeli politics and practices, but to go beyond that now is fraught with genocidal overtones[20] that cannot but harbor an unrecognized antisemitism. Martin Luther King saw clearly when, challenging a Black student who attacked "Zionists," he snapped: "When people criticize Zionists they mean Jews. You're talking antisemitism."[21]

ARAB ANTISEMITISM

The only place in the world today where antisemitism is overtly expressed and practiced with little effort to don it with its anti-Zionist disguise is in Arab or Islamic lands.[22] Already during World War II sympathies for the Nazi cause could be detected among prominent Arab personages, principally, the Grand Mufti of Jerusalem, Haj Amir El-Husseini, who fled to Berlin during the war, where he made clear his approval of the Nazi Holocaust. He was never repudiated by any Arab spokesman, and after the war he was again accepted as the leader of the Palestinian Arabs. Only when Germany's defeat was in sight did Arab countries declare war on Germany, some in 1945. Hitler was often honored in Arab countries, as was Eichmann later. After the war many Nazi officials escaped to Cairo where they enjoyed asylum. After the establishment of the State of Israel, as Arab relations with Israel continued to worsen, Arab propaganda widened its focus against Israel to include the Jewish people and their religion. During the Vatican Council (1962-1965) much could be read in the Arab press and heard on radio about the "deicidal people" and Jewish designs to destroy Christianity. The "blood libel" was revived on at several occasions, on the last of which the late King Faisal of Saudi Arabia was the purveyor. The *Protocols of the Elders of Zion* enjoys a wide circulation in Arab countries and has received public commendations by President Nasser of Egypt and King Faisal of Saudi Arabia. In 1972, before his magnificent peace-making journey to Jerusalem, President Anwar Sadat was able to quote the Koran as to the need to humiliate and degrade Jews. During all of these years the media in most Arab countries were replete with insulting and cruel caricatures not only of Israel but of Jews in stories and cartoons.[23]

In the 1980s the antisemitic attack goes on as Arab propaganda is spread through numerous groups and agents in Europe, Africa, Latin America and United States.

The charge is pressed that the Zionist enemy has stolen Arab land, that they are duplicates of the Nazis, and that their intent against Arabs is genocidal. It has been a lesson well learned in the anti-Zionist world. A ubiquitous myth has taken root: an alien people (the Jews) have expelled an indigenous people (the Arabs) from their homes, forcing them to fester in poverty on the borders of their own homeland. The myth, incredibly, has been swallowed whole by many otherwise intelligent and fair-minded people without the least effort to verify any part of it. The United Nations has been the most receptive. Thanks to an automatic coalition of Arab, Soviet, and Third World countries, the world body has been turned into what appears at times to be no more than an antisemitic world forum.[24]

There are many who attribute Arab antisemitism exclusively to the present Arab-Israeli conflict. Actually, its roots run much deeper, going back through Arab and Islamic history to the Koran itself from which a twofold principle can be distilled: that the *dhimmis* (non-Muslim monotheists) are not to dominate Muslims but be dominated by them, and that they are to be kept in a degraded state. Throughout the centuries a multitude of humiliating customs and practices were enacted against Jews in Muslim lands, all designed to remind them of their inferior position.[25] These customs and practices need not be viewed merely as indulgence in hate or prejudice, but in large part as adherence to Islamic religious principle, a principle that became embedded in Islamic culture and politics. The intensity of Arab resentment of Israel today cannot be fully understood except in light of this traditional principle and practice that has been turned upside down in our time by the Israeli presence and successes in the Middle East.

SOVIET ANTISEMITISM

The most grievous growth of antisemitism in the second half of the century has occurred in Soviet Russia and its satellites, particularly Poland and Czechoslovakia—to which Soviet policies are always promptly exported. The Soviets were among the first to attempt to masquerade antisemitism in the costume of anti-Zionism. One finds, moreover, a strange combining of inconsistency and persistence in Soviet antisemitic practice. This is attributable most likely to the dichotomy of its sources: Marxist theory and the centuries-old Judaeophobia. The inconsistency derives presumably from the first, the persistence from the second.

Ironically, Soviet Russia was one of the most zealous supporters of the creation of the State of Israel, surpassing even the United States in its ardor,[26] which gives the lie to its present contention that Israel is an "imperialist creation." In the early 1950s all this changed almost overnight as Soviet policy took to courting Arab and African states. Straightway Yiddish publications were banned, prominent Jewish litterateurs were executed, thousands of Jews were jailed, and the Jewish Anti-Fascist Committee was abolished. The effort to stamp out Jewish religion and culture was stepped up. It was a successful effort. A handful of rabbis were left in the country; there remained no rabbinical seminary and only a few synagogues; the study of Hebrew was forbidden; and the possession of articles of prayer was outlawed. Discrimination against Jews in education and employment increased.

From this point a relentless anti-Zionist campaign was waged, especially after the Six-Day War of 1967. It soon became clear that a new code word for "Jew" had been found. The Jew was not so much now a "cosmopolitan," a "parasite," etc., but a "Zionist." The controlled media portrayed Israel as a Nazi racist state, and rejected the Holocaust as a myth. Still trumpeting today that there is no antisemitism or Jewish problem in the Soviet Union, the government excoriates "Zionists" on every occasion defining them as reactionary enemies of the revolution and spies for the imperialist West.[27]

Having largely succeeded in weakening the Jewish religion, the government turned its full attention to destroying Jewish nationalism. One of the instruments used to this end was emigration policy. Applied with great inconsistency, the policy was manipulated according to the external and internal needs of the moment, and the gates of exit to Jews who wished to emigrate to Israel were opened and closed accordingly. At first, in the 1960s, some hundreds of thousands were allowed to emigrate; today the emigration is down to a trickle. The very act of trying to procure an exit visa for Israel has become an agonizing one, and the consequences, disastrous: the applicant is likely to lose his/her job, then be accused of "parasitism," if not treason, and possibly jailed. At present there are two thousand of these "refuseniks" (whose application for a visa was rejected), all in a precarious situation. Anatoly Sharansky and Andrei Sakharov, famous names in the West, are among these victims.[28]

In 1980 a new wave of Soviet antisemitism is apparently in progress, for the usual harassments, mistreatments, and repressions have been intensified. Books of a crude antisemitic nature have been published—always with official authorization. The Soviet press, periodicals, and television programs have multiplied negative and insulting references to Jews and Israel. Anti-Jewish material has been distributed to Red Army recruits. Jewish history has been eliminated from elementary and secondary school textbooks, and the Russian pogroms of the late nineteenth century are justified as a legitimate part of the class struggle. No approved Jewish school exists, and private instruction in Hebrew remains forbidden. In Moscow teachers of Hebrew have received threats of banishment.[29]

The export of Soviet antisemitism to Poland was an easy matter, given the endemic Judaeophobia of that country. The Polish Jewish population of the 1930s of 3.5 million had fallen to 150,000 at the end of the war. This decline did not terminate Polish antisemitism. Even after the war pogroms took place in Kielce and Cracow. In 1969 an "anti-Zionist" campaign effected a purge of many Jews from universities and from the economic and political life of the country. The campaign was blamed on a "students' strike" of the year before, supposedly staged by "Zionists." There were at that time only about 25,000 Jews in the entire country. That same year 15,000 of them emigrated. But the end was not yet. In 1981, with only 5,000 to 7,000 Jews left, a public demonstration, apparently officially coordinated, was staged against the "Zionist clique" that supposedly was directing *Solidarity* and influencing the government. Another case of "antisemitism without Jews" in a Jew-free country![30]

Against this sombre background it is heartening to report that this last obviously officially engineered antisemitism did not find any sympathy or backing in the Polish public. One observer has explained: "Antisemitism as an internal weapon has become increasingly less viable largely because the Polish population has to a considerable extent freed itself from this virus."[31] In Poland antisemitism is now mainly government inspired.

Czechoslovakia, though heir to a long moderate tradition and after a serious but fatal flirtation with liberalism under the President Dubcek (crushed by Soviet tanks), was unable to resist the Soviet "anti-Zionist" importation. In the wake of the Six-Day War an antisemitic wave rolled over the country that was to become what was described as a "national plague."[32] Many leading Jews had to leave the country. With only a handful of Jews still in the country, a vocal anti-Zionism continues. One more example of Soviet "antisemitism without Jews."

It is apparent that the Soviets and their satellites have on their hands a problem they cannot solve—the Jewish problem. While denying the very existence of antisemitism or a "Jewish problem," the domestic practice of antisemitism goes on unrestrained. Socialism's dream of a universal classless society had not counted on tenacious ethnic or religious groups that refuse to melt into the faceless proletarian mass, prominent among which was Soviet Jewry. The Kremlin, it appears, has opted to simulate a solution by oscillation, alternating a policy of temporary minor concessions with repression. The prospects for Soviet Jews are accordingly bleak. The best that can be hoped at present is that they be conceded that minimum of rights which other religious bodies and nationalities in the Soviet empire possess. This in itself would be a substantial gain. Meanwhile, since the Soviets have shown themselves to be somewhat sensitive to international opinion, pressures from Western states and churches would do well to continue their demands that human rights be respected and gates of emigration be opened to all Russian citizens, especially to Soviet Jews whose situation is so painful.

RETURN TO THE LEFT

Antisemitism is generally considered by both Jews and non-Jews to be a phenomenon of the Right. And certainly in modern times its most spectacular displays, exemplified by Czarist pogroms, the Dreyfus Affair, Hitler, and chauvinistic demogogues, have tended to justify that interpretation. But this view has tended to eclipse the fact that there has been an uninterrupted strain of antisemitism on the Left.[33] It should not, further, obscure the recrudescence of leftist antisemitism that has developed since the rebirth of the State of Israel. Indeed at present leftist "anti-Zionism" predominates on the antisemitic spectrum—a spectrum running leftward from liberal to socialist to radical to Communist. Prager and Telushkin put the matter succinctly: "The further Left one goes, the greater the antisemitism."[34] W.D. Rubenstein is no less direct: "Today, the main enemies of the Jews and Israel are almost exclusively on the left, most obviously the Communist states, the radical Third World anti-Zionist nations and their sympathizers in the West."[35]

This development comes as no surprise to historians of leftist ideology. From its inception socialist thought took on an antisemitic turn. All the progenitors of socialist theory, with the exception of St. Simon, were bitter antisemites. Marx learned much of his own antisemitism from Proudhon, Bauer, Fourier, Toussenel, Fichte, and others, as did also Engels. The *Protocols* came from socialist sources. In 1891, the Second International Socialist Congress refused to condemn antisemitism without condemning philosemitism at the same time. During the Dreyfus affair socialist leaders refused to counter the rightist attack on the Jewish army officer. Historian Zosa Szajkowski, writing in 1947 after a close study of French socialist literature, concluded that he could not find a single word on behalf of the Jews in the whole of that literature from 1820 to 1920.[36]

In our own day, the strain has continued, and since the Six-Day War has grown in intensity. A number of socialist and radical organizations have mounted an almost frenzied attack on Israel and Zionism—disclaiming antisemitism of course when challenged. In the United States, the Socialist Worker Party, the Young Socialist Alliance, the Progressive Labor Party, and the U.S. Communist Party vie with one another in damning Israel, calling it Fascist and for its destruction. The Students for a Democratic Society together with the Young Students Alliance and other radical student groups collaborate with Arab student groups on numerous campuses in support of the Palestinian cause and condemn Israel often in strident tones. The tendency to support the Arab position and treat Israel severely has been detected also in liberal circles, religious as well as secular.[37] Antisemitism's turn to the Left has been a wide one. Thanks to the anti-Zionist label, it has been often able to align fervent religionists alongside atheistic Communists in a common hostility to Israel and its supporters.[38]

The connection between the ideology of the Left and antisemitism is not accidental. An inevitable tension exists between leftist traditions and those which stress nationality, peoplehood, or religious commitment. The former, best exemplified in history by various brands of socialism, has canonized the conception of an egalitarian classless society that would to one degree or another subordinate ethnic, religious, and national groups to the economic and political policies of the state. A good example of the latter is Judaism. We are at grips here of course with the perennial conflict between universalism and particularism and, to some extent, between the secular and the sacral, which has defied so many attempts at a harmonious solution. Naturally, Judaism, one of the most particularistic of faith-traditions is destined to suffer most from the fall-out of this conflict. Extreme leftist ideologies and traditional Judaism are almost by definition incompatible. This tension diminishes as the leftist position moves rightward towards center, thus explaining the relative tolerance *cum* cool neutrality that liberal opinion is wont to manifest toward Israel and Zionism. The demise or decrease of leftist antisemitism will finally depend on the capacity of leftist theory to moderate its stance vis à vis those cultural and political particularities that are not going to wither away.

A first step toward that end necessarily entails the dissolution of the myth that lies at the root of the leftist hostility to Israel:

that Israel represents a colonial outpost of United States capitalism and imperialism, a creation of the military-industrial complex
that stands in the way not only of the liberation of the Palestinian
people but of the liberation and development of the Third World
as a whole, to which various leftist revolutionaries have dedicated
themselves. The myth can best be dissipated by acceptance of the
realities of the situation: Israel, sole democracy in the Middle
East, is an independent, egalitarian, and moderately socialist state
that has offered and provided technological and agricultural aid
to the Third World countries whenever asked to do so, and that
seeks a lasting peace and mutual cooperation with its Arab neighbors.

THE WESTERN WORLD

Passing from the Soviet and Arabic into the Western world
does not provide an exit from the antisemitic world. Surveying
the situation in the West from the end of World War II, the
chronicler of antisemitism comes to two conclusions: antisemitism has gradually declined, but so also has the sympathy for Israel that followed World War II. All the pieces of the antisemitic
puzzle are in varying degrees and proportions still there. Popular,
governmental, religious leftist, rightist, and pathological forms of
Jew-hate have made frequent appearances in Europe, Latin
America and North America in this period. Most have declined,
however, and some have disappeared, with the exception of the
last category, the pathological, which emulates the level of intensity found in Soviet and Arab models.

LATIN AMERICA

The worst record in the West has been Argentina's, where
some 40,000 Jews live. Their lives have not been happy, indeed
have often been terrorized.[39] For generations they were targeted
for harassments and violence; their synagogues were bombed and
their cemeteries desecrated. In this country, ever falling apart
economically and politically, a scapegoat is always needed, and
this could only be the Jew in Argentina. In this ultra-Catholic society antisemitism was never free of a theological stripe. Fathers

Julio Meinville and Carlos Mujica, well-known antisemites, helped to see to that. Legally Jews were pegged as second-class citizens and, though middle class, branded as purveyors of Communism. A government that welcomed and gave asylum to Nazi war criminals could hardly treat its Jewish citizens justly. After the Eichmann trial their lot worsened, and traditional antisemitism became, as everywhere, an excited anti-Zionism, thanks in considerable part to Arab propagandists. Host of numerous dictatorships and military junta governments, Argentina has, not surprisingly, specialized in right-wing antisemitism. In the 1960s the *Movimento Nazionalista Tacuara* and the *Guardia Restauradora Nacionalista*, Neo-Nazi groups, vandalized the Jewish communities. Less overtly antisemitic, Radical Left groups in university, labor, and clergy circles—all Third Worldist and pro-Arab—were more influential. Both leftist and rightist groups were connected by a common source—Arab propagandists.

In the 1980s the recession of Argentinian antisemitism, initiated temporarily under the Ongania regime in the 1970s, came well into evidence as anti-Jewish bombings, desecrations, and Nazi literature came under attack from the government, church, and prominent figures. Whether it will continue to recede will depend greatly on the fate of the new democratic government of President Paul Alfonsin, who, though faced with formidable internal problems, promises to put Argentina on a new road, a high road, on which the old antisemitism would hardly be viable.[40]

For other countries in Latin America, such as Brazil, Uruguay, and Chile, the story does not differ radically from that of Argentina, once scaled down to much smaller dimensions.[41]

WESTERN EUROPE[42]

In Western Germany, despite its deplorable antisemitic past, antisemitism still exists. Long centuries of Christian teaching of contempt and Nazi indoctrination continue to take their toll. After some years of reluctance, the government made a genuine effort to acquaint the German youth with the truth about the Nazi era, the killing of Jews, and the obligation to bring the Nazi murderers to account. The government considered itself obliged to befriend the state of Israel, but this policy tends to wane. The law requiring arrest of the Nazi criminals was allowed to expire in 1979 amid considerable controversy. Meanwhile extremist and terrorist groups of both the Left and the Right are active. The government is more concerned with the former than the latter. In recent years little has been done educationally to bring home the full horror of the Nazi past, especially the Holocaust. Popular antisemitism has declined, yet eruptions occur from time to time. The "swastika epidemic" begun in 1959 was an example. In 1973, two scathing anti-Zionist articles in *Stern*, a leading magazine, were received with considerable indifference by the public. Germany is still struggling in its soul, and it appears that the worst demons of the past have been overcome. Today some 28,000 Jews live in Germany and, surprisingly, their situation seems stable and their community is slightly growing.[43]

Austria has tried to make amends for its antisemitic past, but not entirely successfully. In the 1950s and 1960s numerous right-wing associations existed, especially among the young, and some old Nazis were still active in public life. In the 1966 election there were antisemitic manifestations and some of the candidates seemed tainted. In 1972 a Gallup poll of Austrians showed that 58 percent of the questioned did not like Jews and 27 percent would not as much as shake hands with one. In recent years the government and the church have made some earnest efforts to keep the climate free of anti-Jewish sentiments. The government has aided transient Jews from Russia allowing them to reside in the Schoenau Castle until it was closed by Chancellor Kreisky, a Jew, under terrorist threats. New camps were established to continue the service.[44]

In Italy a ceaseless flow of anti-Jewish and anti-Zionist actions, ranging from graffiti to attempted arson of synagogues, has clearly pointed to the active presence of Nazi-Fascist and Marxist-Leninist organizations and their probable collaboration with Arab terrorist groups. The government displays a pro-Arab bias and has voted in the United Nations for admission of the PLO as a permanent observer. On the other hand, a group of members of the Italian parliament are solidly in Israel's corner. The mass media in general seem often to take a pro-Arab stance, in any case did so during the Yom Kippur war. An anti-Jewish mood appears to have penetrated the intellectual and cultural world especially the universities. Attacks on the credibility of the Holocaust have been made. On the whole, Italian antisemitism is not of a popular variety, and has more the earmarks of an importation than a home-grown product.[45]

England's antisemitism tends to be urbane, seldom breaking out in overt violent forms, though some potentially dangerous social and political organizations exist. There were some anti-Jewish disturbances in the 1960s and again in the 1979 elections on the part of the National Front, a racist party formed in 1967 that expostulates on mongrelization of the races and domination by Zionist and pro-Zionist conspirators. The government's attitude toward Israel has, from the very issuance of the Balfour declaration in 1916, been profoundly ambivalent. It has voted with the Arab-Soviet bloc in the United Nations on issues concerned with Israel and in 1973 declared an embargo on armaments to the Middle East to the detriment of Israel. Newspapers display a similar ambivalence. On the other hand, Jews and Israel have always had their defenders in the government and in the media. There is an obvious struggle going on between the English sense of fair play and a pro-Arab bias. The struggle becomes an uneven one under the pressure of Arab propaganda in England, especially that stemming from 12,000 Arab students organized in student unions in the universities. In 1973 a high court refused to enjoin the Oxford English Dictionary from defining "Jew" as an "unscrupulous usurer" and a "trader who drives a hard bargain and deals craftily." The outcome of the struggle in the English soul is not as yet predictable.[46]

FRANCE

Five hundred and fifty thousand Jews live in France, the largest Jewish community in Europe. After World War II they lived in relative tranquility. The horror of the Holocaust and the shame of Vichy had effected a taboo on overt antisemitism. Under President De Gaulle both the Left and Right extremists remained restrained. In 1966 a poll in the magazine *Nouvel Adam* found 9 percent of its respondents owning to their antisemitism, 10 percent to not liking Jews, and 60 percent seeing Jews as French as themselves. Many thought French antisemitism was gone. It was not gone, as they were to see, but dammed up, seeking an outlet. The Six-Day War in 1967 provided the required release. President DeGaulle commented publicly on that occasion that Jews were a "domineering people sure of itself," a remark quickly followed by a rash of desecrations of cemeteries. From this point the French government—with the exception of the Poher administration—assumed a decidedly pro-Arab stand: armaments were withheld from Israel, but sold to Libya. Another wave of anti-Jewish incidents, including bombings, began in 1975; and the press, especially of the Left, multiplied attacks on Israel. In late September, 1980, five Jewish buildings, including a synagogue, were machine-gunned. It was in this feverish atmosphere that the culmination came. A bomb was thrown at Temple Simhat Torah on rue Copernic in Paris. Four were killed and twenty injured. This was the first time since World War II that Jews were killed because they were Jews. The popular reaction to the bombing was vigorous and swift, but that of the government, tardy and tepid. Up to 200,000 people from all quarters marched and goaded the government to action against extremism and antisemitic violence. A poll taken by the magazine *Express* found a chastened populace. Fifty-five percent believed that antisemitism is widespread in France and 37 percent that it is traditional in France.[47]

A corner seems to have been turned, but the future of French Jews is not assured. The estimate of Shimon Samuels, European director of the Anti-Defamation League, is a sobering one: "The common denominator in France, as elsewhere, has not changed. It is Jew-hatred, whether in the guise of leftist anti-Zionism, rightist anti-Semitism, or the Arab combination of both."[48]

THE UNITED STATES

What holds true for antisemitic conditions in Europe and Latin America (excluding Soviet and Arab countries) is largely true of the United States.[49] There is no governmental antisemitic policy in this country; the Radical Right and Left, though fragmented and weak, and Arab groups have been active; popular antisemitism has diminished. And there are newcomers on the scene.

The popular decline has been substantiated by several polls and analyses.[50] Important among them is the study conducted in 1981 by Yankelovich, Skelly, and White for the American Jewish Committee.[51] Asking the same questions used in a study by the University of California in Berkeley in 1964, the study came to the following conclusions: that antisemitism today 1) is made up mostly of the usual negative stereotyping of Jews,[52] 2) has undergone a moderate decline, 3) is more common among the old than the young, 4) has increased among Blacks, 5) is found more readily among religiously "orthodox" (in the sense of exclusive and closed), and 6) is less present among the educated. Jews were nonetheless generally seen in a more positive light, for example, as friendly and hardworking. A new correlation was shown in a linkage between antisemitism and unfavorable attitudes toward Israel, though this last finding may have reflected a negative response to the Begin government at the time of the poll, since popular support for Israel remained unchanged.

A new important study undertaken by Quinley and Glock for the Anti-Defamation League and published in 1983, confirmed and amplified these and other findings.[53] It found that antisemitism is no longer virulent in the United States, and loathing of Jews has all but disappeared except in a few eccentric groups. Little discrimination was found against Jews, though some discrimination in club memberships and intermarriage continues. The correlation between antisemitism and the State of Israel that developed since the late 1960s was discovered to be real but weak.

Black attitudes toward Jews constitute a major exception to the general decline. Black acceptance of negative stereotypes of Jews for the period covered from the Berkeley to the Yankelovich study (1964 to 1981) shows a rise of 4.1 percent in contrast with a 7.7 decline among Whites.[54] Other recent surveys have confirmed this finding. The rise comes as a surprise in view of a study in 1967 that found that Blacks tended to be somewhat less antisemitic than Whites.[55] Reasons for the negative rise have been explored. An earlier base of antipathy was generally located in the ghetto where Blacks related to Jews in a role of economic dependency, meeting them almost exclusively as storeowners, landlords, or creditors, a situation hardly destined to endear Jews to Blacks. More recent political developments have added further potential for the rise. One was the resignation of Andrew Young from his post at United Nations, perceived, erroneously, by many Blacks to be the result of Jewish pressures motivated by Young's meeting with PLO leadership. Jewish opposition to quotas in hiring and promotions as part of affirmative action caused further alienation. Meanwhile the influence of antisemitic Black radicals, such as Malcolm X and Stokeley Carmichael in the sixties and Eldrige Cleaver, Louis Farrakhan, the Black Panthers and the Nation of Islam in the seventies cannot be discounted. The tension between the two communities, however, is by no means universal. The Black Caucus in Washington has consistently supported Israel, and Jewish leadership continues to insist that Jews maintain their zeal for justice and rights for Blacks. Co-victims of America's deepest prejudices and traditional allies in the cause of civil rights, Blacks and Jews are not likely to remain at odds indefinitely.[56]

The Radical Right has continued as a fertile spawning ground for antisemitism in the country. That demagogues like Gerald K. Smith, George Lincoln Rockwell, Willis Carto; organizations like the KKK, the John Birch Society, the Liberty Lobby, the Institute of Historical Research, and Neo-Nazi splinter groups; publications like "The Cross and the Flag," "The Thunderbolt," and the "Journal of Historical Review;" political parties like the American Party—that all of these remain on as ringleaders among other similarly inspired individuals, organizations, and publications gives a notion of the dimensions of the rightist contribution to the antisemitic record of the country. And yet their cacophonous rantings have attracted relatively few Americans. Today, splintered and weak, they appeal more and more to the pathological wing than to the bulk of American society. The Radical Left, less extensive and somewhat more subtle, represented by the Communist Party, the New Left, Black nationalist and students' groups, the LaRouche network, and others again, have been more dangerous because of their idealistic rhetoric. All groups of both Right and Left use to the full the nearly universal ploy of clothing antisemitism in anti-Zionist dress. Many, especially on the Left, entertain Arab connections.

The difference separating American from European and South American antisemitism is obviously one only of degree.[57]

A LULL OR A LAST STAGE?

Antisemitism, despite Arab and Soviet Jew-hatred, is at its lowest ebb in centuries—an evaluation that perhaps bespeaks more the virulence of the past than the mildness of the present. At any rate, in all but radical and fanatical groups antisemitism has lost respectability and requires denial or disguise. This in itself may be considered progress, however small. Seen across the centuries, how to interpret it? Is it a temporary lull before another storm, or a waning that will endure until extinction? Looking back over the pages of history that precede, the historically-minded reader would find it foolhardy to accredit the latter alternative. Antisemitism is not in its death throes. A civilization contaminated so long with a toxin so virulent could hardly be detoxified in such short order. Some antisemitism, it is to be hoped, has been dissipated; more still has gone underground. In the 1930s, James Parkes, a pioneer and penetrating student of antisemitism, when asked how long antisemitism would last replied: 300 years. Today, fifty years later, it is realism more than pessimism that urges us to accept the probability of his prophecy.

15
THE ROOTS OF ANTISEMITISM

As the historian of antisemitism looks back over the millennia of horrors he has recorded, an inescapable conclusion emerges: Antisemitism is the longest and deepest hatred of human history. Other hatreds may have surpassed it in intensity for a historical moment, but all in their turn have assumed—or presently commence to assume—their proper place in the dustbin of history. What other hatred has endured some twenty-three centuries and survived a genocide of 6,000,000 of its victims in its twenty-third century of existence[1] only to find itself still intact and rich in potential for many more years of life? The very magnitude of the record, seen as a whole, cries out for explanation. How did this amalgam of undying hatred and oppression come to be? What is it essentially? Who or what was responsible for it?

Many answers have been given to these questions, ranging from simplistic attempts to reduce it to common group-prejudice to profound probings in theodicean and theological theory, yet all fall short. And perhaps inevitably so. So multifaceted a complexus could not but be multiply caused. It is an easy matter to compose a list of causes of antisemitism, and every scholar of the subject seems to have his own. The problem arises in determining which cause or causes are primary and which are secondary, merely precipitating or exacerbating.

284

Before launching into this etiological problem, let us clear some of the terrain by rejecting quite summarily some of the weakest contenders.

To reduce the antisemitic colossus to simple group-prejudice fails to account for the unique persistence and intensity that has set off antisemitism from all other particular manifestations of group-prejudice and, moreover, completely de-Judaizes anti-semitism.[2] Antisemitism may include some or all of the usual attributes of common group-prejudice, but it also includes a certain substratum and other ingredients which inform it with a unique vitality and tenacity. The common-prejudice theory also fails to appreciate the exceptional complexity of the antisemitic motivation which, as the course of history shows, leads the enquirer time and again into the provinces of theology, politics, psychology, sociology, and even the darkest recesses of human irrationality. Antisemitism is an altogether uncommon prejudice.

Another causal explanation should not detain us, indeed should be rejected out of hand. Quite different from the foregoing reducing of the problem, this explanation would inflate it to the very heavens, dignifying the antisemitic development with a divine seal of approval. It was Jacques Maritain who warned against this "blasphemous impersonation of Divine Providence." All have not heeded the warning. The crusaders' cry "God wills it" that accompanied the murder of Jews in the Middle Ages has found its reflection, indeed its actual repetition, in attitudes, utterances, and actions of some contemporary Christians still in the thrall of an anti-Judaic and "deicidal" theology. The trail of the antisemitic culprit does not lead to heaven, and a maligning of God, but rather into the human underground. The study of antisemitism must remain what it essentially is: a study in human perversity.

One of the most widespread—and oldest—theories of antisemitic causation that also fails as a primal explanation traces it to the Jewish economic role in society. In this construction, the Jew is the *homo economicus* of history, the "man of money," a born usurer, a cruel creditor, an addict of sharp practices. The theory falls short by the mere fact that it was first made in the fourth and fifth centuries by Fathers of the Church whose attitudes towards Jews had already assumed a deep hostility. In later centuries again the economic charge was always the product or the concomitant of an already existent antisemitism. The Jews' singular economic role in the Middle Ages is explainable more by the character of that age and society than by any inherent trait in the Jew. There were many practitioners in moneylending and trade in medieval times; the only thoroughly hated representative of those occupations were the "deicidal" ones. And in modern times there were often situations in which Jewish financial and commercial practice did not differ substantially from that of non-Jews but aroused Jew-hatred nonetheless. Throughout history Jews were hated whether rich or poor, capitalist or communist, whether engaged in economic or other fields of endeavor. The place of the Jew in economic affairs derives not from any Jewish character trait but from enforced historical circumstances in which the Jew found himself in Christian medieval society.[3] It cannot be denied, on the other hand, that Jewish involvement in economic affairs has served as a precipitating or aggravating cause of antisemitism. Jewish successes in this—as in other fields of accomplishment— have rarely failed to arouse Gentile fears—and envy. Economic instability or depressions, furthermore, quite independently of Jewish involvement or activity, have been the most fertile spawning ground for outbreaks of antisemitism. In troubled economic conditions scapegoats are needed to transfer blame for or deflect attention from political or social failures. The Jew has always served as the scapegoat here.

Scapegoating has been frequently preferred as the principal agent of antisemitic development, and history has exhibited numerous instances of it. To confer a primary causal status upon it, however, is another attempt to de-Judaize antisemitism and reduce it to the commonality of a universal psychological mechanism. Scapegoating is the constant companion of antisemitic eruptions, but it cannot give a satisfactory accounting of the unique durability and depth of the phenomenon. No better example of the use of Jews as scapegoats can be found than the contumely Hitler heaped upon them in the Nazi period, but is scapegoating sufficient to explain the Final Solution?

We restate our original question: Why have the Jews from time immemorial attracted hostility and inspired fear in almost every age and place? Why from the days of ancient Egypt and Greece to the present have they been the butt of contempt and oppression from Christians, Muslims, rationalists, and atheists?

The antisemite answers promptly that it is clear that the basic root of Jew-hate must reside in the Jew himself. The Jew, in other words, is transcendentally hatable. He is always guilty of what he is accused. With this straightforward answer the antisemite puts us on the right trail, but turns us in the wrong direction. There does exist in Jews a particular quiddity that contributes substantially to the depth and perpetuity of antisemitism. This has, in truth, been the opinion Jews have traditionally held, but in a sense quite in contrast to the answer of the antisemite.

What the antisemite, and many scholars of the subject, indeed some Jews, have overlooked is that antisemitism has a positive base. The first and requisite ground upon which all antisemitism is finally based can be found in the Jews' acceptance and pursuit of their divine calling; in short, their Judaism. Called through God's revelation to become Israel, a holy people and a nation separated from other nations, Jews accepted and strove to fulfill their vocation. Their fidelity to it marked them not only in their own eyes, but also in those of other nations as a people whose faith and worship of the One God engraved upon them a distinctiveness and quality of life that could only draw the attention and admiration but also the envy of those who came within viewing distance of their theophanic venture.[4] The first root of antisemitism, then, takes the shape of the unique moral and religious difference and challenge that Judaism issued to the conscience of the non-Jewish world.

But it is obvious that of itself this positive base is only a potential cause of antisemitism. In the absence of Gentile reaction no antisemitism exists. The reaction can of course be positive or negative. That there was a positive reaction is evident in pre-Christian times, for example, in the philosemitism that often lay behind antisemitic utterances and reactions of ancient Greece and Rome and again in the extensive Judaizing that went on for the first four centuries of the Christian era and thereafter.[5]

The Gentile reaction was, for all that, as this volume amply exhibits, vastly negative. The Jews' religious claim and way of life were a challenge taken in bad grace, and by some as an accusation.

The challenge taken did not come so much from the Jews themselves as from their attributed status as members of a chosen people, a separated nation, and their religious claim to possess God's word. In this way were they burdened with attributions that have always elicited the profoundest passions in the human heart; the ethnic, political, and religious. Whatever attraction Judaism exerted turned to resentment and was looked upon by many as a threat to their own ethnic, national, and religious commitments. It was predictable that following Yahweh would exact a high price from the Jew.

Gentile reaction to the Jewish fact took many forms throughout the centuries and sprung from many motivations, to such a point that it is not possible to consider it a homogeneous development. This must not dispense us, however, from seeking to identify the principal cause, historical or psychological, that best explains the durability and power of this unending animus. Does such a cause stand out? The macroscopic view of its history that we have taken permits an answer: The deicide accusation. It was this theological construct that provided the cornerstone of Christian antisemitism and laid the foundation upon which all subsequent antisemitism would in one way or another build: Slayers and rejectors of God in the person of His Son, Jews were transformed in the Christian mind into an accursed people, hated of God and humankind, doomed to live miserably in expiation for their blasphemous deed. This horrendous accusation proved to be the deepest root of that "powerful, millenary, and strongly rooted trunk" of which Jules Isaac spoke.[6] Throughout Christian history it was the attribute of deicide imposed upon the Jew that tipped the scales and perpetuated the hatred against him regardless of whatever involvement he may have had in situations that ordinarily induce prejudice and persecution. Christian antisemitism thus has always remained in its core theological.

It remained theological, moreover, because Judaism, proclaimed as having been replaced by the Church, lived on as a theological challenge to the Christian claim to be the new and true Israel. The discomfort, indeed the threat that this challenge represented can hardly be overestimated. And the persistent Judaizing among the faithful could only exacerbate the threat. In the minds of the Church Fathers the only solution to this appeal of the old Israel was a drastic one: discredit the Jew theologically, depict him/her as rejected, even cursed, by God, diabolical—the slayer of God Himself; thus only would both his claim and his appeal come to naught. A startling example of theological over-kill! Christian antisemitism originated, in short, in an intense theological rivalry. In retrospect, it is permitted to wonder whether, humanly speaking, a certain inevitability did not affect this conflict between two faiths laying claim to election by the One True God and to a large extent using the same source of revelation to uphold their claim.

The heterogeneous nature of antisemitism comes sharply to the fore as its historical course passes through a declining Christendom into the modern era. The rationalist variety, born of the Enlightenment, while drawing support from its Christian predecessor, can hardly be identified with it. The biting anti-Jewish utterances of a Voltaire paired with his insults to the Church provided striking evidence that a new species of anti-Christian antisemitism was extant. Theological anti-Judaism gave place to a philosophical universalism based on reason alone that found no room for particularistic, faith-traditions, whether Jewish or Christian. Rationalist antisemitism was never to rival the Christian kind in influence or effect but, unwittingly, it paved the way for another more dangerous outgrowth: a racially inspired Judaeophobia. Rationalism abolished not only religious prejudice, but also religious restraints.

Controversy continues to stir the question of the relationship of Christian and modern racist antisemitism. Scholars who have wrestled with the problem divide into two camps. In one, modern racist Jew-hatred is regarded as no more than an intensified phase of the age old demonry that found its sustenance in Christian teachings; in the other, both are sharply distinguished from one another, and the racist development is considered to be as anti-Christian as it is anti-Jewish. The first opinion sees a difference only of degree; the second, a difference of kind.

It is not impossible to mediate these conflicting positions. Each contains a partial truth. Ontologically considered (in essence), Christian and modern racist antisemitism are radically different and opposed; historically they form a continuum. Modern racist antisemitism, as exemplified in its purest culture by the Nazi regime, would not have been possible without centuries of anti-Judaic and antisemitic precedents. From the beginning of his program, Hitler had his target, the Jews, already set up, defenseless, and discredited. Professor Paul Hilberg has been able graphically to document the historical connection by paralleling measures taken against Jews taken by the Church and those taken by the Nazi regime.[7] It is an impressive comparison, and yet insofar as it may suggest an identity linking the Nazi and Christian types of antisemitism, it is deceptive. What does not show up in the parallelism is the fact that the measures taken by the Church were the limit-point of Christian antisemitism, most of them having been enacted during the Middle Ages when the Church and the Christian State had total control of the Jewish circumstance. The Nazi listing, on the other hand, is obviously just the starting point of the Nazi offensive that was relentlessly to pursue its inexorable logic to its conclusion: extermination. The Nazis, in short, took up at the point beyond which the Church could not go. Christianity decreed that Jews, as reprobate unbelievers must be converted and baptized, otherwise quarantined, exiled, humiliated, but *they must not be killed*. In the Nazi design, Jews, constitutionally corrupt and corrupting and unredeemable by conversion or baptism, must be oppressed, quarantined, and when possible, *exterminated*. In Christianity, baptism could turn a Jew into an honored citizen; in Nazi racism it could not prolong his life a single day. Cognizant of this difference separating the two types of antisemitism, Professor Yosef Yerushalmi, commenting on oppressive Christian legislation against Jews in the Middle Ages, had this to say: "Between this and Nazi Germany lies not merely a 'transformation' but a leap into a different dimension. The slaughter of Jews by the State was not part of the medieval Christian world order. It became possible with the breakdown of that order."[8]

Modern racist antisemitism, historically, is doubly rooted. The longer but thinner root, Christian anti-Judaism and antisemitism, supplied a necessary historical preparation. Its proper development began as the process of secularization emerged with the breakdown of the medieval theocentric synthesis. At first, a necessary corrective to the oversacralization of life in the "age of faith," the process took an areligious and then an anti-religious course, passing into the rationalism and skepticism of the French Enlightenment and English Deists, and finally, with the rise of the scientific ethos, took a materialistic and technological turn. Modern racism's complex parentage finds forebears in numerous anti-religious and radical ideologies: Feuerbach's atheism, Fichte and Hegel's statism, social Darwinism, Nietzsche's Promethean will to power, to mention a few of the more conspicuous. From this conglomerate of philosophies the premise emerged that religion as exemplified by Judaism and Christianity stands as the last obstacle to a liberated humankind, the last shackle to be shed for humanity's return to its true instincts and vitality and to the earth to which it properly belongs. Jewish and Christian biblical spirituality and morality were denounced as a massive alienation of humanity from its true natural condition. Only with their abolition could humankind be free and true to itself. Upon this destructive conception the nineteenth century racists, borrowing from a linguistic vocabulary, constructed a pseudo-science of race, dividing peoples into Aryan and Semitic categories, defining the first as ennobling and superior, the second as corrupt and inferior. Centering their attack on Jews and Judaism, they portrayed the Jews as an inferior race corruptive of other peoples, intellectualizers who distort human nature, democratists who legitimize mediocrity, purveyors of a "morality of slaves" that canonizes an ideal of humility and compassion that is suppressive of the natural virtues of courage, strength, victory, and power.

The brunt of the violence emanating from this philosophy was visited upon Jews and Judaism. Christianity, considered an extension and disguise of the Semitic spirit, was given a temporary reprieve for tactical reasons. Here was, in sum, an antisemitism, areligious, murderous, and pagan to the core.

Our etiological quest has netted few hard facts. Antisemitism is a unified phenomenon in its positive base inasmuch as it is a reaction to Judaism and its qualitative impress on the Jew. Antisemitism proper, as a negative reaction to the Jewish fact, is, contrariwise, a heterogeneous development that includes greatly dissimilar, even opposite, kinds of Jew-hatred, despite their his-

torical and sometimes political and social connections. The search
for a unitary causal agency on the historical plane has apparently
failed. Hence does our query reappear in a new form: Can this
hatred that has developed in pre-Christian, Christian, and post-
Christian times; in pagan, monotheistic, and atheistic societies;
in leftist, rightist, and centrist regimes stem from an underlying
agency and unifying explanation that escape the net of historical
enquiry? Must we, otherwise stated, leave the plane of history and
move into subliminal realms of human motivation and behavior
in search of the primary cause of this hatred? Is it possible that,
despite its religiosity, Christian antisemitism is joined by a common bond to the pagan type on other than the historical level? Do
both kinds harbor a common anti-religious impulse that operates
on a lower level of consciousness?

The deeply anti-religious kernel of Hitler's antisemitism is
not difficult to discover. His attack on the Synagogue and the
Church and his acquiescence to Rosenberg's call for a return to
Germany's pagan past shed an important light on his antisemitism. In his *Weltanschauung*, Jews represented symbolically the
demands of a divinely established moral law, which stood in the
way of his racial amoralism and his deification of the German
State and *Volk*. His genocidal decision against the Jewish people
represented, again symbolically, the annihilation of his moral
(Jewish-Christian) conscience, which stood in the way of his grandiose dream of a Thousand Year Reich founded on an apotheosis
of the German *Volk* and of himself as its *Fuehrer* and Savior. This
view is supported by his remarks about conscience as a Jewish
intervention and the need to get the "Thou shall" and "Thou
shall not" out of Aryan blood. Seen in this light, his antisemitism
appears in its ultimate essence as a *nomophobia*, a revolt against
the divinely sanctioned moral law or, religiously speaking, as a
revolt against God.

The anti-religious character of Christian antisemitism is not
so transparent. It has been recognized, however, by numerous
scholars who have varyingly perceived in the hatred of the Jew an
unconscious hatred of Christ, a rebellion against the Christian
"yoke" no longer found sweet (Matt. 11:30); in a word, a *Chris-
tophobia*. Freud who was perhaps the first to see this explained:
"In its depths anti-Judaism is anti-Christianity."[9] Incapable of

hating Christianity consciously, the Christian antisemite, by an unconscious displacement of affect, diverts his animus to the Jews, kinsmen of its Founder. Freud also describes this kind of antisemitism as an attribute of the "badly christened."[10] This undoubtedly is what Thomas Sugrue meant when he wrote: "The anti-Semite is a dead Christian."[11] And Maurice Samuel's judgment on the Nazis: "They (antisemites) must spit on the Jews as 'the Christ-killers' because they long to spit on the Jews as the Christ-givers"[12] can in the same sense be extended to Christian antisemites. It is an observable fact that it is often the rigid Christian who is the most likely candidate for antisemitism. A Torquemada supplies an example from among many in the past, and the antisemitic rigorists of the "Boston heresy" case, one from the present. One might say that in such cases antisemitism is an attribute of the "super-Christian," the Christian who overcompensates for his/her unrecognized anti-Christianity.

Or again, it can be seen as a species of Manichaeism that postulates an evil principle in nature and personifies it in the Jew, a Puritanism that compensates for lofty ideals by casting its shadow on some selected scapegoat. Antisemitism has always displayed this self-contradiction, which marks it as a product of unconscious forces. Throughout history, we recall, this ambivalent character of antisemitism has constantly cast the Jew in contradictory roles. The ambivalence evidently is rooted in a fundamental dichotomy whereby the Jew is represented at once as the divinely elected upholder of the Law and the depraved underminer of morals; or, as the depth analyst might put it, whereby the antisemite struggles against the Jew as a symbol of both the *superego* and the *id*, in the Freudian perspective.[13] Thus to the rigorist (over-repressed) the Jew conveniently serves as a projection screen for the angers generated by rigid standards and at the same time for disowning (by projection) the instinctual self of which his conscience disapproves. Poliakov, interestingly, has extended this interpretation to include Nazi antisemites, several of the most vicious of whom—Himmler, Goebbels, Hoess, and others—he finds, were products of families of a "rigid Catholic piety."[14,15]

According to the foregoing interpretation, which traces hatred of the Jews to the inner forces of the soul, antisemitism is *at its deepest root* a unified phenomenon and from all angles an anti-religious one. In the pagan racist, it is rooted in a revolt against acceptance of a transcendental or divine moral order that would limit human freedom, and focuses on the Jews as the historical source of such a moral order. In the Christian, it derives from the same source, but channels the revolt against Christ, the Jewish God who brought the Jewish concept of God's reign to all nations.

In the perspective of this twofold subliminal revolt the data of history—the contrasting forms of antisemitism and its inexplicable permanence—acquire a measure of coherence and consistency. The positive side of the phenomenon, the attraction the Jews and Judaism have wielded as bearers of God's Word among the nations, and the anti-God impulse in the depths of human consciousness and culture are joined in permanent enmity and conflict. Antisemitism thus is as much a subjective as an objective fact, as much a conflict within a person as among persons. From the subjective depths derive the bewildering and contradictory social, political, and religious shapes the animus has taken through so many centuries. Only a causation of this depth can shed some light on all aspects of its course through history.

On the historical level one of the foremost problems of antisemitism is that of bringing Christians to a full recognition of the enormity of the antisemitic development and the preponderant role played in it by Christians and the Christian churches. There can be no quarter conceded to pious dissimulation or defensive minimizing of the magnitude of the crime committed against the Jews in the Christian era and later in the modern era. The authentic Christian can only deplore that the Church and his/her co-believers were actively—or passively—involved in this tragic story, especially in its latest and most gruesome manifestation, the Holocaust. And he/she can only rue the fact that Christian antisemitism, while milder today, continues to stain the souls of many Christians.

History is of greater value for the light it sheds on the present than as a knowledge of the past, so this chronicle must end with a final question, one that was tacitly present from the outset: How can this endless tragedy be terminated? Many scholars are of the opinion that Christian antisemitism is in irreversible remission. But then secular (or pagan) antisemitism is, if anything, on the rise. Thus a double problem confronts us: the more immediate termination of Christian antisemitism and the eventual defeat of the secular kind. It is a formidable task, and one to which regrettably the generality of Christian clergy and laity is indifferent. The mainline Churches have to their credit excellent and effective documents on antisemitism and Jewish-Christian relations generally, but these, insufficiently promulgated and heeded, risk becoming dead letters on ecclesiastical shelves. The indifference affecting the subject is attributable in the first place to the all but total ignorance of Christians as to what happened to Jews in Christian history and the extent of the involvement of the Church and the Church's teachings. The tale told in this book is still a missing page in our Christian histories and texts. Until it is reinserted, the apathy and general lack of motivation will continue, as will by consequence the longest hatred in history.

Then again, education in history and dialogue is not enough. Antisemitism resides in the heart as much, if not more than, in the head. Education is essential, but more so is a change of heart, that *metanoia* which opens the mind to truth and moves the will to righteous action. More than a problem of education, antisemitism is a matter of conscience.

The tragic story this book has unfolded ends then in the deepest chambers of the spirit. For the Christian reader—for whom it was especially written—it is a tragedy in which Jesus participates, crucified again in the person of His people at the hand of many baptized in His name. The sin of antisemitism contains many sins, but in the end it is a denial of Christian faith, a failure of Christian hope, and a malady of Christian love. And was not this Christianity's supreme defection: that the Christian people to whom persecution was promised by its Master (John 16:2-4) was not the most persecuted people in Christendom, but rather was it the people from whom He came? And the ultimate scandal: that in carrying the burden of God in history the Jewish people did not find in the Christian churches an ally and defender but one of their most zealous detractors and oppressors? It is a story that calls for repentance.[16]

NOTES

INTRODUCTION

1. The first edition of *The Anguish of the Jews*, published by Macmillan Co., N.Y., in 1965, had four reprintings in hardback and seven in paperback reaching a circulation of about 70,000. It was translated into French, Spanish, and Portuguese. Though no statistics on readership are possible, it is the distinct impression of the author that the large majority of its readership was Jewish.

The Christian reception of the book was for the most part positive, even generous. Christians who read it were apparently deeply moved by the tragic tale the book tells, even chastened, and motivated to seek remedies. Some Christian and Jewish writers, however, found it too defensive of the Church—which to a certain extent it was. A few Christians saw it as an unnecessary "washing of the Church's linen in public." The periodical *The Ecumenist* (vol. 3, no. 4, 1965) ventured: "The book may have profound influence on Christian life"; and more recently David Tracy asserted: "The story told by Edward Flannery in *The Anguish of the Jews*, as well as the histories of the church during the Nazi period, calls not only for reform (as almost all admit) but for profound and meaningful repentance . . . " See *Jews and Christians After the Holocaust*, ed. Abraham Peck (Philadelphia: Fortress Press, 1983) p. 94. These desired effects remain as yet a pious wish and hope.

2. The Vatican II Statement on the Jewish People, *Nostra Aetate*, *4*, called for "fraternal dialogue and biblical studies" with Jews. Mainline Protestant churches have also committed themselves in major documents to a new understanding and cooperation with Jews. For a

compilation of these documents, see Croner, *Stepping Stones to Further Jewish-Christian Relations* (New York: Stimulus Books, 1977).

3. Arthur Hertzberg, "The Anguish of the Jews: A Response" (*Continuum*, vol. 4, no. 3, Autumn, 1966) p. 423.

4. See *supra*, p. 179.

5. See Ch. 3, p. 60.

6. See A. Forster and B. Epstein, *The New Antisemitism* (New York: McGraw-Hill, 1974) ch. 1; also N. and R. Perlmutter, *The Real Antisemitism in America* (New York: Arbor House, 1982). The Perlmutters, despite their book's title, are more precise in speaking of "a-Semitic" or neutral issues that "can loose once again classical anti-Semitism." (p. 236).

7. This Hebrew expression literally means "Sabbath Joy" and is used to describe the collation and conversations following the Temple service.

1. THE ANCIENT WORLD

1. We dispense in this work with the distinctions made by historical and biblical scholars between "Jews," "Israelite," and "Hebrew," allowing "Jew" to signify any adherent of the Mosaic faith of any era. The word "Jew," taken from *Judah*, was employed by gentiles in Maccabean times and was finally adopted by the Diaspora. *"Israel"* was reserved for more religious connotations, and today is the name of the Jewish state founded in 1948.

2. In this work the customary designations B.C. and A.D. used to denote historical segments will be replaced by B.C.E. and C.E. which denote "Before the Common Era" and "Common Era", respectively. Since most historians agree that we live in a post-Christian era, the word, "Common" is the more comprehensive denotation since it includes not only the post-Christian era but non-Christian usage as well.

3. See Msgr. Charles Journet, *Destinée d'Israel* (Paris: Egloff, 1945), pp. 199-200.

4. Flavius Josephus, Hellenized Jewish historian of the first Christian century, was at great pains to explain Judaism's dearth of notice by the Greek world. He explained it by the fact that Jews, not occupying a mountainous country, led a sheltered agricultural existence and were less involved in commerce than others. (See *Against Apion*, I, 12; *The Life and Works of Flavius Josephus*, trans., W. Whiston [New York: Holt, Rinehart and Winston, 1962], pp. 862-863.) Unless oth-

erwise indicated, references to Flavius Josephus will be made to this work.

5. Herodotus mentions "Syrians of Palestine" but says no more about them. Theodore Reinach disputes the opinion of Flavius Josephus that the historian here refers to the Jews. (See Reinach, *Textes des auteurs Grecs et Romains relatifs aux Judaisme* [Paris: Leroux, 1895], no. 1, p. 4.) An authoritative compilation of ancient Greek and Roman literary references to Jews, the foregoing work will be employed in this chapter in lieu of the primary sources.

6. J. Juster lists nearly 500 cities and towns in 33 countries in which evidence of a Jewish population was found in the Roman Empire. See *Les Juifs dans L'Empire Romain* (Paris: Guenthner, 1914), I, 179-209.

7. Strabo, the Cappadocian historian writing at the beginning of the Christian era, adds plausibility to such estimates with his claim that the Jews had "already gotten into all cities; and it is hard to find a place in the habitable earth that hath not admitted this tribe of men, and is not possessed by them." (Fl. Josephus, *Jewish Antiquities*, XIV, 7, 2; *op. cit.*, p. 417). Christian missionaries, too, were to discover their truth. The Acts (2:5, 9:11) report that at Pentecost Jews "from every nation under heaven" were in Jerusalem; and St. Paul found Jewish communities wherever he went. The oracle of the Sibyl had almost come true: "Every land shall be full of thee, and every sea" (*Oracula Sibylina*, III, 271).

8. See Reinach, *op. cit.*, no. 5, p. 8.

9. *Ibid.*, no. 7, p. 11.

10. *Ibid.*, nos. 8 and 13; pp. 13 and 39.

11. *Ibid.*, no. 182, p. 326.

12. It is difficult to determine to what extent those writers' views were provocative or merely reflective of the growing popular hostility, whether they shaped or were shaped by history. It seems probable that they were both cause and effect, giving voice to general feelings yet assisting in their creation.

13. See Reinach, *op. cit.*, no. 9, p. 17.

14. *Ibid.*, no. 11, pp. 27-9.

15. *Ibid.*, no. 19, p. 49.

16. *Ibid.*, no. 16, pp. 43-44.

17. The book of Daniel, the apocryphal Book of Enoch, and the Sibylline Oracles appeared in this period.

18. Josephus, *Against Apion*, II, 40; *op. cit.*, p. 899.

19. Reinach, *op. cit.*, no. 145, pp. 262-263.

20. Juster, *op. cit.*, II, 143.

21. Reinach, *op. cit.*, no. 25, pp. 56-58.

22. *Ibid.*, no. 26, pp. 60-64.

23. *Ibid.*, no. 48, pp. 115-117; no. 59, pp. 117-120.

24. *Ibid.*, no. 60, p. 121.

25. Pliny, *Natural History*, Preface, 25; Loeb Classical Library, (3 vols.; Cambridge: Harvard University, 1938), I, 16.

26. See Reinach, *op. cit.*, nos. 62 and 63, pp. 123-134.

27. Josephus, *Against Apion*, II, 8 (H. Thackeray, *Josephus* [9 vols.; Cambridge: Harvard University Press, 1956], I, 329-330).

28. Josephus, *Against Apion*, II, 1; *op. cit.*, p. 880.

29. See Reinach, *op. cit.*, nos. 66-74, pp. 136-150.

30. *Ibid.*, no. 88, p. 168.

31. *Ibid.*, no. 96, p. 176.

32. F. Lovsky alerts us against putting too much stock in Roman philosemitism even on the part of favorably inclined Emperors. Administrative or statutory benevolence, he shows, does not exclude contempt and even hatred toward Jews. (See F. Lovsky, *Antisémitisme et mystère d'Israel* [Paris: Michel, 1955], pp. 67-69.)

33. See Reinach, *op. cit.*, no. 126, pp. 237-238.

34. The senate, for example, forbade access to Greek philosophers in 161 B.C.E.

35. Juster, *op. cit.*, I, 239.

36. Juster's two volumes are an exhaustive study and documentation of Jewish status and privileges under the Roman Empire. See Juster, *op. cit.*, especially I, chs. 1 and 2.

37. The famous text in Suetonius affirming this expulsion, *impulsore Chresto*, is doubted by some because it appears in no other history. But the expulsion is also reported in Acts 18:2. See Giuseppe Ricciotti, *The History of Israel* (Milwaukee: Bruce, 1955), II, 185.

38. Jewish proselytism, begun in the Alexandrian era, continued and expanded under the Roman Eagle. The Roman government had always been concerned about it and took steps against it as early as 139 B.C.E., when the Praetor Hispalis expelled Jews from Rome because of proselytic efforts. In 19 B.C.E., the expulsion of 4,000 Jews, under Tiberius, was decreed because of their religious propaganda. Domitian (81-96 B.E.), similarly motivated, placed a tax on professing Jews. Although Antoninus the Pious (138-161 C.E.) abolished Hadrian's ban on circumcision for Jews, he left it in force for all others. Septimius Severus also forbade conversions to Judaism. Subsequent emperors were generally well disposed, their anti-Christian policies turning their hostilities in another direction.

39. See *supra*, p. 14.

40. See Reinach, *op. cit.*, nos. 128, 136, 150; pp. 242, 249, 267.

41. See *supra*, p. 15.

42. See Reinach, *op. cit.*, no. 126, pp. 238-239.

43. *Ibid.*, nos. 126-127, pp. 237-241.

44. *Ibid.*, no. 127, p. 241.

45. *Ibid.*, nos. 131, 132, 134-135, 138-140; pp. 244-249, 251-257.

46. *Ibid.*, no. 145-146, pp. 262-264.

47. *Ibid.*, no. 172, pp. 292-293.

48. Jules Isaac writes: "Tacitus is incontestably the most beautiful jewel in the crown of anti-Semitism, the most beautiful of all time." (See *Genèse de l'Antisémitisme* [Paris: Calmann-Lévy, 1956] p. 46.)

49. Reinach, *op. cit.*, nos. 174-181, pp. 303-321.

50. *Ibid.*, no. 215, pp. 358-359.

51. Juster, *op. cit.*, II, pp. 313-314. A single warning to "Beware of the Jews" by an Alexandrian merchant at the height of Jewish-Gentile conflicts (*ibid.*, II, 312) and an accusation by Apion of monopolistic tactics on the part of Jewish grain merchants (see Josephus, *Against Apion*, II, 5, p. 884) are hardly enough to constitute a characteristic.

52. This interpretation will be taken up in the final chapter.

53. See Reinach, *op. cit.*, p. *ix*.

54. See Baron, *op. cit.*, I, 194.

55. See J. Isaac, *Gènese de l'Antisémitisme* (Paris: Calmann-Lévy, 1956).

56. An example of this is Grosser and Halperin's *Anti-Semitism: The Causes and Effects of a Prejudice* (Secaucus, N.J.: Citadel, 1976). This otherwise excellent volume purports to be a source-book of anti-semitism, yet commences with the year 70 C.E.

A more modest example is the pressure of the former publisher of *The Anguish of the Jews* to change its subtitle from *23 Centuries of Anti-Semitism* to *2000 Years of Anti-Semitism* despite the book's inclusion of the pre-Christian period.

57. *Op. cit.*, p. 45. Marcel Simon also complains of one of these biases: "They tend, perhaps unconsciously, to make this purely literary anti-Semitism of pagan antiquity something artificial and in this way acquit pagan opinion in order to cast upon the Church the whole responsibility." (*Verus Israel*: Paris: de Broccard, 1948), p. 263. He also imputes the same tendency to Parkes and Juster, and in the latest edition of his book included Isaac (*op. cit.*, 1964: *Postscriptum*, p. 491).

58. See Arthur Hertzberg, *The French Enlightenment and the Jews* (New York: Columbia University, 1968), p. 313.

59. See Samuel Ettinger, "Jews and Judaism as Seen by English

Deists of the Eighteenth Century" (Abstract in English in *Zion* 39, 1964).

See also Milton Himmelfarb's "Response to Shlomo Avineri" in *Auschwitz, Beginning of an Era?* (New York: Ktav, 1974) wherein Himmelfarb is critical of the lack of attention to early pagan antisemitism and its influence on modern antisemitism, pp. 267-72. Meanwhile in a recent thorough study of this period Prof. John Gager has challenged the notion of a pervasive antisemitism in pagan antiquity and evinced a greater degree of philosemitism than generally acknowledged by historians. See J. Gager, *The Origins of Anti-Semitism: Attitudes toward Judaism in Pagan and Christian Antiquity* (New York: Oxford, 1983).

2. THE CONFLICT OF THE CHURCH AND SYNAGOGUE

1. Such designations of Christians are to be found in Tacitus, Pliny the Younger, Suetonius, Minicius Felix, and Marcus Aurelius.

2. Anti-Judaism is understood in the present volume as a theological or apologetical category, which comprehends all opposition to Judaism or Jewish opinion insofar as they run counter to Christian belief or practice, but which falls short of antisemitism, which in turn is understood as any form of hateful stereotyping of the Jewish people *as such*. The denomination purveys no judgment as to the correctness, the appropriateness, or the intensity of the opposition involved.

Marcel Simon has certain scruples concerning the setting off of the term "anti-Judaism" as the contrary of antisemitism: "The choice (of the term)," he writes, "is perhaps not too happy. For myself, I prefer to see 'anti-Judaism' as a more precise and adapted synonym of anti-Semitism, and I would call anti-Jewish apologetics what Lovsky calls 'anti-Judaism.' Whatever term is retained, there is a capital distinction to be made. No doubt, anti-Jewish apologetics can occasionally be, in its form and its argumentation, anti-Semitic, properly speaking. But it is not so either in principle or essence" (*op. cit.*, p. 493). Sensitive to Mr. Simon's refinement, one may yet employ "anti-Judaism" in Lovsky's sense, which has received widespread acceptance. (See Lovsky, *op. cit.*, 103-104, 113-117.)

3. See Jules Isaac, *Has Anti-Semitism Roots in Christianity?* (New York: NCCJ, 1961), p. 40. Bernard Lazare admits as much in his *L'Antisémitisme* (Paris: Jean Crès, 1934) I, ch. 3.

4. For a fuller description of Jewish hostilities see F. Vernet,

"Juifs et Chrêtiens," *Dictionnaire apologetique de la foi chrêtienne,* ed. d'Alès (Paris: Beauchesne, 1911-22), II, cols. 1657-1668.

5. "Letter to the Corinthians" (chs. 4 and 5); FCCH (see below) *Apostolic Fathers,* pp. 12-14. Though St. Clement does not explicitly mention the Jews, he clearly implies that they prompted the Neronian persecution.

References to the Fathers will be, whenever possible, to the series, *The Fathers of the Church* (New York: Christian Heritage, 1946; also New York: Cima, 1947; Washington: Catholic University Press, 1962) (FCCH); *Ante-Nicene Christian Literature* (New York: Scribner, 1886-1905) (ANCL); *Nicene and Post Nicene Christian Literature* (New York: Scribner, 1886-1905) (NPNCL). When English translations are not available, references will be to P.L. Migne, *Patrologia Latina* (217 vols., Paris: Garnier, 1878-1890) (PL), and *Patrologia Graeca* (161 vols., Paris: Garnier, 1857-1866) (PG).

6. See Joseph Klausner, *Jesus of Nazareth* (New York: Macmillan, 1943), p. 41.

7. See *Dialogue with Trypho,* ch. 16; FCCH; *St. Justin Martyr,* pp. 172-173.

8. Simon, *Verus Israel,* p. 144. In the new edition of his book (1964), the author reports that since the publication of the first edition fifteen years earlier no scholar has contested his interpretation of *minim* (p. 500).

9. These letters—also visits by "apostles"—were part of an annual exchange between the Sanhedrin and the Diaspora which usually dealt with financial and disciplinary matters.

10. See James Parkes, *Conflict of the Church and Synagogue* (New York: Meridian, 1961), p. 80.

11. For a competent and succinct account of the debate on this issue see John Pawlikowski, *What Are They Saying About Jewish-Christian Relations?* (New York/Ramsey, Paulist Press, 1980), ch. 1.

12. The charge of antisemitism in the New Testament has centered on John's Gospel and its repeated use of the expression "the Jews" in a pejorative way. Perhaps the most sensitive and nuanced study of John's multi-layered Gospel is that of John Townsend, who in a serried analysis, while conceding the anti-Jewish posture of the Gospel, shows its general Jewish context, and concludes that it is not as anti-Jewish as is frequently claimed, or as anti-Jewish as some of the other gospels. He also points out the philosemitic strain that is not absent in John. Townsend's findings, among those of others again, evidence that the debate on antisemitism in the New Testament is not closed. (See J. Townsend,

"The Gospel of John and the Jews: the Story of a Religious Divorce" (New York/Ramsey, Paulist Press, 1979), pp. 72-97.

13. Some patrologists place *The Letter of Barnabas* in the early second century.

14. *The Didache*, 8:1, FCCH, *Apostolic Fathers*, p. 177.

15. *The Letter of Barnabas*, 4:6-7; FCCH, *Apostolic Fathers*, p. 195.

16. To the Philadelphians, ch. 6; FCCH, *Apostolic Fathers*, p. 115.

17. To the Magnesians, ch. 10; FCCH, *Apostolic Fathers*, p. 99.

18. Parkes, for example, in his *Conflict* (*op. cit.*), tends to tip the balance in favor of the Jews by both inflating the extent of Christian provocation and explaining away Jewish misdemeanors. Vernet performs a like service for the Church in his *"Juifs et Chrétiens"* (*loc. cit.*). Perhaps the safest guide is Marcel Simon who possibly more than any other has succeeded in reaching the necessary degree of objectivity. With respect to the Jewish role in the persecutions, he writes: "What role and responsibility have the Jews assumed in the persecution of Christians? Certain authors have admitted quite uncritically that their part was considerable. Allard on the Catholic side and Harnack on the Protestant are of this number. More recently, the question has been resumed and resolved in a very different sense by Mr. Parkes. Perhaps, giving way to the philo-Semitism that animates his whole work and in reaction against the opposite opinion, he has too readily exculpated the Jews" (*op. cit.*, p. 144).

19. *Dialogue*, ch. 133; FCCH, *St. Justin Martyr*, p. 354.

20. *Ad Nationes* 1:14 (PL, 1:651).

21. Quoted in Eusebius' *Life of Constantine*, 3:18; NPNCL, I, 524.

22. Origen, *In Psalm XXXVII* (PG, 12, 1322); see Parkes, *Conflict*, p. 124.

23. *Martyrdom of St. Polycarp*, 13:1; FCCH, *Apostolic Fathers*, p. 157.

24. *Acta Sanctorum*, (for Feb. 1st) I, 37-46; quoted in Parkes, *op. cit.*, p. 138.

25. *Dialogue*, ch. 110; FCCH, *St. Justin Martyr*, p. 318.

26. *Scorpiace*, ch. 10; ANCL, III, 643.

27. *Letter to Diognetus*, ch. 5, FCCH, *Apostolic Fathers*, pp. 359-360.

28. *Dialogue*, ch. 137; FCCH, *St. Justin Martyr*, p. 359.

29. *Against Celsus*, 1:28, 38; 2:13, 16; ANCL, IV, 408, 413, 436, 438.

30. This scurrilous fable of the life of Jesus is a medieval work, probably written down in the tenth century but whose materials, from the genre of folklore, can be traced back to the third or second century. Though its contents enjoyed a certain currency in the oral traditions of the Jewish masses, it was almost totally ignored by official or scholarly Judaism. Antisemites have not failed to employ it as an illustration of the blasphemous character of the Synagogue.

31. Simon, *op. cit.*, p. 237.

32. Quoted in Parkes, *Conflict*, p. 109.

33. Simon, *op. cit.*, p. 152.

34. Some historians have accused the Church of opportunism in its theological efforts, seeing in its doctrine of the true Israel an *ad hoc* invention geared to wrest from the Jews their place of privilege in the empire. Actually, Christian apologists were elaborating on Christ's claim of anteriority (John 8:58), Paul's concept of the Law as "our pedagogue" and a preparation for Christ (Gal. 3:24-25), and on John's doctrine of Christ as the pre-existing *Logos* (John 1:1).

35. For a description of these see A. Lukyn Williams, *Adversus Judaeos* (Cambridge: Cambridge University Press, 1935), ch. 1.

36. For an illustration of such a charge, see *Dialogue*, ch. 68; FCCH, *St. Justin Martyr*, p. 258.

37. Tertullian, *Apol.* 17:6 (PL, 1:433).

38. Another example of this type in this epoch was the lost *Altercation of Jason and Papiscus* by the Greek writer, Ariston of Pella. (See Williams, *op. cit.*, pp. 28-30.)

39. Williams, *op. cit.*, p. 42.

40. *Dialogue*, ch. 16; FCCH, *St. Justin Martyr*, p. 172.

41. *Letter*, chs. 3, 4; FCCH, *Apostolic Fathers*, pp. 357-358.

42. The introduction and epilogue of this work place it in the fifth century, but critics agree that both were added to the body of the work, which dates from the year 200 C.E. See Williams, *op. cit.*, p. 67.

43. Quoted *ibid.*, p. 54 (PG, 10: 787-794).

44. *Against Celsus*, 4:22; ANCL, IV, 506.

45. For an analysis of these works see Williams, *op. cit.*, ch. 7.

46. *Didascalia*, 21, *Texte und Untersuchungen zur Geschichte des Altchristlichen Literatur* (Leipzig: Hinrichs, 1904), vol. 25, II, p. 108.

47. Duchesne, *Histoire Ancienne de l'Eglise* (3 vols.; Paris: Boccard, 1906-1910), I, 568.

48. Simon's major work, *Verus Israel*, is devoted entirely to this demonstration. See also William G. Braude, *Jewish Proselytizing* (Providence: Brown University Press, 1940).

49. Some observers regard Ebionitism as a moral or ascetic doc-

trine, others as a poverty or simplicity of doctrine. Others again view the heresy as no more than the fossilized survival of the earliest Jerusalemite form of Christianity, which with the development of dogma became *ipso facto* heretical.

50. *Against the Heresies*, 26:2; ANCL, I, 352.

51. "Jewish agnosticism unquestionably antedates Christianity . . . . It is a noteworthy fact that heads of gnostic schools and founders of the gnostic systems are designated as Jews by the Church Fathers" ("Gnosticism," *Jewish Encyclopedia*, V, 631).

52. Joshua Trachtenburg states that: "If Jews were not the malefic sorcerers that Christian animosity made them out to be, they still possessed an ancient and honorable tradition of magic which had been solicitously nourished until the Middle Ages when it reached its highest stage of development" (*Jewish Magic and Superstition* [New York: Meridian, 1961], p. 11). For another meaning of "Jewish superstition," see *infra*, chap. 3, fn. 51.

53. Still other heresies received Jewish support. Quartodecimanism comprised a schismatic group excommunicated by Pope Victor at the end of the second century for persisting in celebrating the Christian Easter simultaneously with the Jewish Passover on the 14th of Nisan. Jews were suspected of involvement in the Donatist heresy, which threatened the orthodoxy of Christian imperial Rome in the late fourth century. Jews also sided with Arians against Catholic orthodoxy (see Simon, *op. cit.*, p. 264).

54. See John Chrysostom, *Homilies Against the Jews*, I (PG, 48: 843-856). Chrysostom's homily is an impassioned plea to the faithful to have done with visiting synagogues, taking Jewish oaths, and celebrating Jewish feasts.

3. A CRITICAL CENTURY

1. The patriarchate embodied the highest authority in Judaism. The *nasi* (patriarch) was the accepted name for the head of the Sanhedrin.

2. Many examples of this method of interpreting could be garnered from the writings of this time. St. John Chrysostom provides one when he likens Jews to "dogs" by simply applying Christ's statement to Jews that the bread reserved for the sons must not be thrown to the dogs (Matt. 15:26) (See *Homilies Against the Jews*, I, 2 [PG, 48:845]).

3. *Evangelical Preparation* (PG, 21) and *Evangelical Demonstration* (PG, 22:13-794).

4. *Commentary on Matthew*, 13:22 (PL, 9:993); also, *Commentary on Psalm*, 51:6 (PL, 9:312).

5. See Juster, *op. cit.*, I, 59-61.

6. See Parkes, *Conflict*, p. 276.

7. Pseudo-Ephraim, *De Magis*, 2:411; quoted in Williams, *op. cit.*, p. 104.

8. *Catecheses*, 12:17 (PG, 33:746).

9. *Against the Heresies* (PG, 41:19-20).

10. *Homilies on the Resurrection*, 5 (PG, 46:685).

11. See Simon, *op. cit.*, pp. 255-271.

12. *Epist.* 121, 5 (PL, 22:1016).

13. *In Ps.* 108 (PL, 25:1054).

14. *In Amos*, 5:23 (PL, 25:1054).

15. *Epist.* 112:13 (PL, 22:924).

16. *Homily* 1:7 (PG, 48:853). The quotations from Chrysostom that follow are taken from his eight *Homilies Against the Jews* (PG, 48:843-942). For the original text with a parallel French translation see *Ioannou tou Krusostomou, ta Eurizkomena Panta, Oeuvres completes de Saint Jean Chrysostome*, ed. J. Bareille (Paris: Louis Vives, 1865), II, 350-513. The first sermon is typical and contains the brunt of Chrysostom's attack. Homilies 2 to 5 are more theological and reasoned in content, but the sixth again takes up the tone of the first, dwelling at length on the theme of perpetual miseries of Jews as a punishment for the deicide. Insulting epithets are scattered throughout. The numeration is from the Vives edition.

17. See Robert Wilkens, *John Chrysostom and the Jews* (Berkeley: Univ. of California, 1983).

18. St. Augustine's opinion of Jews and Judaism is scattered throughout his works. See particularly his *Treatise Against the Jews* (PL, 42:51-64). See L. Williams, *op. cit.*, pp. 312-17; B. Blumenkranz, *Die Judenpredigt Augustins, Ein Beitrag zur Geschichte der Judisch-Christlichen Beziehungen in den Ersten Jahrhunderten* (Basel: Helbing & Lichtenhahn, 1946); J. Isaac, *Genèse*, pp. 166-172.

19. Augustine, *The Creed*, 3:10 (FCCH, 27:301).

20. *Enarratio in Ps. 58*, 1, 22 (PL, 36, 705).

21. *Enarratio in Ps. 56*:9 (PL, 36:666). The "slave-librarian" in Roman society was often well educated and, as teacher of the children of the nobleman, walked behind his master but ahead of his charges. St. Augustine is not far here from St. Paul's view of Israel as our "pedagogue in Christ" (Gal. 3:24).

22. *Epist.*, 137:16 (PL, 33:523).

23. *Commentary on Ps. 50* (NPNCL, 8:177); *Contra Faustus,* 13:10 (PL, 42:207).

24. *Treatise Against the Jews,* 15 (PL, 42:63).

25. For these writings, see Williams, *op. cit.,* pp. 117-132; 139-140; and 295-311.

26. *Ibid.,* p. 304.

27. Sulpicius Severus, 2, 30 (NPNCL, 11:111).

28. *Homily* 6:2 (PG, 48:906-907).

29. *Contra Faustus,* 12:13 (PL, 42:261).

30. *Commentary on Ps. 1* (PL, 15:1032).

31. See Simon, *op. cit.,* p. 272.

32. Eusebius, *Martyrs of Palestine,* 8 (NPNCL, 1:349-350).

33. See Juster, *op. cit.,* I, 311-312.

34. *In Ps. 77;* see Juster, *op. cit.,* I, p. 228.

35. *Sermon 70:2* (PL, 26:1162).

36. See Juster, *op. cit.,* I, 334.

37. Elvira, 49 and 50 (see Mansi: *Sacrorum conciliorum nova et amplissima collectio,* 53 vols. [Paris: Welter, 1901-27], 2:14).

38. Antioch, I (*ibid.,* 2:1307).

39. Nicaea 20 (*ibid.,* 2:683).

40. Laodicea 29, 37, 38 (*ibid.,* 2:571-572).

41. Mr. Isaac sees the early roots of the ghetto in these restrictive canons. Both Christian and Jewish clergy feared commingling and attempted to quarantine their faithful. However, the ghetto's long roots sink deeply into pagan antiquity and also into the nature of Judaism itself.

42. Simon, *op. cit.,* p. 271.

43. The emperor's participation in Chrysostom's disgrace is not certain but probable.

44. *Codex Theodosianus,* ed. J. Gothofredus (6 vols.; Leipzig: Weidmann, 1736) (CT). The numeration in text will refer to book, title, and statute of the foregoing edition of the *Codex.*

45. The patriarchate was abolished in 425.

46. See Isaac, *Genèse,* p. 179.

47. The earliest law concerning synagogues is lost, but a reference in the work of a bishop of Verona (d. 380 C.E.) seems to indicate the existence of such a law before 380. See Juster, *op. cit.,* I, 469.

48. See *ibid.,* II, 263-264.

49. Jewish law and custom discouraged marriage with Christians as strongly as did the Church and imperial law those with Jews. Concerning the Jewish prohibition of marriage with non-Jews, see Juster

(*op. cit.*, II, 45-46), who concludes: "Christianity borrowed from the Jewish religion the prohibition of marriage with infidels and included Jews among the latter; from the Fathers of the Church the prohibition passed into the canons of the councils and thence into the laws of the Empire" (p. 46).

50. This law of Arcadius probably had an economic motive, since it was enacted against Jews in his debt who sought asylum in the Church.

51. In the Codex, as in classical literature, "superstition" (*superstitio*) denoted more a religion at variance with the state religion than an ignorant and unreasonable belief in superhuman forces; *judaica superstitio* was actually one of the official designations of Judaism. See Juster, *op. cit.*, I, 250; Simon, *op. cit.*, p. 420.

52. See CT 16-8-1, 16-9-4, 16-8-6 and 7.

53. *Ibid.*, 16-8-13.

54. *Verus Israel*, p. 267.

55. Basil, *Homily* 24, I (PG, 31:599).

56. Gregory Nazianzen, *Oratio* 4 (PG, 25:668).

57. Sozomenus, *Hist. Eccles.* 5:22 (PG, 67:1283).

58. "The Jews were a seditious people and the anti-Jewish polemic was not wrong in making this reproach." Juster, *op. cit.*, II, 182. For accounts of Jewish violence in this period, see Juster, *op. cit.*, II, 196-204, 207-9; Vernet, "Juifs et Chrêtiens," *Dictionnaire apologetique*, II, col. 1664-5; Isaac, *Genèse*, pp. 184-185; Parkes, *Conflict*, pp. 185-187.

59. Parkes disputes this accusation; see *Conflict*, p. 188.

60. Socrates, *Hist. Eccles.* 7:16 (PG, 67:769-771).

61. Juster, *op. cit.*, II, 204.

62. See Parkes, *Conflict*, p. 234.

63. CT, 16-8-18. On the question of *Purim* drinking, see *The Babylonian Talmud*, ed. I. Epstein (London: Soncino, 1935-48). Megillah p. 38.

64. See Parkes, *ibid.*, p. 234.

65. Socrates, *ibid.*, p. 234.

66. A few Jews were later allowed to return upon baptism, and Juster claims that a hundred years later some Jews reoccupied the city. (See Juster, *op. cit.*, II, 176.)

67. See Parkes, *Conflict*, p. 188.

68. See Simon, *op. cit.*, p. 264.

69. Letter, 40 (NPNCL, 10:440); see also Jacob R. Marcus, *The Jew in the Medieval World* (New York: Meridian, 1960), pp. 107-110. The foregoing is a readily accessible work which presents in a single volume many selections from translations of primary sources.

70. "If it be objected that I did not set the synagogue on fire here, I answer, it began to be burnt by the judgment of God, and my work came to an end. And if the very truth be asked, I was the more slack because I did not expect that it would be punished" (*ibid.*, 40:15 [NPNCL, 10, 440-442]).

71. "The Christian religion takes precedence over the law" (*ibid.*, 40:10 [NPNCL, 10:442]).

72. See Simon, *op. cit.*, pp. 272-273.

73. See Juster, *op. cit.*, II, 312-313.

74. The Judaic attitude toward the earth and its goods is more affirmative than the Christian, even the Christian humanist. (See Baron, *History*, I, 137-39; Simon, *op. cit.*, pp. 251-253.) It is not surprising, then, that in the patristic period when Christian asceticism and monasticism were in process of formation, Jewish attention to earthly comforts and gain appeared to the Fathers as cupidity. St. Jerome's remark is revealing: "The Jews . . . seek nothing but to have children, possess riches, and be healthy. They seek all earthly things, but think nothing of heavenly things: for this reason are they mercenaries." (Quoted in Juster, *op. cit.*, II, 312.)

75. See Graetz, *History*, II, 634. Graetz here tends to blur the richness of the spiritual and intellectual life of the Jewish ghetto in the Middle Ages. See *infra*, Ch. 7.

76. Lovsky, *op. cit.*, p. 113.

77. This brand of apologetics is found, for example, in the late first century in the *Epistle of Barnabas*, in which we read: "Assuredly, God gave the covenant to the Jews, but because of their sins they were not worthy to receive it . . . Moses received the Testament, but the Jews were not worthy" (*Letter of Barnabas*, 14, 1 and 4 FCCH *The Apostolic Fathers*, pp. 213-214). By the fourth century this had become common teaching.

78. (PG, 48:834, 835, 888), also Homily 6, *passim* (*ibid.*, 903-916).

79. See Parkes, *Conflict*, p. 183.

80. The witness-people theory was first adumbrated by Lactantius (d. 330) but gained no currency until Augustine's elaboration.

81. CT, *op. cit.*, 16-8-20, 16-8-3.

82. Principally Matt. 23:28-29; 24:15-16; Luke 21:24.

83. Homily I:6 (PG, 48:852).

84. Simon, *op. cit.*, p. 273.

4. SHIFTING FORTUNES

1. The "Blues" and "Greens" made up two rival factions which performed in the hippodrome of Antioch and in their rivalries interested themselves in religious and political questions.

2. Some of the monks of this period upset our modern concept of the monastic. Apparently, they surpassed all others in anti-Jewish and anti-heretical violence, and neither Church nor State could restrain them. Emperors Arcadius and Theodosius II legislated against them in the Codes (CT: 16, 3, 1-2; Justin. Code [see following note]: 1-3-32) in a fruitless effort to retain them and keep them out of the cities. Though this brand of monastic lawlessness was peculiar to the early medieval East, it was to make sporadic appearances until the beginning of modern times.

3. *Pandectae Justinianeae,* ed. R. J. Pothier (3 vols.; Paris: Belin-Leprieur, 1818) (CJ). The numeration in the text will be to book, title, and statute of this edition.

4. For an English translation of this famous Novella see Parkes, *Conflict,* appendix 2; pp. 392-393.

5. See Isaac, *Genèse,* pp. 201-202.

6. See Parkes, *Conflict,* pp. 253-254.

7. For versions of this episode see Parkes, *Conflict,* pp. 257-263; Isaac, *Genèse,* pp. 210-216; Baron, *History,* III, 18-24; and Graetz, *History,* III, 18-23.

8. The story is told that Heraclius had been warned through a dream that his empire would be destroyed by a circumcised people. Apparently oblivious of the circumcised Arabs, all but at his gates, he turned on the Jews.

9. See *supra,* p. 35.

10. *Epist.,* 1, 47 (NPNCL, 12, 93; PL, 77:510-511).

11. See Mansi, *op. cit.,* 13:751: " . . . *sed aperte sint secundum suam religionem Hebraei.*"

12. *Ibid.,* 7:397, 419.

13. *Ibid.,* 11:946.

14. See *supra.,* fn. 11.

15. Cassiodorus, *Varia,* 3:46 (PL, 69:669).

16. Letter to the Jews of Milan, *ibid.,* 5:37 (PL, 69:669).

17. *Ibid.,* 4:33 (PL, 69:561).

18. See Cassiodorus, *Expositio in Pss. 49 and 81* (PL, 70:357, 595).

19. *Epist.* 8:25 (PL, 77:927-928). This famous text which begins with the words *"Sicut Judaeis"* formed the foundation stone of future

Church policy toward Jews, and supplied the opening words of many of the medieval papal statements concerning Jews.

20. *Epist.* 13:12 (PL, 77:1263).

21. *Epist.* 9:6 (PL, 77:944). On this striking reversal from St. Ambrose's policy (*supra,* p. 60), Salo Baron makes this comment: "The fact that Gregory now threw the whole weight of his revered personality and exalted office behind the old imperial law and indirectly disavowed the famous bishop of Milan (Ambrose) whom he otherwise deeply admired and often imitated, contributed greatly to the re-establishment of that ancient compromise under which the European communities were enabled to carry on their accustomed religious worship" (*op. cit.,* III, 30).

22. *Epist.* 9:109 (PL, 77:1038).

23. *Epist.* 1:35 (PL, 77:489); see also 1:47 (PL, 77:510).

24. *Epist.* 5:8 (PL, 77:30).

25. *Genèse,* p. 234.

26. In the sixth century, under Arian kings, the affairs of the Jews were regulated by the *Breviary of Alaric,* a simplication of the Theodosian Code, which did not substantially change their previous situation. (See *Lex Romana Visigothorum,* ed. Haenel [Leipzig, 1849].)

27. Mansi, *op. cit.,* 9:996. For a typical example of these Visigothic laws, see Marcus, *op. cit.,* pp. 20-23.

28. The term *perfidia* and its derived forms have posed a problem for modern scholars because of the tendency to translate it in the various vernaculars by the cognate term "perfidy" or an equivalent. This has been particularly true in the case of its use in the Good Friday prayer for the Jews which in the Roman liturgy begins *Oremus et pro perfidis Judaeis.* Many scholars have examined the question, and all are in agreement that in its original meaning as well as in the Catholic liturgy the term does not mean "perfidy," "faithlessness," or the like, but rather "unbelief" or "incredulity." The studies of Louis Canet, Erik Peterson, and John Oesterreicher on the question are particularly valuable. (See *infra.*) Msgr. Oesterreicher presents a decisive example from another liturgical work, *The Rite of Baptism for Adults* of the Roman ritual, wherein the term is used with respect to Mohammedan as well as Jewish unbelief (*Horresce Mahumiticam perfidiam*). Erik Peterson presents another example in his quotation from St. Isidore of Seville's *De fide catholica contra Judaeos:* "In order to refute the unbelief (*perfidiam*) of the Jews, we have compiled certain testimonies from the Old Testament" (PL, 83:450). Obviously here is a *perfidia* to be rationally disproved. For studies of the question and bibliography see L. Canet, "*La prière 'pro Judaeis' de la liturgie catholique romaine,*" *Revue des Etudes Juives,* LXI,

122 (April, 1911); Erik Peterson, "Perfidia Judaica," *Ephemerides Liturgicae*, L (1936), 296-311; John M. Oesterreicher, "Pro Perfidis Judaeis," *Theological Studies*, VII (March 1947), pp. 80-96; Kathryn Sullivan, R.S.C.J. "Pro Perfidis Judaeis," *The Bridge*, II, 212-223.

29. *Epist.*, 9:122 (PL, 77:1053-1054).

30. See Isaac, *Genèse*, p. 241.

31. St. Isidore, *Historia Gothorum*, 60 (PL, 63:1073); for text, see A. Ziegler, *Church and State in Visigothic Spain* (Washington, D.C.: Catholic University, 1930), p. 190.

32. See Mansi, *op. cit.*, 10:633-634.

33. Mansi does not limit this decree (10:634, canon 60) to baptized children of Jews as others do; see Bernard Blumenkranz, *Juifs et Chrétiens dans le monde occidental* (Paris: Mouton, 1960), p. 111.

34. Many theologians of today, more attentive to the subjective dispositions requisite for the sacrament, would question the validity of Sisebut's baptisms. For a discussion of the problem see the author's "The Finaly Case," *The Bridge*, I, 292-313. Moreover, Lovsky has pointed out that use of the power of the State was not essentially Catholic, that Jews, Moslems, and Protestants had such recourse in times past when opportunity made it available; rather it was a product of sociopolitical views of medieval times; *Antisémitisme*, pp. 180-181, 190-191.

35. Mansi, *op. cit.*, 10:662.

36. *Ibid.*, can. 3.

37. Isaac contests this indulgence of the Pope, claiming that, quite the contrary, in the letter to Honorius, the Council expressed indignation at his severity toward Jews. It is not impossible to reconcile both views; see Blumenkranz, *op. cit.*, p. 115; Baron, *op. cit.*, III, 40 and 248 fn.

38. Mansi, *op. cit.*, 10:1221.

39. *Ibid.*, 10:1229.

40. *Ibid.*, 11:30-31.

41. *Ibid.*, 11:1035-1036.

42. *Ibid.*, 12:68-69.

43. *Ibid.*, 12:101-103.

44. *De fide catholica ex veteri et novo testamento contra Judaeos* (PL, 83:449-538); see also Williams, *op. cit.*, pp. 215-217.

45. Ziegler, *op. cit.*, p. 197.

46. See Mansi, *op. cit.*, 7:954.

47. Blumenkranz, *op. cit.*, p. xiv.

48. See Parkes, *Conflict*, pp. 322-330.

49. St. Gregory of Tours (c. 538-593) is the chief chronicler of this period in France; see *Historia Francorum* (PL, 71:154-571) in which are

recounted several instances of anti-Jewish violence with royal complicity.

50. See *supra,* p. 69.

51. See Marcus, *op. cit.,* pp. 13-15.

52. For an excellent study of this history see Léon Poliakov's *De Mahomet aux Marranes* (Paris: Calmann-Levy, 1961).

53. See Parkes, *The Jews in the Medieval Community* (London: Soncino, 1938), p. 50.

54. Quoted in Isaac, *Genèse,* p. 272.

55. See Parkes, *Medieval Community,* p. 47. Jules Isaac's justification of the Jewish policy of refusing baptism to slaves because it led to financial ruin for Jews is not wholly true. The Council of Macon (581) had established a compensation (12 *solidi*) for Jewish owners of converted slaves (PL, 104:103); Isaac, *Genèse,* p. 274; Williams, *op. cit.,* pp. 349-350.

56. Henri Daniel Rops, *The Church in the Dark Ages* (New York: Doubleday, 1962), p. 166.

57. The Archbishop's ire was roused when a heathen girl, who was baptized while a slave in a Jewish household, and harshly treated by her master, fled to his court for protection. The Archbishop offered payment to the owner for the loss of the slave, but the slaveowner appealed to Everard, the *Magister,* invoking Louis the Pious' ruling requiring the slaveowner's consent for a baptism. Everard supported the Jewish plaintiff and ordered the girl returned.

58. *De Insolentia Judaeorum* (PL, 104:69-76) and *De Judaicis Superstitionibus* (PL, 104:77-100); for an analysis, see Williams, *op. cit.,* pp. 348-357.

59. See *supra,* p. 37.

60. Controversy has affected the question of whether the change of market day hurt Sunday worship or not. See Williams, *op. cit.,* pp. 354-355; Parkes, *Medieval Community,* p. 52; and J. Isaac, *Genèse,* p. 279.

61. PL, 104:113. Williams attempts to put St. Agobard's criticism in perspective: "No doubt most of Agobard's charges against the theological opinions of Jews are erroneous, and are due to his ignorance of Judaism from within. Yet he cannot be altogether blamed. It was not an age of mealy-mouthed civilities. Jews themselves have never encouraged dissimulation in attack on either side . . . " (*op. cit.,* p. 355).

62. See *supra,* p. 85.

63. See Mansi, *op. cit.,* 14:835.

64. PL, 116:141-184; Williams, *op. cit.,* p. 358.

65. There are very few works in this half-millennium on an in-

tellectual par with those of St. Agobard and Bishop Amulo. The one exception is perhaps *Against the Jews* by St. Isidore of Seville (*supra*, p. 75) which Lukyn Williams describes as "perhaps the ablest and most logical of all early attempts to present Christ to the Jews" (*op. cit.*, p. 217).

66. Probably Lother (954-989); for text see PL, 119:42.

67. See Parkes, *Medieval Community*, pp. 36-37, and Isaac, *Genèse*, p. 315.

68. See Blumenkranz, *op. cit.*, p. 20.

69. See Isaac, *Genèse*, p. 321.

70. The explanation was first given by Amalarius of Metz in the ninth century (PL, 105:1027). It was generally accepted throughout the Middle Ages, and it is not without defenders today.

71. See Oesterreicher, *loc. cit.*, 1947. For a bibliography of this question see "Pro Perfidis Judaeis" by Kathryn Sullivan, R.S.C.J., *The Bridge*, II, 212-223; see Isaac, *Genèse*, pp. 200-205; Blumenkranz, *op. cit.*, pp. 90-92.

72. Thus Felix Vernet in his article "Judaisme," *Dictionnaire de l'archeologie chrêtienne et de la liturgie* (VIII, 1, 1928) col. 181; and Jacques Leclerq, O.S.B., in "De quelques publications liturgiques récentes," *Révue Benedictine* (Maredsous, 1913), III, 122-123.

73. Erik Peterson, *Ephemerides liturgicae*, 1936, no. 64, p. 310; see also Isaac, *Genèse*, pp. 303-304.

74. *Epist.* 14 (PL, 132:1084-1085).

75. Blumenkranz, *op. cit.*, p. xv.

76. See *infra*, pp. 96-98.

77. The term "anti-Judaism" is employed here since the anti-Jewish legislation of this time was chiefly of theological inspiration.

78. Blumenkranz has an excellent survey of Jewish missionary activity in the West at this time: *op. cit.*, Part II, ch. 2.

79. The matter of slaveowning was of especial concern to the Church because of the dangers to the faith of Christian slaves in Jewish households. The Talmud and Jewish traditions forbade keeping uncircumcised slaves in the household; hence the wish on the part of many Jewish slaveowners to Judaize their slaves. (See Israel Abrahams, *Jewish Life in the Middle Ages* [New York: Meridian, 1960], p. 99). In the liberal Carolingian era, in particular, the talmudic prohibition was heeded.

5. THE VALE OF TEARS

1. This title, a Christian expression, is also that of a famous book, *Emek ha-bacha* (Vale of Weeping) by Joseph ha Cohen, sixteenth

century Jewish historian, who recounted the hardships to which Jews were subject through the centuries. (See *Emek ha-bacha* [Leipzig: Leiner, 1958].)

2. Over a dozen sources, Jewish and Gentile, for example, are available for the First Crusade alone, the first skirmish of a continuous onslaught; see Poliakov, *Du Christ*, pp. 57-62.

3. For Christians it was the time of the "Great Fear": The turn of the millennium inspired an apocalyptic awe, centralized government was gone, the prestige of the papacy was at a low ebb, and the Muslim enemy was at the gates.

4. Jules Isaac, in particular, has made this his point of view. (See *Genèse, op. cit.*) In his *Les Prophètes d'Israel*, J. Darmesteter states: "The hatred of the people against the Jew is the work of the Church, and yet it is the Church alone which protects them against the furies which she has unleashed" (p. 183; quoted in Vernet, "Juifs et Chrêtiens," *loc. cit.*, col. 1652). Solomon Grayzel, writing of the Crusades, writes: "After many centuries of internal weakness the Catholic Church finally established its unity and its power. By a slow process the local clergy and the monks obtained a firm hold on the minds of the population of Western Europe." (See *A History of the Jews* [Philadelphia: Jewish Publications of America, 1960], p. 340.)

5. As all others, these times were not without their bright pages. In the late ninth century, Remigius of Auzerre, Benedictine monk, vigorously reasserted the Pauline tradition and warned against blaming the Jews for the crucifixion which, he said, was the responsibility of all the sinners. (See Homily on St. Matthew, 5 [PL, 131:892].) In 1084 Bishop Rudiger of Speyer invited Jews to settle in the city with special protection and privileges for the entire Jewish community; see Blumenkranz, *Juifs et Chrêtiens*, p. 39.

6. Blumenkranz has analyzed these critical developments (*op. cit.*, pp. 380-388); see also Parkes, *Medieval Community*, pp. 34-39; Graetz, *History*, III, 245-258; Baron, *History*, IV, 91-94.

7. Guibert of Nogent, *De Vita Sua*, III, 5 (PL, 156:903).

8. See Marcus, *op. cit.*, pp. 115-120.

9. For good summaries of this and later Crusades see Grayzel, *op. cit.*, p. 339-358; Max Margolis and Alexander Marx, *History of the Jewish People* (New York: Meridian, 1956), pp. 359-361.

10. See Baron, *op. cit.*, IV, 104.

11. See Poliakov, *Du Christ*, pp. 67-69.

12. The name "Rashi" is an acrostic for Rabbi Shlomo son of Isaac (1040-1105), foremost commentator of his time on the Bible and Talmud.

13. See Poliakov, *Du Christ*, p. 101.

14. See Abrahams, *Jewish Life in the Middle Ages* (New York: Meridian, 1960), pp. 13-14.

15. See *infra*, p. 95-97.

16. This cry is believed to stand for *Hiersolyma est perdita* (Jerusalem is lost).

17. Though St. Bernard was the chief defender of the Jews, he nonetheless shared the theological outlook of the time: "The Jews are for us," he wrote, "the living words of the Scripture, for they remind us always of what our Lord has suffered. They are dispersed all over the world so that by expiating their crime they may be everywhere the living witnesses of our redemption." See *Letters of St. Bernard*, ed. Bruno Scott James (Chicago: Regnery, 1953), p. 462.

18. *Ibid.*, p. 465.

19. *Ibid.*, p. 466.

20. *Ibid.*, p. 463.

21. *Epist.* 46, PL, 189:465. Venerable Peter also wrote an earlier tract against the Jews entitled *Tractatus adversus Judaeorum inveteratam duritiam* (PL, 189:507-650; see Williams, *Adversus Judaeos*, pp. 384-393).

22. See *supra*, p. 82.

23. For an example of one of these charters see Marcus, *op. cit.*, pp. 28-33.

24. *Epist.* 8:121 (PL, 215:694).

25. Mansi, *op. cit.*, 22:231.

26. *Letter to the Duchess of Brabant* (*De Regimine Principum* [Turin: Marietti, 1924], p. 117). See also *Summa Theologica*, III a Q. 68, 10. For St. Thomas' attitude toward Jews, see Simon Deploige, *St. Thomas et la question juive* (Paris: Bloud & Barral, 1899).

27. Quoted in Poliakov, *Du Christ*, p. 93.

28. For a bibliography on the theory of Jewish servitude, see Lovsky, *op. cit.*, pp. 182-187; Parkes, *Medieval Community*, pp. 94, 106-108; Vernet, "Juifs et Chrêtiens," *loc. cit.*, cols. 1744-1747.

29. In the medieval world usury signified any interest whatever charged during the agreed time of a loan.

30. See Abrahams, *op. cit.*, pp. 230-250.

31. There is no historical basis for the contention that Jews are possessed of a certain "racial aptitude" for commercial or financial affairs. A well known proponent of this opinion is Werner Sombart, who states in his *The Jew and Modern Capitalism* (New York: Collier Books, 1962): "If anyone wished in a sentence to account for the importance of

the Jews in the world's civilization, and more particularly in modern life, he could do so by saying that it was due to the transplanting of an Oriental people among Northern races" (p. 200). Scholars generally reject Sombart's economic analysis as well as his racial theory.

32. For studies of medieval usury, see Parkes, *Medieval Community*, pp. 269-382; also R.H. Tawney, *Religion and the Rise of Capitalism* (New York: Harcourt Brace, 1926), pp. 3-62.

33. See Abrahams, *op. cit.*, pp. 236-239.

34. See Baron, *op. cit.*, IV, 142-143.

35. Parkes, *Medieval Community*, p. 354.

36. "The older Jewish aristocracy of learning," writes Abrahams, "was replaced by an aristocracy of wealth" (*op. cit.*, p. 43). Lazare is more severe, seeing it as a serious depressant on Jewish character. (See *L'Antisémitisme* [2 vols.; Paris: Crès, 1884] II, 231.) Léon Poliakov, on the other hand, takes another point of view: "Usury and study were not considered incompatible, on the contrary. A text [of the Talmud] even specifies that usury provides the advantage of allowing all the leisure needed for study" (*Du Christ*, pp. 184-185).

37. See Parkes, *Medieval Community*, pp. 285-286.

38. St. Bernard, *op. cit.*, p. 463.

39. Lazare, *op. cit.*, II, 217.

40. See *supra*, p. 13-14.

41. We except the episode at Imnestar in 415 (see *supra*, p. 59) which, if it occurred at all, was more a drunken orgy than a ritual murder.

42. See Marcus, *op. cit.*, pp. 121-126.

43. A famous instance occurred in Brussels in 1370 where twenty Jews were burned and the rest exiled.

44. These accusations place in bold relief the diabolization of the image of the Jew in the Middle Ages. On this subject see Joshua Trachtenberg, *The Devil and the Jews* (New Haven: Yale University Press, 1943).

45. See Poliakov, *Du Christ*, p. 80.

46. For an account see Marcus, *op. cit.*, pp. 127-130. According to this "test" the accuser was believed to be telling the truth or lying depending on whether he sank or remained afloat upon being submerged in a tank of holy water.

47. It may be noted here that this great, free-thinking "archenemy of the papacy" (Margolis and Marx, *History of the Jewish People* [New York: Meridian, 1956], p. 375), despite his patronage of Jewish learning, yielded to none in his disdain for Jews, and actually enforced

the Lateran canons concerning the badge and holding of office. Emperor Frederick is a good example of rationalist antisemitism in the Age of Faith, a type that is to flourish some five or six centuries later.

48. See anonymous *Die Päpstlichen Bullen über die Blutbeschuldigung* (Berlin: Cronbach, 1899), p. 10 (this work contains Latin and German texts of several bulls on ritual murder); for Latin and English text see Solomon Grayzel, *The Church and Jews in the Thirteenth Century* (Philadelphia: Dropsie College, 1933), pp. 269-271.

49. See *Päpstlichen Bullen,* pp. 2-9, 14-17.

50. *Ibid.,* pp. 18-36.

51. For papal attitudes on ritual murder see Vernet, "Juifs et Chrêtiens," *loc. cit.,* cols. 1710-1712. This writer draws an argument for papal disbelief in Jewish ritual murder from the silence of many popes who otherwise criticized Jews and Judaism severely (*ibid.,* col. 1712). See also Elphège Vacandard, "La question du meurtre rituelle chez les Juifs," *Etudes de critique et d'histoire religieuse* (Paris: Gabalda, 1912), pp. 311-377.

52. See Ganganelli, *The Ritual Murder Libel and the Jew,* ed. Cecil Roth (London: Woburn, 1934). Father Vacandard believes that, in accepting the factuality of the cases of Rinn and Trent, the Cardinal was overly influenced by the authorization their cults received from Rome. (See Vacandard, "La Question," *loc. cit.,* p. 258.)

53. The charge was made in Russia in 1911; in Massena, New York, in 1928; in Nazi propaganda; and was the subject of a booklet published in Birmingham, Alabama, in 1962 (Arnold Leese, *Jewish Ritual Murder*), which gives credence to the charge. (See Joshua Trachtenburg, *The Devil and the Jews, op. cit.,* pp. 124-139.)

54. For a more detailed discussion of these cases see Vernet, *op. cit.,* cols. 1703-1713; Vacandard, *op. cit.,* pp. 335-359. The basic work on the ritual murder charge is H. L. Strack's *Das Blut in Glauben und aberglauben der Menschheit mit besonderer Berucksichtigung der Volksmedizin und des judischen Blutritus* (8th ed.; Munich: 1900); English translation: *The Jew and Human Sacrifice* (London, 1909).

55. The most notable of these were Hugh of Lincoln and Simon of Trent, whose cases will be taken up later. Other cases of public veneration and ecclesiastical approval include that of Blessed Domenic of Val approved by Pius IX for the diocese of Saragossa; Blessed Nino of La Guardia for Toledo; Blessed Laurence for the diocese of Vicence in 1867; and Blessed Rudolph for the diocese of Basel in 1869.

56. See Benedict XIV, *De Servorum Dei Beatificatione,* I, 14, 4; III, 5, 6 (4 vols., Padua, 1743); see Vacandard, *loc. cit.,* pp. 350-353; Vernet, "Juifs et Chrêtiens," *loc. cit.,* col. 1710.

57. The question of the infallibility of the Church involved in the process of canonization has been raised. The issue is not relevant since none of these children were formally beatified or canonized. They were given what is called "equivalent beatification." (See Vacandard, *ibid.*, p. 353; Vernet, "Juifs et Chrêtiens," *loc. cit.*, col. 1710.)

58. Vacandard, *op. cit.*, p. 367.

59. Vernet admits this possibility (see "Juifs et Chrêtiens," *loc. cit.*, cols. 1709-1710). So does Lazare, who believes such murders to be "very rare" (*op. cit.*, II, 219). Henry Milman sees the possibility of such by some fanatical Jews "exasperated by the constant repetition of the charge" (*History of the Jews* [New York: Dutton, 1913], II, 359).

60. See Marcus, *op. cit.*, pp. 137-142.

61. See *supra*, p. 73.

62. There is no single volume that contains all papal bulls or statements concerning Jews. Recourse must be made to the usual loci of papal texts, such as Mansi (*op. cit.*) and Migne (*op. cit.*), the Bullarium Romanum, or to a number of compilations and monographs. Most useful among these are Caesar Baronius (Cardinal), *Annales Ecclesiastici*, continued by Odoricus Raynaldus (38 vols.; Lucca: Venturini, 1738-1756); *Die Päpstlichen Bullen über die Blutbeschuldigung* (*op. cit.*); Moritz Stern, *Urkundliche Beitrge ber die Stellung der Päpste zu den Juden* (Kiel: Fiencke, 1893) (Latin texts); Emmanuel Rodocanachi, *Le Saint Siège et les Juifs* (Paris: Firmin-Didot, 1891); Hermann Vogelstein and Paul Rieger, *Geschichte der Juden in Rom* (2 vols.; Berlin: Mayer & Muller, 1896); for thirteenth century, Grayzel, *Church and Jews*, *op. cit.*

63. Namely, Calixtus II, Eugenius III, Alexander III, Clement III, Coelestin III, before Innocent and then by thirteen after him. Other popes may also have used the Constitution without formally promulgating it. Though it was addressed to Jews of Rome and the Papal States, it determined papal policy in its main lines toward all Jewries of Christendom.

64. PL, 214:864-865; Grayzel, *Church and Jews*, pp. 92-95.

65. *Epist.* 10:190 (PL, 215:1291); Grayzel, *Church and Jews*, pp. 126-127.

66. See Mansi, *op. cit.*, 22:1054-1058, 1063.

67. See Num. 15:37-41.

68. See Abrahams, *op. cit.*, pp. 305-306, 424-425.

69. Poliakov enumerates twelve councils and nine royal ordinances that prescribed it. (See *Du Christ*, p. 82.)

70. See Abrahams, *op. cit.*, pp. 302-306; Poliakov, *Du Christ*, pp. 100-108; Graetz, *op. cit.*, III, 558-559.

71. See Abrahams, *op. cit.*, pp. 302-304; Abram Sachar, *A History of the Jews* (New York: Knopf, 1939), p. 195.

72. See Grayzel, *Church and Jews*, 152-178; Stern, *op. cit.*, nos. 170-179, II, 11-23.

73. See Grayzel, *Church and Jews*, 178-248; Stern, *op. cit.*, nos. 189-201, II, 25-42.

74. In most of the minor, and even in some of the great, expulsions of the Middle Ages, Jews went no farther than the nearest border of the realm where they settled, hoping to be readmitted or to find it possible to immigrate unnoticed.

75. See Marcus, *op. cit.*, pp. 41-42.

76. See Vernet, "Juifs et Chrétiens," *loc. cit.*, cols. 1692-1694.

77. Baron, *op. cit.*, II, 427.

78. Some historians believe Donin was a Karaite, the member of a Jewish sect that repudiated the "oral law" and held fast only to the "written law," the Pentateuch. See Grayzel, *Church and Jews*, p. 340.

79. See *supra*, p. 32; Abrahams, *op. cit.*, p. 304.

80. Lovsky, *op. cit.*, p. 130.

81. Hans J. Schoeps, *The Jewish-Christian Argument* (New York: Holt, Rinehart, & Winston, 1963), pp. 24-25. Bernard Lazare, modern socialist Jew, considers the Talmud the chief cause of antisemitism in that it took Judaism out of the mainstream of history and culture, augmented its anti-social character, and prevented participation in the common intellectual life. (See Lazare, *op. cit.*, I, 193-195.) Other scholars see the Talmud as the major "instrument that preserved Jewry in the Diaspora." (See Baron, *op. cit.*, II, 290-292 and 215-217; Graetz, *op. cit.*, III, 571-572.)

82. For discussions of the questions of the Talmud see Vernet, *op. cit.*, cols. 1687-94; Baron, *op. cit.*, II, 215-321; Lovsky, *op. cit.*, 130-131; and Simon, *op. cit.*, ch. 7.

83. See Mansi, *op. cit.*, 23:701.

84. See *infra*, pp. 117-119.

85. See Mansi, 23:1174-1175.

86. See Stern, *op. cit.*, no. 1, I, 5-7.

87. See Marcus, *op. cit.*, pp. 51-55.

88. See Baronius (Raynaldus) *op. cit.*, 6:476-477. Some historians, even modern ones, have held that fewer Jews fell victims than other men. Graetz attributes the fact to their better hygienic conditions. (See *op. cit.*, IV, 101.) Poliakov denies that fewer Jews fell and quotes a chronicler of the time who, commenting on the large number of Jews killed by the plague, declared, "They would have been foolish indeed to have poisoned themselves" (*Du Christ*, p. 129).

89. Quoted in Parkes, *Medieval Community*, pp. 1-18.

90. Quoted in Graetz, *op. cit.*, IV, 106.

91. Quoted in Poliakov, *Du Christ*, p. 128. This is an early example of the inherent anti-Christian and amoral character of antisemitism, of which Hitler gave a more recent example.

92. See Baronius (Raynaldus), *op. cit.*, 6:491-494.

93. See Graetz, *op. cit.*, IV, 132-133.

94. For a history of this legend see Joseph Gaer, *The Legend of the Wandering Jew* (New York: Mentor Books, 1963).

95. See Graetz, *Geschichte der Juden* (Leipzig; Leiner, 1873), VIII, 51, fn. 1.

96. The text of this prayer contains the words: "They [idolators] bow down and pray to naught and to vanity, to a god that cannot save." Scholars explain that the prayer was composed by a rabbi in Babylonia in early third century C.E. who referred to all idolators, not necessarily to Christians, who were extremely few in Babylonia at the time. Some Jewish scholars today, reciprocating Jewish requests for expurgation of Christian literature of presumably anti-Jewish material, have called in a general way for a re-examination of Jewish texts that are possibly offensive to Christians. Thus Rabbi Maurice Eisendrath who states: "We have been—not without much justice—constantly on the qui vive to fend off what we have, often rightly, regarded as insulting and demeaning slurs upon us and upon our faith. But I would hope that we, too, have grown up sufficiently in our religious security and as the world's most adult religion in terms of seniority, that we can now afford to render unto Jesus that which is Jesus' without blanching or self-flagellation" ("The State of Our Union Message of the President" [Chicago: Union of American Hebrew Congregrations, 1963], p. 25).

97. The *Kol Nidre*, to which the accusation refers, was put particularly into practice in Spain by the *marranos* (*infra*, pp. 119) who wished to pray as Jews rather than Christians. The release from oaths did not refer to those assumed in court or among their neighbors. (See "Kol Nidre," *Jewish Encyclopedia*.)

98. The Hussite revolt at this time (1419-1436) proved a disaster for Jews. The Hussites themselves attacked them as usurers, while Christians accused them of connections with the heretical cause. During the crusade, Jews again were the first victims, and so convinced were they that, at the end of hostilities, they would be massacred—as threatened—that they held a day of fast and supplication, praying that they be spared and that the Catholics be defeated. In Austria, under Archduke Albert, things went especially badly as an accusation of Jewish collaboration with Hussites was rumored; all in all, many Jews were

punished by imprisonment, impoverishment, killings, and banishments.

99. See Stern, *op. cit.*, no. 10, I, 22-24.

100. Baronius (Raynaldus), *op. cit.*, 8:503.

101. Stern, *op. cit.*, no. 31, I, 38-42.

102. See Stern, *op. cit.*, no. 34, I, 43-45.

103. See Baronius (Raynaldus), *op. cit.*, 9:398-401.

104. See Mansi, *op. cit.*, 29:98-99.

105. See Baronius (Raynaldus), *op. cit.*, 3:479.

106. See Abrahams, *op. cit.*, pp. 417-418.

107. E. Flournoy, *Le Bienheureux Bernardin de Feltre* (Paris, 1896), p. 70; quoted in Poliakov, *Du Christ*, p. 165.

108. *Ibid.*, p. 122.

109. Graetz, *op. cit.*, IV, 297.

110. *Acta Sanctorum*, p. 910; quoted in Milman, *op. cit.*, II, 424.

111. See *supra*, p. 100; also Vacandard, "La question du meurtre rituel," *loc. cit.*, p. 353.

112. See Marcus, *op. cit.*, pp. 155-158.

113. *Ibid.*, pp. 131-136.

114. Jewish historians generally admit the truth of this charge; Abrahams, for example, declares that the evidence is "too well attested for me to deny or palliate it" (*op. cit.*, p. 104). Christians were also involved in the offense.

115. See Mansi, *op. cit.*, 22:1772, 1774.

116. See Margolis and Marx, *op. cit.*, p. 389.

117. See Milman, *op. cit.*, p. 366.

118. See Baronius (Raynaldus), *op. cit.*, 4:10-11.

119. Amends have been made by the present administration of the Lincoln Cathedral, which has had a plaque of repentance erected.

6. AN OASIS AND AN ORDEAL

1. Rodocanachi, *Les Juifs et la Saint Siège* (Paris: Firmin Didot, 1891), p. 2.

2. Poliakov, *Du Mahomet*, p. 303.

3. The custom dates back at least to Calixtus II (1119-1124). It began as a joyful one, but took on a more somber note in the course of time. When Martin V (1417-1431)—a friend of the Jews—received them he addressed them with these words, which became a part of the rites: "You have the Law, but understand it not. Old things are passed; all things are new"; see Franz Wasner, "The Popes' Veneration of the To-

rah," *The Bridge*, IV, 274-293; Rodocanachi, *op. cit.*, pp. 128-130, 139-147.

4. This Benjamin, a twelfth century Jew, traveled to many Jewish communities across Europe and Asia, and reported his findings. For an English edition, see *The Itinerary of R. Benjamin of Tudela* (London: Frowde, 1907).

5. Quoted in Rodocanachi, *op. cit.*, p. 133.

6. Poliakov, *Du Mahomet*, p. 304.

7. See Milman, *op. cit.*, II, 416.

8. Graetz, *op. cit.*, IV, 407.

9. *Ibid.*, IV, 285; III, 135.

10. Abrahams, *op. cit.*, p. 400.

11. Poliakov, *Du Mahomet*, p. 304.

12. This severity was often influenced by complaints and appeals for action against Jews by churchmen and rulers in nonpapal regions.

13. *Op. cit.*, p. 121. Abrahams states the same fact less adroitly when he writes: "Theology seemed to rule with a stronger hand as it drew farther from Rome" (*op. cit.*, p. 401).

14. See *supra*, p. 124.

15. See *supra*, p. 73.

16. Martin V (1429); see Stern, *op. cit.*, p. 39.

17. For an account of the condition of Jews under the papacy see Rodocanachi, *op. cit.*, pp. 120-222; Vernet, "Juifs et Chrêtiens," *op. cit.*, col. 1730-1732.

18. Roth, *The History of the Jews in Italy* (Philadelphia: Jewish Publication Society of America, 1946), p. 177.

19. The *Kabbalah* is a mystical Jewish tradition and literature, dealing with divine emanations and God's immediate relations to man. The classical work of the *Kabbalah* is the *Zohar*, assumed by its followers to have derived from the second century C.E. or earlier but to have been committed to writing in the thirteenth. See *"Kabbalah," Jewish Encyclopedia*.

20. See *supra*, p. 81.

21. Milman, *op. cit.*, II, 370.

22. Americo Castro; quoted in Poliakov, *Du Mahomet*, p. 82.

23. Simon Dubnow, *Weltgeschichte des judischen Volkes* (Berlin: 1926), IV, 131.

24. See Poliakov, *Du Mahomet*, p. 155.

25. *Ibid.*, pp. 116-119.

26. See Marcus, *op. cit.*, pp. 34-40.

27. See *supra*, p. 25; ch. 2, note 2.

28. Cited in Poliakov, *Du Mahomet*, p. 163. In referring to the

damnation of Jews who die in their Judaism, St. Vincent expressed the belief prevalent in his time that all outside the visible Catholic church could not be saved, an interpretation rejected finally by the Holy See in the so-called "Boston heresy case." (See T. Bouscaron, *Canon Law Digest* [Milwaukee: Bruce, 1954], pp. 526-529.)

29. Menendez y Pelayo: quoted in Poliakov, *Du Mahomet*, p. 162.

30. See *supra*, pp. 74-78.

31. See August Potthast, *Regesta Pontificum Romanorum* No. 1479 (Berlin: Decker, 1874-75), I, 131. Not all Church authorities were of the same mind on this matter. Honorius I (625-638) doubted the validity of such baptisms, and allowed Jews so converted to return to their Judaism (PL, 80, 667-670). St. Thomas demonstrated the necessary role of "intention" and "will" in receiving baptism (*Summa Theol.*, III, q, a, 9), and concluded that "since God does not force men to justification, it is clear that whoever approaches baptism insincerely (*ficte*) does not receive its effects" (*ibid.*). Contemporary theology is more attentive still to the subjective requirements for receiving the sacraments. The Code of Canon Law (1917) requires that the subject be *sciens et volens* (knowing and willing) (can. 752, 1).

32. Other improbable derivations of the term *marrano* (also written *marano*) have been sought in Hebrew and Arabic vocabularies, as also in the anathema "Marantha" (The Lord Comes) of Paul (I Cor. 16:22). The word did not usually appear in formal writings of the time. See Cecil Roth, *History of the Marranos* (New York: Meridian, 1959), pp. 27-28.

33. See Williams, *op. cit.*, pp. 277-281.

34. See James J. Broderick, S.J., "St. Ignatius Loyola and Jews," *The Bridge*, IV, 300-301.

35. See *supra*, p. 105.

36. The Portuguese expression for "act of faith"; in Spanish, *auto de fè*.

37. For an excellent study of the *marranos* and the Inquisition, see Cecil Roth's *History of the Marranos* (*op. cit.*). The classical study of English of the Inquisition is that of Henry Charles Lea, *A History of the Inquisition in Spain* (4 vols.; New York: Macmillan, 1906-07). A competent Catholic study is E. Vacandard's *L'Inquisition, Etude Historique et critique* (Paris: Bloud, 1907). See also Paul van K. Thomson, "The Tragedy of the Spanish Inquisition," *The Bridge*, IV, 171-196.

38. A somewhat amusing story is told by Roth of the Portuguese nobleman who, in order to save his physician who, under torture, had confessed to Judaizing, seized the inquisitor himself and extracted from

him a confession of the same crime by the same means. (See *History of the Marranos,* p. 386, fn. 6.)

39. Quoted in Dubnow, *op. cit.,* V, 39.

40. See Vacandard, "Meurtre Rituel," *loc. cit.,* pp. 341-342.

41. See Poliakov, *Du Mahomet,* p. 198; Marcus, *op. cit.,* 51-55.

42. See Graetz, *op. cit.,* IV, 348; Milman, *op. cit.,* II, 401.

43. Graetz, *op. cit.,* IV, 396.

44. Cleared in 1492 of its most industrious bourgeois citizens, Spain, after its imperial triumphs following Columbus's discoveries, failed to take its place in the general economic and industrial expansion of the modern world. (See Milman, *op. cit.,* II, 400; Poliakov, *Du Mahomet,* p. 193.)

45. See Marcus, *op. cit.,* pp. 56-59.

46. See Roth, *History of the Marranos,* pp. 355-378.

47. See Oesterreicher, *The Apostolate to the Jews* (New York: America Press, 1948), pp. 51-54; Lovsky, *op. cit.,* p. 188.

48. R. Anchel; quoted in Lovsky, *op. cit.,* p. 188.

49. Guido Kisch, "The Jews in Medieval Law," in *Essays on Anti-Semitism,* ed. Koppel, Pinson (New York: Conference on Jewish Relations, 1942), pp. 64-65.

50. See Parkes, *Conflict,* p. 339. In his *History of the Jews,* Milman features extensive data of Jewish involvement in usurious practices; see *op. cit.*

51. See Sombart, *op. cit.,* pp. 159-260.

52. Poliakov, *Du Christ,* p. 174.

53. Petrus Abelardus, *Dialogus inter Philosophum, Judaeum, et Christianum* (PL, 178:1617-18).

54. See Trachtenburg, *The Devil and the Jews,* pp. 11-31; Joseph Reider, "Jews in Medieval Art," in Pinson, *loc. cit.,* pp. 45-56; Poliakov, *Du Christ,* pp. 140-171.

55. See Poliakov, *Du Christ,* p. 100.

56. *Ibid.,* p. 179.

57. Karl Thieme, "Der religiose Aspekt der Judenfeindschaft," *Freiburger Rundbrief,* X, 33 (Oct., 1957) (Reprint).

58. R. Travers Herford, "The Influence of Judaism on Jews" in *The Legacy of Israel* (Oxford: Clarendon Press, 1927), p. 122.

7. THE AGE OF THE GHETTO

1. The origin of the term is not certain. It is probably from the Italian word *gèto,* meaning "iron foundry," beside one of which the first

Italian ghettos in Venice were situated. See "Ghetto," *Jewish Encyclopedia;* Abrahams, *Jewish Life in the Middle Ages,* p. 62.

2. See Parkes, *Medieval Community,* p. 160; Abrahams, *op. cit.,* pp. 62-64.

3. See Mansi, *op. cit.,* 29:99.

4. See Grayzel, *A History of the Jews,* p. 475.

5. Roth, *A Short History of the Jewish People* (Oxford: East and West, 1935), pp. 308-309.

6. Solomon Grayzel describes the situation thus: "In my study of Talmud and Midrash, men could forget time and place. Though physically they resided in Frankfurt, or Vienna, or Rome, mentally they dwelt in the Palestine of kings and prophets, or in the academies of Sura and Pumpeditha. Their hopes were centered not upon any earthly rulers who, as far as they were concerned, were hostile or greedy, but on the promise made to their ancestors of a Messiah who would come to redeem them"; see *History,* p. 489.

7. Abraham J. Heschel, *The Earth Is the Lord's* (New York: H. Schuman, 1950), p. 10.

8. *Ibid.,* p. 100.

9. Jacob Katz, *Exclusiveness and Tolerance* (London: Oxford University Press, 1961), p. 136.

10. Cecil Roth, *A Short History,* p. 308.

11. See Marcus, *op. cit.,* pp. 367-372.

12. Lee Levinger, *Anti-Semitism Yesterday and Tomorrow* (New York: Macmillan, 1936), p. 81.

13. See Poliakov, *Du Christ,* chs. 8 and 9.

14. Pascal, *Pensées,* (ed. Brunschvicg), especially nos. 607-610, 622, 747-750 (Paris: Crès, 1913), pp. 251-255, 264, 337-338. It should be noted that the term "carnal" as used by Pascal denotes more the idea of attachment to earthly things than abandonment to the flesh.

15. Bossuet, *Oeuvres Oratoires* (Paris: Lebarg, 1913), p. 158. For further evidences of antisemitism at this time, see Poliakov, *Du Christ,* pp. 193-216.

16. Historians disagree on the character of Pfefferkorn. Many, following Graetz, regard him as a "despicable wretch" (Graetz, *op. cit.,* IV, 424); Poliakov finds him "sincere and moderate" (*Du Christ* p. 233).

17. Quoted in Graetz, *op. cit.,* IV, 435.

18. Quoted in Graetz, *op. cit.,* IV, 447-448.

19. See Marcus, *op. cit.,* pp. 159-164.

20. Reuchlin's enemies became known by this term after the appearance of an anonymous satire, written at that time, entitled *Epistolae*

Obscurum Virorum (Letters of Obscure Men), which lampooned the Dominicans and anti-Reuchlinists.

21. Luther, "That Jesus Christ Was Born a Jew" (1523); see *Luther's Works*, ed. I. Brandt (55 vols.; Philadelphia: Muhlenberg Press, 1962), XLV, 200-201.

22. Luther, "Von den Juden und Ihren Lgen," see *Luthers Reformations-Schriften* (22 vols.; St. Louis: Concordia, 1890), XX, 1861-2026.

23. Luther, *Schem Hamphoras, ibid.*, 2029-2109.

24. See Poliakov, *Du Christ*, p. 240; Marcus, *op. cit.*, pp. 165-169.

25. Eisenmenger, *Entdecktes Judentum* (Dresden: Braudner, 1893).

26. See Rodocanachi, *Les Juifs et le Saint Siège*, pp. 159-160.

27. See Stern, *op. cit.*, no. 100, pp. 98-102.

28. *Magnum Bullarium Romanum* (25 vols.; Turin: Dalmuzzo and Vecco, 1860-72), VI, 498-500. Most of these measures were promulgated in Paul IV's bull *Cum nimis absurdum* of 1555; for an analysis, see Rodocanachi, *op. cit.*, pp. 160-165.

29. For an account of the period following Paul IV's reign, see Rodocanachi, *op. cit.*, pp. 177-220.

30. See J. Aronius, *Regesten zur Geschichte der Juden im frankischen und deutschen Reichen*, no. 724, can. 12 (Berlin, 1902).

31. See *supra*, p. 115.

32. Margolis and Marx, *op. cit.*, p. 552.

33. Many historians consider the second figure exaggerated and the first a minimum.

34. Hasidism was the creation of Israel ben Eliezer, who received the popular name Baal Shem Tob (also the Besht) (1700-60), or Israel of the Good Name. This deeply spiritual man, with no intention of creating a sect, emphasized simple relations with God, candor in prayer, and joyous living under a spiritual guide. People flocked to him, and after his death a pietistic tradition called Hasidism flourished but stirred up several countermovements in Judaism. The Jewish philosopher Martin Buber partook of the Hasidic tradition. See Oesterreicher, "The Hasidic Movement," *The Bridge*, III, 122-186; Jacob Katz, *Tradition and Crisis* (New York: Free Press of Glencoe, 1961), pp. 231-44.

35. See *supra*, p. 100.

8. THE STRUGGLE FOR EMANCIPATION

1. Hugo Valentin, *Anti-Semitism* (London: Gollancz, 1936), p. 47. Heine, the poet, was typical of some of these converts. He frankly

confessed to accepting baptism as a sort of ticket into Christian society. "I was baptized, not converted," he wrote, and complained, "Judaism is not a religion, but a misfortune." (Quoted in Abram Sachar, *A History of the Jews*, p. 289.)

2. Dohm, *Ueber die bürgerliche verbesserung der Juden* (Berlin: Nicolai, 1781).

3. At the time of the Revolution, some 500,000 Jews lived in France, 50 per cent of whom inhabited Alsace and Lorraine. Other communities were at Bordeaux, Bayonne, and Marseilles, sprung from settlements of Portuguese *marranos*, and a few lived in Paris.

4. Suffering at the hands of the Revolution and shocked at the blasphemies perpetrated in its name, the Church, both in France and Rome, took a dark view of the Revolution as a whole. Pius VII fought its work as French "infidelity." In America the Catholic journalist Orestes Brownson saw it as the work of Satan. (See *Works*, ed. Orestes Brownson [Detroit: H. F. Brownson, 1884], IX, 220.) In our own day, Paul VI has assessed the mixed character of the great event differently. In addition to the "anti-Christian, secularistic, irreligious" in the revolution, he saw a "combination of the great principles of the Revolution that had done nothing more nor less than appropriate to itself certain Christian concepts—fraternity, liberty, equality, progress, the desire to lift up the lower classes . . . ." (Address on occasion of Canonization of St. Vincent Pallotti.) See *The Pope Speaks*, IX, no. 2 (1964), p. 176.

5. See Graetz, *op. cit.*, V, 470; see also Jacob S. Raisin, *Gentile Reaction to Jewish Ideals* (New York: Philosophical Library), pp. 585 ff.

6. See *supra*, p. 94; ch. 5, note 16.

7. Sachar, *op. cit.*, p. 295.

8. See Lazare, *op. cit.*, II, 225-260.

9. See Lazare, *ibid.*, II, 46.

10. See Karl Marx, *A World Without Jews* (New York: Philosophical Library, 1959), pp. 37, 45. Hannah Arendt in her *The Origins of Totalitarianism* [New York: Meridian, 1958], p. 34), as well as Lovsky (see *op. cit.*, p. 276), refuses to place Marx in the antisemitic bracket, yet it would seem that his rigid and scornful identification of Jewry with the pursuit of gold betrays more than a purely economic judgment.

11. Both Jewish and Christian commentators have recognized the reformist and progressive inclination at the heart of Judaism and in Jewish pursuit of social justice. The phenomenon is largely explained as a combined product of the Jewish prophetic tradition and a reaction to oppression undergone throughout the centuries. It is to be clearly distinguished from a reformism, or radicalism, of a more destructive kind,

such as Marxist-Leninism, to which Judaism as such has no bond. One can see, however, how the impulse derived from the religious tradition could tend to feed the socialist movement. See Baron, *op. cit.*, I, 84-91: Lazare, *op. cit.*, II, 150-181.

12. R. H. Tawney, in opposition to Sombart, has argued convincingly that the spirit of capitalism and free enterprise sprang from a Calvinist or Puritan ethic which sought the "triumph of the economic virtues," rather than from Jewish economic or financial activities. See *Religion and the Rise of Capitalism, op. cit.*

13. See Bertram W. Korn, *American Reaction to the Mortara Case: 1858-59* (Cincinnati: American Jewish Archives, 1957).

14. See A. Delacouture, *Droit canon et Droit naturel dans l'affaire Mortara* (Paris: Cantu, 1958).

15. The defenders of the action of the Holy Office cited the superior rights of the supernatural order established by baptism and found canonical precedents in the fourth and seventeenth councils of Toledo (Mansi, *Sacrorum conciliorum*, 10: 634; 13: 103). (See *supra*, p. 100.) These canons were promulgated again by Benedict XIV in his letter *Postremo Mense* of 1747 (Denziger, *Enchiridion*, 407-411) and incorporated in the Code of Canon Law of that time. The present Code (1917) makes no reference to the matter. Present theological opinion may best be gauged by the discussions of the similar Finaly Case of 1950, wherein most Catholic theologians argued that divine law does not abrogate natural law; that recourse to the "secular arm" is not a necessary or permanent part of the Church's mission to teach or govern; and that the discipline of removing children did not constitute a general law of the Church. (See Edward Flannery, "The Finaly Case," *The Bridge*, I, 292-313.)

16. Louis Greenberg, *The Jews in Russia* (2 vols. [New Haven: Yale University Press, 1951]), I, 73.

17. Brafman's lack of culture is comically evinced by an attested story that he once asked the imperial librarian about a "book" called *Ibid.* or *Ibidem*, "which authors quote so often." (See Greenberg, *ibid.*, I, 94.)

18. The term "rationalism" in this work does not connote the use or rule of reason but that philosophy which erects reason as the sole source and arbiter of truth to the exclusion of faith or religious experience as well as other non-rational sources of truth.

19. Spinoza, *Theologico-Political Treatise*, ch. 17; *Chief Works* (2 vols.; New York: Dover, 1951), I, 229.

20. See especially "Abraham," "Lois," *Dictionnaire Philosophique;* "Philosophie d'Histoire," *Essai sur les Moeurs (Oeuvres Completes*

de Voltaire [70 vols.; Paris: Imprimerie de la Société Littéraire, 1785], XXXVII, 41-62; XLI, 463-518; XVI, 166-220).

21. See *supra*, pp. 12-13.

22. Voltaire, *Essai sur les Moeurs*, 103 (*ibid.*, XVII, 530-534); art. "Juifs" and "Julien," *Dictionnaire Philosophique* (*ibid.*, XLI, 136-182, 182-196).

23. Voltaire, *Essai sur les Moeurs*, XCIV (*ibid.*, XVII, 467).

24. Voltaire, *Lettres*, (Dec. 14, 1773); *Sermon des Cinquantes* (*ibid.*, LXII, 279; XXXII, 381).

25. Voltaire, "Juifs," *Dictionnaire Philosophique* (*ibid.*, XLI, 152).

26. Voltaire's "l'infâme" (the infamous one) was, of course, the Church.

27. Adolf Hitler, *Secret Conversations* (New York: Farrar, Straus, and Young, 1953), I, 84, 87, 124.

28. See Lovsky, *op. cit.*, pp. 268-269.

29. *Ibid.*, p. 273; see also Poliakov, *Du Christ*, p. 6.

30. See Toussenel, *Les Juifs, rois de l'épogue, Histoire de la féo-dalite* (Paris: De Gonet, 1847).

31. Quoted in Lovsky, *op. cit.*, p. 274.

32. Paul Johnson demonstrates the consistently, though at times covert, antisemitic character of Marxism. See "Marxism vs. the Jews" in *Commentary* (April, 1984) pp. 28-34. See also R. F. Byrnes who describes the determining role Socialism played in the evolution of anti-semitism between the years 1840 and 1870, especially in France. Byrnes, *Anti-Semitism in Modern France* (2 vols.; New Brunswick: Rutgers, 1940) I, 115, 125, 134.

33. Lovsky insists that antisemitism is essentially of a traditionalist and conservative derivation. Lovsky, *op. cit.*, pp. 476-77.

9. THE RACIAL MYTH AND ITS CONSEQUENCES

1. W. Marr, *Der Sieg des Judentums über des Germanentums* (Berne: Costenoble, 1879).

2. G. W. F. Hegel, *Philosophy of Right*, III, 3; *Great Books of the Western World*, ed. R. Hutchins, vol. 46; *Hegel* (Chicago: Enc. Britannica, 1952), pp. 80-114; also *Philosophy of History*, IV, *ibid.*, pp. 315-369.

3. See C. Lassen, *Indische Altertumskunde* (4 vols.; Bonn: Koenig, 1847-61). Renan believed that Jews, as Semites, comprised "a really inferior combination of the human race" (*Histoire generale des langues Sémitiques* [Paris: Imprimerie Imperiale, 1878], I, 16). Later, Renan

protested the exaggerations of the racists, and admitted that modern Jews were not strictly Semites. (See Lovsky, *op. cit.*, p. 281.)

4. M. Gobineau, *Essai sur l'inégalité des races* (Paris: Firmin-Didot, 1884).

5. Anthropologists today reject the entire ideological basis of racial antisemitism as without scientific foundation. The Jews in particular are not considered as constituting a race. Descended from a number of early peoples, not all semitic, they commingled in the course of their history with neighboring peoples: Greeks, Romans, Celts, Germans, Khazars, and others. It has been justly pointed out that in-groups of Jews differ as much among themselves as Jews do as a whole from other peoples. Bernard Lazare described Jews as "the most heterogeneous of all peoples, that one which presents the greatest varieties. This supposed race, whose stability and resistance both friends and enemies are at one in vaunting, presents us with the greatest multiplicity of opposite types which extends from white Jews to the black Jews by the way of yellow Jews, to say nothing of secondary divisions such as blond, redheaded, brunette, and black-haired Jews" (Bernard Lazare, *op. cit.*, II, 107).

6. August Rohling, *Der Talmudjude zur Beherzigung für Juden und Christen aller Stände* (Munich: Russell, 1871).

7. Some historians, including Abram Sachar and Hugo Valentin, accuse Pope Pius IX of stirring sentiment against the Jews in his Christmas message of 1872. Writes Sachar: "Pope Pius IX celebrated Christmas of 1872 by issuing a diatribe denouncing Jews as enemies of Christ and a pernicious influence in civilized society" (*History*, pp. 340-341; also Valentin, *op. cit.*, p. 49). An examination of the Christmas message reveals no mention of Jews, explicit or implicit. The Pope's criticism seems to be leveled exclusively against the German leadership. For an English translation of the message, see *The Tablet* (London, Jan. 4, 1873), I, 16-17.

8. James Parkes has evinced the purely political motivation of Bismarck, and used it as an example of the invariable way in which Jews are made a scapegoat for purely political reasons. (See *An Enemy of the People* [New York: Penguin Books, 1946], pp. 5-11.) Hannah Arendt has argued against over-reliance on the "scapegoat" theory. The theory, she argues, "implies that the scapegoat might have been anyone else as well," and thus avoids the possibility of any distinction of the victim. (See Arendt, *The Origins of Totalitarianism* [Cleveland: World Publishing, 1927], pp. 5-7.)

9. H. von Treitschke, *Ein Wort über unser Judentum* (Berlin, 1888).

10. T. Fritsch, *Antisemiten-Katechismus* (Leipzig: Fritsch, 1892).

11. H. S. Chamberlain, *Die Grundlagen des neunzehnten Jahrhunderts* (2 vols.; Munich: Bruckmann, 1889); English translation: John Lees (New York: John Lane, 1914).

12. M. Stirner (pseudn., Johann Kasper Schmidt), *Der Einzige und sein Eigentum* (Leipzig: Wigand, 1845).

13. Nietzsche had some good things to say about Jews but in the final account holds them responsible for the "slave-morality" and vulgarization of morals. "It is with them," he writes, "that the slave-insurrection in morals commences" ("Beyond Good and Evil"; *The Philosophy of Nietzsche* [New York: Modern Library, 1954], p. 486). Comparing them to the "aristocratic" Germans and Chinese, he finds Jews "fifth rate" ("The Genealogy of Morals," *ibid.*, p. 664).

14. For a masterly analysis of this period in Germany and of the oppositions and cross-fertilizations affecting Christian and anti-Christian racist antisemitism, see Uriel Tal, *Christians and Jews in Germany: Religion, Politics, and Ideology in the Second Reich (1870-1914).* (Ithaca: Cornell Univ., 1975). See also Lovsky, *op. cit.*, pp. 278-92.

15. See *infra*, p. 188.

16. E. Drumont, *La France Juive* (15th ed.; 2 vols.; Paris: Marpon & Flammarion, 1886).

17. A. Leroy-Beaulieu, *Les Juifs et l'antisémitisme, Israel chez les nations* (Paris: Levy, 1893); English translation: *Israel Among the Nations* (New York: Putnam, 1895).

18. See Hannah Arendt, "From the Dreyfus Affair to France Today," Pinson, *op. cit.*, p. 194.

19. See Joseph N. Moody, "Dreyfus and After," *The Bridge* (New York: Pantheon, 1956), II, 184-187.

20. See H. Arendt, "From the Dreyfus Case to France Today," *loc. cit.*, pp. 188-191. Miss Arendt need not be considered anticlerical; rather her sources seem tainted. Only 10 per cent of the French general staff were educated by Jesuits and only one member entertained close relations with a Jesuit. Jesuit schools were numerous, but there is no reason to believe that they were more antisemitic than any other. In those days the non-Jesuit daily, *La Croix*, was as antisemitic and influential as they. For a discussion of the question see Moody, "Dreyfus and After," *loc. cit.*, pp. 184-187.

21. See *supra*, p. 158.

22. Gougenot de Mousseaux, *Le Juif, le Judaisme et la Judaization des peuples chrétiens* (Paris: Wattelier, 1869).

23. This term may be rendered in English as "resentment."

24. Lovsky, *op. cit.*, p. 340.

25. This Russian word originally meant "storm" or "devasta-

tion," but came to signify any planned attack on a defenseless group, especially Jews, and including looting, rapine, torture, and even murder. The word crept into other languages after the turn of the century and was widened to mean almost any violent attack on Jews.

26. The emigration had begun on a smaller scale in 1869.

27. A relaxation of the restrictions was granted to Jewish women who were permitted to enter the universities provided they wore the yellow circle of the prostitute.

28. See *infra*, p. 256.

29. Pierre Charles, S.J., "The Learned Elders of Zion," *The Bridge, op. cit.*, I, 171.

30. Valentin, *op. cit.*, p. 181.

31. See Lovsky, *op. cit.*, pp. 252-260.

32. See ch. 14, pp. 269-270.

33. See *ibid.*, p. .

10. A WAR WITHIN A WAR

1. Psychologists point out that one of the unvarying causes of antisemitism is the presence of political and social unrest. (See Otto Fenichel, "Elements of a Psychoanalytic Theory of Anti-Semitism," in *Anti-Semitism: A Social Disease;* ed. Ernest Simmel [New York: International Universities Press, 1946], pp. 11-32.)

2. On Jewish participation in leftist revolutions see *infra*, p. 232.

3. Valentin, *op. cit.*, pp. 94-95.

4. *Ibid.*, p. 94.

5. See Salo Baron, "European Jewry Before and After Hitler," *American Jewish Yearbook* (Philadelphia: Jewish Publication Society of America, 1962), LXIII, 26; also James Parkes, *A History of the Jewish People (op. cit.)*, p. 198.

6. See ch. XI.

7. Baron, "European Jewry," *loc. cit.*, p. 34.

11. THE FINAL SOLUTION

1. Raul Hilberg, *The Destruction of European Jewry* (Chicago: Quadrangle, 1961), p. 3.

2. See *infra*, p. 263.

3. What profiteering by Jews there was during the inflation was vastly overshadowed by the same activity on the part of "Aryan" Germans, the most notable example of which was the industrialist Hugo

Stinnes who, by financial manipulations, earned for himself his first billion dollars in a short time.

4. See Valentin, *op. cit.*, ch. 11. These charges were illustrations of the classic double standard of antisemites. Gentiles who were successful were hailed for their drive and achievements. Jews who succeeded were regarded as sinister conspirators; their success was explained as a result of their "Jewishness" which made them "pushy" and "unscrupulous."

5. Hitler's antisemitism was not original in itself. One might say that his animus was his own, but his ideas were derived from his mentors. The foremost National-Socialist philosopher of antisemitism was Alfred Rosenberg, a neo-pagan who expounded his views in his *Der Mythus des neunzehnten Jahrhunderts* (Munich: Hohenneichen, 1934), which is little more than a reworking of Chamberlain's opus (*supra,* p. 181). Nazism's racial anthropology was the work of Hans F.K. Guenther, whose major antisemitic work was *Rassenkunde des judischen Volkes* (Munich: Lehman, 1931).

6. See *supra,* p. 182.

7. Adolf Hitler, *Mein Kampf* (Boston: Houghton Mifflin, 1943).

8. Many of Hitler's backers, of course, were not convinced Nazis but rather voters of protest who did not take him seriously enough and who believed that he would moderate his radicalism with the assumption of power. They looked to him merely as one who would arrest the "Red menace," abolish the Weimar Republic, and curb the Jews. What support he received from the churches derived mostly from such considerations.

9. *Ibid.,* ch. 6. Hitler counsels that all propaganda be directed to the masses alone, that its intellectual content be as low as necessary, that a few visceral truths or falsehoods be hammered home endlessly. He puts it plainly: "All propaganda must be popular and its intellectual level must be adjusted to the most limited intelligence among those it's addressed to . . . . The art of propaganda lies in understanding the emotional ideas of the great masses" (*ibid.,* p. 180).

10. "The transformation of a liberal into a totalitarian nationalism, appealing to the masses and uniting them under the leadership of Hitler, was accomplished under the banner of antisemitism." Waldemar Gurian, "Anti-Semitism in Modern Germany," in Pinson, ed., *Essays on Anti-Semitism,* p. 251.

11. The source books of this antisemitism are Hitler's writings and speeches; see *Mein Kampf (op. cit.); Hitler's Secret Conversations, 1941-44 (op. cit.); Hitler's Secret Book* (2 vols.; New York: Grove Press, 1961); *The Speeches of Adolf Hitler* (New York: Oxford Press, 1942).

12. Hitler, *Mein Kampf, op. cit.,* p. 65.

13. On the subject of the religiosity of Nazism see Léon Poliakov, *Bréviaire de la Haine* (Paris: Calmann-Lévy, 1951), pp. 6-9. For an English translation of this important work, see *Harvest of Hate* (Syracuse: Syracuse University Press, 1954). References in this book are to the French edition.

14. "Anti-Semitism is a useful revolutionary expedient. Antisemitic propaganda in all countries is an almost indispensable medium for the extension of our political campaign. You will see how little time we shall need in order to upset the ideas and criteria of the whole world, simply and purely at attacking Judaism. It is beyond question the most important weapon in my propaganda arsenal." Hitler to Rauschning; quoted in Parkes, *An Enemy of the People: Anti-Semitism* (New York: Penguin, 1946), p. 50.

15. See William L. Shirer, *The Rise and Fall of the Third Reich* (New York: Simon and Shuster, 1960), pp. 1123-1126.

16. On the basis of counting "quarter Jews" and "half Jews," Nazi propaganda put the Jewish population of Germany at 3,000,000 or 5 per cent of the population. Jewish research placed the number of these "non-Aryans" at 252,000 and the number of "whole" Jews in Germany in 1935 at 450,000, to give a total of 700,000. For an analysis of Nazi definition of Jews, see R. Hilberg, *op. cit.,* pp. 43-53.

17. Valentin, *op. cit.,* p. 121.

18. A. Sachar, *Sufferance is the Badge* (New York: Knopf, 1939), p. 63.

19. Cited in Poliakov, *Bréviaire,* p. 20.

20. After the war government documents relating to the organization of the "demonstrations" were found. Though mostly the work of Reinhardt Heydrich, second in charge of the SS troops, they were approved and encouraged by Hitler, as were also the economic measures we are about to see. (See Shirer, *op. cit.,* pp. 430-431.)

21. Antisemitism had known internationalization before, of course, in the 1870s, for instance, when international congresses were held, and in the early efforts to export Nazi propaganda; but in these cases the nationalist inspiration still predominated.

22. The greatest portion of our knowledge of the extermination program comes from the Nuremberg trials, whose material has been published in several editions. A German edition printed in Nuremberg in 42 volumes, *The Trial of German Major War Criminals* (Nuremberg, 1947-1949), has for the greater part been published in an American edition, *Nazi Conspiracy and Aggression* (11 vols.; Washington, D.C.: State Department, 1946-48). Among first-rate secondary sources are Polia-

kov, *Bréviaire de la Haine (Harvest of Hate), op. cit.;* Reitlinger, *The Final Solution* (New York: Beechhurst, 1953); Hilberg, *The Destruction of European Jews, op. cit.;* Davidowicz, *The War against the Jews* (New York: Holt, Rinehart & Winston, 1975).

23. Quoted in Poliakov, *Bréviaire,* p. 208.

24. Cited in Poliakov, *ibid.,* pp. 143-145.

25. Quoted in Poliakov, *ibid.,* p. 172.

26. For an unfortunate example of one such baptism and the *cause célèbre* it became, see E. H. Flannery, "The Finaly Case," *The Bridge,* I, 292-313.

27. In 1953 the Israeli government established by law a national memorial to commemorate the martyrs and heroes of the Holocaust. According to Article Nine of the establishing Act it was stipulated that a "place and name" (*Yad Vashem*) be given to Christians who acted to save Jews during the Holocaust. A permanent committee was established to record and assess all testimonies from inclusion among these "righteous of the nations," and an "Avenue of the Righteous" was paved and lined with trees to be planted, when possible, by the "righteous" themselves. Seven hundred trees enclose the Avenue.

The numerous publications of *Yad Vashem*'s research center contain the records of the "righteous" ones, but these have not been assembled in a single volume. Information concerning these records may be obtained by writing to: *Yad Vashem,* Martyrs and Heroes Remembrance Authority, Har Ha-Zikaron, Jerusalem, P.O.B 3477. Many individual unofficial but reliable accounts of these heroes and their activities have appeared. See Philip Friedman's *Their Brother's Keeper* (New York: Crown, 1957); Philip Hallie, *Lest Innocent Blood be Shed* (New York: Harper and Row, 1980); Alexander Ramati, *The Assisi Underground* (Stein and Day, 1978); and Peter Hellman, *Avenue of the Righteous* (New York: Bantam, 1980).

28. On the record of the Churches, see Gordon C. Zahn, *German Catholics and Hitler's Wars* (New York: Sheed and Ward, 1962); Guenter Lewy, *The Catholic Church and Nazi Germany* (New York: McGraw Hill, 1964); Johan Snoek, *The Grey Book* (Assen: Van Gorcum, 1969); A. Cochrane, *The Church's Confession Under Hitler* (Philadelphia: Westminster, 1962); *The German Church Struggle and the Holocaust,* ed. F. Littel and H. Locke (Detroit: Wayne State, 1974); Poliakov, *Bréviaire (op. cit.).*

29. See Poliakov, *Bréviaire, op. cit.,* pp. 293-95.

30. Johan Snoek, *The Grey Book, (op. cit.),* p. 289.

31. *Ibid.,* p. 289. See also Turi Suhl, *They Fought Back: The Story of Jewish Resistance in Nazi Europe* (New York: Schocken, 1973).

32. From the considerable literature that has grown about the Pope's silence, the following volumes, among others, may be read with profit. They are arranged according to their position on the subject.

Among the defenders of the Pope: See Pinchas Lapide, *Three Popes and the Jews* (New York: Hawthorn, 1967); Anthony Rhodes, *The Vatican in the Age of the Dictators (1922-1945)* (New York: Holt, Rinehart and Winston, 1973); Edgar Alexander, *Hitler and the Pope: Pius XII and the Jews* (New York: Thomas Nelson, 1964); Dr. Joseph Lichten, "A Question of Judgment: Pius XII and the Jews" (Pamphlet) (Washington, NCWC, 1964).

Among the Pope's critics, Guenter Lewy, *The Catholic Church and Nazi Germany* (New York: McGraw Hill, 1964); Carlo Falconi, *The Silence of Pius XII* (Boston: Little, Brown, 1965); John Morley, *Vatican Diplomacy and Jews During the Holocaust, 1939-1943* (New York: Katav, 1980).

Critics with reservations: Saul Friedlander, *Pius XII and the Third Reich: A Documentation* (New York: Alfred Knopf, 1966); Leon Poliakov, *Bréviaire, (op. cit.)*. The playwright Rolf Hochhuth "The Deputy" (DerStellvertreter), which gave impetus to some of this literature, cannot be considered a serious contribution to the question because of dramatic license he used for his gross caricature of the Pope. See Hochhuth, *The Deputy* (New York: Grove, 1964).

33. For the case against the United States see Arthur D. Morse, *While Six Million Died* (New York: Random House, 1967); also Henry Feingold, *The Politics of Rescue: The Roosevelt Administration and the Holocaust, 1933-45.*

34. See Yerushalmi, *Auschwitz: Beginning of a New Era?* ed., Eva Fleischner (New York: Ktav, 1977), p. 104.

35. See Lapide *(op. cit.,)* p. 215.

36. See Morley, *Vatican Diplomacy and the Jews during the Holocaust*, 1939-1943. (New York: Katv, 1980), p. 209.

37. See Poliakov, *Bréviaire (op. cit.)*, p. 341.

38. *Ibid.*, pp. 257-262.

39. See Hannah Arendt, *Eichmann in Jerusalem* (New York: Viking, 1963), p. 111. Miss Arendt's criticism is debated by many, notably Norman Podhoretz, editor of *Commentary*, who writes: "The truth is— *must be*—that the Jews under Hitler acted as men will act when they are set upon by murderers, no better and no worse: the Final Solution reveals nothing about the victims except that they were mortal beings and hopelessly vulnerable in their powerlessness." ("Hannah Arendt on Eichmann," *Commentary*, XXXVI, 3 [Sept., 1963], p. 208.)

40. The classical estimate of Jewish casualties under Hitler is six

million—more than half of European Jewry or one third of world Jewry. It is a round but reasonably accurate figure; and, moreover, that of Adolf Eichmann. Absolutely precise computation here is, of course, impossible, given the dearth of Nazi documentation. Hence many estimates have been made: for example, 4,200,000 to 4,600,000 (Reitlinger); 4,700,000 (Anglo-American Committee of Enquiry on Palestine); 6 to 7,000,000 (Frumpkin); 6,093,000 (Lestchinsky); and so on. Most historians agree on 6,000,000 as the most probable figure. Three methods of computing are used: the evidence of Nazi documents, analysis of death-camp records, and demographical comparison of the Jewish population before and after the war. The triple results converge upon the figure 6,000,000. For a brief treatment of the subject see Poliakov, *Bréviaire*, Annex I; Reitlinger, *op. cit.*, Appendix I; William Keller, "Ledger of Death," *The Bridge, op. cit.*, I, 283-291.

12. RED ANTISEMITISM

1. Among other American hate sheets, *The Thunderbolt* (published in Birmingham, Alabama, by the National States Rights Party) pursues this line.

2. Even in the Communist camp, protestations against antisemitism occasionally occur. In 1964, for example, when following the publication of an antisemitic book, *Judaism Without Embellishment*, by Trofim K. Kichko, under the auspices of the Academy of Science of the Soviet Republic of the Ukraine, *Tass*, official press agency in Moscow, ran a criticism of the book. The criticism, however, followed other critical comments in European Communist publications. For a more recent Communist repudiation of Kichko's book, see the editorial article " 'Soviet Anti-Semitism': the Kichko Book," *Political Affairs*, LXIII, 6 (June 1964), pp. 1-12; "Soviet Anti-Semitism; the Status of Soviet Jews": *ibid.*, LXVII, 7 (July 1964), pp. 1-15. See also Moshe Decter, "Judaism Without Embellishment':—Recent Documentation of Soviet Anti-Semitism" (*New Politics*, III, no. 1 [Winter, 1964], pp. 102-118). Decter likens Kichko's book to an "updated and refurbished version of the *Protocols of the Elders of Zion*" (p. 112).

For an example of present-day Communist position on Soviet antisemitism, see Herbert Aptheker, "The Fraud of Soviet Anti-Semitism" (New York: New Century, 1962); Sofia Frey (Moscow) "The Truth About the Jews in the Soviet Union" (New York: New Century, 1960).

3. See *supra*, p. 167.

4. See *supra*, p. 176.

5. Quoted in Solomon Schwarz, *The Jews in the Soviet Union* (Syracuse: Syracuse University Press, 1951), pp. 40, 53.

6. Quoted in Solomon Schwarz, "The New Anti-Semitism of the Soviet Union," *Commentary*, VII, 6 (June 1949), p. 537. The jester, incidentally, took part in antisemitic activities during the civil war.

7. Advocacy of national hatred or contempt was made punishable in the Criminal Code of the RSFSR and other Union republics by imprisonment of two years, or in serious circumstances, by death and confiscation (Art. 59, para. 7). (See Andrei Vishinsky, *The Law of the Soviet State* [New York: Macmillan, 1951], p. 604.)

8. The Soviet Constitution contains these words: "Equality of rights of citizens of the U.S.S.R., irrespective of their nationality or race, in all spheres of economic, government, cultural, political, and other social activity, is an indefeasible law.

"Any direct or indirect restriction of rights of, or, conversely, the establishment of any direct or indirect privilege for citizens on account of their race or nationality, as well as any advocacy of racial or national exclusiveness or hatred and contempt, are punishable by law." (Constitution [Fundamental Law] of the Union of Soviet Socialist Republics, as amended by the seventh session of the fifth Supreme Soviet of the U.S.S.R. [Moscow: Foreign Language Publ. House, 1962], p. 101.)

9. As early as 1918, the Council of the Peoples' Commissars stated that "national enmity weakens our revolutionary ranks, disunites the labor front, joined together regardless of nationality, and helps only our enemies." Quoted in Schwarz, "The New Anti-Semitism of the Soviet Union," *loc. cit.*, p. 536.

10. Schwarz, *The Jews in the Soviet Union*, p. 106.

11. Schwarz, *ibid.*, p. 103.

12. Howard M. Sachar, *The Course of Modern Jewish History* (New York: World Publishing, 1958), p. 348.

13. The motives of the government were not altogether pure in this project. The Birobidzhan experiment was at once an anti-Zionist move and a scheme to populate a large frontier region the Chinese were in the habit of infiltrating.

14. See Schwarz, *The Jews in the Soviet Union*, pp. 258-273.

15. *Ibid.*, p. 298.

16. Schwarz, "The New Anti-Semitism of the Soviet Union," *loc. cit.*, p. 542.

17. See Peter Meyer, "Stalin Follows in Hitler's Footsteps," *Commentary*, XV, I (January 1953), p. 12.

18. For accounts on the situation in the satellites, see F. Fejto, *Les Juifs et l'Antisémitisme dans les pays Communistes* (Paris: Plon, 1960),

pp. 37-88. This volume, two thirds of which contain a wide assortment of documents, gives a first-hand sampling of the Soviet antisemitism. See also Peter Meyer, "The Jewish Purge in the Satellite Countries," *Commentary*, XIV (September 1952), pp. 212-218; and Béla Fabian, "Hungarian Jewry Faces Liquidation," "The New Soviet Anti-Semitism," *loc. cit.*, pp. 32-37.

19. See Fejto, *op. cit.*, p. 14.

20. See Moshe Decter, "The Status of the Jews in the Soviet Union," *Foreign Affairs*, XLI, 2 (January 1963), p. 422.

21. Quoted in *The New York Times*, June 6, 1956; see W. Keller, "Anti-Semitism in the Soviet Union," *The Bridge*, 309-310.

22. C. L. Sulzberger in *The New York Times*, July 9, 1956.

23. See Decter, *loc. cit.*, p. 422.

24. See Fejto, *op. cit.*, pp. 54-56.

25. See Decter, *loc. cit.*, p. 422.

26. Fejto, *op. cit.*, p. 45; also see Keller, *loc. cit.*, p. 310, and Decter, *loc. cit.*, p. 429.

27. See Decter, *ibid.*, p. 426.

28. See Decter, *ibid.*, p. 430.

29. See Chapter XIV.

13. POLITE ANTISEMITISM

1. Carey McWilliams presents an illustration of this view. See his *A Mask for Privilege: Anti-Semitism in America* (Boston: Little, Brown, 1948).

2. See Lee Levinger, *Anti-Semitism in the United States* (New York: Bloch Publishing Co., 1925), p. 12.

3. Another sample of this approach is provided by Oscar Handlin, whose *Adventure in Freedom* (New York: McGraw-Hill, 1954) sees Jewish history in American in its rosiest hue.

4. From Emma Lazarus' *The New Colossus;* see H. E. Jacob, *The World of Emma Lazarus* (New York: Schocken Books, 1949), pp. 178-179.

5. Lazarus, *ibid.*, p. 178.

6. See J. S. Raisin, *Gentile Reactions to Jewish Ideals* (New York: Philosophical Library, 1953), p. 771.

7. See *supra*, p. 169.

8. See J. Higham, "Social Discrimination Against Jews in America, 1830-1930," *Publications of the American Historical Society*, XLVI, 1 (Sept., 1957), p. 9.

9. Higham, *op. cit.*, p. 11; also McWilliams, *op. cit.*, p. 3.

10. From 1881 to 1891, some 135,000, and from 1881 to 1920 a total of 3,000,000 Russian Jews entered the United States.

11. Ignatius Donnelly, *Caesar's Columns* (Cambridge: Harvard University Press, 1890).

12. Carey McWilliams has well analyzed this "schizoid" character of American tradition; see McWilliams, *op. cit.*, especially ch. 3.

13. J. F. Fraser, *The Conquering Jew;* quoted in McWilliams, *op. cit.*, p. 24.

14. M. Grant, *The Passing of the Great Race* (New York: Scribner's, 1926).

15. L. Stoddard, *The Revolt Against Civilization* (New York: Scribner's, 1922).

16. B. Hendrick, *The Jews in America* (New York: Doubleday, 1923).

17. Handlin, *op. cit.*, p. 196.

18. Quoted in G. Myers, *History of Bigotry in the United States*, (New York: Capricorn Books, 1960), p. 203.

19. See *supra*, p. 191.

20. *The International Jew, the World's Foremost Problem* (Dearborn: Dearborn Publishing, 1920), see Preface; quoted in Myers, *op. cit.*, p. 282.

21. This compilation was issued in four volumes, published by the Dearborn Publishing Co., Dearborn, Michigan, and entitled, consecutively: *The International Jew, The World's Foremost Problem* (1920); *Jewish Activities in the United States* (1921); *Jewish Influences in American Life* (1921); and *Aspects of Jewish Power in the United States* (1922).

22. The republication of *The International Jew* under Ford's name was announced by the Christian Nationalist Crusade, under the directorship of J. K. L. Smith; see *The Thunderbolt* (September 1963). The book was also serialized in the same publication throughout the same year. *The Thunderbolt* also advertised the sale of the *Protocols* at $1.00 a copy.

23. McWilliams, *op. cit.*, p. 35.

24. Quoted in Myers, *op. cit.*, p. 353.

25. See Myers, *ibid.*, p. 368.

26. *Social Justice*, July 25, 1938; quoted in Myers, *op. cit.*, p. 377.

27. *Ibid.*, p. 378.

28. *Ibid.*, p. 386.

29. See "Victory and Peace," Statement of Archbishops and Bishops of the United States (Washington, D.C.: NCWC, 1942); also in *Our Bishops Speak* (Milwaukee: Bruce, 1952), p. 113.

30. *Des Moines Register*, Sept. 12, 1941; quoted in Wayne S. Cole,

America First (Madison: University of Wisconsin Press, 1953), p. 144. Many refuse to consider Lindbergh antisemitic or even pro-Nazi, but merely anti-interventionist. (See *ibid.*, pp. 148-151.) His awkward remarks, in any event, provided antisemitism with a fresh impetus.

31. Morris S. Lazaron; quoted in McWilliams, *op. cit.*, p. 41.

32. See Benjamin Epstein and Arnold Forster, *Some of My Best Friends* (New York: Farrar, Straus, and Cudahy, 1962).

33. For a survey of these organizations, personages, and literature see the American Jewish Yearbooks (Philadelphia: Jewish Publication Society of America, 1961, 1962, 1963) under "Anti-Jewish Agitation."

14. THE LAST TWENTY-FIVE YEARS

1. In the United States, for example, the press, both secular and religious, expressed doubts about the validity of the trial and their uncertainties about Eichmann's accountability. An ill-disguised sympathy for Eichmann was manifest in many cases. See *The Eichmann Case in the American Press* (New York: Institute of Human Relations Press, American Jewish Committee, 1962).

2. At the time of the trial the German bishops asked all German Catholics to recite the following prayer:

> Lord God of our fathers! God of Abraham, of Isaac, and of Jacob! . . . We confess before you: Countless men were murdered in our midst because they belonged to the people from which comes the Messiah, according to the flesh. We pray: Lead all of those among us who became guilty through deed, omission, or silence that they may see their wrong and turn from it. Lead them so that they examine themselves, be converted, and atone for their sins. In your limitless mercy forgive, for the sake of your Son, that limitless guilt no human atonement can wipe out.

(Quoted in *The Bridge, op. cit.*, I, Preface, pp. 18-19.)

3. For compilations of these and other various documents, Catholic and Protestant, European and American, on the subject of Jewish-Christian relations, see *Stepping Stones to Further Jewish-Christian Relations: An Unabridged Collection of Christian Documents*, ed. Helga Croner (New York: Stimulus Books, 1977); *Les Eglises devant le Judaisme: Documents Officiels*, 1918-1978, ed. Hoch and Dupuy (Paris: Cerf, 1980); and L. Sestieri and G. Cereti, *La Chiese Cristiane e l'Ebraismo: 1947-1952* (Rome: Marietti 1983).

4. For samples of "revisionist" anti-Holocaust literature, see Austin J. App, *The Six Million Swindle* (Takoma Park: Coniface Press, 1973); Arthur R. Butz, *The Hoax of the Twentieth Century* (Surrey, England: Historical Review Press, 1976); the "Journal of Historical Review" published quarterly by the "Institute for Historical Review" (P.O. Box 1306, Torrance, California); and "Holocaust Revisionism: A Denial of History," in *Facts* (New York: Anti-Defamation League, 1980), June, vol. 26, no. 2.

5. The "Identity" doctrine was largely the creation of Dr. Wesley Swift who in the 1950s founded the "Christian Defense League." Not a church in any strict sense of the word, the "Identity" movement in the United States is given expression by a handful of clergymen and a number of organizations, such as, "Aryan Nations," "Posse Comnitatus," the "Christian Patriots Defense League," and again in publications of the KKK and neo-Nazi factions. For a summary of this movement and its adherents see "The 'Identity Churches': A Theology of Hate" in *Facts, Ibid.* (1983, Spring, no. 1).

6. See Glock and Stark, *Christian Beliefs and Antisemitism* (New York: Harper and Row, 1966), and Quinley and Glock, *Antisemitism in America* (New Brunswick: Transaction, 1979), ch. 6. While these volumes inaccurately equate Christian "orthodoxy" with certain fundamentalist doctrinal views, they succeed in establishing a definite correlation between these religious views and mythologizing and stereotyping of Jews of a secular character.

7. Positive contacts between Evangelicals and Jews have become numerous in recent years. Such prominent Evangelicals as Billy Graham, Jerry Falwell, Pat Robertson, and Bailey Smith have been vocal in their support of Israel not only theologically but as a modern democracy and in their personal affection for the Jewish people. On this trend see Nathan and Ruth Perlmutter, *The Real Antisemitism* (New York: Arbor House, 1982), ch. 7; also Merrill Simon, *Jerry Falwell and the Jews* (New York: Jonathan David, 1984).

8. See *New York Times* (February 6, 1983), p. 1.

9. See John Pawlikowski, *Christ in the Light of the Jewish-Christian Dialogue* (New York: Paulist Press, 1982), pp. 59-75.

10. James Parkes in England, Jacques Maritain in France, Karl Thieme in Germany, and Msgr. John Oesterreicher in this country stand out among these pioneers.

11. Bibliographical listings of the more prominent thinkers in the field of Jewish-Christian relations may be found in Michael McGarry, *Christology After Auschwitz* (New York: Paulist Press, 1977); John Pawlikowski, *What Are They Saying about Christian-Jewish Relations?* and

Christ in the Light of the Jewish-Christian Dialogue (Paulist Press, 1980 and 1982); also Eugene Fisher, "A New Maturity in Christian-Jewish Dialogue: An Annotated Bibliography: 1973-1983" in *Face to Face: An Interreligious Bulletin*, vol. XI.

12. Such include Hans Kung, Edward Schillebeeckx, Wolfhart Pannenberg, Jurgen Moltmann, Johannes Metz, and David Tracy.

13. Dr. Ruether considers antisemitism intrinsic to traditional Christology, comprising its "left-hand," and finds Christian antisemitism ideologically continuous with the modern racist development. See Ruether, *Faith and Fratricide: The Theological Roots of Antisemitism* (New York: Seabury, 1974); also her "Anti-Semitism and Christian Theology" in *Auschwitz: Beginning of an Era?* (New York: Ktav, 1974).

14. For a variety of responses to Dr. Ruether's theses see *Anti-Semitism and the Foundations of Christianity*, ed. Alan T. Davies (New York: Paulist Press, 1979). See also Walter Burkhardt and Josef Hayim Yerushalmi's responses in *Auschwitz: Beginning of an Era?* (*op. cit.*); also John Oesterreicher, "The Anatomy of Contempt," Institute of Judaeo-Christian Studies Papers, no. 4 (Fall 1975).

15. This point of view is represented by Jakob Jocz, A.F. Knight, Jean Danielou, and Urs von Balthasar. For a summary of their views see McGarry (*op. cit.*), pp. 64-68. A concise example of this position is also found in James Hitchcock, "What Price Harmony?" in *Face to Face* (*loc. cit.*), pp. 18-20.

16. See Georges Passsalecq, "The View from Belgium," in *Face to Face: An Interreligious Bulletin* (New York: Anti-Defamation League, vol. VII, Summer, 1980), pp. 12-13.

17. Etymologically, anti-Zionism and antisemitism are obviously not synonymous. Theoretically it is possible to be anti-Zionist without being antisemitic. To be so in practice is another matter. Close observation shows that non-antisemitic anti-Zionists are in reality rarities among non-Arabs. They may of course for obvious reasons be more readily found among Arabs but not in every case. See *supra*, p. 269.

18. The habit some anti-Zionists have of pointing to supposedly anti-Zionist Jews is countered by Dennis Prager and Joseph Telushkin in these words:

> Anti-Zionists would be hard put to find any affirmatively identifying Jew who would not view them as mortal enemies. Studies and opinion polls have shown that 99 percent of American Jewry identifies with the right of Jews to the Jewish state. For religious Jews, as we have seen, Israel and Jewish nationhood are part of their religious creed. An anti-Zionist

is therefore an enemy of religious Jews. As for secular and less religious Jews, anti-Zionists oppose the one aspect of Judaism which they passionately affirm—Israel.

See D. Prager and J. Telushkin, *Why the Jews? The Reason for Antisemitism* (New York: Simon and Shuster, 1983), p. 172.

19. During the war the leadership of the mainline churches, represented by the National Catholic Welfare Conference (NCWC) of the Catholic Church and the National Council of Churches (NCC) of the Protestant and Orthodox churches, preserved a scrupulous neutrality. Recommending peace in very general and even-handed terms, they refused to make any reference to the right of all states in the area to exist in peace within secure borders. The Jewish community looked for no more than this, and accurately interpreted anything less as inimical to the interests of Israel, given the declared intention of the pan-Arab and PLO leadership to eliminate the state of Israel.

The neutrality of the churches has persisted. The NCWC has maintained a cool neutrality, irrespective of the real involvements, and the NCC, a neutrality verging on hostility to Israel that has been manifest, for example, in pronouncements recommending cessation of all supply of arms to either side of the conflict. It is to be sincerely hoped that that organization was innocent of the destructiveness implicit in such a proposal. The Soviets unquestioningly would continue to supply Arab countries. Should the United States heed the proposal the inevitable outcome would in the long run be the extinction of Israel. The anti-Zionism informing such statements can hardly be seen as altogether benign.

For a Jewish view of the churchly approaches, see N. and R. Perlmutter, *op. cit.*, ch. 7.

20. Amos Kenan brings this point out with clarity:

It appeared that a slogan of this sort (that Jews should be driven into the sea) was not good public relations for the Arab cause. So today, only the Zionists are to be thrown into the sea. The only trouble is that when the Arabs get through pushing all the Zionists into the sea, there won't be a Jew left in Israel. For not a single Jew in Israel will agree to less than political and national sovereignty. We are now a nation that has shaken off the dust of a thousand years. Anyone who deludes himself into believing that he means to drive only the Zionists into the sea should know what he is really talking about.

See "New Left Go Home" in *The New Left and the Jews*, ed. M. Chertoff (New York: Pitman, 1971), p. 311.

21. Quoted in Prager and Telushkin, *op. cit.*, p. 174.

22. The word "antisemitism," a misnomer, does not denote hatred of Semites, but of Jews. Arabs as well as non-Semitic people, so to say, can fall within its focus.

23. See A. Forster and B. Epstein, *The New Antisemitism* (New York: McGraw-Hill, 1974), ch. 9; Prager and Telushkin, *op. cit.*, ch. 9; "Arab Antisemitism" in *ADL Facts*, vol. 16, no. 4; also the *1967 Supplement, ibid*; and "A Summary of Information Concerning the Situation of Jewish Communities in Arab Countries" (American Jewish Committee, Foreign Affairs Department), Unpublished manuscript, September 22, 1967.

24. To evince the anti-Zionism/antisemitism of the United Nations one has much from which to choose. For example: the numerous predictable denunciations of Israel through the instrumentality of an automatic Arab-Soviet-Third World vote on all issues touching Israel and the resolution in 1975 condemning Zionism as racism. But the ultimate in proof is no doubt reached in its embrace of Idi Amin that same year. None have better described the shocking scene than Paul Johnson, who wrote:

The history of hostility to the Jews over more than two millennia is rich in episodes of human cruelty and folly, but it contains few such disgraceful scenes as that enacted at the United Nations on the occasion of the state visit by President Idi Amin of Uganda, on October 1, 1975. By that date he was already notorious as a mass murderer of conspicuous savagery; he had not only dispatched some of his victims personally, but dismembered them and preserved parts of their anatomy for future consumption—the first refrigerator-cannibal. He had nevertheless been elected President of the Organization of African Unity, and in that capacity he was invited to address the U.N. General Assembly. His speech was a denunciation of what he called 'The Zionist-American conspiracy' against the world, and he demanded not only the expulsion of Israel from the U.N. but its 'extinction.' This blatant call for genocide was well received by Marxist, Arab, and many other Third World delegations. The Assembly awarded him a standing ovation when he arrived, applauded him periodically throughout his speech, and again rose to its feet when he left. The next day the U.N. Secretary General Assembly gave a public dinner in his honor.

See Paul Johnson, "Marxism vs. the Jews" in *Commentary* (April, 1984, p. 34).

25. For an excellent background of Arab-Jewish relations see S.D. Goitein, *Jews and Arabs: Their Contacts Through the Ages* (New York: Schocken Books, 1955); also Joan Peters, *From Time Immemorial* (New York: Harper & Row, 1984).

26. It is difficult today to believe that in 1974 Andrei Gromyko, Soviet ambassador to the United Nations, delivered a forceful pro-Zionist speech at the United Nations, that the Soviets voted for the creation of the new Israeli state in 1948, and was one of the first countries to recognize the new state after its foundation.

27. For further background see Boris Smokar, *Soviet Jewry: Today and Tomorrow* (New York: Macmillan, 1971); Elie Wiesel, *The Jews of Silence: A Personal Report on Soviet Jewry* (New York: Holt, Rinehart and Winston, 1966). For a more recent survey see Forster and Epstein, *op. cit.*, pp. 222-45; and M. Kampelman, "The Facts about Soviet Antisemitism" in *ADL Bulletin* (March, 1982, pp. 11-13).

28. For a thorough study of the emigration problem in Russia, see William Korey, *The Soviet Cage: Antisemitism in Russia* (New York: Viking, 1973).

29. See Forster and Epstein, *loc. cit.*; also M. Kampelman, *loc. cit.*

30. See Abraham Blumberg, "A Heritage Roundtable: Antisemitism in the Modern World" (Washington, D.C.: The Heritage Foundation, 1984), pp. 9-13; see also Forster and Epstein, *op. cit.*, pp. 244-49.

31. See Abraham Blumberg, *ibid.*, p. 14.

32. Forster and Epstein, *op. cit.*, p. 250.

33. For an analysis of left antisemitism see George Lichstein, "Socialism and Jews" in *Collected Essays* (New York: Viking, 1973), pp. 413-47.

34. Prager and Telushkin, *op. cit.*, p. 143.

35. W.D. Rubenstein, "The Left, the Right and the Jews" (New York: Universe Books, 1978), p. 77; quoted in "A Heritage Roundtable," *op. cit.*, p. 4.

36. See Zosa Szajkowski, "The Jewish Saint-Simonians and Socialist Antisemitism in France" in *Jewish Social Studies*, January, 1947: cited in Prager and Telushkin, *op. cit.*, p. 142.

37. On the anti-Zionism of the religious Left see Forster and Ep-

stein, *op. cit.*, pp. 79-80; N. and R. Perlmutter, *op. cit.*, pp. 154-165; and Prager and Telushkin, *op. cit.*, pp. 149-150.

38. Some of the bitterest attacks this writer has encountered when engaged in a defense of Israel has come from committed Christians, Catholic and Protestant, clerical and lay, all ostensibly of liberal persuasion. The intensity of their reaction could hardly be reducible to political differences alone.

39. For a personal account see Jacobo Timmerman, *Prisoner Without A Name, Cell Without A Number* (New York: Knopf, 1981).

40. See Forster and Epstein, *op. cit.*, pp. 268-81; also *Encyclopedia Judaica: Decennial Book* (1973-1982) (New York: Macmillan, 1982), pp. 162 ff.

41. Forster and Epstein, *op. cit.*, pp. 281-84; and *Encyclopedia Decennial, ibid.*, pp. 281-84.

42. See *La montee de l'antisemitisme en Europe* in *Sens* (XXXIV, no. 21, 1983).

43. See Forster and Epstein, *loc. cit.*, pp. 256-57, also *Encyclopedia Decennial, loc. cit.*, pp. 261 ff.

44. Forster and Epstein, *ibid.*, p. 257; also *Encyclopedia Decennial, ibid.*, pp. 168 ff.

45. Forster and Epstein, *ibid.*, p. 257-58; *Encyclopedia Decennial*, p. 412.

46. Forster and Epstein, *ibid.*, p. 261-68; *Encyclopedia Decennial*, p. 235 f.

47. See Abraham Foxman, *Memorandum: Antisemitism in France*, ADL, New York, October, 1980; also Richard Eder, "The Jewish Question in France" in *New York Times Magazine* (Sunday, November 13, 1980); also Forster and Epstein, *ibid.*, pp. 258-60.

48. Quoted in Foxman, *ibid.*, p. 7.

49. An annual source of information on American antisemitism is found in annual audits and analyses of antisemitic incidents throughout the country published by the Anti-Defamation League of B'nai B'rith. See also the *American Jewish Yearbook*, prepared by the American Jewish Committee with general annual summaries (Philadelphia: Jewish Publication Society).

50. For a listing of recent studies see Harold Quinley and Charles Glock, *Antisemitism in America* (New Brunswick: Transaction Books, 1983). Prominent among these studies are seven undertaken by the Anti-Defamation League, under the title *Patterns of American Prejudice* (listed *passim* in Quinley and Glock). For an earlier study see Charles H. Stember, *Jews in the Mind of America* (New York: 1966).

51. See Gregory Nartire and Ruth Clark, *Antisemitism in the United States* (New York: Prager, 1982).

52. The common stereotype casts Jews as unethical, dishonest, aggressive, pushy, clannish, and conceited.

53. See Quinley and Glock, *op. cit.*

54. See Quinley and Glock, *ibid.*, p. *xx*.

55. See Gary Marx, *Protest and Prejudice: A Study of Belief in the Black Community* (New York: Harper and Row, 1967), pp. 163-180.

56. For a survey and discussion of Black antisemitism see Forster and Epstein, *op. cit.*, ch. 10; and Quinley and Glock, *op. cit.*, ch. 4.

57. See N. and R. Perlmutter, *op. cit.*; Quinley and Glock, *op. cit.*, ch. 9; Forster and Epstein, *op. cit.*, chs. 8, 12, and 13.

15. THE ROOTS OF ANTISEMITISM

1. To this figure must be added the millions murdered before the Holocaust, estimated between 7 and 10 million by historians.

2. "Dejudaization" here means that nothing unique or distinctive is attributed to antisemitism, and that what happened to Jews happens similarly to other groups in different times and places. It is tantamount to a denial of the problem of antisemitism.

3. See *supra*, pp. 95-97.

4. Prager and Telushkin argue convincingly that Judaism and its positive impact on the Jew is the essential root of all antisemitism. It is an important contribution, but does not sufficiently respect the complexity of the antisemitic reaction since it fails to sound the depths and vagaries of the negative reaction of the antisemite. See Prager and Telushkin, *op. cit.*, part 1.

5. In his study of the Jewish-Gentile relationship between the third century B.C.E. and the fourth century C.E. Professor John Gager has offered strong evidence of philosemitic tendencies in the ancient world and Judaizing in the early Christian centuries, thus tempering the common notion of a widespread and deep antisemitism in these periods. See Gager, *op. cit.*

6. See *Genèse*, pp. 17-18.

7. Raul Hilberg, *op. cit.*, pp. 5-6.

8. Yosef Yerushalmi, "A Response to Rosemary Ruether" in *Auschwitz: Beginning of an Era?* (New York: Ktav, 1977), p. 104.

9. S. Freud, *Moses and Monotheism* (New York: Vantage Books, 1955), pp. 116-17.

10. *Ibid.*, p. 117.

11. See his Introduction in Malcolm Hay, *The Roots of Christian Anti-Semitism* (New York: Freedom Library Press, 1981), p. vi.

12. M. Samuel, *The Great Hatred* (New York: Knopf, 1948), p. 128. See also J. Maritain, *Ransoming the Time* (New York: Scribner, 1946), pp. 144-45.

13. See Rudolph M. Lowenstein, M.D., *Christians and Jews, A Psychoanalytic Study* (New York: Delta Books, 1963), p. 186. For psychological analyses of antisemitism see Douglas W. Orr, "Anti-Semitism and the Psychopathology of Everyday," in Simmel, *Anti-Semitism: A Social Disease (loc. cit.*, pp. 85-95); Otto Fenichel, "Elements of a Psychoanalytic Theory of Anti-Semitism," *ibid.*, pp. 11-32; N. Ackerman and M. Jahoda, *Anti-Semitism and Emotional Disorder: A Psychoanalytic Interpretation*, ed. M. Horkheimer and S. Flowerman (New York: Harper Bros., 1950).

14. Poliakov, *Bréviaire*, p. 350.

15. The theory of a rigorist origin of antisemitism seems to break down in face of the near universality of antisemitism among Christians. Most Christians are not rigorists. An adjustment and reformulation of the theory is necessary: To the extent that a Christian finds his/her Christianity a burden, he/she will tend to be antisemitic. Christianity, obviously, is not a yoke found easy, a burden found light, by many Christians.

16. The word "repentance" here is used metaphorically in the sense of expressing sorrow and regret, since progeny cannot be guilty of the sins of its forebears, unless of course it is still open to those sins. The openness of many Christians to antisemitism today provides sufficient grounds, it would seem, for real as well as metaphorical repentance.

INDEX

Aaron of Lincoln, 118
Abelard, Peter, 142–43
Acheson, Dean, 240
Acta Sanctorum, 36
Act Concerning Jews, 119–20
Acts of Philip, 40
Acts of the Martyrs, 54
Adler, Viktor, 201
Ad Quirinum, 40
Adversus Haereses, 41
Adversus Judaeos (anonymous),41
Adversus Judaeos (Tertullian), 40
Ad Vigilium, 41
Aelia Capitolina (Jerusalem), 21
Affirmative action, 282
Against Apion, 16, 17
Against Celsus, 37, 41
Agatharchides of Cnidus, 12
Agnosticism, 305
Agobard, St., 83–85
Agriculture, slavery and, *see* Slavery
Akiba (rabbi), 32
Albert (emperor), 95
Albert II (Austria), 109, 111, 113, 321
Albert the Great, St., 105
Albigensians, 102, 106
Alenu prayer, 112, 321
Alexander II (pope), 128
Alexander III (pope), 101, 102
Alexander IV (pope), 123

Alexander VI (pope), 126
Alexander I (Russia), 171–72
Alexander II (Russia), 172–73
Alexander III (Russia), 189–90
Alexander the Great, 10
Alexandria (Egypt), 10, 11, 21, 25
Alfonsin, Paul, 277
Algiers, 202
Alliance Israelite Universelle, 170, 195
Almohades, 101, 127, 128
Alphonso VI (Castile), 128
Alphonso VIII (Castile), 128
Alphonso X (Castile), 130
Alphonso XI (Castile), 130
Ambrose, St., 47, 54, 60, 61
Amenophis, 12
American Jewish Committee, 195, 265
American Joint Distribution Committee, 197
American Nazi Party, 258, 262
American Party (modern), 282
American Protective Association, 253
American Standard, The (New York), 256
American Vigilante Intelligence, The, 258
Amin, Idi, 346–47
Amulo, 85
Anacletus II (antipope), 123
Anastatius I, 67, 69

André, Joseph, 224
Andrew of Rinn, 100
Anglo-Jewish Association, 195
Animal sacrifices, 10
Anti-Christianity, 41
Anti-Christian antisemitism, 181–82, 290–91
Anti-clericalism, 180, 184, 187
Anti-Defamation League, 254, 280
Anti-Judaism:
    antisemitism distinguished, 5, 29, 33, 38–46, 62–66, 88–89
    theological, 265–67
    U.S.S.R., 231, 233–34, 271
Antioch, 21–22
Antioch, Council of, 55
Antiochus IV Epiphanes, 13, 15, 17
Anti-Semitic Catechism, 181
Antisemitism (generally), 2, 4–5, 284–89
Anti-Zionism, 5, 240–41, 274–75
    antisemitism and, 344–45
    Arab, 194, 264, 267–69, 274, 279
    U.S.S.R., 238, 239, 241, 243, 271, 339
Antoninus, the Pious, 299
Aphraates, 45, 49
Apion, 12, 16–18, 21
Aquinas, Thomas, St., 90, 96
Arabia, 81–82
Arabs, 194, 202, 267–68, 269
    Palestinians, 267
    Six-Day War, *see* Six-Day War
    Yom Kippur War, 279
Aragon, 127, 128, 129, 133, 137
Arcadius, 56, 308, 310
Arendt, Hannah, 188, 228, 332, 337
Argentina, 276–77
Arians, 59, 305
Aristobulus, 14
Aristotle, 105
Armleder massacres, 109
Aryan associations, 213
Aryan nation, 343
Aryan race, 179
Ashkenazim, 163

Assassinations, 191
Assault on Christians forbidden, 78
Assembly of Jewish Notables, 164
Assimilationism, 13, 161–62, 173, 179–80, 195
Associations, Jewish, 195
Asylum, right of, 58
Athanasius, St., 59
Augustine, St., 47, 52–53, 54, 64
Augustus, 20
Aurelius, Marcus, 301
Auschwitz death camp, 223
Austria, 166, 179, 182–83, 201, 278
    massacres, 107, 109, 111, 201, 217
Autos-da-fé, 90, 137, 324
Avignon, Papal, 123
Avincebron, 80
Avitus, St., 79–80

Baal Shem Tob (Israel ben Eliezer), 327
Babi Yar, 238
Babylonia, 8, 61
Badges of Shame, 82, 90, 103–04, 106, 113–14, 120, 163, 194, 224
    France, 103, 106
    Germany, 103, 154, 213, 217
    Italy, 123, 155
    Spain, 103, 128, 130–32
Balfour Declaration, 199, 279
Balkans, 149
Baptism, forced, 101, 324
    children, 76, 77, 115, 140, 169–70, 224
    crusades, during, 92, 93
    France, 79–80, 108
    Germany, 115, 116
    papal opposition, 71, 74, 102, 107, 110, 113
    Poland, 157
    Portugal, 140
    Roman Empire, 69–71
    Spain, 75, 132–34
Baptism, slaves of Jews refused, 83
Barbarian invasions, 72
Bar Kokba, Simon, 32, 36

Barnabas, St., 30, 34
Baron, Salon, 26
Barrès, Maurice, 202
Baruch, Bernard, 240, 258
Basel, Council of, 114, 146
Basil, St., 59
Basil I, 70
Bauer, Bruno, 168, 177, 274
Bauer, Otto, 201
Bavaria, 115, 202
Begin, Menachem, 281
Beilis, Mendel, 191–92, 255
Belgium, 109, 197, 202
Belloc, Hilaire, 202
Belzec death camp, 221, 223
Benedict XII (pope), 109
Benedict XIII (antipope), 134
Benedict XIV (pope), 76, 158, 329
ben Eliezer, Israel (Baal Shem Tob), 327
ben Israel, Manasseh, 150
Benjamin of Tiberias, 69
Benjamin of Tudela, 123, 323
Bergson, Henri, 202, 203
Berlin, 153
Berlin Treaty, 174
Bernardinus of Feltre, St., 116
Bernard of Clairvaux, St., 93, 94, 98
Beziers, Council of, 106
Bill of Rights, 163
Birch Society, John, 282
Birobidzhan, 235
Bismarck, Otto von, 180
Black Caucus, 282
Black Death, 109–11, 129
Black Hundreds, 191
Black Panthers, 282
Bloch, S. (rabbi), 183
Blood Accusation, *see* Ritual Murder accusation
Blum, Léon, 202
Blumenkranz, Bernard, 79
B'nai B'rith, 254
Bodo, 83, 85
Bohemia, 112, 153
Boleslav V (Poland), 156

Bolsheviks, 198, 201, 232
Book burning, 213
Bossuet, Jacques, 149, 188
Bracton, Henri de, 96
Brafman, Jacob, 173
Breslau, Council of, 156
Breviary of Alaric, 76, 311
Brownson, Orestes, 328
Bruna, Israel, 115
Buber, Martin, 327
Bulgaria, 223
Bundists (Russian), 231–32
Burning alive, 99–102, 107, 109–10, 115, 116, 117, 155, 171
autos-de-fé, 90, 137, 324
Byzantine Empire, 67

Caesar, Julius, 20
Caesarea, 22
Caesar's Columns, 252
Cahiers de la Quinzaine, 188
Caligula, 18, 20, 21
Calixtus II (pope), 319, 322
Callinicus, 60
Canon Law, 58, 76
Caorsini, 119, 124
Capistrano, John, St., 115, 156
Capitalism, 142, 147, 160
Caraffa, Giovanni, *see* Paul IV (pope)
Carmichael, Stokeley, 282
Carolingian Period, 82
Carto, Willis, 282
Casimir III, the Great (Poland), 156
Casimir IV (Poland), 115, 156
Cassignac, 188
Cassiodorus, 72
Cassius, Dio, 28
Castile, 127, 128, 129, 130, 133, 137
Catherine II (Russia), 171
Celsus, 18, 28, 37, 41, 175
Cerenthians, 43, 44
Chaeremon, 12, 16
Chalcedon, Council of, 71
Chamberlain, Houston, 181, 208, 254
Charlemagne, 66, 82

Charles II, the Bald (France), 83, 85, 86
Charles III, the Simple (France), 86
Charles IV (emperor), 110
Charles IV (France), 108
Charters, 95
Chateaubriand, François, 165
Chaucer, Geoffrey, 121
Chelmo death camp, 221
Chesterton, G. K., 202
Childebert, I., 79
Chilperic II, 80
Chintila, 76
Chmielnicki, Bogdan, 157
"Chosen People" concept, 8, 287–89
Christ, 29, 39–41, 43, 46
  Jewish insults to, 37, 53, 59, 84, 105, 113
Christian X (Denmark), 224
Christian Defense League, 343
Christian Front, 260
Christiani, Pablo, O.P., 114
Christianity:
  converts to, 34, 57
  insults to, 77, 120
  opposition to, 30–33, 41, 180, 181–82, 189, 290–291
Christian-Jewish dialogue, see Jewish-Christian dialogue
Christian Mobilizers, 260
Christian Patriots Defense League, 343
Christians, 32
  Jewish sect, as, 28, 29
  persecution of, 28–31, 35–38
Christian Socialist Party (Austria), 201
Christian Social Workers Union, 181
Christian theology of Judaism, 265–67
Christology, 267
Chrysostom, John, St., 45–47, 50–52, 54, 56, 61, 63, 64, 305, 306
Church:
  Holocaust and, 224–27
  true Israel, as, 35, 39

Cicero, Marcus Tullius, 19, 22
Circumcision, 45, 57, 299
Citizenship, 21, 160–61
Civil Rights, 162–64
Claudius (emperor), 20, 64
Clearchus of Soli, 9
Cleaver, Eldridge, 282
Clemenceau, Georges, 185–86
Clement III (antipope), 93
Clement III (pope), 319
Clement IV (pope), 117, 129
Clement VI (pope), 110
Clement VII (pope), 127
Clement VIII (pope), 155
Clement XIV (pope), 100, 158
Clementine Recognitions, 40
Clement of Alexandria, St., 45
Clement of Rome, St., 31
Clovis, 79
Codex Theodosianus, 56–57, 59, 67, 68, 72, 78, 84
Coelestin III (pope), 319
Collaborators, Jewish, 229
Common Sense, 261
Communism, 199, 203, 233, 257, 260
  German fear of, 207, 210, 217
Communist Party (U.S.), 275
Concentration camps, 221–23
  gentiles in, 223
Concerning the Civic Amelioration of the Jews, 162
Concubinage, 103
Confiscation of property, 97, 113
  England, 118, 119
  France, 86
  Germany, 109–10
  remission of debts, see Moneylending
  Spain, 77, 137–38
Congress of Vienna, 165
Conrad III (emperor), 93, 95
Conscription, 172
Conspiracy accusations, 108, 173, 252
Constance, Council of, 113
Constantine, 35, 48
Constantius I, 56

Constitutio pro Judaeis, 102, 112–14, 126, 319
Contra Judaeos (Isidore), 78
Conversion of Jews, 85–86
  forced, *see* Baptism, forced
Conversions to Judaism, 14, 91
Conversos, 132, 133–34
Cornelius, 29
Cosmas, Bishop of Prague, 92
Coughlin, Charles E., 259–60
Council of the Four Lands, 156, 158
Councils of the Church, 79, 85
  (*See also* individual Councils.)
Counter-Reform, 127, 154–55
Creditors, remission of debts to, 94, 101, 103, 104, 111, 113, 131, 132
Crematoria, 222
Cremieux, Adolphe, 169
Crimea, 235
Cristiani, Pablo, 129
Cromwell, Oliver, 150
Cross and Flag, 261, 282
Crosses, desecration of, 57, 59
"Crusade of Spain," 91
Crusades, 90
  debts of crusaders, 94, 103
  First, 91–93, 128, 315
  Second, 93–95, 99
  Third, 101, 118–19
Crypto-Jews, 70–71
Cyprian, St., 40
Cyrenaica, 22
Cyril of Alexandria, St., 59–60
Cyril of Jerusalem, 49
Czechoslovakia, 201, 217, 239–40, 271, 273

Dagobert, 80
Dante (Alighieri), 90, 124
Dark Ages, 66
Darre, R. Walter, 211
Daudet, Léon, 202
Dearborn Independent, The, 193, 256
Deatherage, George, 258
de Bonald, 165, 188
de Bouillon, Godfrey, 92

Declaration of the Rights of Man, 163
Declaration on the Relationship of the Church to Non-Christian Religions (Nostra aetate), 296
Defense League of Registered Americans, 261
DeGaulle, Charles, 279–80
de Gobineau, Arthur, 179, 183
DeGrelle, Léon, 202
Deicide accusation, 285, 288
  Good Friday, humiliations, 86, 87
  Middle Ages, 86–87, 102–03, 109, 112, 141
  modern, 266, 269
  Patristic period, 39–41, 46, 48, 51–54, 63
  Vatican II on, 263
Deism, English, 27
del Medigo, Elias, 124
de Lyra, Nicholas, 151
Demi-proselytes, 45
Democritus, 16
Demonology, 90
Demonstratio Adversus Judaeos, 40–41
De Montibus, Sina et Sion, 41
Denikin, Anton, 198
Denmark, 224
Deportations:
  Babylonian exile, 8
  Roman Empire, 20
  Russia, 197
Depression, 257–58, 261, 262
de Santa Fe, Geronimo, 133, 134
Desecration of Hosts accusation, 107, 113
  Germany, 99, 109, 117
  Poland, 156, 157, 158
  Spain, 139
de Spina, Alphonso, 136, 137
Dezhavin, G. R., 171
D'Holbach, Paul Henri, 176
Dialogue (Justin), 63
Dialogue between a Philosopher, a Jew, and a Christian, 142–43
Dialogue of Athanasius and Zaccheus, 53

Dialogue of Timothy and Aquila, 40
Dialogue with Trypho, 35, 39–40, 46
Diaspora, 7–9, 13–14, 18, 49
Didache, 34
Didascalia, 41–42, 46, 54
Diderot, Denis, 176
Dietary Laws, 23, 77–78
Diocletian, 28
Discours sur l'Histoire Universelle, 149
Discussion Concerning the Law between Simon, a Jew, and Theophilus, a Christian, 53–54
Disraeli, Benjamin (Beaconsfield), 194
"Doctor's Plot," 230, 240–41
Dohm, Christian Wilhelm, 162
Dominicans, 113, 114, 120, 121, 151
  Spain, 129, 132, 137–38
Domitian, 299
Donatists, 305
Donin, Nicholas, 104–05
Donnelly, Ignatius, 252
Dress Regulations, *see* Badge of Shame
Dreyfus, Alfred, 185–89, 255, 274
Drumont, Edouard, 184–85, 186, 188, 189
Dubcek, Alexander, 273
Duchesne, Louis, 42
Duehring, Eugen, 182
Duma, 191

Easter, Passover and, 305
Ebionites, 43, 304–05
Economic basis for antisemitism:
  Middle Ages, 112, 116–17
  moneylending, *see* Moneylending
  Roman empire, 25, 61
Economic crimes, U.S.S.R., 244–45
Edict of Milan, 48
Educational restrictions, 81, 114, 172–73
  quotas, 190, 200
  seminaries, 243, 271
Edward I (England), 119
Egibert, Bishop of Treves, 92

Egica, 77
Egypt, 7–12, 21, 25, 169
Ehrenburg, Ilya, 237, 238, 239, 243
Eichmann, Adolph, 218, 221, 223, 263, 264, 269, 338
Einsatzgruppen, S.S., 219
Einstein, Albert, 203, 213
Eisenmenger, Johann, 154
Eisner, Kurt, 202
El Husseini, Haj Amir, 269
Eliezer (rabbi), 31
Elizabeth (Russia), 171
Elkasites, 43
Elphantine, 8, 9
Elvira, Council of, 55, 75
Emancipation, 160–64, 174
Emanuel (Portugal), 140
Emicho, Count, 92
Emigration of Jews, 190, 213, 214
Engels, Friedrich, 274
England, 166, 190, 191, 197, 279
  arrival, 117–18, 150
  expulsion, 98, 107, 120
  massacres, 118, 119
  ritual murder accusation, 99, 121, 318
Enlightenment, 26–27, 161
Entdecktes Judentum, 154
Ephesus, 22
Ephraim, St., 45, 49
Epiphanius, St., 43, 49
Erasmus of Rotterdam, 151
Erwig, 77–78
Essay on the Inequality of Human Races, 179
Esterhazy, Major, 185, 186
Esther, Book of, 10
Ethnic Antisemitism, *see* Racial antisemitism
Eugenius III (pope), 94, 319
Eugenius IV (pope), 114, 126
Eusebius of Caesarea, 32, 37, 49
Evagrius, 53
Evangelical Churches, 265
Expulsion of Jews, 8, 9, 113
  England, 98, 120

France, 79–80, 88, 98, 101, 107
 Germany, 91, 98, 112, 115, 153,
  212, 215, 218
 Papal States, 155
 Portugal, 140
 Russia, 170
 Spain, 75, 76, 139

Faisal (Saudi Arabia), 269–70
Falwell, Jerry, 343
Farrakhan, Louis, 282
Fascism, 202
Fellowship Forum (Washington), 256
Ferdinand I (Castile), 127
Ferdinand IV (Castile), 130
Ferdinand V (Castile), 137, 139
Ferrer, Vincent, St., 114, 133–34
Ferriol, St., 79
Fettmich, Vincent, 153
Feudalism, 124, 160
Feuerbach, Ludwig, 291
Fichte, Johann, 165, 176, 274, 291
"Final Solution," 205–06, 211, 218–
  29, 290
Finaly case, 224, 329
Finland, 224
Flaccus, 18, 22
"Flagellants," 110
Flogging, 76
Florentines, 124
Ford, Henry, 193, 256
Fortalitium Fidei, 136
Foundations of the Nineteenth Century,
  181, 254
Fourier, Charles, 183, 274
France:
 anti clericalism, 180, 184, 187
 emancipation, 161–64, 166
 expulsion, 79–80, 88, 98, 101, 107
 Middle Ages, 78, 82, 90–94, 98,
  101, 103–04, 106–10, 149–50
 racial prejudice, 179, 181, 183–89
 Third Republic, 184, 187, 279–80
 World War II, 223, 227
France Juive, La, 184
Franciscans, 114, 124, 136, 137

Francis of Assisi, St., 90
Frank, Anne, 224
Frank, Leo, 254–55
Frankfurt ghetto, 146, 153
Frankists, 158
Fraternization, discouragement of,
  55
Frederick II (emperor), 100
Frederick II (Prussia), 154, 176
Freemasons, 188, 192
French Revolution, 161, 162, 163
Freud, Sigmund, 203, 292, 293
Friends of the New Germany, 259
Fritsch, Theodor, 181

Gabirol, Solomon ibn (Avincebron),
  80
Gamaliel, 31
Gamaliel VI (patriarch), 58
Ganganelli, Cardinal, *see* Clement IV
Genocide, 205–06, 218
German-American *Bund*, 259
Germany:
 badges, 103, 107, 213
 crusaders, 92–94, 101
 emancipation, 161, 165, 166
 expulsions, 91, 98, 112, 115, 153,
  212, 215, 218
 massacres, 92–94, 101, 107, 109–
  11, 166, 215–16
 Nazism, 209–29
 racial prejudice, 165, 179, 180–82
 readmission, 111
 Weimar, 206, 207, 210, 334
 World War I, 197
Germany, West, 277–78
Gershom, Rabbi, 135
Ghettos, 90, 103, 114, 145–59, 166,
  218, 227
 opening of, 160, 164
 self-segregation, 10, 145–46
Glagau, Otto, 181
Gnosticism, 38, 43–44
Godfrey of Wuerzburg, 115
Goebbels, Joseph, 211, 213, 215,
  219, 227

Goedsche, Hermann, 193
Goering, Hermann, 211, 216, 219
Goethe, Wolfgang von, 165
"Golden Bull," 111
Gondebaud, 78
Good Friday, 86, 87
Gospel of Peter, 40, 46
Gougenot de Mousseaux, 183, 188
Graebe, Hermann, 219–20
Graham, Billy, 343
Grand Mufti, 269
Grant, Madison, 254
Grant, Ulysses S., 174, 251
"Great Fear," 315
Great War, 31
Greece, 201–02
Green Mountain Boys (Nazi), 258
Gregoire, Abbé, 163
Gregory I, St. (the Great), 66, 71, 73–75, 80, 102, 126
Gregory VII (pope), 90, 128
Gregory IX (pope), 104
Gregory X (pope), 100, 107, 126
Gregory Nazianzen, St., 59
Gregory of Nyssa, St., 47, 50
Gregory of Tours, 80
Grenada, 132–33
Grynspan, Herschel, 215
Guenther, Hans F. K., 334
Guibert of Nogent, 91–92
Guilds, 97, 120

Hadrian, 11, 21
Hakim, 91
Halevi, Judah, 80
Haman, 10
Handlin, Oscar, 254
Hapsburg dynasty, 182
Harassments, 153–54
Harnack, Adolph von, 177
Hasidic movement, 158–59, 327
Hasmonean dynasty, 13
Hebrew language, 234, 243, 271, 272
Hebrew studies, 150
Hecataeus of Abdera, 11–12
Hegel, Georg, 176, 179, 291

Hellenic Period, 10–18, 24
persecution during, 15
Hellenized Jews, 13
Hendrick, Burton V., 254
Henry I (England), 118
Henry II (emperor), 90, 91
Henry III (England), 119, 120
Henry IV (emperor), 93, 95
Henry VI, 90
Henry, Archbishop of Mainz, 94
Henry, Colonel, 186
Henry of Trastamara, 131
Heraclius, 69, 70, 80, 310
Herder, Johann, 177
Heretics, Jews contrasted with, 64
Hermann, Archbishop of Cologne, 92
Hermes the Deacon, 36
Hermippus, 9
Herod, 22
Herod Agrippa I, 30
Herodians, 49
Herodotus, 8, 298
Hertzberg, Arthur (rabbi), 3, 26–27
Herzl, Theodor, 187, 268
Heydrich, Reinhardt, 218, 219, 223, 335
Hilary of Poitiers, 49
Himmler, Heinrich, 211, 218, 219
Hippolytus, St., 37, 40–41, 46
History of Asia, 12
History of Egypt (Apion), 16
Hitler, Adolf, 176, 183, 206–11, 219, 229, 269, 292
Hoess, Rudolph, 223
Holocaust, 4, 205–06, 264, 266, 271, 294
Holy Sepulcher, destruction of, 91
Honorius III (pope), 104
Honorius IV (pope), 120
Horace, 22–23
Hormizd IV, 81
Horseback riding, Jews banned from, 82
Horthy, Nicholas, 201
Horthy regime, 224

Housing discrimination, 252, 257, 261
Hugh of Lincoln, 121, 318
Humanism, 150–52, 154–55, 159
Hungary, 179, 182–83, 201, 239
emancipation, 166–67
World War II, 224
Hussites, 113, 321
Hypatia, 60

Identity Churches, 265, 343
Ignatiev, 189
Ignatius of Antioch, St., 34–35
Immanuel (Jewish poet), 124
Immigration Law of 1924, 253
Imperial cult (Roman), 19
Indifference, 294–95
Industrial Revolution, 167
Inheritances, regulation of, 154
Innocent III (pope), 90, 96, 102–03, 126, 128, 136
Innocent IV (pope), 100, 105
Innocent VIII (pope), 139
Inquisition:
papal, 137, 151, 155
Spanish, *see* Spanish inquisition
Institute of Historical Research, 282
Institute of Research on Judaism, 213
Internationalist Socialist Congress of 1891, 177
International Jew, The, 256
International trade, 167
Ionia, 22
Iran, 81, 194
Irenaeus, St., 41, 43
Isaac, Jules, 26, 74, 300
Isabella of Castile, 137, 139
Isidore of Seville, St., 75, 78, 311
Islam, 81–82, 91, 103, 202, 270
Almohades, *see* Almohades
conversions to, 127, 169
Spain, 77, 127
Isolationism, 255, 260
Israel, 227, 265, 297
Arabs and, 264, 267–69, 274, 279

U.S.S.R. and, 238, 239, 241, 243, 271
U.S. and, 276
Israelitische Allianz, 195
Italy:
counter reformation, 154–55, 167
ghettos, 146, 166, 167
Middle Ages, 122–27
modern, 224, 278–79
Mortara case, 170
Papal States, *see* Papal States
Rome, *see* Rome
Ivan III (Russia), 170

J'Accuse, 186
James, St., 30
James I (Aragon), 129
James the Less, St., 30
Jan Albrecht (Poland), 156
Jan Casimir (Poland), 157
Jazdegert II, 81
Jerome, St., 32, 45, 47, 50, 54–55, 61, 151, 309
Jerusalem, 10, 12–13, 69–70, 92
destruction of, 20–21, 31, 34
Jeshua (Jason), the High Priest, 13
Jesuits (Society of Jesus), 188
"Jew," etymology, 297
Jewish-Christian Dialogue, 2–3
Jewish Colonization Society, 195
Jewish rebellions, 19–21
Jews, Kings of the Epoch, The, 177
Jews in America, The, 254
Job discrimination, 253, 261, 271
John (England), 119
John II (Portugal), 140
John XXIII (pope), 225
John of Ephesus, 68
John the Evangelist, St., 33, 44, 302
Johnson, Paul, 346
Johnson Bill, 257
Joly, Maurice, 193
Jordanes, 15
Joseph II (Austria), 163
Josephus, Flavius, 14, 17, 297, 298
Journal of Historical Review, 282

Judaeo-Christianity, 29–30, 32, 34, 38, 43
Judaism:
  anti-Judaism, *see* Anti-Judaism
  basis for antisemitism in, 287
  civil status, 55–58, 60–62
    Justinian Code, 68–69, 71
  conversion to prohibited, 57, 71
  excommunication from, 68
  Gnosticism and, 43–44
  paganism and, 47
  separatism, 10–11, 13, 15, 23, 24, 62, 143–44, 146
  socialism and, 275
  U.S.S.R., 271
Judaizing, 81, 152
  Christians, 32, 34–35, 42, 44–46, 48, 50–51, 58, 66, 71, 73, 79, 157, 170, 287
  marranos, *see* Marranos
Judas, 52
Judith of Bavaria, 83
Juifs et l'antisémitisme, Les, 185
Julian the Apostate, 47, 52, 56, 59, 63
Julius II (pope), 127
Junkers, 207, 209
Justin, St., 31, 32, 35–37, 39–40, 44, 45, 54, 63
Justinian I, 66, 68
Justinian Code, 68–69, 71
Juvenal, 23, 45

Kabbalah, 127, 130
Kaganovich, 232
Kamenev, Lev, 198, 232, 236
Kammerknechtschaft, 95–96, 101, 128
Kant, Immanuel, 162
Karaism, 80, 158
Kavadah I, 81
Kavadah II, 81
Kemal, Pasha, mustafa (Ataturk), 202
Kenan, Amos, 345
Kerensky Regime, 198
Khaki Shirts, 258

Khazar Kingdom, 80
Khosru II, 81
Khrushchev, Nikita, 231, 242, 243
Kichko, Trofim K., 338
King, Martin Luther, 269
Knights of the White Camellia, 258
Know-Nothings, 253
Kopecky (Russian Minister), 240
Koran, 270
Koshru II, 69
Kreisky, Bruno, 278
Krystallnacht, 215–16
Kuhn, Bela, 201
Kuhn, Fritz, 259
Kulturkampf, 180
Ku Klux Klan, 255, 258, 261, 282, 343

Labor union movement, 168
Lactantius, 309
Landon, Alfred M., 258
Langton, Stephen, 120
Laodicea, Council of, 55
Lapide, Pinchas, 226
LaRouche Network, 282
Lassalle, Ferdinand, 168
Lassen, Christian, 179
Lateran Councils, 96, 101, 103, 126, 128
Latin America, 276–77
Lazare, Bernard, 185
Lazarus, Emma, 249, 340
League of Nations, 216, 217, 255
League of Russian People, 191
Leftist antisemitism, 282
Lenin, Nicolai, 198, 232, 233
Leo I, The Great, St., 55
Leo VII (pope), 88
Leo X (pope), 127, 151–52
Leo XIII (pope), 189
Leonis, Pedro, 123
Leo the Isaurian, 70
Leprosy, exodus as expulsion for, 12
Leroy-Beaulieu, Anatole, 185, 188
Lessing, Gotthold, 162
Letter of Barnabas, The, 34

Letters of Protection, 83, 95
Letter to Diognetus, 37, 40, 46
Levi, Solomon, 133
Levinger, Lee, 248
Liberalism, 180
Liberation (Magazine), 259
Liberation theology, 265
Liber Contra Judaeos, 85
Liberty Lobby, 282
Libre Parole, La (Newspaper), 184, 186
Libya, 280
Lilienthal, Max, 172
Lindbergh, Charles A., 260–61
Lithuania, 112, 155, 156
Loeb, Judah (rabbi), 148
Logos, 39
Lombards, 124
Lothar, 313
Louis I, The Pious (emperor), 82–84
Louis IV, The Bavarian (emperor), 108, 115
Louis VII (France), 93, 101
Louis VIII (France), 95
Louis IX (France), 104
Louis X (France), 108
Louis Philippe (France), 169
Lovsky, F., 26, 299, 301
Lowell, Abbott, 257
Lueger, Karl, 183, 209
Luther, Martin, 152–53, 155
Lynchings, 254, 255
Lysimachus, 12, 16

Maccabees, 13, 60
Madagascar Plan, 218
Magister Judaeorum, 83
Magus, Simon, 43
Maidanek death camp, 221, 223
Maimonides, 80, 106
Malcolm X, 282
Malesherbes, Chretien, 163
Malik, Yakov, 268–69
Manetho, 12
Manichaeism, 293
Marcion, 34

Marcionism, 38
Maria Theresa (Austria), 153
Maris, 242
Maritain, Jacques, 285, 343
Market Day, change in, 84
Marr, Wilhelm, 179, 180, 181
Marranos, 71, 124, 126, 127, 136–41, 155
Marriage:
  ban on intermarriage, 55, 58, 75, 78, 79, 103, 213
  limitation on Jewish, 154
Martin V (pope), 100, 113–14, 322
Martinez, Ferrand, 132
Martyrdom, Jewish, 93
Martyrs, burial of, 31
Marx, Karl, 168, 177, 231, 274
Masaryk, Thomas, 201
Massacres of Christians, 69–70
Massacres of Jews, 109, 113, 176, 317, 332–33
  Byzantine Empire, 67, 69–70
  crusaders, by, 92, 94, 98, 119
  England, 118, 119
  France, 99–100, 107, 108, 109
  Germany, 99, 100, 107, 109, 166, 215–16
  Islamic countries, 194
  Poland, 100, 157–58, 200, 272
  Portugal, 140
  Roman Empire, 21, 59, 60, 64
  Russia, 188–91, 197–99, 238
  Spain, 109, 130, 132, 136
Mauritius, 70
Maury, Abbé, 163
Maximilian I (emperor), 151
Maximum, 60
McFadden, Louis V., 258
McGinley, Conde, 261
McWilliams, Carey, 256
Meaux, Council of, 85
Medicine, practice of, 106, 127, 130, 147
Medina, 81
Megasthenus, 9
Mein Kampf, 209, 210

Meinville, Julio, 277
Meir (rabbi), 37
Mendelssohn, Moses, 148, 162, 175
Mensheviks, 232
Metternich, Clemens von, 169
Michael II, 71
Midrash, 148
Minicius, Felix, 301
Mirabeau, Honore, 163
Misanthropy, allegations of, 12
Mishnah, restriction, 68, 69
Mnaseas of Patros, 12, 16
Modestus, 70
Mohammed, 81–82
Molon, Apollonius, 12, 15–16, 22
Molotov, Vacheslav, 236, 237
Monasticism, Byzantine Empire, 68,
    310
Moneylending, 96–98, 101, 103, 104,
    108, 142–43, 147, 168, 180,
    285–86
  Act Concerning Jews, 119
  cancellation of debts, 94, 101, 103–
    04, 110–13, 131, 132
  England, 117–18
  Italy, 124
  Kammerknechtschaft, 95–96
  Spain, 127, 131
Montefiore, Moses, 169, 172
Montes pietatis (credit unions), 124
Moorish conquest of Spain, 77, 80
Morgenthau, Henry, 240
Morley, John, 226
Morocco, 194, 202
Mortara, Edgardo, 169–70
Mosaic Law, 13, 29, 30, 39, 43
Moses, 12, 16
Mosley, Oswald, 202
Mujica, Carlos, 277
Mulot, Abbé, 163
Munk, Solomon, 169
Mussolini, Benito, 202
Mystery Cults, 44

Nachman, Rabbi, 129
Nahardea, 81

Napoleon Bonaparte, 164–65
Nasi, *see* Patriarchate, abolition of
Nasser, Gamal Abdel, 269
Nathan the Wise, 162
National Catholic Welfare Council,
    345
National Council of Churches, 345
National Democratic Party (Poland),
    194
National gods, monotheism and, 10
Nationalism, German, 180
National Liberal Party (German),
    180
National Socialist German Workers'
    Party, *see* Nazism
National States Rights Party, 261,
    338
Nation of Islam, 282
Nativism, 250, 255
Navarre, 127, 130
Nazarenism, 43
Nazism, 4, 193, 199, 206–09, 212,
    290
Neo-Nazism, 282, 343
Nero, 30–31
Netherlands, 150, 224
New Deal, 257
New Economic Policy (NEP), 235
New Left, 282
New Testament, 33, 302
Nicaea, Councils of, 55, 71
Nicholas I (Russia), 172
Nicholas II (Russia), 191
Nicholas II (pope), 102, 126
Nicholas III (pope), 114
Nicholas V (pope), 100, 136
Nicolaites, 44
Nietzsche, Friedrich, 182, 208,
    291
Nilus, Sergei, 192, 193
Nobel Prizes, 203
Nostra Aetate, 263–64, 265, 296
Numerus Clausus, *see* Quota systems
Nuremberg Laws, 213, 214, 217
Nuremberg trials, 229, 263

Oaths, special, 113
Occupational restrictions, 57, 58, 61, 68, 212, 244
Odo, Bishop, 105
Oesterreicher, John, 343
Office-holding by Jews, 128, 249
 ban on, 75, 79, 96, 103, 114, 130, 212
 restrictions, 71, 173
Old Testament, 38, 68, 162
Olligen, Peter, 130
Omar, 81, 82
On Jewish Superstitions, 84
On the Insolence of the Jews, 84
On the Jews (Democritus), 16
Oppas, Archbishop, 77
Oppenheimer, Samuel, 154
Order of Seventy-Six, 258
Origen, 36, 37, 40, 41, 45
Orleans, Councils of, 79
Ostracism, U.S.S.R., 237, 238
Ovid, 23
Oxford, Councils of, 120

Pacifism, 228
Paganism:
 Diaspora and, 8, 28, 48, 64–65
 neo-paganism, German, 208, 210–11
Pale of Settlement, 171, 172, 190
Palestine, 12–13, 107, 149
 see also: Israel
Palestine Liberation Organization, 278, 282
Palestinian Mandate, 199
Palestinians, 276
Panama Canal scandal, 185
Pan-Slavism, 170, 171
Papal States, 125–27, 155, 169–70
Parasitism charge, 168, 171, 174, 177, 210, 231, 235, 272
Parkes, James, 283, 343
Partisans, World War II, 227, 237
Pascal, 149
Passing of the Great Race, The, 254
Passover, Christians celebrating, 55, 68

Pastoreaux, 129
Patent of Tolerance, 163
Patriarchate, 49, 58
 abolition, 47, 58, 61, 305
Patristic Period, 34, 38–46, 285, 288–89
Paul, St., 29, 30, 33, 44, 54, 94, 141
Paul III (pope), 100, 127, 155
Paul IV (pope), 127, 155
Paul VI (pope), 328
Paul of Palestine, 54
Pawnbroking, 98, 147
Pedro the Cruel, 131
Pelley, William, 258
Pepin, 82
Peroz, 81
Persia, 81, 194
Persian Empire, 9
Peter, St., 29, 40, 44
Peter the Great (Russia), 171
Peter the Hermit, 92
Peter of Cluny, 94–95
Petlyura, 198, 202
Petronius, 23
Pfefferkorn, Joseph, 151
Phatir, 80
Philip II, Augustus (France), 101
Philip III (France), 106
Philip IV, the Fair (France), 96, 106, 107, 108
Philip of Heraclea, St., 36
Philo, 17, 21
Philostratus, 18
Phocas, 69, 70
Pico della Mirandola, Giovanni, 124
Picquart, Colonel, 185, 186, 188
Pilsudski, Joseph, 200
Pionius, St., 36
Pius IV (pope), 155
Pius V (pope), 155
Pius VII (pope), 166, 328
Pius IX (pope), 114, 167, 170, 331
Pius XII (pope), 225–26
Placitum, 77
Pliny the Elder, 16, 22
Pliny the Younger, 301

Plutarch, 18
Pobedonostsev, Konstantin, 189
Podhoretz, Norman, 337
Pogroms, *see* Massacres
Poisoning accusations, 109
Poland, 115, 215, 239
  badges, 103
  ghettos, 221, 222, 227
  golden age, 149, 155–57
  holocaust, 221–23, 227
  invasions, 157, 171
  massacres, 109, 111, 157–58, 188,
    190, 200, 221–23, 272
  Russia and, 171, 194, 271–73
Poliakov, Léon, 293
Polycarp, St., 36
Pompey, Trogus, 23
Poppaea, 31
Porphyry, 28, 38
Portugal, 127, 130, 133, 140
Portuguese Inquisition, 140
Poseidonius, 12, 15
Posse Commitatus, 343
Prager, Dennis, 274, 344
Pravda, 236, 241
Prayers for the Jews, 54–55, 311
Press, American, 256
Preuss, Hugo, 207
Printing houses, 151
Priscus, 80
Privilegia Odiosa, 58
Pro Flacco, 19, 22
Progressive Labor Party, 275
Propaganda, Nazi, 207, 213–14, 217,
  237
Proselytizing:
  Christian, 49, 57
  Jewish, 14, 15, 18, 19, 21, 42, 45–
    48, 57, 71, 89
Protocols of the Elders of Zion, 108,
  173, 192–93, 200, 202, 256, 260,
  269
Proudhon, Pierre, 177, 183, 274
Provocative behavior, 57
Prussians, 208
Pseudo-Aristeas, 14

Pseudo-Hecataeus, 14
Psychological factors, 292–94, 295
Ptolemy Lagus, 12
Ptolemy Physcon, 14
Pumbeditha, 81
Purges:
  Czechoslovakia, 240
  U.S.S.R., 235, 236, 239
Purim, 57, 59

Quartodecimanism, 305
Quintilian, 23
Quislings, 218
Quota systems, 257, 261, 282

Rabaud, Pastor, 163
Racial antisemitism, 4, 177–78, 179–
  95
  humanism and, 159
  Nazism, 207–08, 212–14
  rationalism, 4, 26, 106, 175, 289–
    91
Radek, K., 198, 232, 236
Radulph, 94
Rashi (Rabbi Shlomo, son of Isaac),
  93, 135, 315
Rathenau, Walther, 207, 208
Rationalism, 4, 26, 106, 174–77, 289,
  291
Raymond of Penaforte, St., 114, 129
Reccared, 75
Recceswinth, 76
Refugees, 124, 126, 133, 214
  Palestinians, 276
  Polish, 155–56, 158, 215
  Spanish, 133, 139–40
Refuseniks, 272
Regnard, 182
Reichstag Fire, 209
Reinach, Theodore, 26
Religio licita status, 56, 71
Religious goods, 243–44, 271
Remigius of Auzerre, 85, 315
Renan, Ernest, 179
Repentance, need for, 2–3, 296
Restrictive covenants, 257

Reuchlin, Johann, 151–52, 155
Revolt Against Civilization, 254
Revolts, Jewish, 59–60, 67
Revolutionaries, 180
Revolutions, 161, 162, 163
Rewbell, 176
Richard I (England), 118–19
  coronation massacre, 118
Richard of Cornwall, 119
Riesser, Gabriel, 166
"Righteous" (rescuers), 223–25
Rindfleisch, 107
Riots:
  Germany, 212, 214, 215
  Roman Empire, 18, 22
Ritual Murder Accusations, 99–101,
    113, 176
  Arabs, 169, 269
  Austria, 183
  Byzantine Empire, 59
  Christians, against, 28, 99
  England, 99, 120–21
  France, 99–100, 107
  Germany, 99, 100, 112, 116–17,
    181, 182
  Hungary, 183
  Poland, 100, 156, 157, 158
  pre-Christian, 16–17, 99
  Russia, 173, 191–92, 236
  Spain, 139
  United States, 255, 257
Robertson, Pat, 343
Robespierre, Maximilien, 163
Rockwell, George Lincoln, 262, 282
Rohling, August, 180, 181, 183
Roman Empire, 9, 18–25, 27, 299
Romania, 173–74, 193–94, 200–01,
    223, 239
Roman law, religious aspects, 58
Romanos I, 70, 71
Rome, 8, 18, 122–23, 125–27, 146,
    155, 167
Roncalli, Angelo, *see* John XXIII
    (pope)
Roosevelt, Franklin D., 258
Rosenberg, Alfred, 211, 213, 292, 334

Rothschild, House of, 167
Rothschild, Lionel de, 166
Rousseau, Jean Jacques, 176
Rubenstein, W.D., 274
Rudiger, John, 92, 146, 315
Rudolph of Hapsburg, 107
Ruether, Rosemary, 266
Rumkowski, Chaim, 228
Russia, 171–73, 230–46, 271–74
  anti-religious policies, 233–34
  conscription, 172, 173
  emigration, 190, 191, 238, 245,
    272
  exclusion, 170, 235, 239
  massacres, 189–91, 198–99, 219–
    21, 235
  Nazi era, 219–21, 237
  1917 Revolution, 198, 232
  restrictions, 171–73, 179, 189–92,
    196–97
Ruthard, Archbishop of Mainz, 92
Rutilius, Namatianius, 24

Sabbath observance, 12, 16, 23, 24,
    81, 234
Sabbatians, 158
Sadat, Anwar, 270
Safe-conducts, 153–54
St. Étienne, 163
Sakharov, Andrei, 272
Salonika, 201–02
Samuel, Herbert, 191
Samuel, Maurice, 293
Samuels, Shimon, 280
Sanhedrin, Napoleonic convocation,
    164
San Remo Conference, 199
Sardinia, 139
Sassanids, 81
Scapegoating, 187, 206–07, 212, 247,
    276, 286, 293, 331
Schacht, Hjalmar, 216
Schervakov, Alexander, 241
Schleiermacher, Friedrich, 165, 177
Schmidt, Johann Kasper, 181, 332
Schoenerer, Georg, 183

Scholasticism, 80
Schools, Jewish, 81
  seminaries, 243, 271
Searchlight (Atlanta), 256
Second International Socialist
  Congress, 274
Secularism, 180, 188–89, 290–91
Sedition, Hellenic accusations of, 15
Sejanus, 20
Self-government, Poland, 156
Seligman, Joseph, 251
Seminaries, 243, 271
Semitic race, 179
Seneca, 14, 23
Senior, Abraham, 139
Separatism, 10–11, 13, 15, 23, 24,
  62, 143–44, 146
Sephardim, 163, 249
Septimus Severus, 299
Septuagint, 38, 68
Sergius of Amida, 68
Sermons, mandatory, 77, 113–15,
  120, 129, 134, 155, 167
Servitude, *see Kammerknechtschaft*
Severus, Sulpicius, 54, 67
Shapiro, Aaron, 256
Shapur II, 81
Sharansky, Anatoly, 272
Shemoneh, Esreh, 28, 32
Shoenerer, Georg, 209
Sicily, 104, 139
Sigismund (emperor), 113
Sigismund II (Poland), 156
Silver Shirt Legion, 258
Simeon, St., 36
Simeon of Ctesiphon, 59
Simlai (rabbi), 41
Simon, Marcel, 37, 42, 301
Simon of Trent, 100, 116, 318
Sisebut, 75, 80
Sisinand, 75
Six Day War, 264, 267, 271, 274,
  280
Sixtus IV (pope), 127, 137, 138
Sixtus V (pope), 117, 155
Slansky, Rudolph, 230, 239–40

Slavery:
  Christians owned by Jews, 57, 61,
    68, 71, 73, 75, 79, 83, 84, 96
  Jews reduced to, 77
Slave trade, 88
Smith, Bailey, 343
Smith, Gerald K., 261, 282
Sobibor death camp, 221
Social discrimination, United States,
  248, 250–62
Socialism, 168, 177, 180, 194, 274–
  75
Socialist Worker Party, 275
Social Justice, 260
Socinians, 157
Solidarity, 273
Sorcery, accusations of, 83
Soviet Bloc, 271
Sozomenus, 59
Spain, 90, 122, 190
  badges, 103
  expulsion, 139
  golden age, 80–81
  Inquisition, *see* Spanish Inquisition
  Marranos, 71, 124, 126, 127, 136–
    41, 155
  massacres, 109
  Visigoths, 74–78
Spanish Inquisition, 127, 137–39
Spanknoebel, Heinz, 259
Spengler, Oswald, 208
Speranski, M. M., 172
Spinoza, Baruch, 175
Stalin, Josef, 230, 232, 236, 238
Stephen, St., 29, 30, 40, 54
Stephen (England), 118
Stern (magazine), 278
Stinnes, Hugo, 333–34
Stirner, Max, 181, 332
Stoddard, Lothrop, 254
Stoecker, 181
Strabo, 298
Streicher, Julius, 211, 213
Stroop, 227
Students for a Democratic Society, 275
Stuyvesant, Peter, 249

Stylites, Simon, St., 61
Suetonius, 301
Sugrue, Thomas, 293
Suicides, 92, 93, 108, 110, 115, 132,
   213–14, 227, 240
Suidas, 16
Superstition, 44, 143
Sura, 81
Swift, Wesley, 343
Switzerland, 109
Symmachians, 43
Synagogue at Jabne, 43
Synagogues:
   attacks on, 60–61, 67
   closing, 69, 234, 243, 271
   construction, 84, 120
   conversion to churches, 60, 68, 73,
      117
   desecration, 208, 261, 280
   destruction, 72, 73, 80, 81, 92,
      102, 155, 181, 216
   regulation of, 58, 120
Syria, torture, 169
Szajkowski, Zesa, 274

Tacitus, 12, 23–24, 301
Talmud, 129, 155
   Babylonian, 62
   destruction, 104–05
   offensive passages, 104–06, 129,
      134, 154
   Palestinian, 37
   printing, 151–52
Talmudic Studies, 147–48
Talmud Jew, The, 180
Tam, Jacob, 94
Tannenbaum, Mark, 265
Tarphon (rabbi), 37, 39
Tartars, 107, 157
Taxes, special, 61, 97, 108, 136
   Temple tax, 10, 21
Telushkin, Joseph, 274, 344
Temple (Jerusalem), 13, 63
   destruction of, 31, 34
"Temporary Laws" (Russia), 190,
   196–97

Tertullian, 31, 35, 37, 40, 45
Testament of the XII Patriarchs, 40,
   46
Testimonies, 38
Testimony restrictions, 96
Theobald, 99
Theodoric, 66, 72
Theodosian Code, *see Codex*
   Theodosius
Theodosius I (the Great), 56, 60
Theodosius II, 57, 61, 310
Theophilus of Antioch, 38
Theophrastus, 9
Theresienstadt concentration camp,
   223
Thieme, Karl, 343
Third Crusade, 118–19
Third Reich, 209, 211–29
Thomas, Father, 169
Thunderbolt, the, 261, 282
Tiberias (emperor), 16, 20, 299
Tibullus, 23
Titus, 21, 95
Titus-Levy, 22
Toledo, Councils of, 75–77, 136,
   329
Toledot Yeshu, 37, 84, 304
Tolstoy, Leo, 191
Torah, 24
Torquemada, Thomas, 137, 138–39,
   293
Torture, 110, 115–17, 119, 138
Toussenel, Alphonse, 177, 183, 274
Trajan, 21
Travel restrictions, 77, 153–54
Treason, accusations of, 86
Treason, heresy as, 70
Treatise Against the Jews, 53
Treblinka death camp, 221, 223,
   227–28
Treitschke, Heinrich von, 181
Tribunals, Jewish, 58
Tridon, 182
Tripoli, 202
Trotsky, Leon, 198, 232, 236
True Account, 41

Trullo, Council of, 71
Truman, Harry, 240
Trypho (rabbi), 31
Tunis, 202
Turkey, 140, 149, 157, 194, 197, 202

Ukrainians, 157, 235
Union Génerale, 182, 184
Union of Soviet Socialist Republics,
    see Russia
Unitarians, 157
United Kingdom, 217
    see also: England
United Nations, 270, 346
United States, 247–48, 280–83
    blacks, 281
    Civil War, 250, 251
    colonial period, 249
    constitutional rights, 163
    immigration, 250–53, 256–57
    Israel and, 276
    U.S.S.R. and, 190, 191, 217
Usury, *see* Moneylending
Uvarov, Count, 172

Vadislaw (Bohemia), 97
Valentin, Hugo, 162, 327–28
Valladolid, Council of, 128
Vannes, Council of, 78
Varro, 22
Varus, 20
Vatican II Council, 263–65, 296
Vayol, Hans, 116
Versailles, Treaty of, 199, 206, 210
Vespasian, 21, 95
Vichy Regime, 186
Victor (pope), 305
Victor of Palermo, 73
*Victory of Judaism Over Germanism,
    The,* 179, 180
Vienna, 153
Vienna, Council of, 107
Voltaire, François de, 26, 27, 176
Vom Rath, Ernst, 215, 228

Von Hindenburg, Paul, 209
Von Plehre, Viacheslav, 191
Von Rundstedt, 221
Voting rights, 249

Wagnerian group, 208
Wannsee conference, 219
Warsaw ghetto, 221, 227
Watson, Tom, 254–55
Watson's Magazine, 254
Wecelinus, 91
Weimar Republic, 206, 207, 210,
    334
Wenceslaus (emperor), 111
Wertheimer, Wolf, 153
Wheeler, Burton K., 260
White Terror, 232
William (bishop), 86
William Rufus (England), 118
Williams, Roger, 163
Wilson, Woodrow, 200
Winrod, Gerald B., 258
Withdrawal, *see* Separatism
Witiza, 77
Witness-people theory, 53, 64, 141,
    309
World Court of Justice, 255
World War I, 196–97
    aliens, treatment of, 197
World Zionist Congress, 192

Xenophobia, 7, 11, 25

Yakuts, 242
Yehiel (rabbi), 104–05
Yemen, 81, 194
Yerushalmi, Yosef, 226, 290
Yevsektsiya, 234
Yevtushenko, 238
Yiddish, 233, 234, 239, 242, 271
Yom Kippur War, 279
York Massacre, 119
Young, Andrew, 282
Young Socialist Alliance, 275
Young Students Alliance, 275

Zamora, Council of, 131
Zamosc Ghetto, 222
Zaporozhti, 157
Zeno (emperor), 67
Zhandov, Andrei, 241

Zinoviev, Grigori, 198, 232, 236
Zionism, 187, 194–95, 199, 232, 268
Zohar, 323
Zola, Emile, 185–86
Zossima, 170–71

Other Books in the Stimulus
Studies in Judaism and Christianity Series:

Stepping Stones to Further Jewish-Christian Relations: An Unabridged Collection of Christian Documents, compiled by Helga Croner (A Stimulus Book, 1977).

Helga Croner and Leon Klenicki, editors, *Issues in the Jewish-Christian Dialogue: Jewish Perspectives on Covenant, Mission and Witness* (A Stimulus Book, 1979).

Clemens Thoma, *A Christian Theology of Judaism* (A Stimulus Book, 1980).

Helga Croner, Leon Klenicki and Lawrence Boadt, C.S.P., editors, *Biblical Studies: Meeting Ground of Jews and Christians* (A Stimulus Book, 1980).

Pawlikowski, John T. O.S.M., *Christ in the Light of the Christian-Jewish Dialogue* (A Stimulus Book, 1982).

Martin Cohen and Helga Croner, editors, *Christian Mission-Jewish Mission* (A Stimulus Book, 1982).

Leon Klenicki and Gabe Huck, editors, *Spirituality and Prayer: Jewish and Christian Understandings* (A Stimulus Book, 1983).

Leon Klenicki and Geoffrey Wigoder, editors, *A Dictionary of the Jewish Christian Dialogue* (A Stimulus Book, 1984).

More Stepping Stones to Jewish-Christian Relations: An Unabridged Collection of Christian Documents 1975–1983, compiled by Helga Croner (A Stimulus Book, 1985).